Slavery in Mississippi

SOUTHERN CLASSICS SERIES

Mark M. Smith, Series Editor

SLAVERY IN MISSISSIPPI

CHARLES S. SYDNOR

New Introduction by John David Smith

THE UNIVERSITY OF SOUTH CAROLINA PRESS

*Published in Cooperation with the Institute for
Southern Studies of the University of South Carolina*

© 1933 American Historical Association, renewed 1959
New material © 2013 University of South Carolina

Cloth edition published by D. Appleton-Century, 1933
This paperback edition published by the University of South Carolina Press,
Columbia, South Carolina 29208

www.sc.edu/uscpress

Manufactured in the United States of America

21 20 19 18 17 16 15 14 13   10 9 8 7 6 5 4 3 2 1

Library of Congress Cataloging-in-Publication Data
Sydnor, Charles S. (Charles Sackett), 1898–1954.
  Slavery in Mississippi / Charles S. Sydnor ; new introduction by
John David Smith. — Paperback edition.
    pages cm. — (Southern classics series)
  "Published in cooperation with the Institute for Southern Studies
of the University of South Carolina."
  Originally published: New York : D. Appleton-Century Company,
Incorporated [c1933]
  Includes bibliographical references and index.
  ISBN 978-1-61117-332-1 (pbk.)
  1. Slavery—Mississippi. 2. Slaves—United States—Social conditions.
3. African Americans—Mississippi—History. I. Title.
  E445.M6S92 2013
  306.3'6209762—dc23
                        2013020628

Publication of the Southern Classics series is made possible in part
by the generous support of the Watson-Brown Foundation.

To my parents, Evelyn Sackett Sydnor and Giles Granville Sydnor

CONTENTS

SERIES EDITOR'S PREFACE

Charles S. Sydnor's study *Slavery in Mississippi* had the feel of a classic as soon as it was published in 1933. As noted historian John David Smith observes in his elegant and deeply informed introduction to this reprinting, Sydnor's book remained immensely influential in the field of southern history for thirty years. Much of what Sydnor wrote about the nature of slavery in Mississippi was based in detailed, original, even groundbreaking research, allowing him to think and write meaningfully about the workings, the significance, and the complexity of the peculiar institution. For these reasons, among many others, *Slavery in Mississippi* remains an important book for the study of antebellum slavery generally.

MARK M. SMITH

INTRODUCTION

John David Smith

On the final page of his influential *Slavery in Mississippi* (1933) University of Mississippi historian Charles Sackett Sydnor (1898–1954) forthrightly summarized the book's thesis. "Except for the omnipresent danger of being sold—and no slave was beyond the shadow of this," Sydnor wrote, "being a slave was not for the average negro a dreadful lot." The thirty-five-year-old Georgia native then underscored slavery's complexity and the contingencies that lay at the heart of the "peculiar institution." "How distasteful life was under these conditions depended on two very variable factors: the character of the masters and the desire for freedom in the hearts of the slaves."[1] Responding to Sydnor, Mississippi essayist and novelist Stark Young remarked that Sydnor's book illuminated how the "aristocratic section that freely admitted the evils of slavery was outvoted by a democratic section whose political leaders denied any imperfections in the institution." This political "impasse," according to Young, "put some of the best minds in the South at a disadvantage." This scenario prefigured "the solid South we all know of."[2]

Slavery in Mississippi immediately became a classic, required reading for historians of slavery, and it remained a staple in the field for three decades. Writing in *Social Studies,* the historian Harold J. Jonas argued that Sydnor's "reasoned, impartial book" deserved a wide audience.[3] The *Boston Evening Transcript* touted Sydnor's "comprehensive and scholarly study," one that successfully overcame the paucity of sources and the problem of "contradictory evidence" that nagged all students of slavery.[4] London's *Times Literary Supplement* suggested that Sydnor's use of obscure newspaper advertisements for slave runaways demonstrated his "ingenuity" as a researcher. The reviewer noted that while Sydnor recognized slavery's "dark side," his argument was "that in many respects the social condition of the negro was far from being as deplorable as is sometimes supposed."[5] And University of North Carolina historian Joseph Grégoire de Roulhac Hamilton, a leading authority in the field of southern history, found Sydnor's arguments most congenial. Hamilton ranked *Slavery in Mississippi* "one of the most valuable contributions yet made to the history of American Negro slavery"; it provided "the most complete picture that has so far appeared for any state."[6]

Remarkably, Sydnor's *Slavery in Mississippi* continued to influence slavery scholarship following World War II and up through the modern civil rights movement. In 1951 the historian Chase C. Mooney described it as "the most comprehensive single" state study on slavery.[7] Eight years later the historian Stanley M. Elkins ranked Sydnor's book as the best of the so-called Phillips school state studies inspired by Ulrich Bonnell Phillips, whose landmark *American Negro Slavery* (1918) surveyed slavery across the South. Elkins also observed how closely the chapter headings in Kenneth M. Stampp's revisionist *The Peculiar Institution: Slavery in the Ante-Bellum South* (1956) mirrored those addressed by Sydnor almost a quarter century earlier.[8] The historian Daniel Calhoun has mused that Stampp had "engaged in a point-for-point for moralism" with Sydnor that circumscribed much of the then extant historiography of African American slavery.[9] And writing in 1965, Eugene D. Genovese remarked that thirty years following its first appearance, Sydnor's *Slavery in Mississippi* still "enjoys pride of place."[10]

Sydnor, according to the historian Fred Arthur Bailey, began his career as a traditional, fact-driven, "scientific" narrative historian whose early work subscribed to the apologetic, reactionary "Lost Cause" orientation common to early-twentieth-century southern historians. Influenced significantly by what he considered the political demagoguery of 1930s Mississippi politics, Sydnor changed course, emerging as a free-thinking intellectual who ruminated on the negative results of excessive democracy in both Old and New Souths. By the 1940s Sydnor ranked as one of the South's foremost historians and influential scholars. He eventually came to challenge the neo-Confederate bias held by most white southern historians of his generation. In 1945, upon publishing "The Southern Experiment in Writing Social History," Sydnor ordered one hundred reprints of his article, he said, determined to show his "cynical friends that southern history may have other objectives than to praise the South and damn the North."[11]

Just as he faulted southern leaders of the 1850s for succumbing to extremist sectionalist views regarding slavery and disunion, Sydnor found wanting 1950s southern demagogues who rode to power championing segregation and anti-Communism. Though Bailey undervalues Sydnor's essential conservatism, he accurately portrays the historian's intellectual evolution and significance as one of the deans of twentieth-century southern historiography. Sydnor ultimately transcended the narrowness and provincialism of his upbringing and his environment, developing into a critical, introspective, and rigorous intellectual. Over time he came to write "thesis-oriented history designed as much to influence the future as to illuminate the past."[12]

Born in Augusta, Georgia, to a Presbyterian minister, Giles Sydnor, and his wife Evelyn, Charles S. Sydnor grew up in a world of elite professionals who considered their social status an indicator of noblesse oblige. In the early decades of the twentieth century, Sydnor imbibed the romanticized ideas, images, and literature of the Old South, the Confederacy, and the Lost Cause perpetuated by neo-Confederate patriotic groups.

After studying at the Darlington School in Rome, Georgia, Sydnor entered Virginia's Hampden-Sydney College, graduating in 1918. He taught secondary-school mathematics in Rome, Georgia, and in Chattanooga, Tennessee, before enrolling in the doctoral program in history at the Johns Hopkins University. Hopkins, along with Columbia University, ranked as one of the early twentieth century's foremost centers for the study of "scientific" history. In Baltimore, Sydnor specialized in British history, completing his dissertation, "Press Censorship in England, 1534–1603," in 1923.[13] After teaching briefly at Hampden-Sydney, in 1925 Sydnor assumed the chairmanship of the history department at the University of Mississippi (Ole Miss). Upon relocating to Mississippi, Sydnor changed his specialty from English medieval history, a field difficult to research in southern libraries, to the history of the American South. Early in the twentieth century the southern states led the nation in establishing state archives and historical libraries.[14] Sydnor took special advantage of these collections and their opportunities for research and publication.

Sydnor's years at Ole Miss were both productive and formative. While in Oxford he published (with Claude Bennett) an elementary-school textbook, *Mississippi History* (1930), and *Slavery in Mississippi* (1933), plus important articles on free black persons, slaves, and frontier life in the Old South.[15] Bailey notes correctly that these "early historical works evidenced a comfortable scholar little inclined to challenge contemporary social values." The Mississippi state history textbook, for example, "was replete with the Negrophobic, anti-Yankee tone typical of southern school literature of the period," while Sydnor's slavery volume, certainly more significant to professional historians, nevertheless "projected a paternalistic image

of the peculiar institution." "Stultifyingly dull," according to Bailey, Sydnor's first two books "were laden with the carefully worded, sterile prose
of the scientific school and both conformed to conclusions amenable to the
region's guardians of historical orthodoxy." In 1930, when Mississippi's
populist-racist governor Theodore Bilbo fired Ole Miss's president and
dismissed one-quarter of its faculty, "Sydnor developed a keen sensitiv-
ity to the struggles between the South's intransigent elites and the restive
under classes which found voice in the demagogic Bilbo."[16] Sydnor and
his department were spared in Bilbo's academic purge, but he remained
shaken by the experience.[17]

Disappointed by the intellectual constraints, limitations for research,
and, especially, the overt interference by politicians into academic freedom
at Ole Miss, in 1936 Sydnor departed for the more academically liberal
confines of North Carolina's Duke University. He taught in Durham for
the remainder of his career, rising from associate professor to professor
and chair of the department of history.[18] In 1952 Sydnor became dean of
Duke's Graduate School of Arts and Sciences and retained his position as
chair of the Department of History.[19] In 1950–1951 Sydnor held the Harold Vyvyan Harmsworth Lectureship of American History at Oxford University. He was the first scholar from the South to receive this prestigious
guest professorship.

Sydnor maintained the highest standards of critical historical scholarship. In an early publication he underscored the importance for historians to present facts and avoid ethical questions. "Sometimes considerable
reading is necessary to form an opinion that can be expressed very briefly,"
he added.[20] Years later Sydnor encouraged and praised scholars who carefully examined source materials "that are often distorted and biased." He
believed that the best historical work resulted from teasing out the "fine
distinctions" in "controversial evidence."[21] Sydnor demanded fair, thoughtful, and rigorous analysis and deplored shoddy scholarship.

For example, in a book review on the role of African Americans during
the Civil War, Sydnor attacked the Marxist historian Herbert Aptheker's
The Negro in the Civil War (1938) for arguing that the Union Army played
a minimum role in emancipation and that the black population "'*had, for
all practical purposes, killed slavery.*'" Challenging Aptheker's conclusion,
Sydnor wrote that although Aptheker's collection of readings might prove
of "interest to students of current propaganda techniques, its obvious deficiency in research and its one-sidedness of interpretation render it valueless to the historian." In the same critique Sydnor exhibited condescension

toward the black historian Joseph C. Carroll who, in his *Slave Insurrections in the United States, 1800–1865* (1938), "managed to remain comparatively dispassionate in interpreting the facts even though they are of a
sort to stir the emotions, especially of a negro historian."[22]

In contrast, Sydnor praised Bell Irvin Wiley's *Southern Negroes, 1861–
1865* (1938) for examining black life and culture in the South during the
Civil War for its "wealth of detail . . . frequently enlivened by quoting
Negro dialect." Sydnor remarked that Wiley's study demonstrated that
"abundant evidence is marshaled to prove that the slaves did, despite contrary traditions, want their freedom, and they were keenly concerned over
the outcome of the fighting. But the notion that freedom was of much immediate benefit to the Negroes is disproved."[23]

Sydnor's career reached new heights in the late 1930s when he began
systematically researching the antebellum South, according to Bailey, a
region and a time that Sydnor considered "a vanished tradition of enlight-
ened aristocratic statesmen who had created a model society beneficial to
those of high estate and low." Sydnor's widely acclaimed *A Gentleman of
the Old Natchez Region: Benjamin L.C. Wailes* (1938), a pen portrait of
society in the antebellum Mississippi Valley, was the first significant fruit
of this labor. Admiring Wailes's promotion of education and cultural uplift
in frontier southwestern Mississippi, Sydnor also appreciated the Mississippian's nationalism in the midst of southern secessionism, his coura-
geous defense of the Union in 1861.[24]

Sydnor made an even more significant contribution to southern historiography, and signaled another break with neo-Confederate historiography, with the publication of *The Development of Southern Sectionalism,
1819–1848* (1948). This nuanced analysis of southern sectionalism between
the Missouri Compromise and the Treaty of Guadeloupe Hidalgo was no
apologia for the antebellum South. Rather Sydnor presented a critical as-
sessment of the origins of the Confederacy, especially what Bailey terms
the "excesses of democracy that empowered sectional demagogues to . . .
lead the South on its ill-omened path to secession and defeat." Sydnor
blamed the ruinous Civil War on destructive sectionalism and attacked
the chauvinism of southern partisans who he believed recklessly destroyed
the Union.[25]

The historian Arthur Schlesinger Jr. singled out Sydnor's *Development
of Southern Sectionalism* for "its pervading quality of thoughtful and dispassionate judgment." Schlesinger suggested that "this quality is especially
to be prized in dealing with the question of slavery—a problem that seems

to provoke almost as much acrimony today as it did a century ago." Avoiding the "neo-Confederate school" that Schlesinger believed had "risen to give a kind of Dixiecrat reading of the events leading to the war, with the responsibility for bloodshed placed exclusively upon the northern abolitionists and upon the blundering statesmanship of northern presidents," Sydnor remained "unimpassioned without becoming evasive."[26]

Sydnor followed *The Development of Southern Sectionalism* with the engaging *Gentlemen Freeholders: Political Practices in Washington's Virginia* (1952; republished in 1965 as *American Revolutionaries in the Making: Political Practices in Washington's Virginia*). In this book Sydnor detailed how local politics, especially the county courts and justices of the peace, operated in pre-Revolutionary Virginia. Celebrating what later historians would term "deferential democracy," a syncretic blend of aristocracy and democracy, Sydnor underscored how friendship, free liquor, rowdyism, and violence shaped electioneering in the days of Thomas Jefferson, James Madison, John Marshall, and George Washington. Despite having property and religious qualifications for voting, Sydnor explained, the economically homogeneous landed gentry produced quality statesmen who ruled and represented their lower-class neighbors judiciously.

Sydnor's *Gentlemen Freeholders* appealed to readers in the 1950s who, during the tumultuous age of the Cold War and desegregation, sought responsible conservative leaders with strong grassroots support. In the book, according to Bailey, "Sydnor let reign his faith in the uplifting value of a cultured and compassionate elite that shared with its less-favored peers the bounties of a well-ordered society."[27] One reviewer, Syracuse University's T. V. Smith, praised Sydnor's work as "informative, amusing, and reassuring: the roots of sin were in early Virginia, but they did not uniformly produce the fruits of unrighteousness."[28] Leonidas Dodson of the University of Pennsylvania found suggestive Sydnor's identification of shared interests between governors and the governed.[29] A third critic concluded that Sydnor's book established "a high standard for those who write on Virginia history, or, for that matter, any history."[30] Publication of *Gentlemen Freeholders* catapulted Sydnor to the top tier of the historical profession.

Nineteen fifty-four promised to be a banner year for Sydnor. His busy schedule included invitations to present the distinguished Claiborne Lectures at Ole Miss, a speech at the Mississippi Historical Society in Biloxi, and then the Walter Lynwood Fleming Lectures at Louisiana State University. Sydnor's Biloxi address, "Historical Comments on American Democracy," focused on what the historian considered a pattern of undemocratic tendencies at home and abroad under the sway of demagogic leaders. Sydnor implored the audience to reject leaders "who usurp functions that do not properly belong to them" and, no doubt thinking of the Virginia Dynasty that he had idealized in *Gentlemen Freeholders,* select only decision makers of the highest quality, those endowed with "wisdom, character and courage." Sydnor urged moderation whether in interpreting the meaning of the Civil War or in contemporary international or race relations or politics. A day following his Biloxi address, on March 2, 1954, Sydnor suffered a massive heart attack and died. His family buried him in Chattanooga, Tennessee.[31]

Decades earlier Sydnor had begun to publish widely on the history of black Mississippians. In his 1930 school text, *Mississippi History,* Sydnor addressed many of the topics and questions that he would examine three years later in *Slavery in Mississippi,* including the origins of slavery in the state and the role of slaves in Mississippi's cotton fields. In *Mississippi History* Sydnor described slavery in the Magnolia State as a benign institution. According to Sydnor, "on some plantations each slave was given a certain amount of work to do in a day. He had to plow so many acres of land or pick a certain number of pounds of cotton. If the slave worked rapidly, he might have some time free from labor." Similarly, "on some plantations the slaves were given rewards if they did more or better work than was usually done." Most slaves received sufficient food and clothing. Their masters required the bondsmen to do little more than "a reasonable amount of work." When Sydnor described the negative aspects of slavery in Mississippi, he usually presented them as positively as possible and with qualified criticism.[32]

In his description of the causes of the Civil War, Sydnor displayed a clear pro-southern bias. While he identified slavery as the main point of contention between north and south, Sydnor nonetheless held northern abolitionists largely responsible for igniting the conflict. When describing abolitionists, Sydnor declared, "Not realizing all the difficulties in the way of setting free all the slaves at once, they worked night and day to make other people believe as they did." He maintained that abolitionists regularly helped slaves run away and refused to help masters capture fugitive slaves. Consequently, Sydnor suggested that white southerners considered themselves under fire and lobbied Congress to force "abolitionists to cease making disturbances." When Abraham Lincoln, a Republican opposed to slavery, won the 1860 presidential election, many southerners believed that they had no choice but to secede.[33]

In *Mississippi History* Sydnor left the distinct impression that he favored the doctrine of secession. He maintained that the original thirteen colonies had joined the Union voluntarily and that "at different times some of the northern states had said that a state could separate from the other states if it wanted to." Sydnor also pointed out that in the early days of the Republic several northern states threatened to leave the Union. Resembling most southern historians of his day, Sydnor recognized the legitimacy of state rights and secession, openly sympathizing with Mississippi's course in the War Between the States. Sydnor clearly viewed the armed conflict of 1861–1865 not as a civil war but rather as a war between two sovereign nations.[34]

Despite his southern sympathies, Sydnor nevertheless identified negative sides to slavery. Writing in 1929 in the *South Atlantic Quarterly,* he underscored the painful separation of families that resulted from the domestic slave trade, considering the breakup of families the most heinous aspect of the "peculiar institution." Sydnor explained that their determination to reunite families or friendships motivated slave runaways. Others "escaped to avoid deserved punishment for some misdeed," burglary or even murder. Tellingly, however, Sydnor concluded that the majority of slaves "left for no outstanding cause." He contended that "the irksomeness of regular and compulsory work, coupled with the call of the road, created a temptation [to run away] that was occasionally irresistible."[35] The slaves' determination to be free thus undermined Sydnor's interpretation of slavery as a patriarchal institution.

So too did Sydnor's research on Mississippi's free persons of color. As early as 1927 he published the results of his research on Mississippi free black persons in the *American Historical Review* based on a close reading of the state's antebellum law codes. Sydnor found that the mere presence of free black people as a class instilled fear "in the hearts of the slave-owners of Mississippi" and, not surprisingly, Sydnor discovered that free black individuals faced harsh discrimination in a state where white residents presumed every person of color "to be a slave." Under Mississippi law, in order to retain one's three-year certification as a free man or woman of color, a person had to appear before a court, pay a fee, and give proof of "his non-servile condition." If a free black person failed to maintain his registration, or if he lost his certificate, he became subject to arrest, capture, and sale into slavery. Furthermore, even with the certificate of registration, free black life remained circumscribed. Free black individuals could not move about the state freely, sell certain goods, or possess firearms. They also remained excluded from a wide range of possible jobs.[36]

Frederic Bancroft, the veteran gentleman scholar and raconteur who specialized in the history of the domestic slave trade, assisted Sydnor in his transition from a British historian to a specialist in Mississippi slavery. Bancroft studied history at Columbia University under Professors John W. Burgess and Munroe Smith. His doctoral dissertation, *A Sketch of the Negro in Politics, Especially in South Carolina and Mississippi* (1885), drew heavily on oral history interviews that Bancroft had conducted in Mississippi as early as in 1884. Bancroft, who in July 1927 praised Sydnor's "model" article, "The Free Negro in Mississippi before the Civil War," became the junior scholar's mentor and sounding board for his research on Mississippi slavery. In return Sydnor critiqued Bancroft's work on the slave trade and slave prices.[37]

In March 1929 Sydnor informed Bancroft of his interest "in the matter of the length of life of slaves as a factor throwing some light on the treatment and conditions of life of slaves." Sydnor found from using the research on cemetery records by Prudential Insurance statistician Frederick L. Hoffman that "there was very little difference between the average length of life ahead of a twenty year old slave in Mississippi and the white population of the same age and territory. I do not think that the difference was more than about two years." Bancroft suggested that mild winters in the lower southern states might have contributed to slave longevity, assuming they did not live under the control of "severe masters or overseers."[38] Sydnor published his findings in an influential and innovative article, "Life Span of Mississippi Slaves," arguing that "the negro as a slave had a longer life in comparison with his white master than he has as a free man in comparison with the white people of Mississippi today." He was quick to point out "that to prove that the slave lived a reasonably long life does not prove that the life of the slave was pleasant or even reasonably bearable."[39]

Bancroft also assisted Sydnor in quantifying Mississippi's slave population and the slave trade in the state by using tax data.[40] Bancroft's own revisionist work, *Slave-Trading in the Old South*, appeared in 1931.[41] Sydnor gushed over Bancroft's book in the *American Historical Review*, praising it as the definitive work on domestic slave trading and remarking that "no other phase of slavery has been handled with more skill and care." Sydnor took special note of Bancroft's comments on inflated slave prices and pondered the causative effect on secession.[42]

In April 1931 Sydnor sent several chapters of his slavery manuscript to the senior scholar for his review. In his reply Bancroft urged him not to rush into print, maintaining that "the books that are re-re-revised" are generally those "that give an author the best results." Over the summer of 1931 Bancroft critiqued Sydnor's drafts. Bancroft considered it essential that Sydnor include a chapter on slavery as an economic system—"its profits, its losses, its excuses and its follies," which would constitute an especially original contribution to historical scholarship on slavery. Bancroft implored Sydnor to develop a degree of "self-criticism," especially in terms of his exposition, without which he could not "do justice to the certain superior natural qualities" he already possessed. Bancroft lamented that Sydnor's opening chapter contained "much that is crude, labored, wordy, rather than thoughtful, concise and clear" and complained that Sydnor's footnotes were unnecessarily complex. Bancroft also implored Sydnor to contact the Mississippi planter-sociologist-historian Alfred Holt Stone "and pump him to the limit." Finally, Bancroft reminded Sydnor to pay close attention to the numerous extant state studies on slavery and free black persons.[43]

In addition to criticism and research assistance from Bancroft, Sydnor received a Social Science Research Council grant in the summer of 1932 to fund work at the Library of Congress.[44] Because Mississippi libraries contained few primary source materials on slavery, he also went to great lengths to locate obscure sources, most notably plantation account books, diaries, and manuscripts, in private collections.[45] For example, Natchez native Laura Baker provided Sydnor access to the last will and testament of Elizabeth Kirkland Green, a source that provided information as to how masters transferred slaves to heirs. "I have not often found proof of much humanity in disposing of slaves," Sydnor informed Baker. "I have believed that this existed among the better slaveholders, but the historian is embarrassed in stating what he has not proof of. This will is clear proof and I shall be very glad to be allowed to cite it, of course acknowledging my indebtedness to you for permitting me to use it."[46]

In November 1933 the American Historical Association's Carnegie Revolving Fund published Sydnor's *Slavery in Mississippi* under the imprint of New York's D. Appleton-Century Company.[47] The *Mississippian*, the Ole Miss student weekly, announced Sydnor's monograph as "an interesting analytical study of slavery in Mississippi during the years prior to the Civil War. It gives a more complete picture of the actual conditions under which slaves lived than does any other single volume."[48] Bancroft's congratulatory note to Sydnor no doubt carried special meaning to him. Bancroft wrote that "you have written a thoroughly scholarly, comprehensive and unanswerable a work, which will never need to be done again. That is the best criterion, the highest satisfaction."[49] Sydnor's *Slavery in Mississippi* did in fact pass the test of time, appearing in reprint editions in 1959, 1965, and 1966.[50]

Sydnor's *Slavery in Mississippi* painted an unmistakably benign picture of slavery. The author noted that notwithstanding common assumptions about the severity of slavery in the lower South, slavery in the Magnolia State was neither more harsh nor laborious than in the upper slave states. Conditions of slave life depended largely on the character of the individual masters, Sydnor averred. Mississippi slaves' food and raiment, discipline, work routine, and medical care were neither better nor worse than bondsmen experienced elsewhere. He acknowledged that Mississippi masters generally paid little attention to educating and providing religious and moral training for their slaves. Brutal punishments were rare, though Sydnor noted that all slaves lived under the specter of being sold and separated from their loved ones.

Sydnor considered the living and working conditions of Mississippi slaves to be quite reasonable. Slave owners generally treated their slaves fairly and responsibly. Abuses by slaveholders were the exception not the rule. Sydnor questioned the economic efficiency of slavery, however, arguing that free labor represented a more profitable alternative to forced labor. Most important, Sydnor maintained that slaveholders responded first and foremost to economic considerations. Financial factors determined the quality of slave life.

Sydnor wrote that Mississippi had a vibrant domestic slave trade. He observed that Mississippians purchased more slaves than they sold and that most of these bondsmen came from the upper South. This proved unsurprising, Sydnor reasoned, given that Mississippi territory formed in 1798, the African slave trade to the United States ended in 1808, and Mississippi statehood occurred in 1817. Sydnor explained that "on the journey south, slaves were well fed and not pushed too fast" (149).[51]

Sydnor divided Mississippi's slave population into three categories: domestic slaves, town slaves, and plantation slaves. The work of domestic slaves, who cooked, cleaned, gardened, and provided child care was, according to Sydnor, "far more pleasant than that of the field hand." Sydnor observed that house servants frequently received the same food and clothing as their white families, although their clothing consisted of hand-me-downs. Moreover, a larger percentage of domestic slaves learned to read and write than did plantation slaves. Sydnor went so far as to say that some masters actually pampered their domestic slaves. A prize domestic slave, Sydnor averred, "was more of a favored pet than a slave" (4). Town slaves worked as mechanics, carpenters, or blacksmiths or plied trades on steamships or assisted with railroad construction. Because these tasks required considerable skill, Sydnor reasoned, most contemporaries considered town slaves the most intelligent among the bondsmen. He pointed out, however, that white carpenters, mechanics, and blacksmiths often refused to train slaves, fearful not only that slave tradesmen would take work away from them, but also that their skills would diminish "their self respect" (8).

The vast majority of Mississippi slaves, however, worked as field hands on plantations. Sydnor conceded that plantation life represented the most laborious form of slavery but disagreed with the journalist Frederick Law Olmsted, who judged slavery both immoral and inefficient, and who alleged that Magnolia State slave owners worked their field hands excessively. In Sydnor's opinion "the average slave did not perform an unreasonable amount of work in a day" (252). He maintained that with proper discipline, slaves could have become even more productive. He contended "that skilled slaves with proper encouragement could pick two or even three times as much cotton as the average slave picked in a day. The average slave under normal conditions was, therefore, not driven to the limit of his powers" (16). Sydnor went on to explain that though slaves worked long days, "movement of body was slow and energy expended was small. Considered as a machine, the slave turned out about the same product in a day and used about the same fuel as his free grandchildren of to-day" (252).

Sydnor concluded that "with the usual qualification as to exceptions, the food and clothing of Mississippi slaves were reasonably satisfactory" (252). While Sydnor acknowledged that white people almost always enjoyed better food than the slaves, he nevertheless disagreed with Olmsted's characterization of slave food as "indigestible" (31). Northerners and southerners had distinct diets and different ways of preparing food, Sydnor explained. Thus, while Olmsted cared little for the food allotted to southern slaves, Mississippians most likely would have preferred their hog meat and hoecake diet to the beef and Irish potatoes consumed north of the Mason-Dixon line. Sydnor concluded that at the very least, "slaves did not often suffer hunger," a circumstance, he said, that found support in travelers' accounts, including Olmsted's (39).

While conceding that the slaves' clothing was "cheaper and coarser" than that of white persons, Sydnor maintained that slave garments "would probably compare favorably with that of the agricultural laborer of the same region in more recent times" (30). Specifically, Sydnor pointed out that owners provided clothing appropriate to seasonal changes and to ensure the health of their slaves. For example, slaves received a new pair of shoes in the winter when the weather became cold. He also pointed out that slave owners commonly provided their bondsmen coats or wraps, flannel shirts, shifts, and warm socks as protection from morning chills and to prevent contagious diseases such as cholera.

Sydnor proved more willing to accept criticism of Mississippi slaves' housing. He recognized that Mississippi law offered no protection to bondsmen against poor housing. Slaves often lived in small, crowded quarters, Sydnor acknowledged. Exhibiting Jim Crow–era condescension at best, and gross insensitivity at worst, he asserted that most slaves did not appear to be dissatisfied in their housing arrangements because, like children, they found ways to amuse themselves, despite less than optimal circumstances. Sydnor argued that, in any case, slave cabins never constituted homes in the traditional sense; rather they "were little more than places to sleep" and, during most of the day in fact, slave cabins remained deserted. Contextualizing, if not rationalizing, the slave experience, Sydnor remarked that "civilization was still in the pioneer stage in at least half of Mississippi at the beginning of the Civil War" (41). Many slave owners themselves resided in equally incommodious homes, meager log houses.

Sydnor emphasized that most slave owners provided their bondsmen with satisfactory physical and medical care. While conceding that plantation records documented that slaves missed a considerable number of work days due to sickness, he nonetheless argued that ill health did not necessarily mean that owners provided their slaves with insufficient medical treatment. Sydnor cited mortality rates from antebellum Mississippi to support his point, maintaining that slaves became ill only slightly more often than white persons. Much like the old slaveholders, Sydnor observed a "prevalence of sickness when there was a large amount of work to be done" (48). As evidence, Sydnor cited plantation records that described slave illnesses as little more than indications of slothfulness.

Sydnor extolled masters' treatment of older slaves, arguing that "as slaves grew old, their tasks were lightened in proportion to their failing strength." Masters continued to maintain slaves even when they no longer could perform enough work to compensate for the cost of their sustenance.

xxiv INTRODUCTION

Sydnor went so far as to assert that "no instance has been found of a master's failing to care for such slaves and they generally seem to have been treated as well as able-bodied field hands" (66). Sydnor did, however, acknowledge the high rate of infant mortality among slaves, explaining that it may have resulted from the fact that "managers of slaves thought that negro women needed very little care at such times" (49). Because slaveholders considered women valuable as field workers, they received minimal time off to take care of their newborn.

Sydnor conceded that the punishment of slaves was an inevitable part of a system of forced labor because "the ordinary incentives to labor which operate on free men were lacking in slavery" (86). He noted that masters commonly whipped their slaves to induce them to work faster. While Sydnor admitted that brutal punishments occurred under Mississippi slavery, he nonetheless maintained that "these revolting extremes were rare" (91). Most masters "took no delight in the lash" because excessive "whipping indicated a poorly run plantation" (89, 87). On balance, Sydnor wrote, "the vast majority [of slaves] seem to have accepted an occasional whipping as a matter of course, and were not greatly affected" (94). Sydnor pointed out that a master who meted out cruel punishments to slaves could be punished by state law.

On a happier note Sydnor remarked that masters often rewarded slaves for performing their tasks well. Incentives included tips, "free" time to visit friends and families on neighboring plantations, and presents at Christmas and seasonal holidays. On some estates slaves received wages for work after the completion of routine labor. Other slaves cultivated garden truck patches and raised farm animals. Some masters even set their slaves free after an unusually good deed.

Sydnor credited either white overseers or black slave drivers with providing plantation management. He argued that overseers rarely forced slaves with legitimate illnesses to work in the fields and described the typical overseer as "kind and sympathetic in prescribing for a slave who he believed was really sick" (45). The slave driver, according to Sydnor, gained status and received material advantages in return for assuming responsibilities for marshaling the slave work force. It was difficult, Sydnor argued, for slaveholders to find effective slave drivers and, realizing the complications with the system of privileging one slave over others, he often reduced the slave driver's ability to punish other bondsmen. The driver, Sydnor noted, "must generally have been unpopular among the other slaves" (75).

So too were the overseers. Sydnor considered finding an overseer who could treat slaves fairly and still manage a profitable plantation one of the most formidable challenges facing slaveholders. On the one hand, he understood that overseers tended to treat slaves more harshly than masters because "they had no permanent interest in the slaves, either as persons or as property" (69). Moreover, their wages depended almost entirely on the profits yielded from large cotton crops. Accordingly, the overseer "could hardly be expected to deal gently with the negroes" (70). At the same time, however, owners had an economic incentive to eschew hiring brutal overseers. Ideally, slave owners sought plantation managers who treated their most valuable resources, slaves, with care while concomitantly producing abundant crops.

Masters favored treating their slaves kindly, Sydnor argued, not because of altruism but rather out of economic self-interest. Though he characterized most slave owners as "men of conscience," Sydnor nevertheless maintained that their motivation stemmed from their quest for profits, not from philanthropy (106). As slaves represented a valuable and expensive commodity, it made economic sense for masters to treat them well. Consequently, Sydnor asserted that "for economic reasons, planters at the very least wanted their slaves so treated as not to endanger health or life" (72). He pointed out that injury or damage to a slave "might easily offset the proceeds from a large crop" (70). Slaveholders thus had an economic incentive to provide good medical care and to refrain from overworking slaves and handing out unusually harsh punishments.

Sydnor admitted, however, that the slave owners' economic interests often resulted in decisions that proved unbeneficial to the slaves. Most slave owners opposed educating their bondsmen, reasoning that educating slaves rarely made them better workers or provided owners with economic benefits. Slaves who learned to read and write might prove more inclined to run away, encouraging owners "to keep slaves ignorant" (53). Though state law outlawed teaching slaves to read and write, some bondsmen nonetheless received the rudiments of an education. Sydnor wrote that while few slaves became educated, many bondsmen learned agricultural and domestic trades. Training slaves in specific tasks benefited the owner financially and equipped the slaves with marketable skills if they obtained freedom.

Slaveholders, according to Sydnor, cared less about the moral and religious education of their slaves than they did about their physical well-being. Religion did little to increase the market value of slaves and some slave owners even believed that religion made slaves lazier. Even so, Syd-nor found evidence that some slaveholders tried to correct the so-called immorality among their slaves, particularly regarding marriage, while "others left the negroes to their own sins, made no attempt to teach moral-ity, took cognizance of conditions only when quarrels or disturbances broke out, and then warned or flogged all participants" (63). Although slave marriages were not legally sanctioned, Sydnor insisted "that the fail-ure to respect marriages between slaves, particularly when they were sold, was much criticized and rightly so" (64).

Though he devoted much of *Slavery in Mississippi* to assessing the conditions of slave life, slavery's implications as an economic force ran through Sydnor's book like a leitmotif. By the 1830s the "practical prob-lems of making the investment pay" preoccupied planters (249). Slave owners, Sydnor insisted, paid up-front costs of from $500 to $1,800 for the privilege of owning their labor and then incurring the obligation of their lifelong sustenance. Soil depletion and exhaustion also ate into their profit margins.

Rarely, Sydnor explained, did increased cotton production offset the high costs of slave ownership and plantation management. Not only did slaves generally underperform, but owners also refrained from overwork-ing them, fearful of damaging their most valuable economic asset. Beyond this, Sydnor maintained that increased profits from cotton in the 1850s precipitated a greater demand for slaves. The swell in demand also re-sulted in inflated slave prices. Sydnor argued that the increased demand for and cost of slaves associated with the rise in cotton production gener-ally negated substantial profits for planters ("their investments showed an inadequate return" [198]). They believed that if the market value of slaves decreased, their net worth would decline precipitously. Conse-quently, slave owners continually bought slaves to keep the demand and price of slaves elevated. Sydnor concluded that "economics demanded that the slave-owner be an expansionist, for without a market slave prices must soon have declined" (202).

Sydnor asserted that not only did many planters fail to turn a profit, but many succumbed to debt as well. He pointed out that the lure of cot-ton profits tempted many planters to increase their labor force by buying slaves on credit. Sydnor's research in sheriffs' and trustees' sales records, the account books of New Orleans merchants, and slave traders' ledger books provided "evidence that cotton plantations were not sure roads to wealth" (198). He maintained that even in the economic flush times of the early 1830s and late 1850s, the high cost of keeping slaves, along with fluctuating cotton prices, made it nearly impossible for planters to make significant profits. They probably would have reaped larger gains from free labor. "From an economic standpoint," Sydnor concluded, "it is very questionable whether slaves were a good investment year in and year out even in Mississippi" (200).

The large number of fugitive slaves in Mississippi, according to Sydnor, constituted an additional problem for slave owners. Not only did runaway slaves translate into financial loss to planters, but the disruption of work also led to some degree to "the breakdown in the morale of the working force" (102). Sydnor considered the problem of slave runaways a major concern for the region's economic and social welfare. A slave known for running away could not be trusted because he could convince other slaves to abscond. "By boasting of his exploits he could easily spread discontentment among slaves who were ordinarily satisfied" (106).

Sydnor speculated on the motives of slave runaways. Anticipating later scholars, he supposed that most slaves absconded in order to reunite with family or friends. Sydnor conceded that some slaves fled because of undeserved punishment but insisted that slave owners generally treated their slaves well for economic reasons. He contended that slaves often ran away to avoid justifiable punishment for some misdeed, explaining that "sometimes the slave deserved punishment, sometimes not, but there were certainly a number of instances of both kinds" (107). Sydnor also argued that slaves took flight "to avoid the times of greatest work" (104). He pointed out that most runaways occurred in June and September, when work on plantations became most laborious. In the end Sydnor found no conclusive cause for slave runaways. "Many, possibly most, of the runaway slaves left for no outstanding reason," he said. Borrowing language from his 1929 article on pursuing slave fugitives, Sydnor wrote that "the irksomeness of regular and compulsory work, coupled with the call of the road, created a temptation that was occasionally irresistible" (111).

Sydnor considered the presence of free Negroes in Mississippi another problem for slaveholders. Though the state contained only a small number of free black individuals (fewer than 800 in 1860), most free persons of color resided in areas where black people outnumbered white. Sydnor wrote that free black persons as a class had a nefarious influence on the slaves. "Slaveholders feared that the mere existence of free negroes among slaves might make the latter dissatisfied, and there was always a possibility that some of the free negroes might actively endeavor to create discontent" (203). As a step in eradicating this "problem," Mississippians established the Mississippi Colonization Society (MCS) in 1831 in order to facilitate the removal of free black individuals from their state. Sydnor remarked that though the society intended originally only to remove free Negroes from Mississippi, in practice it served to repatriate freed men and women to Africa.

The MCS established a colony for freed slaves from Mississippi in Greenville, in southeastern Liberia at the mouth of the Sinoe River. Sydnor considered Mississippi's Liberian settlers "superior to the average negroes in Mississippi," crediting them with developing Liberia and civilizing neighboring Africans. He noted, however, the poor state of Greenville in the 1930s and insinuated that many of the town's contemporary residents descended from its original founders, men "whose conduct has recently brought condemnation upon their country" (238).

Sydnor explained that despite slavery's economic weaknesses and other liabilities, most white Mississippians wholeheartedly embraced the "peculiar institution." Though before 1830 some in the Magnolia State occasionally tolerated slavery as a necessary evil, by the late 1830s "public opinion became nearly unanimous in extolling slavery as an unmixed blessing both for the slaves and the white people" (241). The dramatic increase in cotton production in the 1830s solidified slavery's importance to the state. Over time white Mississippians came to fear so-called renegade white abolitionists who they believed would destroy slavery and their "southern way of life." Slaveholders and others, at first unsure "of the excellence of slavery," ultimately became "convinced by their own and their neighbors' arguments that it was most desirable" (246). They joined hands in defending slavery and combating the abolitionists.

Sydnor concluded *Slavery in Mississippi* by discussing the degree to which white Mississippians' increasing reverence for slavery during the 1830s influenced the well-being of their slaves. On the one hand, life became more difficult for "a few intelligent and skilled slaves" who gradually lost hope of purchasing their freedom and hiring their own time. On the other hand, however, Sydnor surmised that overall "slaves do not appear to have been affected by what their masters thought of the institution; for there seemed to be little relation between the degree to which a man would go in defending slavery and his treatment of his own slaves" (249).

In the end Sydnor argued that it made economic sense for planters, even those with no moral qualms about enslaving African Americans, to become benevolent slaveholders. Compassionate treatment of slaves resulted in greater productivity and reduced the probability of financial loss from the serious injury or death of an expensive slave. Sydnor insisted, however, that a slave owner might genuinely define his slave as more than a "machine for making money." He judged "him a person for whom he might have kindly feelings or even true friendship" (249–50).

Sydnor's *Slavery in Mississippi* received a cordial reception from many lay readers and scholars. Writing from Church Hill, Mississippi, for example, Winbourne Magruder Drake congratulated Sydnor on what he considered "a fine piece of work." Drake found the book especially agreeable "because it carries the tone of the historian, whereas many previous works on Mississippi history have had the tone of the advocate."[52] The *Chattanooga Daily Times*'s reviewer judged *Slavery in Mississippi* "as good a presentation of the southern attitude" toward slavery and secession as was available. He welcomed Sydnor's differentiation between large planters (whose economic interests predisposed them against disunion) and politicians (who mobilized non-slave-owning white individuals to support slavery and state rights).[53]

Esteemed University of Richmond colonial historian Maude H. Woodfin also praised Sydnor's book. She suggested that in *Slavery in Mississippi*, "Professor Sydnor finds the distinctive difference of slavery in Mississippi from the upper tier of the slave states or the old South in the facts that the region was a buyer of slaves—and Virginia born and bred slaves were highly desired on that market—that it was more the character of a frontier civilization, and that it was almost wholly devoted to cotton culture." Woodfin compared Sydnor's analysis with the "realistic fiction" of the late-nineteenth-century Mississippi journalist John Macon. Sydnor's book possessed "a pleasurable quality often lacking in so careful a monograph." In her opinion close reading of *Slavery in Mississippi* revealed that "every now and then the personality of a specimen triumphed over the system of bondage. The thread of human interest enlivens the sociological and economic treatise."[54]

Dwight L. Dumond, who studied history with the historian Ulrich Bonnell Phillips at the University of Michigan, agreed with Woodfin, referring to Sydnor's *Slavery in Mississippi* as "the most important study of the institution of slavery since Phillips' *American Negro Slavery* appeared in 1918 and, without exception, the most comprehensive and exhaustive analysis ever made." Dumond praised Sydnor for tracing slavery's evolution in one state and for assessing the complexities of the day-to-day lives of the bondsmen. His research was so thorough that he could provide only "a highly generalized picture of the institution," proving that "there was no such thing as a typical plantation." Dumond also appreciated that Sydnor went beyond studying slave life and labor to examine the conflict between planters and slave traders, the colonization movement, and proslavery ideology.[55]

Not all historians, however, greeted Sydnor's *Slavery in Mississippi* uncritically. Rosser H. Taylor, an authority on slavery in North Carolina, questioned Sydnor's economic analysis, particularly his emphasis on the high cost of Mississippi slaves. "This was unquestionably an important factor in estimating profits when a person was buying slaves," Taylor admitted, "but as it cost no more to feed and clothe a high-priced slave than a medium-priced slave already in possession, it would appear that the profitableness of slavery would depend in most cases upon the cost of operations and the price of the crops produced."[56]

V. Alton Moody, an expert on Louisiana slavery, suggested that while Sydnor's monograph offered "a thoroughgoing study of the daily life of slaves and of the profitableness of slavery," it nonetheless contained weaknesses. Moody challenged Sydnor's argument that the slaves' food supply came from local sources, usually from within the plantation itself. Rather, Moody suggested that plantations rarely were self-sufficient, usually abandoning diversified farming in favor of importing foodstuffs, especially bacon and pork, from the Midwest. Moody also critiqued Sydnor for paying short shrift to several important topics, such as slave crime, the compensation of slave owners when the state sentenced their bondsmen to life imprisonment or capital punishment, changes in slave birth and death rates over time, and threats of slave revolt. Finally, Moody faulted Sydnor for drawing more heavily on slave codes rather than on session laws as evidence and for overstating slaves' access to plantation livestock.[57]

William K. Boyd, Sydnor's future Duke University colleague, praised *Slavery in Mississippi* for contributing to the modern trend of examining the "practical, everyday problems, rather than the legal and statistical aspects" of slavery. But Boyd nonetheless had reservations about Sydnor's book, including about the author's failure to consult medical journals to document slave medical care. "Conservatism characterizes the work," Boyd continued. "The harsher aspects of the slave system are not exploited. Apparently the Negro was satisfied with his lot. Nor is reflection made concerning the reaction of the presence of a servile race on the minds of a master class and on those who did not own slaves." Boyd also regretted that Sydnor was "cautious" in his assessment of the slave profitability question, failing to consider the full range of "limitations resulting from combining labor and capital in one investment."[58]

Black scholars found much to criticize in *Slavery in Mississippi*. For example, the controversial Josephite priest John T. Gillard attacked Sydnor for describing Mississippi slaves impersonally, more as "mules and machines" and less as "men and women." Gillard reminded readers that "human souls looked out with pleading eyes as the slave-driver's whip seared scars into sinews; human hearts were broken as the auctioneer's hammer smashed family ties upon the slave block; moral minds were in those black women who taught their children to hate the white blood which violence so often sent surging through black veins. Slavery's stinging lash may have left its awful marks upon the souls of white masters. Soul scars are the crueler heritage."[59]

Howard University sociologist E. Franklin Frazier argued that Sydnor fell short of disproving Mississippi's reputation as the most heinous of slave states and the state with the worst record of post-emancipation lynchings. Frazier found unconvincing Sydnor's conclusion that, except for slave housing, slavery in Mississippi was no worse than the "peculiar institution" elsewhere in the South. He wrote that "if one looks more closely into the manner in which the author has used his sources, one is inclined to doubt that we have a real cross-section study of the institution of slavery." Though Frazier conceded that the availability of sources limited Sydnor's study, he nonetheless questioned the historian's reliance on "sentimentalized" accounts and criticized his failure to consider ecological, economic, and social forces that rendered Mississippi slavery unique.[60] Similarly, Alain Locke, the philosopher and writer who also taught at Howard, doubted Sydnor's objectivity and the viability of his economic determinism. Like Frazier, Locke concluded that Sydnor failed in his attempt to absolve "Mississippi of the unenviable reputation of having been the darkest spot in American slavery . . . insisting that there was as much division of camps and opinion there on the slavery question as anywhere else; and the facts almost prove it."[61]

Carter G. Woodson, the veteran editor of the *Journal of Negro History*, leveled the most serious criticisms at *Slavery in Mississippi*. Woodson wrote that though Sydnor paid more attention to slaves as persons "than one customarily finds in the sectional treatises on slavery," he nevertheless fell short in developing "the human side of the equation. Herein the slaveholder is made not only the chief performer, but the performance it-self." Beyond this, Woodson faulted Sydnor for allowing his personal bias to obstruct his attempt at writing "with restraint and care."[62]

Woodson charged that Sydnor, "like most persons who defend the South," explained away slavery's cruelties and hardships except in a small minority of cases and for the omnipresent fear on the part of the bondsmen of being sold. He pointed out examples where Sydnor's anecdotal evidence contradicted his argument that slavery was essentially a benign institu-tion dependent on the individual master's character. Woodson took special umbrage at Sydnor's assertion that slave life differed little from that of white agricultural laborers except for the fact that the master controlled every facet of the slave's life. Woodson found "utterly untenable" Sydnor's contention that slaves received "kind treatment" from a class of men and women who denied slaves opportunities to purchase their freedom, who radiated contempt for free black persons, and who denied the bondsmen religious and educational training. "It is evident," Woodson concluded, "that when most whites write about Negroes they have in mind a double standard. What was 'kindness to the slave' was not 'kindness to a white man.'" He asked: "Can men of such bias write history?"[63]

Notwithstanding such serious criticisms, most historians have taken aim at Sydnor's economic analyses, especially his argument that slavery generally was financially unprofitable, not his description of slavery as a generally mild institution. Writing in 1942, the historian Thomas P. Govan noted "many objections and questions" regarding Sydnor's economic as-sessment. He charged that Sydnor miscalculated slaveholders' profits by failing to include interest on investment and wages for management as profit, by not taking into account the increasing value of slaves as profit, by overstating depreciation of land, and by ignoring changing slave prices and values over time.[64] In 1958, in his *Agriculture in Ante-Bellum Mis-sissippi,* John Hebron Moore, unlike Sydnor, found slavery profitable on Mississippi plantations depending on circumstance—time, place, and the ability and fortune of the individual planters.[65] In 1974 two economic his-torians, Robert W. Fogel and Stanley L. Engerman, pounced on Sydnor's inexperience in working with economic questions generally and with de-mographics and statistics in particular. They charged that among other lapses, Sydnor failed to analyze appropriate variables, misinterpreted equations that he derived from demographics handbooks, made serious computational errors, and drew incorrect conclusions from his data.[66]

These methodological weaknesses aside, Sydnor's *Slavery in Missis-sippi* remains important because, as the best of the "Phillips school" of state-level slavery studies, it filled in details in Phillips's larger, more com-prehensive story. Seeking to test Phillips's conclusions and to expand upon his work on the local level, Sydnor in fact portrayed slavery as an even more varied and complicated institution than Phillips had realized. Most significantly, *Slavery in Mississippi,* alone among the "Phillips school" volumes, calculated the average rate of profit for slaveholders based on estimated average normal expenses (prices of slaves, depreciation, man-agement, and equipment) and income (cotton production). In addition, Fogel and Engerman credit Sydnor with pioneering the systematic use of records detailing daily cotton picking rates.[67]

Avery O. Craven, one of the leading southern historians of the 1930s, praised Sydnor for recognizing the essential diversity of slavery as a labor system and the plantation as an agricultural unit. Sydnor emphasized the role of Mississippi's small planters, the Cotton Kingdom's "small men," not the stereotypical large planters who oversaw palatial estates. Large planters, Craven explained, occupied a far less dominant place in Missis-sippi agriculture than those slaveholders who lived more modestly and sought upward mobility. Craven also credited Sydnor with underscoring the small proportion of slaveholding to non-slaveholding whites and the degree, directly or indirectly, to which slavery touched all Mississippians.[68]

Sydnor established that slave runaways occurred more frequently dur-ing the state's pioneer period than later and maintained that Mississippi's slave laws proved to be harsher on the statute books than in execution. In terms of the treatment of the slaves (housing, food, clothing, conditions of work) Sydnor largely agreed with Phillips and, in assessing the domes-tic slave trade, with Bancroft. Sydnor argued that slaves' lives generally compared favorably with laborers under other contemporary economic systems except that they were forbidden to be educated, that their punish-ments were more severe, that their marriages were forbidden, and that slaves could be sold without consideration of separating families. Like Phillips, Sydnor considered slavery an economic liability. He went so far as to suggest that in cotton production at least, free white labor would have been preferable to slave labor.[69] As Fred Arthur Bailey observed more re-cently, "Sydnor approached *Slavery in Mississippi* as a journeyman work-ing confidently through a complicated historical problem, thoroughly studying available primary sources (largely produced by proslave whites), and in the end he drew conclusions that confirmed rather than challenged the prevailing views of his own time."[70]

Yet even when evaluated within the context of his day, Sydnor's *Slavery in Mississippi* exhibited weaknesses. Clearly undervaluing the hardships of slave life, Sydnor exaggerated what he considered the planters' benevolent treatment of their bondsmen, including the care of the elderly as well as their allowance of clothing, food, and housing. Based on his own central thesis—that slaveholders operated largely out of economic self-interest—what economic incentive would planters have had to take good care of unproductive older slaves and to clothe, feed, and house the general slave population beyond mere subsistence?

Sydnor's assertion that economic forces led slave owners continually to purchase slaves, thereby escalating slave prices and keeping the value of slave owners' most valuable assets high, also is problematical. Based on the author's evidence, it would have made equally wise economic sense for slave owners to have allowed slave prices to drop, thereby decreasing their initial investment with hopes of returning a larger profit.

Finally, the large number of slave runaways Sydnor documented provides palpable evidence that he exaggerated the favorable conditions of Mississippi slavery. If "being a slave was not for the average Negro a dreadful lot" why, then, did so many undertake the serious risks involved with fleeing their masters? Even if some slaves absconded to avoid punishment, the sheer number of Mississippi fugitive slaves suggests that bondsmen found slavery a less than pleasant existence. Like Phillips's other disciples, then, Sydnor misread both "the character of the masters and the desire for freedom in the hearts of the slaves" (253).

Quick to contextualize African American slavery within the experiences of other laboring groups, Sydnor ultimately proved blind to the broad meaning of slavery and freedom for people of color. "Generally, the chief difference between a slave and a free agricultural laborer lay outside the realm of food, clothing, shelter and work," he wrote. "The difference was that the slave was ordered to his work; his food and clothing were allowanced; his movements were restricted; his every act was watched; he was sometimes punished and he might be sold" (253). As later generations of historians would argue with a vengeance, these constituted large differences indeed.

My thanks go to Lisa F. Andrusyszyn, Ann Davis, Elizabeth Dunn, Charles W. Eagles, James J. Harris, Jon Helmandollar, Chuck McShane,

William J. Maher, Randall M. Miller, Chris Ruehlen, Lois Stickell, and Robert B. Townsend for their research assistance in the preparation of this introduction. Alex Moore and Mark Smith exhibited their usual generosity, patience, and support while awaiting its completion.

NOTES

1. Charles Sackett Sydnor, *Slavery in Mississippi* (New York: D. Appleton-Century, 1933), 253.

2. Stark Young, "Two Slavery Books," *New Republic* 79 (May 23, 1934): 48.

3. Harold J. Jonas, review of *Slavery in Mississippi,* by Charles S. Sydnor, *Social Studies* 26 (February 1935): 133–34.

4. "Slavery in Mississippi," *Boston Evening Transcript,* January 17, 1934, p. 2.

5. Anonymous review of *Slavery in Mississippi,* by Charles S. Sydnor, *London Times Literary Supplement,* no. 1676 (March 15, 1934): 199–200.

6. Joseph Grégoire de Roulhac Hamilton, review of *Slavery in Mississippi,* by Charles S. Sydnor, *Social Forces* 16 (March 1938): 446.

7. Chase C. Mooney, "The Literature of Slavery: A Re-Evaluation," *Indiana Magazine of History* 47 (September 1951): 259.

8. Stanley M. Elkins, *Slavery: A Problem in American Institutional & Intellectual Life* (1959; repr., New York: Grosset & Dunlap, 1963), 14, 22n29.

9. Daniel Calhoun, "Call to Quarters: A Review Essay," *Agricultural History* 49 (April 1975): 448.

10. Eugene D. Genovese, *The Political Economy of Slavery: Studies in the Economy and Society of the Slave South* (New York: Vintage Books, 1965), 289.

11. Fred Arthur Bailey, "Charles S. Sydnor's Quest for a Suitable Past," in *Reading Southern History: Essays on Interpreters and Interpretations,* ed. Glenn Feldman (Tuscaloosa: University of Alabama Press, 2001), 89–90; Bethany Leigh Johnson, "Regionalism, Race, and the Meaning of the Southern Past: Professional History in the American South, 1896–1961" (Ph.D. diss., Rice University, 2001), 375. Sydnor's article appeared in *Journal of Southern History* 11 (November 1945): 455–68. Unless otherwise cited, biographical information on Sydnor derives from Bailey's excellent article.

12. Bailey, "Charles S. Sydnor's Quest for a Suitable Past," 102.

13. Warren F. Kuehl, *Dissertations in History: An Index to Dissertations Completed in History Departments of United States and Canadian Universities, 1873–1960,* 2 vols. (Lexington: University of Kentucky Press, 1965), 1:182.

14. See John David Smith, "'Keep 'em in a fire-proof vault'—Pioneer Southern Historians Discover Plantation Records," *South Atlantic Quarterly* 78 (Summer 1979): 376–91, and John David Smith, "The Historian as Archival Advocate: Ulrich Bonnell Phillips and the Records of Georgia and the South," *American Archivist* 52 (Summer 1989): 320–31.

15. See, for example, Charles S. Sydnor, "Letter from Alexander M. Clayton to J. F. H. Claiborne Relative to Cuban Affairs," *Hispanic American Historical Review* 9 (August 1929): 364–68, Charles S. Sydnor, "The Beginning of Printing in Mississippi," *Journal of Southern History* 1 (February 1935): 49–55, and Charles S. Sydnor, "Diary of a Journey in Arkansas in 1856," *Mississippi Valley Historical Review* 22 (December 1935): 419–33.

16. Fred Arthur Bailey, "Charles Sackett Sydnor," http://www.olemiss.edu/depts/south/ms_encyclopedia/sydnorcharlessample.htm (accessed January 10, 2012), and Bailey, "Charles S. Sydnor's Quest for a Suitable Past," 95, 100.

17. David G. Sansing, *Making Haste Slowly: The Troubled History of Higher Education in Mississippi* (Jackson: University Press of Mississippi, 1990), 106.

18. "Historian is Named Dean of Duke Graduate School," *New York Times,* July 7, 1952, p. 7; "Charles Sydnor, Dean at Duke, 55," ibid., March 3, 1954, p. 27.

19. "Historian is Named Dean of Duke Graduate School."

20. Charles S. Sydnor, "The Free Negro in Mississippi before the Civil War," *American Historical Review* 32 (July 1927): 787.

21. Charles S. Sydnor, review of *John Tyler: Champion of the Old South,* by Oliver Perry Chitwood, *Journal of Southern History* 6 (May 1940): 266–67.

22. Charles S. Sydnor, review of *The Negro in the Civil War,* by Herbert Aptheker, and *Slave Insurrections in the United States, 1800–1865,* by Joseph C. Carroll, *Mississippi Valley Historical Review* 26 (June 1939): 94 (emphasis in original).

23. Charles S. Sydnor, review of *Southern Negroes 1861–1865,* by Bell Irvin Wiley, *South Atlantic Quarterly* 38 (January 1939): 113.

24. Bailey, "Charles S. Sydnor's Quest for a Suitable Past," 101.

25. Ibid., 105.

26. Arthur Schlesinger Jr., review of *The Development of Southern Sectionalism, 1819–1848,* by Charles S. Sydnor, *Columbia Law Review* 48 (December 1948): 1264–65.

27. Bailey, "Charles S. Sydnor's Quest for a Suitable Past," 101.

28. T. V. Smith, review of *Gentlemen Freeholders: Political Practices in Washington's Virginia,* by Charles S. Sydnor, *William and Mary Quarterly,* 3rd ser. 10 (January 1953): 142.

29. Leonidas Dodson, review of *Gentlemen Freeholders: Political Practices in Washington's Virginia,* by Charles S. Sydnor, *Pennsylvania Magazine of History and Biography* 77 (July 1953): 362–64.

30. David J. Mays, review of *Gentlemen Freeholders: Political Practices in Washington's Virginia,* by Charles S. Sydnor, *Journal of Southern History* 19 (February 1953): 77.

31. Bailey, "Charles S. Sydnor's Quest for a Suitable Past," 110.

32. Charles S. Sydnor and Claude Bennett, *Mississippi History* (New York: Rand McNally & Company, 1930), 175–78. Sydnor admitted to a friend that his

"only excuse for" undertaking the school history "is that I needed the money, and I am glad it is about over and I can return to things more interesting and more worthwhile." Sydnor to Frederic Bancroft, April 11, 1930, Charles S. Sydnor Papers, Rare Book, Manuscript, and Special Collections Library, Duke University.

33. Sydnor and Bennett, *Mississippi History*, 181.

34. Ibid., 182, 180.

35. Charles S. Sydnor, "Pursuing Fugitive Slaves," *South Atlantic Quarterly* 28 (April 1929): 152, 154, 155.

36. Sydnor, "The Free Negro in Mississippi before the Civil War," 786–87, 769–71.

37. Bancroft to Sydnor, July 11, 1927, March 3, 1930, April 20, July 12, 1931, Sydnor Papers. On Bancroft, see Jacob E. Cooke, *Frederic Bancroft, Historian* (Norman: University of Oklahoma Press, 1957), John David Smith, "Historical or Personal Criticism? The Case of Frederic Bancroft vs. Ulrich B. Phillips," *Washington State University Research Studies* 49 (June 1981): 73–86, and John David Smith, "Frederic Bancroft's 'Notes Among the Negroes': Writing Contemporary History in Bourbon-Era Mississippi," *Journal of Mississippi History* 66 (Fall 2004): 227–64.

38. Sydnor to Bancroft, March 1, 1929; Bancroft to Sydnor, April 5, 1929, Sydnor Papers.

39. Charles S. Sydnor, "Life Span of Mississippi Slaves," *American Historical Review* 35 (April 1930): 573–74. Privately Sydnor admitted to Bancroft feeling "a little uncertain about" this article. See Sydnor to Bancroft, April 11, 1930, Sydnor Papers.

40. Bancroft to Sydnor, May 30, 1930, Sydnor Papers.

41. Frederic Bancroft, *Slave-Trading in the Old South* (Baltimore: J. H. Furst Company, 1931).

42. Charles S. Sydnor, review of *Slave-Trading in the Old South,* by Frederic Bancroft, *American Historical Review* 36 (July 1931): 834–35.

43. Bancroft to Sydnor, April 26, June 7, 1931, January 7, 1932; Sydnor to Bancroft, December 19, 1931, Sydnor Papers.

44. Charles S. Sydnor to Carl Hamilton Pegg, September 24, 1932, Carl Hamilton Pegg Papers, Southern Historical Collection, Manuscripts Department, Wilson Library, University of North Carolina at Chapel Hill.

45. Patricia Galloway, "Archives, Power and History: Dunbar Rowland and the Beginning of the State Archives of Mississippi (1902–1936)," *American Archivist* 69 (Spring / Summer 2006): 113; Sydnor to P. H. Hunter, July 19, 1930; Henry Minor to Sydnor, August 1, 1930; Sydnor to Louise Mabry Terry, May 30, 1931; Mrs. Hal Terry to Sydnor, September 24, 1931, Sydnor Papers.

46. Sydnor to Baker, July 28, 1931, Sydnor Papers. See Sydnor, *Slavery in Mississippi,* 257, for the author's acknowledgment of Miss Baker.

47. The American Historical Association's Carnegie Revolving Fund began in 1926 and ended in 1956.

48. "Dr. Sydnor's New Book is Off Press," *Mississippian*, December 2, 1933, clipping in Sydnor Papers. The *Mississippian* was a weekly until September 22, 1961. In 1968 the newspaper changed its name to the *Daily Mississippian* to reflect the increased frequency of publication.

49. Bancroft to Sydnor, November 25, 1933, Sydnor Papers.

50. These were published by Louisiana State University Press in 1959 and 1966 and by Peter Smith in 1965. In 1952 Sydnor had difficulty finding a copy of *Slavery in Mississippi* for sale. When a book dealer located a copy for fifteen dollars Sydnor responded: "I do not want a copy badly enough to pay $15.00 for it, though I do confess to surprise, and perhaps even to pleasure, to know that a copy has been priced at this level." See Isabel Smith to Sydnor, April 24, 1953; Sydnor to Smith, April 30, 1953, Sydnor Papers.

51. References to Sydnor's *Slavery in Mississippi* are parenthetical and refer to this University of South Carolina Press edition.

52. Drake to Sydnor, May 19, 1934, Sydnor Papers.

53. Gilbert E. Govan, "Roaming the Book World," *Chattanooga Daily Times,* December 31, 1933, p. 11.

54. Maude H. Woodfin, "'Slavery in Mississippi' Gives Mirror of Life Under Old System," *Richmond News Leader,* n.d., clipping in Sydnor Papers.

55. Dwight L. Dumond, review of *Slavery in Mississippi,* by Charles S. Sydnor, *Mississippi Valley Historical Review* 21 (June 1934): 94–95.

56. Rosser H. Taylor, review of *Slavery in Mississippi,* by Charles S. Sydnor, *North Carolina Historical Review* 11 (October 1934): 317.

57. V. Alton Moody, review of *Slavery in Mississippi,* by Charles S. Sydnor, *American Historical Review* 39 (July 1934): 746–47.

58. William K. Boyd, review of *Slavery in Mississippi,* by Charles S. Sydnor, *Journal of Southern History* 1 (February 1935): 94–96.

59. John T. Gillard, "Slavery's Poison," *Commonweal* 20 (February 23, 1934): 471–72. On Gillard, see Stephen J. Ochs, *Desegregating the Altar: The Josephites and the Struggle for Black Priests, 1871–1960* (Baton Rouge: Louisiana State University Press, 1990).

60. E. Franklin Frazier, review of *Slavery in Mississippi,* by Charles S. Sydnor, *American Journal of Sociology* 42 (March 1937): 765–66.

61. Alain Locke, "New Light on an Old Problem," *Survey Graphic* 23 (April 1934): 197.

62. Carter G. Woodson, review of *Slavery in Mississippi,* by Charles S. Sydnor, *Journal of Negro History* 19 (July 1934): 332.

63. Ibid., 333–34.

64. Thomas P. Govan, "Was Plantation Slavery Profitable?" *Journal of Southern History* 8 (November 1942): 520–22.

65. John Hebron Moore, *Agriculture in Ante-Bellum Mississippi* (New York: Bookman Associates, 1958). In an article Moore chided Sydnor for failing in his

later books to cite other historians of slavery, most notably Lewis C. Gray, who disagreed with Sydnor and Phillips that slave-worked cotton plantation had turned a profit. See John Hebron Moore, "A Review of Lewis C. Gray's *History of Agriculture in the Southern United States to 1860,*" *Agricultural History* 46 (January 1972): 25.

66. Robert William Fogel and Stanley L. Engerman, *Time on the Cross: Evidence and Methods—A Supplement* (Boston: Little, Brown and Company, 1974), 183–85, 191–92, 231, 241–42.

67. Ibid., 182, 231.

68. Avery O. Craven, "Slavery Reconsidered," *Virginia Quarterly Review* 10 (April 1934): 291. Craven applied the same conclusions to another contemporary monograph on slavery, Ralph Betts Flanders's *Plantation Slavery in Georgia* (1933).

69. Craven, "Slavery Reconsidered," 292–93.

70. Bailey, "Charles S. Sydnor's Quest for a Suitable Past," 98.

PREFACE TO THE ORIGINAL EDITION

The population of the Natchez region at the time it came under the control of the United States in 1798 was, excluding Indians, scarcely 8,500, about 5,000 white people and 3,500 slaves. Nearly all of these lived in or close to Natchez, and this was the only settlement of importance in the area that has subsequently become the State of Mississippi. This outpost of civilization, which was accessible only by river in its early days, was ruled successively by France, England, and Spain; it continued to be governed as a colony for more than twenty years after the thirteen seaboard colonies determined to separate themselves from England. The smallness of its population, the changes in governmental policy with each change of owner, and the remoteness of the region from each of the home governments tended to make its administrative policy more of a benevolent despotism than the governments of the older seaboard colonies. Under such a régime a detailed code of law was not developed, for control was by orders rather than by laws. In brief, when the United States acquired the Natchez region, slavery existed, but there was little established law on the subject.

Under American control a mighty stream of immigrants began to pour in from the older States, and the crest of the flood was reached between 1830 and 1840. The numerous white settlers brought an even more numerous army of slaves, and consequently the need of an ample slave code arose. Though there was much bickering between Democrats and Federalists over land titles and sundry personal issues in the early days of this new territory of the United States, there seems to have been none over slavery. Most of the population of Natchez, in 1798, was of English ancestry, and a part of it had come from the seaboard colonies. There was, therefore, no conflict between the divergent attitudes of two different civilizations toward slavery. By common consent slavery was retained. As the need for laws arose, since there was no established body of conflicting law, these were drawn on the basis of information supplied by those who had come from the older and more populous slave States; for with their slaves they had brought this knowledge as well as the practices and customs of the institution.

Before Mississippi attained statehood slavery was a matured institution of the South with well-established attitudes and informal customs as well as formal law. As increasing amounts of the fresh land of Mississippi were opened to settlement this established institution spread over the State. It appears, therefore, that the form of slavery that flourished in Mississippi was an offshoot of the same institution in the older slave States rather than an indigenous growth. To trace the development of the system of slavery that existed in Mississippi from the time it attained statehood until the Civil War, one must follow the stream of immigrant masters and slaves to their sources in the older States; for it was there that slavery, as it existed in the State of Mississippi, had its origin. Fortunately for the present study, this task has in a large measure been performed; there have been careful investigations of the development and history of slavery in the older States, and the results of these studies have been integrated in descriptions of the institution for the South as a whole.

It appears, therefore, that the most desirable approach to a study of slavery in Mississippi is through an investigation of how the institution functioned in this particular region instead of the narration of how it developed; for the growth of slavery in Mississippi was a numerical increase of slave units rather than an evolution of the system. The comparatively brief span of years—scarcely more than fifty —in which slavery was an important institution in this State further emphasizes the need for an analytical description rather than a chronological narrative. For this reason the plan followed in this study is widely different from that which has usually prevailed in similar studies of the older slave States.

Mississippi differed from the upper tier of slave States in that it was a buyer of slaves, that it had more of a frontier civilization, and that it was given over almost entirely to cotton planting. *A priori,* these facts should have made the life of slaves harder and more laborious in this State than in the upper slave States, and it is, therefore, proper in this study to give close attention to the daily life of the average slave. Another reason for this emphasis is that in general the Gulf States, of which Mississippi was one, have been less closely studied in respect to slavery than the upper slave States. Also, a knowledge of the daily life of the slaves is essential for an adequate treatment of the more frequently discussed economic, political, and moral phases of slavery. The quantities of food and clothing supplied to slaves, the amount of work required of them, and the systems of managing them, all of which were important elements in their daily lives, must all be considered in appraising the economic profitableness of slavery. The political question of the extension or restriction of slavery was often argued according to different beliefs as to the treatment of the slaves. Any consideration of the ethics of slavery is closely related to the question of slave treatment, and this in turn is an important index to the character of the dominant slaveholding class of the Old South.

For these reasons, it has seemed best to present a cross-section of slavery in Mississippi rather than a story of its development and, in doing this, to proceed from the particulars of the daily life of the slaves to later generalizations about the system.

CHARLES SACKETT SYDNOR

University, Mississippi
September, 1933

ACKNOWLEDGMENTS

For careful reading of the manuscript of this book and for many helpful criticisms I am indebted to the Committee of the Carnegie Revolving Fund of the American Historical Association, to my colleagues in the faculty of the University of Mississippi, Professor Calvin S. Brown and Associate Professor P. L. Rainwater, and to my wife. To those who aided me in my search for manuscript material in private hands and to those who with great generosity allowed me to use diaries, letters, and other papers I wish to express my gratitude. Their names appear in the section of the bibliography which deals with manuscripts in private hands.

C. S. S.

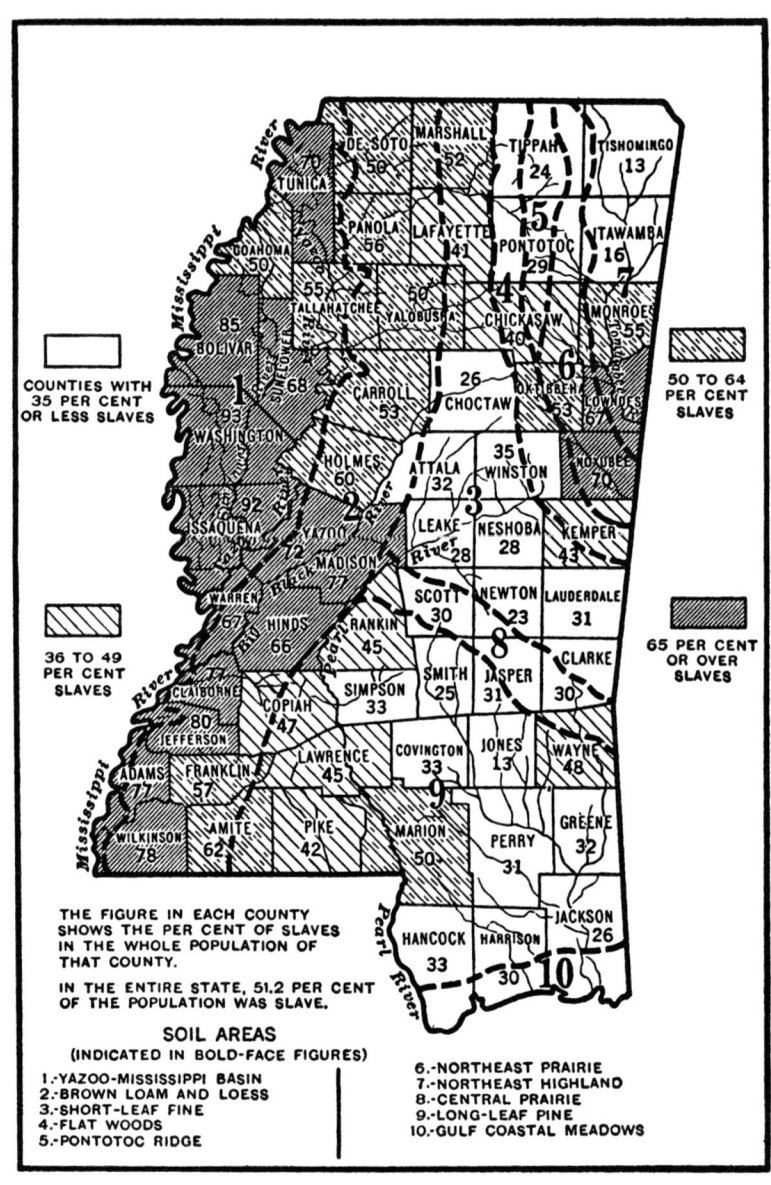

COUNTIES WITH
35 PER CENT
OR LESS SLAVES

36 TO 49
PER CENT
SLAVES

50 TO 64
PER CENT
SLAVES

65 PER CENT
OR OVER
SLAVES

THE FIGURE IN EACH COUNTY
SHOWS THE PER CENT OF SLAVES
IN THE WHOLE POPULATION OF
THAT COUNTY.

IN THE ENTIRE STATE, 51.2 PER CENT
OF THE POPULATION WAS SLAVE.

SOIL AREAS
(INDICATED IN BOLD-FACE FIGURES)

1.-YAZOO-MISSISSIPPI BASIN
2.-BROWN LOAM AND LOESS
3.-SHORT-LEAF FINE
4.-FLAT WOODS
5.-PONTOTOC RIDGE

6.-NORTHEAST PRAIRIE
7.-NORTHEAST HIGHLAND
8.-CENTRAL PRAIRIE
9.-LONG-LEAF PINE
10.-GULF COASTAL MEADOWS

RELATION OF DISTRIBUTION OF SLAVES TO SOIL AREAS IN MISSISSIPPI IN 1850

The per cent of slaves in each county was computed from the figures in the
Compendium of the Census of 1850, p. 260. The soil areas are based on Mississippi
State Geological Survey, Bulletin No. 14, p. 172.

SLAVERY IN MISSISSIPPI

CHAPTER I

Work

The ownership of slaves has generally originated in the desire of mankind to escape work and increase wealth. Whether slaveholding was profitable to the masters will be discussed in a later chapter. Here economics will be avoided, and the kinds and amounts of work done by slaves will be described.

Local newspaper advertisements of the sale or hiring of slaves often announced the occupations in which they were most proficient. Much specialization was evident, and only rarely was the same slave proclaimed a first-rate field hand and an equally good house servant. One negro woman was so described, and to explain this unusual claim, it was stated that she had been "raised in the field" until her sixteenth year and had since served in the house.[1] More frequently, if the slave was classed as "first-rate" in one, he was considered only "tolerable" in the other.[2] House and field were far apart, and this was particularly true on the larger estates, where "the domestic slaves and the field slaves are two distinct classes . . . and never interchange labor, save indeed, when a refractory house servant is sometimes sent into the field, to toil under the hot sun as punishment, for a week or so." [3]   .

On large plantations, the house servants and field hands were the major groups only; within each of these there was much partitioning of labor. In the domestic establishment of a well-ordered plantation, "a gardener, coachman, nurse, cook, seamstress, and a house-maid, are indispensable. Some of the more fashionable families add footmen, chamber-maids, hostler, an additional nurse, if there be many children, and another seamstress. To each of these officials is generally attached a young neophyte. . . ." [4] An ambitious overseer on

[1] *Woodville* (Miss.) *Republican,* Jan. 24, 1846.
[2] *Ibid.,* July 20, 1833.
[3] J. H. Ingraham, ed., *The Sunny South; or, The Southerner at Home,* p. 35.
[4] [J. H. Ingraham], *Southwest by a Yankee,* II, 252–253.
Advertisements of slaves who were specialists in most of these varieties of domestic services can be found easily, *e. g., Woodville Republican,* Apr. 15, 1837; Jan. 26, 1839.

a Hinds County plantation reminded his employer that there were twenty-seven servants in the house.[5] Of course, in humbler homes, where only one or two slaves could be afforded, each had to fill several of the rôles that were separated on large estates.

On the whole, the life of the house servant was far more pleasant than that of the field hand. His food was likely to be the same as was served to the white family. Clothing was frequently identical, subject to the qualification that the servant enjoyed it second-hand. A larger per cent of house servants could read and write. Generally they copied the manners of the owner, and the dignity of the house was usually safe in their hands.[6] They took pride in having a master of wealth and high rank in society—a pride that was partly generous and partly selfish, for the house servant considered himself far above the "corn field nigger," as is indicated in a brief conversation between a smartly dressed coachman and a footman.

"You know dat nigger they gwine to sell, George?"

"No, he field nigger; I nebber has no 'quaintance wid dat class."

"Well, nor no oder gentlemens would." [7]

In general, the larger the establishment the more pleasant was the life of the domestic slave, for in a small family there was more for each servant to do, and the slave was more likely to suffer from undignified treatment.[8]

The journeys of the white family broke the monotony of life for many favored domestics. Some of them traveled extensively, and on a few of the steamboats that plied the Mississippi River there were separate cabins for negroes.[9]

Though domestic servants normally had their full stint of work to do, some were pampered. Seargent S. Prentiss had a body servant, Burr, who was more of a favored pet than a slave. This diminutive negro was supposed to minister to his master on his travels to Washington and New England, as well as when in Mississippi. Burr was allowed, with astonishing results, to choose his own costume; he was well supplied with pocket money and spent much of his time playing marbles. In traveling, he was as hard to keep track of as baggage, and in crowds would have been completely lost but for the fame

[5] Susan Dabney Smedes, *Memorials of a Southern Planter*, p. 83.
[6] *Southwest by a Yankee*, II, 30–31, 247–249.
[7] *Ibid.*, II, 30, 56.
[8] Frederick Law Olmsted, *A Journey in the Back Country*, pp. 173–174.
[9] *Woodville Republican*, Mar. 16, 1839. Sir Charles Lyell, *A Second Visit to the United States of North America*, II, 158.

of his master and the good-natured directions of those who knew him. Prentiss offered to free Burr in Maine, but the latter refused and reported the following conversation with a gentleman of Portland, who asked Burr whether he would not like to be free.

"Yes," Burr replied, "I like it very much."

"But," said the man, "do you think yourself free now?"

"If I ain't, what am I?"

"Why, wouldn't you like to work, and have all your earnings to yourself?"

"No!" said Burr.

"Why?"

"Because I don't like to work. I plays, and Mr. Prentiss finds all the money."

Such was the life, and attitude toward life, of a favored domestic slave.[10]

A number of Mississippi slaves, neither domestic servants nor agricultural laborers, were commonly spoken of as "town slaves," because they worked at miscellaneous tasks in the towns. In 1840 only one ninth of the slaves of Adams County lived in the little city of Natchez, though three fifths of the white population of the county were there. Town slaves were relatively few, for there were half as many slaves as whites in Natchez but six times as many in the rest of Adams County.[11] Approximately the same proportions prevailed at the time of the next census.[12] In Vicksburg and its county of Warren, there were almost twice as many whites as slaves in the city, but elsewhere

[10] [George Lewis Prentiss], *Memoir of S. S. Prentiss*, II, 59–62.

Prentiss was an exceptionally gentle master. "His own treatment of the colored man, whether bond or free, was always most kind. Nothing could show this better than the fact that, many years before his death, a young free negro 'squat' upon his premises insisted upon becoming his servant, and did serve him, in the most faithful and affectionate manner, to the last day of his life. He was at full liberty to go when and where he pleased, but attachment to Mr. Prentiss seemed to be his ruling passion."—*Ibid.*, II, 459.

The very favorable descriptions of slavery sometimes written by a wife or daughter of a planter are often due to their having seen more of the domestic servants than of the field hands.

[11] Natchez population in 1840: white 2,994; slave 1,599. Population in Adams County, including Natchez: white 4,910; slave 14,241.—*Compendium of the Census of 1840*, pp. 56–58.

[12] Natchez population in 1850: white 2,710; slave 1,511. Population in Adams County, including Natchez: white 3,948; slave 14,395.—*Compendium of the Census of 1850*, pp. 260, 397.

between two and three times as many slaves as whites.[13] Natchez and Vicksburg were the only Mississippi cities listed in the federal census of 1840, and they contained only 2,664 slaves. In the whole State there were 195,211 slaves. If three times as many slaves be allowed to the smaller towns as the number in Natchez and Vicksburg, we should still find that only a small part of the slaves lived in the towns; possibly one out of twenty would be a liberal estimate.[14] Since many of these were domestic servants, only a small fraction of the negroes in the State could be classed as town slaves. Nevertheless, the diversity of their work makes a study of them peculiarly interesting.

Ingraham made two general remarks about town slaves. He believed they were distinguished as a class by superior intelligence and acuteness but also by a deeper degradation of morals.[15] He judged also that most of them belonged to neighboring planters who hired them to the townspeople.[16] His stricture on the morals of town slaves may be explained by remembering that their hirers had no permanent interest in them or responsibility for them and were only concerned with their work during a limited time. Superior skill or special training caused the town slaves to be hired, and this doubtless accounts for their higher average intelligence.

Town slaves labored chiefly as mechanics, draymen, hostlers, common laborers, or washwomen; or as assistants to white cabinet-makers, blacksmiths, carpenters, wheelwrights, or builders.[17] There were in Natchez a number of establishments which we may reasonably suppose employed negro laborers: foundries; tin, copper, sheet iron, and brass works; carriage factories and blacksmith shops; as well as establishments for making saddles and harness, cotton-gins, bricks, shoes and boots, and lumber, including shingles.[18] A Natchez cotton

[13] Vicksburg population in 1840: white 1,968; slave 1,065. Population in Warren County, including Vicksburg: white 5,223; slave 10,493.—*Compendium of the Census of 1840*, pp. 56–58.

[14] The free negroes, on the other hand, lived mainly within the towns. In 1840, 73 per cent of the free colored population of Adams County lived in Natchez, and about the same condition existed in Vicksburg and Warren County. —Charles S. Sydnor, "The Free Negro in Mississippi before the Civil War," in *American Historical Review*, XXXII, 782.

[15] *Southwest by a Yankee*, II, 253.

[16] *Ibid.*, II, 251.

[17] *Ibid.*, II, 249.

[18] An excellent survey of the manufacturing situation in Natchez was quoted from the Natchez *Free Trader* in *De Bow's Review*, V, 379.

mill employed twenty negro men, six women, and four children;[19] while in Jackson, the capital, forty-five negroes, mostly children, were employed in a similar establishment.[20] Owners of tanneries supplemented their own efforts with the labor of negro slaves who were trained in currying, tanning, and shoemaking.[21]

Mississippi railroads claimed a share of negro laborers, particularly in construction work. A number of these workers were plantation field hands whose owners had contracted to grade a short section of the roadbed, either through or close to the plantation. They were used for this work at seasons when they could be spared easily from routine tasks.[22] At other times slaves were purchased outright for railroad work. In 1838, it was reported that $159,000 had been spent for 140 slaves to be used in building a railroad between Jackson and Brandon, Mississippi.[23] Slaves were also used in the operation of completed railroads. This was true of the West Feliciana, one of the earliest lines in the United States. For ten years a negro slave, Emanuel, who belonged to the company, was the engineer on this road. It should be added that only one serious accident marred his record.[24]

In river transportation slaves were also employed. Steamboats on the Mississippi and the smaller rivers were manned in part by them. The cooking was frequently done by negro men,[25] as was the roustabout work at the docks.[26] They were also employed as firemen.[27] Among the killed and wounded on the *Helen McGregor*, which blew up, in 1830, at Memphis, just a few miles from the Mississippi

[19] *Ibid.*, VI, 296.
[20] *Ibid.*, VII, 176.
[21] *Woodville Republican*, Dec. 22, 1831; May 11, 1833.
[22] Leigh MSS. Planters' Bank of Tennessee *v.* Conger *et al.*, 20 Miss. 527. This form will be used in citing the reports of cases tried before the Supreme Court of Mississippi. As the early cases are sometimes cited according to the reporter, a table of reporters is supplied in the bibliography.

At the beginning of 1837, it was stated that 700 hands were at work on the Woodville-St. Francisville railroad; 800 hands on the Vicksburg-Jackson; between 500 and 600 on the Grand Gulf-Port Gibson; and between 500 and 800 on the Natchez-Jackson. What share of these "hands" were slaves was not reported. —*Woodville Republican*, Jan. 7, 1837.
[23] Petrie's executors *et al. v.* Wright *et al.*, 14 Miss. 647. U. B. Phillips, *American Negro Slavery*, p. 377, citing *Niles' Register*, LVI, 130.
[24] Natchez *Daily Free Trader*, July 6, 1859.
[25] *Woodville Republican*, Sept. 5, 1840.
[26] *Southwest by a Yankee*, II, 17.
[27] *Woodville Republican*, Nov. 10, 1838.

boundary line, were two negro firemen who may have been slaves.[28]

As wood was burned in the engines of the early steamboats, frequent stops were made to replenish the supply of this bulky fuel. A number of men lived by chopping wood, stacking it at some convenient spot on the bank of the river, and selling it to the first steamer that came to shore in search of fuel. These wood-cutters were frequently aided by one or two slaves whom, in some instances, they neither owned nor hired. Particularly in the southwestern part of the State, wood-cutters often gave refuge to fugitive negroes.[29]

As one would expect, professional men used negro slaves to keep their offices in order,[30] and town merchants sometimes bought or hired an old negress to care for the "bachelors' halls," or rooming places which many of them kept over their shops.[31] In the hotels and taverns there were negro servants, sometimes rendering poor service and grumbling when the proffered gratuity was small.[32]

The craft of cigar-making, learned in far off Richmond, was understood by one slave, but there is no record of whether he ever practiced his trade in Mississippi.[33] One is also surprised to find a negro employed as keeper of two chained bears and bravely leading them through the courtyard of the Mississippi Hotel in Natchez.[34]

White mechanics generally objected to slaves being trained as carpenters, blacksmiths, or tanners, for this injured their business and possibly hurt their self-respect.[35] One white artisan was offered the services of three slaves for six years, if he would teach them his trade. He refused with indignation saying that he would starve before he helped a slave become a mechanic.[36]

"The last and lowest link in the chain of the human species," according to a Mississippian by adoption, was the class of negroes who

---

[28] Ibid., Mar. 13, 1830.

[29] Southwest by a Yankee, I, 253; II, 10. U. B. Phillips, Life and Labor in the Old South, p. 339, citing Tyrone Power, Impressions of America, II, 118. Basil Hall, Travels in North America, III, chapters 13–15. Memphis Commercial Appeal, June 15, 1931. Woodville Republican, June 11, 1831; July 23, 1836.

[30] Cabaniss et al. v. Clark, 31 Miss. 423.

[31] Southwest by a Yankee, II, 60.

[32] Back Country, p. 17.

[33] Woodville Republican, Oct. 9, 1846.

[34] Ibid., Dec. 19, 1835.

[35] A one column protest against "negro mechanics" appeared in ibid., Sept. 18, 1847.

[36] Back Country, pp. 180–181.

labored on the great plantations and small farms of the State.[37] Yet there was a tendency to consider each of these agricultural laborers as especially fitted by body, mind, or training for some particular kind of work. This does not necessarily imply any great skill, but it does mean that subdivision of labor was the rule, especially on the larger plantations.

Agriculture in Mississippi was built upon the hoe gang and the plow gang. Both of these, together with all other slaves who could be put into the field, were converted into a great army of cotton-pickers when the proper season of the year came around.[38] In some respects it seems that a greater variety of occupations consumed the time of plantation slaves than of their brothers in the towns. The near approach of the larger plantations to economic independence was made possible in large part by the negroes who were skilled in various kinds of labor. Among the slaves on an average plantation there was a rough carpenter, a blacksmith, a coal-burner, as well as weavers, shoemakers, brickmakers, and shinglemakers.[39] Several of this list could be found on most of the larger plantations. One also finds slaves who were proficient as ox-drivers,[40] mechanics,[41] wagoners,[42] operators of steam-engines in sugar mills,[43] and hog-tenders.[44]

On a very large estate there was still more division of labor, as the following list indicates. In addition to sixty-seven field hands, there were three mechanics (blacksmith, carpenter, and wheelwright), two seamstresses, and one each of the following: stable servant, cattle-tender, hog-tender, teamster, driver of the hoe gang, foreman of the plow gang, cook for the slaves, midwife and nurse, in addition to the house servant of the overseer. The owner did not reside on the estate, otherwise the number of domestic servants would have been larger.[45]

[37] *Southwest by a Yankee*, II, 254.
[38] *The Cultivator*, n. s., II, 272.
[39] *Woodville Republican*, Nov. 13, 1830.
[40] *Ibid.*, Dec. 27, 1831.
[41] *Ibid.*, Apr. 13, 1833.
[42] *Ibid.*, May 29, 1830.
[43] *Ibid.*, Aug. 26, 1837.
[44] Wailes, B. L. C., Diary, MS., XIX, 63.
"At Burleigh there were two carpenters in the carpenter-shop, two blacksmiths in the blacksmith-shop, two millers in the mill, and usually five seamstresses in the house. . . . Two of the negro men were tanners and shoemakers. . . . In the laundry were two of the strongest and most capable women on the plantation . . ."—*Southern Planter*, p. 82.
See also, *De Bow's Review*, X, 621-626.
[45] *Back Country*, p. 47.

One of the many tasks of the overseer or owner was to put each slave in the position where he could serve most efficiently. Very little judgment was required to collect the antiquated or crippled negroes who were unfit for field work and place them in a "loom house" to manufacture coarse stuff for clothing the hands or making shoes.[46] More judgment was needed in appointing a driver or in selecting an intelligent boy to be apprenticed to the blacksmith or carpenter. Possibly most judgment was needed to find a new and more agreeable task for the slave who was constantly shirking or fleeing from the work to which he had been previously assigned.[47]

A slave often had opportunity to use native or acquired skill in his work. In laying out hillside ditches, a master discovered that one of his negro boys had a most accurate eye for levels, which was profitable to the owner and gave zest to the work of the boy.[48]

Even for the common field hand there was some variety of occupation, depending mainly on the changes of the seasons of the year. The details of plantation routine show what his tasks were. The following table summarizes the amount of slave labor devoted to various tasks on the Wheeless plantation during the fall of 1858.

picking cotton	788
sick	179
out [sic]	256
ginning	63
baling	26
repairing road	5
halling brick [sic]	10
hunting oxson [sic]	2
harvesting peas	8
harvesting corn	24
housing corn and potatoes	60 [approximate]
clearing up pasture	8
Total	1,429

[46] *Ibid.*, pp. 76–77.

[47] Maria, on President Polk's Mississippi plantation, was a very unsatisfactory field hand, but when taught to weave seems to have learned quickly and to have caused no more trouble.—John S. Bassett, *The Plantation Overseer,* pp. 144, 150–151.

"Seeing a wench ploughing, I asked him [the overseer] if they usually held the plough. He replied that they often did; and that this girl did not like to hoe, and, she being a faithful hand, they let her take her choice."—A. de Puy Van Buren, *Jottings of a Year's Sojourn in the South,* p. 170.

[48] *The Cultivator,* n. s., II, 303.

This shows some variety of occupation even in the cotton-picking season, which was probably the busiest time of the year.[49] From twelve to fifteen hands were accounted for each day for a period of nineteen weeks. The numbers that appear after each occupation represent the total number of days devoted to that task by all slaves during this period.

If the whole year is considered, agricultural routine included many other kinds of work. After cotton was picked, the slaves began knocking down the old stalks, repairing fences, clearing new ground, banding trees, burning brush, and mauling rails. During the fall and winter the bales of cotton were hauled to market by ox teams. Goading six or eight yoke of oxen all day and camping by night was the winter routine of many of the negro men.[50] Then came spring plowing and planting, and the plowing, hoeing and replanting of the crops. If at any time the hands completed one of these routine tasks before the next needed to be done, they cleaned up the grounds about the houses and barns, repaired plantation equipment, cleaned out wells and cisterns, burned charcoal, made bricks, and did the dozens of other things necessary for the success of the plantation.[51]

Rain often interrupted scheduled plantation work, though for a few tasks, such as setting out sweet potato slips, a rainy day was preferred.[52] In spite of rain, plowing and hoeing sometimes continued, particularly in the southwestern part of the State. There the soil was a sandy loam which could be cultivated without injury while wet, and as the estates were large and discipline more strict than elsewhere, there was less consideration of the comfort of the slaves.[53] However, on some plantations overseers were instructed not to work the slaves in the rain.[54] Occasionally, weather sheds or rough shelters were erected near the center of outlying fields.[55]

[49] Compiled from the Wheeless Plantation Account Book, MS.

[50] *Southwest by a Yankee*, II, 170.

[51] One of the best discussions of the cultivation of a cotton crop can be found in a paper prepared by Dr. J. W. Monette, of Mississippi, and printed as an appendix to *Southwest by a Yankee*, II, 281–291. In addition to this description of the seasonal duties of the hands, each of the plantation account books or diaries mentioned throughout this study indicates numerous kinds of work performed by the plantation slaves.

[52] U. B. Phillips, ed., *Plantation and Frontier Documents*, I, 231–244. Franklin L. Riley, ed., "Diary of a Mississippi Planter," in *Publications of the Mississippi Historical Society*, X, 347. Citations of the latter publication will hereafter be abbreviated thus: *P. M. H. S.*

[53] *Back Country*, p. 14.

[54] *De Bow's Review*, X, 626; III, 420.

[55] *Ibid.*, X, 623. Leigh MS.

Indoor tasks were generally provided when the weather was inclement. The chief of these for the women were: spinning, weaving, knitting socks, making and mending clothes, and, on a few plantations, grinding corn into meal or hominy. The men usually shelled corn. To a less extent they thrashed peas, cut potatoes for planting, platted shucks, cleaned the corn crib, or, if they were skilled workers, repaired any plantation equipment that needed it. Naturally, more days were so spent in winter than in summer.[56]

It is noticeable that the indoor occupations of the men and women differed rather widely. Outdoors the women and boys were occasionally classed as the "light force" and assigned to easier tasks. But women seem usually to have done about as much plowing as men and on one large estate did most of this work.[57] On another plantation women were in the gang that rolled logs, one of the heaviest of all plantation tasks.[58]

It is evident that Mississippi slaves, whether domestic, town, or agricultural laborers, performed many different kinds of work. Indeed, their masters could order them to do anything, subject to a very few legal restrictions. These, enacted to safeguard public interests, may be briefly summarized. Slaves could not be employed legally as typesetters in printing establishments, for this would encourage the education of slaves and enable them, if they so desired, to print inflammatory matter to be circulated among their fellows. Neither could they keep houses of entertainment nor sell goods, especially liquors, within the State.[59]

One general limitation of the labor of slaves should be mentioned here, though it is more fully discussed in another connection. Legally, the slave must always labor under the supervision of a white man. Wherever he was working, and even in his cabin at night, the slave was always, according to the laws of the State, under the control and subject to the orders of a white man.[60]

The only description of the daily work of the slaves that will be attempted will be the following brief outline of their duties in the cotton-picking season, the most important part of plantation routine.

[56] *Southern Planter*, p. 74. *Plantation and Frontier*, I, 231–244. *Back Country*, p. 141.
[57] *Back Country*, p. 81. Leigh MSS. *Southwest by a Yankee*, II, 281, 285.
[58] "Diary of a Miss. Planter," in *P. M. H. S.*, X, 341–342.
[59] Hutchinson, *Code of Mississippi, 1798–1848*, p. 948.
[60] *Ibid.*, p. 526.

"Then begins another push, which continues until the whole crop is gathered and housed. During 'picking time' . . . the hands are regularly roused, by a large bell or horn, about the first dawn of day, or earlier so that they are ready to enter the field as soon as there is sufficient light to distinguish the bolls. As the dews are extremely heavy and cool, each hand is provided with a blanket coat or wrapper, which is kept close around him until the dew is partially evaporated by the sun. . . . The hands remain in the field until it is too dark to distinguish the cotton, having brought their meals with them. For the purpose of collecting the cotton, each hand is furnished with a large basket, and two coarse bags about the size of a pillow case, with a strong strap to suspend them from the neck or shoulders. The basket is left at the end of the row, and both bags taken along; when one bag is as full as it can well be crammed, it is laid down in the row, and the hand begins to fill the second in the same way. As soon as the second is full, he returns to the basket, taking the other bag as he passes it, and empties both into the basket, treading it down well, to make it contain his whole day's work. The same process is repeated until night; when the basket is taken upon his head and carried to the scaffold-yard, to be weighed. There the overseer meets all hands at the scales, with the lamp, slate, and whip." [61]

It is interesting to note the variety of occupations that were performed by slaves and to observe that most of the negroes were usually bound to a particular task or group of tasks; but for the purpose of judging the degree of hardship that characterized the bondman's existence, the amount of work is more important than its variety.

It was Olmsted's opinion that slaves in the old Southwest, of which Mississippi was the heart, were forced to work harder than slaves to the east or north of this region. "They are constantly and steadily driven up to their work, and the stupid, plodding, machine-like manner in which they labor, is painful to witness." [62] This was the commonly accepted view: that slaves in the Southwest worked harder than elsewhere, which creates an additional reason for investigating the amount of work that was done by Mississippi slaves.

Mississippi planters expected each slave to produce on the average from five to seven bales of cotton each season, the bales weighing 400 pounds, which was the standard weight of that time. Where the land was fresh, the soil fertile, and the plantation large, seven bales a hand might be secured. On old land, or in the hills, or on a small plantation

[61] *Southwest by a Yankee*, II, 285–286.
[62] *Back Country*, pp. 81–82.

or farm, five bales a hand was a good crop. The size of the plantation was an important factor, for on small farms field hands had
many duties that field hands on a large estate escaped. On the latter
there were special slaves to perform everything necessary outside the
actual work of cultivating the crop.[63]

Estimates varied widely as to the number of acres cultivated by
each slave. In addition to the cotton crop, most planters attempted to
produce enough corn for the plantation. The acres in corn were generally from one-half to two-thirds as many as in cotton, and, of
course, the corn had to be cultivated by the slaves who produced the
cotton. One planter considered six acres of cotton sufficient for one
slave, but he expected to make from a bale to a bale and a half an
acre.[64] Another estimated that he cultivated ten acres of cotton and
six of corn to the hand.[65] Dr. M. W. Philips, taking an average for
a number of years, planned for each hand to care for eight and one-
half acres of cotton, four and one-half acres of corn, and one and
one-quarter acres of such crops as oats, potatoes, millet, rice, and
peas.[66] On the whole, these statements are probably a little high,
partly because most of them are estimates, and partly because there
were frequently more negroes in the field than were counted as hands
—a subject that will be discussed within a few pages.

[63] A farmer, who was an ex-overseer, with three hands expected to make five
bales to the hand.—*Plantation Overseer*, p. 92.
"The quantity of cotton raised and secured by good management most commonly averages about five or six bales to the hand: and the quantity . . . more
frequently falls below, than rises above this estimate."—This was the opinion of
J. W. Monette in *Southwest by a Yankee*, II, 291.
Ingraham, whose observations were chiefly in the neighborhood of Natchez,
where land was fertile and estates large, estimated that each slave ought to
average from seven to eight bales, especially on new lands.—*Ibid.*, II, 90.
Mr. R. Abbey, an intelligent planter of Yazoo County, thought that "six to
nine bales to the hand [was] as much, generally more, than can be picked in
good order."—*De Bow's Review*, II, 134.
"From four to eight bales to a hand they generally get; sometimes ten and
better, when they are lucky."—*Back Country*, p. 28.
See below, pp. 195–196.
[64] R. Abbey, writing in *De Bow's Review*, II, 134.
[65] *Ibid.*, X, 625; an estimate of ten acres of cotton and five of corn was reported
in *Back Country*, p. 28.
[66] "Diary of a Miss. Planter," in *P. M. H. S.*, X, 312, 362, 403, 431, 441, 445–
446, 452, 461, 465.
At the beginning of most years, Philips made estimates of the amount of land
he expected to plant in the different crops and of the number of hands at his
disposal. The statements given above are based on a summary of these estimates
for nine years.

Probably the simplest and most easily measured of all farm operations in Mississippi is cotton-picking. Then, as now, the worker used nothing but a bag in which to place the cotton as it was gathered, and no development in tools or equipment has changed the process through the years. Slaves were more likely to be driven hard during the picking season than at other times,[67] which is doubtless why they ran away in larger numbers at that time.[68] The reason for this pressure of work is set forth in the common-sense statement of William Dunbar, who, in 1799, wrote to his partner in Philadelphia that "a well managed gang of negroes can cultivate fifty per cent. more cotton than they will be able to pick from the fields, and the loss from the deterioration of the staple, by exposure after Christmas, is very great." [69] While the variety of cotton known to Dunbar made this statement truer of his day than in later years, cotton-planters to-day are sometimes unable to pick all the cotton they have raised.

The earliest estimate which I have discovered of the amount of cotton picked in a day appears in another letter written, in 1800, by William Dunbar. He stated that the usual daily task of a slave was 75 to 80 pounds. In regard to this estimate, which seems very small, the historian Claiborne makes the following note.

"This refers to the black seed cotton which grew in a small, pointed boll, and the picker seldom exceeded one hundred pounds. Of pure Sea Island seed from fifty to seventy pounds was the average picking. But with the introduction of the Petit Gulf variety the hands usually brought in an average of one hundred and fifty pounds, some of them gathering as high as three hundred pounds. Women are usually the best pickers." [70]

This Petit Gulf variety was possibly the most important of the strains that were bred from Mexican cotton, which became popular in Mississippi during the 'twenties. B. L. C. Wailes, who prepared the first geological survey of the State, agreed with Claiborne that it was more easily picked. In 1854 he wrote: ". . . fifty years since, fifty pounds a day was accounted fair work. Now the children double this; and

[67] *Southwest by a Yankee*, II, 281–291.
[68] See below, pp. 45–46, 103–104.
[69] J. F. H. Claiborne, *Mississippi, as a Province, Territory and State*, p. 144.
[70] *Ibid.*, p. 144, note.
Another, and highly reputable, authority estimated that fifty or sixty pounds of cotton was the ordinary amount gathered a day in the period at which William Dunbar wrote.—B. L. C. Wailes, *Report on the Agriculture and Geology of Mississippi*, p. 131.

two hundred pounds is not infrequently the average of the whole gang of hands . . ." [71] The amount of cotton gathered a day was of course larger at the height of the season than at the beginning or the end, and it varied somewhat with the planters' insistence on clean picking. It was commonly believed that the average for all hands on a plantation for a whole season was but little, if any, over 150 pounds per day.[72]

A few instances in which very large amounts of cotton were picked a day by single slaves shows that 150 pounds a day was not excessive. While some hands averaged only from seventy-five to 100 pounds, there were extraordinary workers who could bring in from 400 to 500 pounds, working of course at top speed.[73] On September 27, 1830, a force of fourteen slaves on a Mississippi plantation picked 4,520 pounds of clean seed cotton, an average of 323 pounds per hand. The largest amount picked by any one slave on this day was 415 pounds and the smallest was 240. The work was closely observed because it was done on a wager, and the results were sufficiently unusual to call for newspaper notice.[74] It is thus evident that skilled slaves with proper encouragement could pick two or even three times as much cotton as the average slave picked in a day. The average slave under normal conditions was, therefore, not driven to the limit of his powers.

Plantation records verify the estimates already stated and give further information on individual variations among slaves. In these records the daily weights of the pickings of each slave were commonly entered. Sometimes the cotton was weighed three times a day—morning, midday, and evening—and the number of pounds picked by each slave was set down opposite his name.[75] The chief possibility of error was that slaves sometimes tried to cheat the overseer and make the day's work seem larger than it was.[76] As for the planter,

[71] *Agriculture and Geology*, p. 154.
[72] "The average weight picked by all hands on a place, will seldom exceed 150 or 160 lbs., in good picking."—*Southwest by a Yankee*, II, 287.
"I think when the picking is good, I generally make from 150 to 200 lbs. per day to the hand. Earlier or late in the season of course less."—R. Abbey in *De Bow's Review*, II, 138.
See also, *Plantation Overseer*, p. 209.
[73] *Southwest by a Yankee*, II, 287. *Southern Planter*, 69.
[74] *Woodville Republican*, Oct. 2, 1830.
[75] *Southern Planter*, p. 70.
[76] *Southwest by a Yankee*, II, 286.

one would no more expect a man willfully to distort his cotton records than to falsify any other private business memorandum.

In the account book of the plantation owned by F. W. Wheeless is a complete record of the number of pounds each slave picked each day through the fall of 1858. Picking was begun on August ninth and finished December seventeenth. Ginning was finished six days later. The records of this plantation, kept mainly by an overseer, show that the largest number of hands in the field on any one day was fifteen. The total number of days devoted to cotton-picking by the aggregate hands was 788. The largest amount of cotton picked by any hand in one day was 348 pounds and, what is more important, the average amount of cotton picked per day by all the slaves was 145.9 pounds.

To give further information concerning individual variations, as well as to illustrate the way the accounts of this and other plantations were kept, the record of one week will be copied. Because of rain, no cotton was picked during the first two days of this week in September.

	W. 16	T. 17	F. 18	S. 19	Total
Osburn	264	260	269	261	1,054
Pole	253	256	263	263	1,035
Fremon	224	231	247	232	934
Sam	170	196	195	103	664
Simon	182	196	193	178	749
Tim	169	204	195	187	755
Hardy	200	208	232	200	840
Ellin	190	211	216	201	818
Betsey	168	192	173	179	712
Willis	112	167	119	106	504
Rachel	——	97	100	116	313
					6,578 [77]

On a Lafayette County plantation during the four days, January 13 through 16, 1851, the slaves performed seventy-seven days' work

[77] Wheeless MS.

This plantation was probably located on the Yazoo River, sixteen miles below Yazoo City, for there is inserted in the plantation book a printed permit, the blanks filled in by pen. It was issued by an "Asst. Special Agt., Treas. Dept. for leasing abandoned plantations." It is a reconstruction document, authorizing F. W. Wheeless to occupy and cultivate his own plantation, located sixteen miles below Yazoo City, and the plantation was described as containing about 500 acres of tillable land.

picking cotton and brought in a total of 6,946 pounds, an average of slightly over ninety pounds a day for each negro.[78] They picked 7,718 pounds from January twentieth to twenty-fifth, using eighty-seven days' work, which gives an average of slightly under eighty-nine pounds a day.[79] These averages of about ninety pounds a day were made at the end of the season, when the amount of cotton in the fields and its condition did not permit weights to be large. However, there are more complete records for the following fall. Between September 1 and November 11, 1851, the crop was harvested, except for a very small amount. During this time the hands were in the field 54 days and brought in a total of 117,301 pounds. There were about seventeen hands at work each day, if we may assume that the force was of the same size that it had been in the previous January. It therefore follows that the average for one hand during the whole season was not far from 130 pounds a day.[80]

Present-day practical farmers of the regions that have been discussed state that a gang of cotton-pickers should average at least 150 pounds a day. This is the same average that was set by Claiborne, and Wailes in 1854 closely agreed with this estimate. The records that have been analyzed of two Mississippi plantations in the 1850's show that the slaves did not quite reach this standard. Twenty years earlier under favorable conditions and with sufficient incentive, a gang of slaves picked more than twice this average.

A great disparity was evident between the amounts that the various slaves picked. If the task system were used, the allotted task should have been individual for each slave for they differed widely in the amounts of work they did. Indeed, daily variations of the same slave were too large to allow one to suppose that this system was used.

What proportion of the slaves on an average plantation was considered active workers, or, conversely, what per cent of the slaves was non-productive because of youth, old age, or other reasons?

The following figures were taken from typical advertisements in

[78] Bowles MS.
Reference is made only to the slaves residing on this estate, and the work of slaves borrowed from a neighboring plantation is not counted.
[79] A few of the individual weights that made up this total were evidently estimated.
[80] A fragment of a cotton-record book of the estate of Greenwood Leflore has been saved. It deals chiefly with November, and the year is not recorded. The average amount of cotton picked per day by the average hand was well under 100 pounds.—Leflore MSS.

the *Woodville Republican*. There was offered for sale a plantation of 800 acres together with thirty-three negroes, among whom, it was stated, were twenty first-rate hands.[81] In another group of sixty-three negroes were forty-eight hands.[82] In other advertisements we find from gross totals of sixty, fifty, twenty-six and twenty-six slaves that forty, thirty-five, twenty and seventeen respectively were rated as hands.[83] In these six cases we have a total of 258 negroes of whom 180, or about 70 per cent, were rated as hands. This high proportion of workers can be explained by remembering that the estimates were made by those who wished to sell. Naturally, in a borderline case they described the slave as a first-rate hand, for they wanted the estate to appear in the most favorable light. In scattered instances, an even higher proportion of workers can be found.[84] But it seems probable that in the actual operation of plantations the owner was fortunate if 60 per cent of his slaves could be classed as hands. Dr. Philips once rated his fifty-nine negroes as twenty-seven hands.[85] On a large plantation observed by Olmsted there were 135 slaves. Of this number the overseer counted sixty as field hands, though sixty-seven slaves went to the field daily, and there were thirteen negroes who performed specialized tasks, most of which were out of the field.[86]

Of course, all hands were not even approximately equal as workers. For instance, in the Wheeless account book, great differences are evident among the workers. On the same four working days, two negroes picked, in round numbers, 1,000 pounds apiece, two picked 800 pounds, three picked 700 pounds, and one each picked 600, 500, and 300 pounds. This difference in capacity and willingness to work caused planters sometimes to employ the term "hand" or "field hand," as a more or less abstract standard by which slaves could be measured. This is suggested in one of the *Woodville Republican* advertisements just used, in which the advertiser stated that among his twenty-six slaves were twenty-two workers, or twenty effective hands. Excellent examples of the appraisal by a planter of his work-

[81] *Woodville Republican*, Oct. 24, 1835.
[82] *Ibid.*, June 11, 1836.
[83] *Ibid.*, June 11, May 14, 1836; Feb. 18, 1837; June 1, 1839.
[84] A letter from Wm. Gwin to J. F. H. Claiborne, dated May 8, 1841, describes a plantation of which ". . . 300 acres are planted in cotton, 200 in corn, 150 in oates. There is [sic] 30 negroes of which 27 are hand[s] 10 mules and horses. The negroes and mules I do not wish to sell if I can sell the place without them." —Library of Congress, J. F. H. Claiborne MSS., vol. I, no. 39,348.
[85] "Diary of a Miss. Planter," in *P. M. H. S.*, X, 461.
[86] *Back Country*, p. 47.

ing force, as well as of the process by which such an estimate was made, can be found in the diary of Dr. M. W. Philips. In December, 1852, he wrote: "I rate my hands as follows, considering though some are not hands themselves, yet with others will be so, through the year. For instance, Mary will be a full hand in picking, the most important, and in hoeing ordinary." [87] Instead of giving the appraisal that here follows, a later and more illuminating one will be quoted.

"I will send off 2 more hands to factory, Jim and Manuel, and rate hands thus (Cyrus out to attend garden, etc.): 1, Jerome; 2, Prince; 3, Bill; 4, Esau; 5, Moses; 6, Paris; 7, David; 8, Anthony; 9, Amy; 10, Charity; 11, Emily; 12, Ann; 13, Fanny; 14, Milly (1st); 15, Mary; 16, Amanda; 17, Hannah; 18, Betsey; 19, Milly; 20, Jacob; 21, Ellen; total 20 full hands. The following half hands (under 15 years): 1, William; 2, Zack; 3, Caesar; 4, Cicero; 5, John; 6, Jimmy; 7, Sambo; 8, Richmond; 9, Louisa; total, 4½ hands.

"Will send Tom, Ben, Isaac, and Cordelia out to keep out of mischief, though too small to carry water.

"I add Wyatt and Hardy together with Rosetta and Scott, will make 2 hands more . . .

"This will make, in all, say 26 hands, at *utmost*." [88]

The length of the field hand's working day depended mainly on the number of hours of daylight. On one of the largest estates in Mississippi there were no rules as to hours of work; each overseer followed his own judgment.[89] According to countryside gossip, the slaves on another estate were roused by a bell at three-thirty in the morning and sometimes worked until nine at night.[90] On the other hand, it was reported of the Dabney plantation that negroes were not roused by horn or bell in the morning, and that they went to the field when they chose, which was frequently well along in the morning.[91] As a general rule, work was begun pretty soon after daylight,

[87] "Diary of a Miss. Planter," in *P.M.H.S.*, X, 441.
[88] *Ibid.*, X, 465.
A number of other appraisals can be found in this diary.
In a penciled note on the back of a list of the slaves on one of his plantations, Greenwood Leflore divided his slaves into four groups, and thereby revealed his views on the effect of the age of a field hand on his usefulness. The groups were: (1) children, (2) those between 13 and 40 years old, (3) those between 40 and 50, and (4) those over 50.—Leflore MSS.
[89] *Back Country*, p. 80.
[90] *Ibid.*, p. 182.
[91] *Southern Planter*, p. 58.

"except 'tis in pickin' time," as one overseer stated, "then maybe I get 'em out a quarter of an hour before." [92]

Work continued through the day with time out for breakfast in some cases and for dinner in all. When the days were longest, the dinner hour was extended into a resting period, usually one hour and sometimes two or three. Plow hands generally had a longer time of rest at noon than did hoe hands.[93]

Slaves were not often required to do plantation work after dark, though an occasional task, such as shelling corn to be ground next day [94] or weighing and putting away cotton,[95] might continue after sundown. However, they frequently had to clean their own cabins or clothes, or cook their own food at night after being in the field all day.

During the year there was respite from work on occasional holidays. Practically every slave enjoyed a day of freedom at Christmas, and the period was sometimes extended to a week. The average was about four or five days.[96] No case has been noticed of a slave being compelled to work Christmas day. Only one objection has been found to the granting of this holiday, and this was not based on any consideration of the amount of labor lost. The objector was protesting against the demoralization and possible danger of permitting all the slaves of the whole countryside to be unrestrained at the same time, wandering about freely and many of them drunk.[97] It was said that most of the slaves considered the holidays incomplete unless one day was spent in a neighboring town.[98] Though the Fourth of July was sometimes celebrated as a holiday,[99] it was more usual for all holidays, except at Christmas, to be granted on the occasion of some local event such as a wedding, the laying by of crops or the finishing of cotton-picking, and there was generally feasting, frequently in the

---

[92] *Back Country*, p. 49. *Plantation and Frontier*, I, 114, 243. *Southern Planter*, p. 74. "Diary of a Miss. Planter," in *P. M. H. S.*, X, *passim*.

[93] *Southern Planter*, p. 57. *De Bow's Review*, X, 623. *Back Country*, pp. 49–50. Frederick Law Olmsted, *A Journey in the Seaboard Slave States*, p. 697, citing a letter of Dr. M. W. Philips in the New York *Tribune*.

[94] *Southern Planter*, p. 164.

[95] *De Bow's Review*, X, 626.

[96] Bowles MS. Leigh MSS. "Diary of a Miss. Planter," in *P. M. H. S.*, X, 435. *Southern Planter*, p. 161. *Sojourn in the South*, pp. 116–118.

[97] *Woodville Republican*, Dec. 22, 1832.

[98] *Southern Planter*, p. 161.

[99] *Ibid.*, p. 58.

form of a barbecue. Sometimes slaves from a neighboring plantation were invited to the celebration.[100]

Sunday work was commonly prohibited, frequently by the written orders of the owner to the overseer.[101] Only one infraction has been noted.[102] Of course such routine work as feeding the stock, milking, and cooking had to go on.

Only one Mississippi plantation has been noted on which the slaves were said to have worked six full days a week through the entire year, and only one on which the slaves always had at least one half holiday a week.[103] With these two exceptions, every plantation of which we have record gave respite from work on some Saturdays but not all.[104] Pressure of plantation work determined when these rest periods should come, and the half holiday was sometimes sadly stunted.[105] At the other extreme, there was a plantation on which the slaves stopped work at eight o'clock on Saturday mornings, except at picking time or sometimes when the crop was badly in grass.[106] On another estate of fifty slaves, the laborers did no work from Friday night until Monday morning the year around.[107] A protracted period of bad weather in January or February usually resulted in several days of idleness.[108]

[100] Bowles MS. *Southern Planter*, p. 58.

[101] *De Bow's Review*, X, 626. *Back Country*, p. 49.

[102] June 21, 1840, "Light shower. Jacob hauled 5 loads of oats *Sunday* as it is."—"Diary of a Miss. Planter," in *P. M. H. S.*, X, 328.

[103] *Back Country*, p. 182.

[104] For example, "Diary of a Miss. Planter," in *P. M. H. S.*, X, 318–319, and *passim*.

[105] "Saturday, 6th. . . . All hands stopped at 4 P.M."—*Plantation and Frontier*, I, 244.

[106] *Back Country*, p. 49.

[107] *Ibid.*, p. 182.

[108] "Diary of a Miss. Planter," in *P. M. H. S.*, X, 340–341.

CHAPTER II

CLOTHING, FOOD, AND SHELTER

Those who lived among slaves apparently considered their clothing too commonplace to deserve detailed description. While travelers from afar were more attentive, they usually commented only in vague and general terms. As intentional descriptions are, therefore, not satisfactory, one's knowledge of how slaves were dressed must be secured from such sources as plantation account books and those newspaper advertisements which listed the various articles town merchants proposed to sell to planters.

Most of the clothing of slaves was evidently bought between September and February. During this span of months, numerous notices appeared in the newspapers concerning shoes, garments, and cloth from which the latter could be made. Through the spring and summer such notices were rarely printed. There were probably two reasons for this seasonal fluctuation. Winter chills made more clothing necessary, and planters had better credit about the time the cotton crop was sold. Fortunately for the negro, his own need for clothes and his master's ability to supply this need came in the same part of the year.

In practically all advertisements, a distinction was made between clothing for negroes and clothing for white people. The former, when advertised for sale, was designated as negro clothes, and, if the merchant's stock of goods warranted it, there was a separate description of "fashionable clothing for gentlemen." [1]

The following summary of Stanwood and Bulkley's advertisement illustrates the kind and amount of negro clothing in a store in Woodville. In the fall of 1839, this firm offered for sale:

1500 pr. Negro Brogans	2 bales brown Linseys
2 bales plaid Linseys	2 cases super Kerseys
2 bales red and blue Linseys	2 cases Glascow Jeans
6 bales Lowell cotton [2]	

[1] *Woodville Republican,* Nov. 23, 1824.
[2] *Ibid.,* Sept. 14, 1839 to Jan. 29, 1840.

A competitor in this same year offered 600 pairs of negro blankets, 300 pairs of kerseys and linseys, and 700 negro brogans.[3] In addition to these staple goods, a purchaser might find such fancy articles as, "servants Japanned hats with gold and silken bands, cotton lion skins, and fear noughts and strong shoes." [4] Most of the slave clothing that was advertised by Mississippi merchants had been manufactured outside the State, New York and Boston apparently being the chief points of supply.

Homespun was largely worn on many plantations, especially in the more recently·settled and less accessible parts of the State.[5] When bad weather interrupted work in the field, negro women were frequently required to spin or weave, and naturally in the winter months a large part of this work was done.[6] Many slaves who were unfit for field work because of age or infirmity regularly labored in the "loom house," carding wool, spinning cotton and wool, weaving, dying, and making clothes.[7] Homespun was often dyed with hickory bark or with the juices of berries, though indigo was sometimes purchased.[8]

Although homespun was not on the market, in later years it was possible for the Mississippi planter to purchase, in limited quantities, cloth of domestic manufacture. The Woodville Manufacturing Company,[9] incorporated in 1850 with a capital of $175,000,[10] manufactured cotton and woolen yarns and fabrics. Within two years the work was progressing as the following advertisement testifies:

[3] *Ibid.*, Nov. 2, 1839.

[4] Natchez *Mississippi Messenger,* Sept. 29, 1807.

[5] "All of the cotton clothing and part of the woolen is spun and woven by women" on the Leigh plantation.—Leigh MSS. *De Bow's Review,* VII, 381.
Also, Olmsted, *Back Country,* pp. 76–77, 141.

[6] *Back Country,* p. 141.

[7] Bassett, *Plantation Overseer,* pp. 144, 150–151. *Back Country,* pp. 76–77.

[8] *Woodville Republican,* Nov. 5, 1825; statements of ex-slaves.

In the Leigh MSS. is a record of the amount of cotton spun a day over a period of some months.

The following is a memorandum in the Bowles plantation book:

Expense of making Jeans,
warp 20 yards	1.50
Indigo and madder	1.50
Carding the wool	3.00
dying the wool	1.50

[9] Sometimes called the Wilkinson County Factory.

[10] *Laws of Mississippi,* 1850, pp. 462 ff.

"AGENCY FOR THE WILKINSON COUNTY FACTORY.

"The undersigned having received the agency of this *Home Manufactory* would call attention to the following described goods which he offers at Factory prices.

"4–4 Osnaburgs,

"7–8 Osnaburgs,

"4–4 Kerseys,

"4–4 Lindseys,

"Cotton yarns 6 to 10, etc.

"It is hoped that all friends of Southern enterprise will at least call and look at these goods.

"Clean wool *in any quantity* wanted for this factory for which a fair price will be paid

"Sept. 13   H. S. FULKERSON, Agent." [11]

On the whole, most of the fabric which clothed Mississippi slaves seems to have been manuactured in the East and England; a moderate amount of homespun was in use; and a relatively small part of the cloth was factory-made in the State.

In the neighborhood of Woodville, the same locality from which our clothing advertisements were largely drawn, there were a number of domestic sources of supply for negro shoes. In addition to the merchants, who imported shoes from New York and Boston, there were local establishments that manufactured shoes, including the tanning of the leather.[12] Judging by newspaper advertisements, most of the negro shoes were made in the State. The number of shoes advertised yearly by each tannery ranged between 1,000 and 2,500. The elements involved in purchasing negro shoes, such as price, credit, and even the fit, are better understood, if the following advertisement is perused.

"LOOK AT THIS

"The undersigned offers for sale at his tanyard, one mile south of Woodville,

---

[11] *The Southern Reveille,* Port Gibson, Miss., Nov. 3, 1852.
This manufacturing company was destroyed during the Civil War, as well as the home of Judge McGehee, its founder. With the home the records of the venture presumably turned to ashes. The development of the company and its death in the war, are significant. A prospectus of the enterprise, describing the building and equipment of the factory, appeared in *De Bow's Review,* X, 564.

[12] Among those in the business were: John Connell, whose advertisements appeared between 1826 and 1828; G. A. Irion, 1826; James Leech, 1828–1833; W. P. Perkins and D. Stewart, 1828; J. Riddle, 1831; and W. Arbuthnot, 1831. See *Woodville Republican* under proper years.
Among the boot and shoe manufacturers of Natchez in 1848 were Messers. Swain, Hughes, Essig, and Batterson.—*De Bow's Review,* V, 380.

1800 PAIR OF NEGRO SHOES

at the accommodating price of ten bits per pair, cash in hand, or drafts on Merchants in New Orleans, payable the first of February next. If payment should be delayed to a subsequent period, fourteen bits will be required for every pair.

Customers must take a proportion of the different sizes, or give a little more.

"August 24, 1826.   G. A. IRION" [13]

Occasionally more shoes were placed on the market than could be disposed of during the fall and winter. Rather than carry the surplus over through the summer, the price was sometimes lowered "two bits" around the first of June.[14]

Negro shoes were slightly cheaper than those of white men, though the material in them was a little more expensive. The shoe was roughly made out of good leather, according to the superintendent of the State penitentiary, who estimated that ten hands would make an average of forty pairs of negro brogans a day, or thirty pairs of shoes for white men. The former would sell for $1.12½ per pair, the latter for $1.25. The cost of material per pair was estimated at $0.60 for the shoes for negroes, and $0.55 per pair for white persons.[15]

As a complement to newspaper advertisements, one can examine the orders sent from the larger plantations to commission merchants. The following is a selection of the major items of slave clothing that appeared in a Mississippi plantation order for the year 1855.

> 6 gross large buttons for servants
> 140 yds. Kentucky Jeans.
> 140 yds. plain linsey.
> 40 yds. bright plaid linsey.
> 400 yds. Lowells
> 40 yds. dark blue Georgia Stripes
> 40 yds. gay calico for negroes
> 2 doz. campeachy hats
> 20 pr. good negro blankets
> 1 box Russet brogans [16]

So much do we learn of the wardrobe of the slave from newspaper advertisements and from the order of a particular plantation.

---

[13] *Woodville Republican*, Sept. 2, 1826.
[14] *Ibid.*, June 5, 1830; Sept. 7, 1833.
[15] *De Bow's Review*, VII, 456.
[16] From "Orleans Memorandum, Plantation & House Sent to Messers Buchanan Carroll & Co., mailed in Coffeeville, Miss., 13th of Jany. 1855," by P. Randolph Leigh.—Leigh MSS.

The first leaves us wondering what the planter actually bought, and the latter is not sufficiently precise in telling the details of the outfit of any one negro. As to the quantity of clothing allowed the slaves, one planter stated: "I give to my negroes four full suits of clothes with two pair of shoes, every year, and to my women and girls a calico dress and two handkerchiefs extra." [17] This was twice as generous as Olmsted found to be the rule on a large estate he visited in Mississippi.[18] Dr. M. W. Philips allotted yearly to each slave two summer suits, two winter suits, one straw hat, one wool hat, and two pairs of shoes.[19]

More precise descriptions of slave clothing can be found in the advertisements of fugitive negroes that jailers and sheriffs prepared and published in the newspapers. While it was their legal duty to insert these notices, it is surprising what a knowledge of fabrics these gentlemen of the law possessed. This should be qualified by remarking that a smaller range of terms was used in describing the clothing of the negro women who were captured. While there were not nearly as many women as men who fled from the plantations, the jailer may have been under a natural disadvantage in describing feminine clothing.

The clothing of the women was classed as dresses, frocks, or shifts, and the materials from which they were made were linen, cotton, homespun, cambric, domestic, calico, and woolen goods.[20] There was more variety in the clothing of the men. The essentials were trousers and shirt. The latter were made from such materials as were used in the dresses of the women and many other kinds also. Trousers differed from each other in weave, color, and material, and a full list of all the combinations would not fall short of a hundred. Some of the more usual materials were nankeen, homespun, woolen goods, twill, tow, oznaburgs, plains, broadcloth, linsey woolsey, cassinet, casimere, duck, kersey, bombazett, leather, corduroy, domestic, French drilling, cottonade, Kentucky jeans, and Lowell cotton. Add to these a numerous array of colors and some variation in weaves and the result is amazing.

Other items of clothing of the men were vests, jackets, coats, hats

---

[17] *De Bow's Review*, X, 624.
[18] *Back Country*, p. 80.
[19] Olmsted, *Seaboard Slave States*, p. 697.
[20] These and the following statements about clothing of fugitives are taken from the *Woodville Republican*, 1832–1848, *passim*.

and shoes. There were surtouts, round coats, frock coats, waist coats, and several other kinds, differing in color, weave, and fabric almost as much as the trousers.

Socks were apparently not essential in clothing slaves, though they were knit on some plantations.[21] They were very rarely advertised by the merchants, although one of them offered for sale fifty dozen pairs of Kentucky socks.[22] Hats were generally described simply as woolen,[23] though some were of the type known as campeachy, and one gang of slaves wore "blue Scotch bonnets."[24] There were, naturally, many individual variations, such as the old straw hat covered with green oilcloth which was worn by one negro. It was sometimes said that hats were not as generally supplied as shoes, and they were certainly less frequently for sale. On the other hand, in notices of fugitives, hats were more often mentioned and described than shoes, possibly because they varied more widely and, therefore, better served to identify runaways. The possession of both hats and shoes varied with the weather. The general practice seems to have been to provide a pair of shoes for each negro when the days began to grow chilly, and these he would wear until they were beyond use. But by this time warm weather had come, and shoes were no longer necessary. Shod in winter and barefoot in summer was the rule, with a good many exceptions each way.

In addition to adapting the slaves' clothing to seasonal changes, planters in other ways considered the health and comfort of their negroes. Blanket coats or wrappers were provided cotton-pickers to protect them against the heavy dews of early morning.[25] When the dread cholera was in the land, flannel shirts and shifts and warm socks were often issued.[26]

Bedclothes, consisting entirely of blankets together with a few comforts and quilts, were issued to slaves at more or less regular intervals. On the Dabney estate one blanket was given yearly to each man, woman, and child.[27] Dr. Philips, in alternate years, distributed blankets worth two dollars apiece.[28] In the Leigh plantation book is a

[21] Smedes, *Southern Planter*, p. 74.
[22] *Woodville Republican*, Nov. 12, 1836.
[23] *Ibid.*, Feb. 25, 1832.
[24] *Back Country*, pp. 14–15.
[25] [Ingraham], *Southwest by a Yankee*, II, 285.
[26] William D. Jenkins, "The Cholera in 1849," in *P. M. H. S.*, VII, 277.
[27] *Southern Planter*, pp. 73–74.
[28] Riley, "Diary of a Miss. Planter," in *P. M. H. S.*, X, 337, 395, 439. *Seaboard Slave States*, p. 697.

record of the distribution made in 1859. To each family of slaves were given two or three blankets, and to each unmarried adult, one. These new blankets were in addition to those left over from previous years, which generally amounted to two or three blankets per slave. The latter must have been in moderately good condition, for they did not include those dismissed as "some old ones." [29]

The clothing of the negro children is most easily described. It was simply a one-piece garment, in appearance a slightly lengthened shirt. This was the maximum for week day use.

There was a newspaper statement that might indicate that slaves were put in uniform on certain plantations. A planter wrote that his two runaway slaves, Richard and Minor, took a supply of clothing, "part of which was their negro uniform, corduroy jacket and trousers, and small new black hats." [30] The purchase of clothing in wholesale lots by large plantations would naturally lead to something like a uniform system of clothing, which a traveler of the time noted in at least one instance.[31] However, had there been any widespread practice of clothing alike all the slaves on each estate, it seems that more use would have been made of this in tracing fugitive slaves. There was certainly a wide range in the clothing combinations worn by runaway slaves.

The individual tastes and desires of the slaves worked against any uniform system of clothing. Left to their own desires, they tended to diversification. Some of the most startling outfits were worn by fugitive negroes, and in a later chapter a few of these will be described. But these hardly seem typical and were doubtless in part the result of the runaway's attempt to take all his valued finery with him. The simplest way to do this was to wear it. We shall here mention briefly but one or two unorthodox combinations. One negro, except for a linen shirt, was dressed as an Indian. Another was arrayed in two pairs of trousers, white underneath and black canton crêpe on top. A third case of superfluous clothing was the following: two pairs of pantaloons, one cotton, the other satinet; two round jackets, one a soldier's jacket and the other corduroy; and brogan shoes.[32]

If a negro wore such finery as a "swansdown waistcoat," or a

[29] Leigh MSS.
[30] *Woodville Republican,* June 30, 1832.
[31] *Back Country,* pp. 14–15.
[32] *Ibid.,* Feb. 25, 1832; July 21, 1827; Apr. 27, 1833.

"silk waistcoat," [33] or a swallow-tail coat, or a hoop-skirt with ruffles and ribbons,[34] one may reasonably suppose that it had been received after the master or mistress had tired of it. Naturally, the house servant was in a better position to receive such bounty than the less fortunately placed field hand. The desire of the master to have the corps of house servants present a good appearance frequently called for a dress costume or uniform for the butler or coachman.[35]

Though slaves were generally dressed in clothes that were cheaper and coarser than those of the white people, most of them were clad comfortably. Their raiment would probably compare favorably with that of the agricultural laborer of the same region in more recent times.

The food of slaves, as well as their clothing, was not generally described by competent witnesses; yet this was one of the most bitterly debated of all phases of slavery. Abolitionist literature had much to say on the subject, and while this was not often accurate, one extract will be quoted. Though the writer very frankly states his purpose in the first sentence, he does seem to have made an attempt at fairness and he discredits one of the extravagant rumors of how the slaves were underfed.

"I now proceed to show that they are underfed. But, in the first place, I will say that the stories that have been sometimes circulated in the North, about planters at the South feeding their slaves on cotton seed, are all a humbug. There may have been some instances of the experiment's being tried; but that it is commonly, or even occasionally brought into regular practice, is false. The general rule of feeding is to give just what will supply the demands of nature, and no more. Slaves are almost universally allowanced. Their rations are usually a peck of meal, and three or three and a half pounds of meat a week. This is dealt out on some plantations weekly, and on others daily; which is the more common practice, I am not able to say. Some add a half pint or a pint of molasses a

[33] *Ibid.*, July 21, 1829.
[34] *Southern Planter*, p. 71.
[35] Leigh MSS.

"But the dignity of the turn-out chiefly reposed in the coachman, an obese old black man, who should have been a manufacturer of iced root-beer in a cool cellar, but who had by some means been set high up in the sun's face on the bed-like cushion of the box, to display a great livery top-coat, with the wonted capes and velvet, buttoned brightly and tightly to the chin, of course, and crowned by the proper narrow-brimmed hat, with broad band and buckle; his elbows squared, the reins and whip in his hands, the sweat in globules all over his ruefully-decorous face, and his eyes fast closed in sleep." Such was a scene viewed by Olmsted a few miles from Natchez.—*Back Country*, p. 36.

week. As a general thing, the bread stuff is given them ground, and not whole, as has been sometimes represented. On most plantations there is a cook, who prepares their breakfast and dinner, which are always eaten in the field. Their suppers they prepare for themselves after they return from work. Some allowance them only in meat, giving what meal they want; the general rule, however, is a peck of meal and three pounds of meat a week. This allowance is frequently very much shortened when corn or meat is scarce or high. So that on almost every plantation, the hands suffer more or less from hunger at some season of almost every year. I have conversed with some very candid slaves on this subject; and they say that they can do very well on a peck of meal and three and a half pounds of meat a week, except in the winter, when their appetites are keener, and crave particularly more meat." [36]

Undoubtedly, the diet of the slaves in Mississippi, and in the rest of the South, was composed chiefly of corn and meat. Meat in most cases was synonymous with pork. This is no place to investigate the value of these foods from the standpoint of dietetics. The opponents of slavery contended that insufficient amounts of them were furnished, and Northern travelers in the South sometimes contended that they were not palatable. For instance, Olmsted wrote, with worn patience, "that bacon, corn-bread and coffee invariably appeared at every meal" on his journey through Mississippi. These and other articles such as "biscuit invariably made heavy, doughy and indigestible with short-ening" that were from time to time added to the fare he did not like.[37] And Olmsted sought, though he did not always secure, good accommodations in his travels. But one must remember that there is a sectionalism in foods as much as in politics. This may have been a case where one influenced the other ever so slightly. Though Olm-sted did not like the various ways of serving maize and pork, it is at least likely that a Mississippi slave, serving his master on a Northern tour, might have yearned for these very things, even in the face of plentiful supplies of beef and Irish potatoes.

There was almost no criticism of the amount of meal furnished the slaves. It is hardly conceivable that the slave would have suffered a shortage in this, for in feeding the stock he had frequent access to

[36] *Liberty*, pp. 140–144, an anti-slavery pamphlet published in 1837, without naming the editor or publisher. This particular letter was written May 24, 1835, by Asa A. Stone, a theological student, who resided near Natchez, in 1834 and the following year.

For other abolitionist statements concerning the food of slaves in Mississippi, see [Theodore Dwight Weld], *American Slavery As It Is: Testimony of a Thousand Witnesses*, pp. 28, 31, 35, 99 ff.

[37] *Back Country*, pp. 161–162.

the crib. Furthermore, planters, whose estimates can be checked or who estimated closely in other items of foodstuff, stated in regard to meal that they were not "particular about the measure of that, . . . and wish them to have all they will eat without wasting it." [38] In practically every case where meal was rationed, a peck a week for each slave was considered the standard measure. [39]

Planters hoped to raise enough corn and meat to supply the needs of their estates. One informed his overseers that, if they failed to do this, they would not be employed the following year. [40] Few Mississippi plantation managers lived up to such a rule. [41] It appears that there was more often a shortage of pork than of corn, possibly because on larger estates it was difficult to keep slaves from stealing and roasting the young pigs. [42]

Generally speaking, in Mississippi, between three and four pounds of pork was supplied to each slave weekly. Except for a rumor, no instance has been found in which the allowance fell below three pounds. [43] On a plantation where three pounds was the amount rationed, Olmsted noted that the negroes seemed well fed and had "often more than they could eat." [44] The amount was usually larger. Two Mississippi planters, John T. Leigh and Col. Joseph Dunbar, wrote that they supplied three and a half pounds of bacon a week, [45] and a third planter allowed four. [46] On a large estate, controlled by an overseer in the absence of the owner, the weekly allowance was four pounds, which was increased to five when vegetables were not available. [47] On the Dabney estate twelve pounds of meat were issued each fortnight to the men, and ten to the women, or an average of five and a half pounds a week to each adult slave. [48]

[38] De Bow's Review, VII, 380.
[39] Back Country, pp. 41–42, 50, 75. De Bow's Review, III, 420.
[40] Ibid., X, 626.
[41] "Diary of a Miss. Planter," in P. M. H. S., X, passim. The Cultivator, n. s., II, 272. Bassett, Plantation Overseer, passim. During the first decade of the exploitation of Polk's plantation there was each year a failure to produce enough pork.—Ibid., p. 171.
[42] Back Country, pp. 46–47, citing, Russell, North America: Its Agriculture, etc., p. 265.
[43] Back Country, pp. 41–42.
[44] Ibid., p. 74.
[45] De Bow's Review, VII, 380–382.
[46] Ibid., X, 623; III, 420.
[47] Back Country, p. 50.
[48] Southern Planter, p. 71.

In his private plantation accounts P. R. Leigh, son of the John T. Leigh just mentioned, noted toward the beginning of 1853 that the pork on hand was "not less than 13,800 pounds, which is more than necessary by 1,500." [49] He had forty-nine slaves, of whom thirty were working hands. Supposing the owner's family to have included five persons, there were about 230 pounds of pork per person during the year, or almost four and a half pounds a week. This does not anticipate using the 1,500 pounds of reserve, and it counts the whole plantation population as full hands, when, as a matter of fact, quite a few were small children or infants.

In other plantation books either the number of pounds of pork for the year or the number of slaves are not stated. There are merely notations that hogs were killed on certain days, and the weight for one day was frequently in excess of two thousand pounds.[50] On the cold days that were chosen for hog-killing, meat was plentiful, for much that could not be salted or otherwise preserved was distributed to the negroes.[51] In all seasons of the year an occasional hog, often one that was wild, was killed and used as fresh pork.[52]

Though corn meal and pork were staple foods, they were not the only articles of diet.[53] The census of the United States of 1860[54] lists many other products, both meat and vegetable, for the State of Mississippi, and it is fair to suppose that a considerable quantity of these were consumed by the slaves. Most of the plantation accounts tell of the planting and harvesting of many forms of foodstuffs. Possibly the most favorable account is that given by Mrs. Smedes.[55] The greatest variety of all kinds of food were produced by Dr. M. W. Philips,[56] but he was a born experimenter, and much that he raised was produced for scientific purposes rather than for food. The Bowles account book records the operation of a more typical cotton plantation. While the overseer did not note the exact amount of the products of field, garden, orchard, and barnyard of the estate, one can learn what these were, and some idea of quantity can be

[49] Leigh MSS.
[50] Bowles MS.
[51] *Southern Planter*, p. 163.
[52] Bowles MS.
[53] *De Bow's Review*, VII, 380–382; *ibid.*, X, 623.
[54] *Census of 1860 (Agriculture)*, 84–87.
[55] *Southern Planter*.
[56] "Diary of a Miss. Planter," in *P. M. H. S.*, X, *passim*.

gained by observing the amount of work devoted to their care or harvesting. The list could be approximately equaled by a study of any of the extant records of Mississippi plantations.

In addition to large numbers of hogs, sheep and beeves were killed several times during the year on the Bowles plantation. Most of the sheep and cattle were slaughtered in the fall, after the weather was cool, but before it was cold enough for killing hogs. Poultry and fish were not mentioned, though we know that on many estates slaves were allowed to keep their own hen-houses and to fatten the chickens from the corn in the master's crib. On some estates fish were provided for the slaves, sometimes being purchased by the master,[57] and sometimes being caught by the negroes themselves.[58] Further impressions of the meat supplies of Mississippi plantations can be gained from newspaper advertisements of the livestock on estates advertised for sale.[59]

In addition to corn, there was produced on the Bowles estate oats, wheat, and rye and such vegetables as potatoes, peas, cabbage, turnips, and pumpkins. Of the vegetables, potatoes and peas were the more important. There were two pea patches, one of seven acres and the other of twenty-three. Many days' labor were expended in cultivating potatoes, which were mainly, perhaps wholly, sweet potatoes.

Also, on the Bowles estate there was a garden, the size and produce of which is not known. However, a large amount of work was done in it, for sometimes as many as five slaves worked there together, and its products must have been too many by far to have been consumed by the white residents of the estate. Vegetables were often mentioned as a part of the food of the slaves,[60] and on the Leigh estate Solon Robinson found the slaves provided with "sweet potatoes, turnips, squashes, onions, green corn, and various other vegetables, as well as melons and peaches, by untold quantities."[61] Leigh, as well as Philips, had extensive orchards.

These were the domestic food products of typical Mississippi plantations. The quantity of each is not known, but a considerable amount

[57] *Southern Planter*, p. 59.
[58] At least they were permitted to go fishing occasionally.—"Diary of a Miss. Planter," in *P. M. H. S.*, X, 368, 433.
Ely, a negro driver, was permitted to have a fish trap in a pond on his master's estate.—Ned and Taylor *v.* The State, 33 Miss. 364.
[59] E. g., *Woodville Republican*, Jan. 8, 1848. Also *The Cultivator*, n. s., II, 272.
[60] *De Bow's Review*, III, 420; X, 626. *Back Country*, pp. 50, 74.
[61] *The Cultivator*, n. s., II, 272.

of time was devoted to their production, and the lack of a close check on their volume indicates that they were for home consumption. Cotton, the money crop, was closely weighed at various stages of production and detailed records kept.

Though most of the food of slaves was undoubtedly raised on the plantation, some articles were bought from the market cities. In the absence of any description of this on the Bowles estate, other than the notations on several consecutive days that the wagons were hauling groceries from the neighboring steamboat landing, some other estate must be investigated. The following items were taken from the order sent to New Orleans in 1854 by P. R. Leigh.

> 3 barrels Molasses
> 2 best brown sugar
> 1 common brown sugar
> 80 lbs. loaf sugar
> 200 lbs. Java coffee
> 100 lbs. Rio coffee
> 100 lbs. rice
> 8 sacks fine salt
> 5 coarse
> 8 barrells best flour, not of the Union
>   brand, that does not keep well

Some of these were doubtless used by the household of the planter, and there were other entries of small amounts of spices, cheese, and similar articles that certainly were not purchased for the negroes. But the list gives a fair example of the food purchased off the plantation for the use of the plantation population, both white and black. With the exception of molasses, most purchased foodstuffs were doled to the slaves as luxuries or rewards. Molasses was frequently looked upon as a substitute for meat, or possibly vegetables. On one plantation, a quart of molasses a week was issued to each slave during the months when vegetables were scarce.[62] In another case, when molasses was issued a certain amount of meat was withheld, the choice being left to the individual slave.[63] On a large absentee-owner plantation, each family of slaves received a barrel of molasses, together with large amounts of coffee, tobacco, and other articles, at Christmas. This was said to have been rather common in Mississippi though the amount was generally not so generous. The amount of this "Christmas

[62] *Back Country*, p. 75.
[63] *De Bow's Review*, VII, 380–381.

food" was often in proportion to the value of the last crop sold, and was thus an approach to the share system.[64]

The cost of feeding slaves varied with the times, and was naturally higher in town than in the country. With this in mind, the following facts may be of interest. In the 1850's, slaves engaged in railroad work in northern Mississippi were boarded at fifteen cents a day.[65] A few years earlier, twenty cents a day was allowed for the board of each of forty-five negroes employed in a cotton factory at Jackson. Only nine of them were adults. In the same establishment were seven white men, whose board was thirty cents a day.[66] A German resident of Natchez told Olmsted that it cost eight dollars to board a negro a month in town, but less in the country, where there were no "extras," and "where they did not get anything but bacon and meal . . ." [67]

No general rule was followed in preparing the meals of slaves. On small plantations or farms, one cook served for the master and the slaves. As this arrangement was once described, the negroes ate in the kitchen, the master in the dining room, with an open door between them and their food came "right out of the same frying-pan." [68] This was impracticable when the slaves were numerous. The planter then had each negro family prepare its own food, or else a common kitchen was built and one slave set apart to cook for all the rest.

There was some encouragement to orderly family life in having each family of slaves remain to itself at meal times. However, after laboring a full day in the fields, slaves were severely taxed when required to secure wood, sometimes a half mile from the quarters, before a fire could be kindled and supper cooked. Even though the better planters provided wood conveniently located, cooking in addition to field work made too long a day and sensible men recognized that this was bad economy.[69] However, many adhered to this foolish and oppressive system, "each family being provided with an oven, skillet, and sifter, and each one having a coffee-pot, (and generally some coffee to put in it,) with knives and forks, plates, spoons, cups, etc. of their own providing." [70] Intelligent managers of large planta-

[64] Back Country, p. 51.
[65] Leigh MSS.
[66] De Bow's Review, VII, 176.
[67] Back Country, p. 41.
[68] Ibid., p. 153. Southern Planter, p. 105.
[69] De Bow's Review, X, 623-624; III, 419.
[70] Ibid., X, 623.

tions established a separate "cook house" [71] and set apart one or more negroes to prepare food for the others. Cooking was doubtless more closely supervised when the communal kitchen was used.[72]

A number of those who struggled with problems of plantation management found it advantageous to use a combination of the two systems just described. On one estate each family was a unit in cooking and eating, but there was a common kitchen for the single slaves.[73] On another, dinner was prepared at the quarters and brought to the field hands at noon, but families separately prepared their breakfasts and suppers.[74] The season of the year also helped determine what system should be followed. During the winter and for a short time in summer when crops were laid by, each family cooked and ate separately; when work was pressing, the food of the field hands was prepared in a central kitchen.

Slaves were more often rationed when each family did its own cooking. The food was usually apportioned to the slaves each Saturday or, sometimes, each Sunday.[75] Occasionally the allowance was given out daily and on a few plantations fortnightly.[76]

In a few cases slaves returned to the quarters for every meal, but supper was the only meal that almost universally was eaten at home. With but few exceptions, dinner was carried to the field, sometimes being taken in individual pails by the slaves when they started out in the morning, at other times being sent out hot at noon. At noon on one large estate, one cart took the dinner to the plow gang, and another to the hoe gang.[77]

Breakfast was, in some respects, the most movable feast. When days were short, it was generally eaten at the quarters before work was begun. But in the summer, when there was much to be done and days were long, the slaves generally reached the field soon after dawn. Breakfast was then brought to them about eight o'clock.[78]

When breakfast and dinner were eaten in the field, half an hour

[71] *Seaboard Slave States*, p. 697.
[72] *De Bow's Review*, III, 419; VII, 382. *American Slavery As It Is*, p. 99.
[73] *De Bow's Review*, VII, 380.
[74] *Ibid.*, X, 623.
[75] *Plantation and Frontier*, I, 244.
[76] *Southern Planter*, p. 72.
[77] *Back Country*, pp. 49, 153.
[78] *Ibid.*, p. 80. *Plantation and Frontier*, I, 114, 243. *Liberty*, pp. 140–144. *Southern Planter*, p. 74.

was allowed for the former, and an hour for the latter.[79] The cotton fields were frequently extensive. Doubtless some planters begrudged the time lost in going to and from shade trees at the edge of the field at meal time. Partly because of this, weather sheds were sometimes built in the middle of wide fields and to these the slaves could resort to eat their noon meal. However, there were negroes who preferred to sit in the direct rays of the sun, a practice which overseers were sometimes ordered to discountenance.[80]

Though most of the food of the slaves came from the plantation supplies, either home-grown or bought, they were permitted on many estates to have their own garden patches, or their separate flocks of chickens.[81] By diminishing allowances, some managers may have virtually compelled their negroes to produce privately part of their supply of food, but outside of abolitionist writings no instance has been found in which this was true. As the slaves could either consume or sell their garden truck or poultry, the frequent use of the latter alternative indicates that the negroes did not need all that they produced to satisfy their own hunger.[82] Rarely, the money secured by a slave through the sale of his products, or through rewards, was carefully saved, with the hope of purchasing his freedom. But most of it was spent soon after it was secured. Bright garments or silk dresses, whiskey, confectionery, and other luxuries were bought,[83] or a more sober slave was thereby enabled to place his coin in the collection plate on Sunday.[84]

Some slave owners, though they encouraged the negroes to cultivate their own gardens, or to tend their own chickens, did not permit any of the produce to be sold.[85]

There can be no doubt that the food of the slaves was generally inferior in quality to that of their masters. For instance, slaves were

[79] *Back Country*, p. 80. *De Bow's Review*, III, 420.

[80] *Back Country*, p. 49. *De Bow's Review*, VII, 382; X, 623. Leigh MSS.

[81] *De Bow's Review*, VII, 380–381; X, 624.

[82] *Plantation and Frontier*, I, 114.
There are entries of "amounts of negroes corn sold at Christmas" in Bowles MS.
In *Southern Planter*, pp. 70–71, it is said that one of the slaves raised as many as five hundred chickens in a year.
See also a letter of William Dunbar quoted in Claiborne, *Mississippi*, p. 144.

[83] *Southern Planter*, p. 71.

[84] *Ibid.*, p. 106. E. P. Southall, "The Attitude of the Methodist Episcopal Church, South, toward the Negro from 1844 to 1870," in *The Journal of Negro History*, XVI, 365.

[85] *De Bow's Review*, X, 624.

more likely to receive pork middlings and joints than ham and bacon.[86] In plantation purchases there was frequently a significant difference in the grades of coffee, sugar, or flour. Here, as in other conditions of life, it is probable that the house servants fared better than the field hands, for the former frequently ate the same quality of food as was prepared for the master and mistress.[87] However, slaves did not often suffer hunger. Olmsted and other travelers rarely, if ever, found an estate on which the negroes seemed underfed, and the former frequently made such statements as, "the negroes appeared to be well taken care of and abundantly supplied with the necessaries of vigorous physical existence." [88]

On Mississippi plantations there were probably wider differences in respect to the housing of negroes than in kinds and amounts of food. A planter who lived near the edge of the swamp of the Big Black River pointed out the extremes of practice in regard to housing slaves in a description he gave of his own negro quarters.

"My first care has been to select a proper place for my 'Quarter,' well protected by the shade of forest trees, sufficiently thinned out to admit a free circulation of air, so situated as to be free from the impurities of stagnant water, and to erect comfortable houses for my negroes. Planters do not always reflect that there is more sickness, and consequently greater loss of life, from the decaying logs of negro houses, open floors, leaky roofs, and crowded rooms, than all other causes combined; and if humanity will not point out the proper remedy, let self-interest for once act as a virtue, and prompt him to save the health and lives of his negroes, by at once providing comfortable quarters for them. There being upward of 150 negroes on the plantation, I provide for them 24 houses made of hewn post oak, covered with cypress, 16 by 18, with close plank floors and good chimneys, and elevated two feet from the ground. The ground *under* and around the houses is swept every month, and the houses, both inside and out, white-washed twice a year. The houses are situated in a double row from north to south, about 200 feet apart, the doors facing inwards, and the houses being in a line, about 50 feet apart. At one end of the street stands the overseer's house, workshops, tool house, and wagon sheds; at the other, the grist and saw-mill, with good cisterns at each end, providing an ample supply of pure water." [89]

Beyond these broad outlines, the detail varied from plantation to plantation. While this was doubtless an accurate description of the

[86] Leigh MSS. "The Cholera in 1849," in *P. M. H. S.*, VII, 276–277.
[87] *Southern Planter*, p. 57.
[88] *Back Country*, p. 74.
[89] *De Bow's Review*, X, 623.

quarters on this estate, conditions there were in several respects better than on many other plantations. The planter himself intimates as much,[90] and so the other side will be stated. On a small plantation in the northern part of Mississippi,

"The negro cabins were small, dilapidated and dingy; the walls were not chinked, and there were no windows . . . which, indeed, would have been a superfluous luxury, for there were spaces of several inches between the logs, through which there was unobstructed vision. [This was summer. It was sometimes the practice to knock out the chinking in the spring, and fill the cracks with fresh mud in the fall.] The furniture in the cabins was of the simplest and rudest imaginable kind, two or three beds with dirty clothing upon them, a chest, a wooden stool or two, made with an ax, and some earthenware and cooking apparatus. Everything within the cabins was colored black by smoke. The chimneys . . . were built of splinters and clay. . . ."[91]

These slaves did not seem unhappy in their quarters, for the following scene was witnessed inside one of these huts at night. "A man sat on the ground making a basket, a woman lounged on a chest in the chimney-corner smoking a pipe, and a boy and two girls sat in a bed which had been drawn up opposite to her, completing the fireside circle. They were talking and laughing cheerfully."[92]

Another description of slave houses was written by Eleazar Powell, of Pennsylvania, who plied his trade of masonry in Adams and Jefferson Counties, in the winter of 1836–1837. "The huts are generally, of split timber, some larger than rails, twelve and a half wide and fourteen feet long—some with and some without chimneys, and generally without floors; they are generally without daubing, and mostly had split clap-boards nailed on the cracks on the outside, though some were without even that: . . . "[93]

There is no doubt that the housing of slaves was more open to criticism than their food, or even their clothing. According to modern ideas, they were crowded, and the houses were frequently mean. Two statements, however, should be made.

[90] William B. Trotter, in his *History and Defense of African Slavery*, supplements his defense by advising planters how to feed, clothe, and house their slaves, and how to manage a plantation. But Trotter shows the same lack of judgment as does this correspondent in *De Bow's Review*. He frequently advises planters to correct various evils commonly practiced in the management of slaves, and thus largely nullifies his own defense of the institution. Something of Trotter's own relationship to slavery may be found in Trotter *v.* McCall, 26 Miss. 410.

[91] *Back Country*, p. 140.

[92] *Ibid.*, p. 142.

[93] *American Slavery As It Is*, pp. 99 ff.

The cabin of the slave was not a home in the full sense of the word. On many plantations they ate in a community dining room. Children were generally cared for in the house set apart as the nursery. Negro cabins were little more than places to sleep. They were closed and locked, and the slave quarters were generally deserted through the entire day, except for the nursery, hospital, and cook house.[94]

In the second place, civilization was still in the pioneer stage in at least half of Mississippi at the beginning of the Civil War.[95] The plantation homes of many well-to-do planters were of logs. The residence of the intelligent Dr. M. W. Philips was properly known as "Log Hall," and the master whose slaves lived in unchinked cabins himself dwelt in a house of logs.[96] As time went on, the homes of the masters were weatherboarded on the outside and ceiled inside. The cabins of the slaves naturally were uncovered logs for a longer time.

When new land was taken up, the first task was the building of houses. While this was being done, the slaves were sometimes sheltered in tents, and the master likewise, unless he was invited to the house of a neighbor.[97] Clearing new ground, building fences, planting crops, and, in general, creating a plantation left little time for building houses. Naturally they showed the ill effects of hurried construction. When President Polk's Mississippi planting venture was commenced, eighteen days were spent in putting up houses (one for the overseer, four for the slaves, a smoke house, and a kitchen) and in making a lot for the stock. Into their four houses were crowded thirty-seven slaves.[98] The owner was doubtless dissatisfied with this as a permanent arrangement, but these were pioneer conditions; and in pioneer life there was frequently but little difference, except in size, between the cabins of slaves and the home of the owner or overseer.[99]

As time went on, there was a gradual improvement in houses, though changes were retarded by the pressure of other plantation

[94] De Bow's Review, X, 626.
[95] Most of northern Mississippi, as well as much of the land in the southwest, had been settled not over twenty years in 1861.
[96] "Diary of a Miss. Planter," in P. M. H. S., X, 305–306. Back Country, pp. 140–142. The Cultivator, n. s., II, 272, 365.
[97] Southern Planter, p. 63.
[98] Plantation Overseer, p. 262.
[99] De Bow's Review, VII, 380. Back Country, p. 74.

duties always waiting to be done. Some log cabins were weather-boarded; others were entirely replaced by frame cabins, and, incidentally, more space could then be given to windows. On a few estates, brick houses for the slaves began to appear.[100] Among other improvements, plank floors began to replace dirt or puncheon floors, and planters rather generally realized that floors should be elevated at least two feet above the ground.[101]

Olmsted observed the evolution of cabins on a plantation of several hundred slaves. Though some of the slaves lived in small, mean, log huts, these were being replaced by well-built cottages, with broad galleries in front. Each contained two rooms, with a loft above, and was built for one family, averaging five slaves.[102] The attic space was also used on some other plantations, the approach usually being by means of a ladder inside the house.[103]

Separate cabins for each family were doubtless more sanitary and conducive toward peacefulness and were, therefore, more generally used, even though there was an economy in building a larger structure to house several families. However, in rare cases the dormitory plan was used. The slave quarters on the Nutt estate, near Natchez, were both attractive and unusual. There was a large brick building, one room thick, a number of rooms long, and two stories high, with a two story porch across the front. Shaded by large oaks, the location was pleasant.

There were usually from ten to thirty cabins in one slave village.[104] As the number of slaves grew, it was usually deemed advisable to form one or more new quarters rather than to expand the old settlement. To save time in going to and from work, the new cabins were constructed at some distance from the old in a different part of the estate.[105]

[100] For instance, there are brick cabins for slaves, and a large wooden house for the master, still standing on the Bailey plantation on the outskirts of Oxford, Miss.

[101] De Bow's Review, III, 419.

[102] Back Country, p. 74.

[103] As was the case on the Dunbar plantation near Woodville.—Woodville Republican, Oct. 4, 1845.

[104] [George Lewis Prentiss], Memoir of S. S. Prentiss, I, 74-75. Letter dated from Natchez, June 23, 1828.

[105] "There were two quarters on this plantation (Tarbert); the old quarters, very near the river, and the new or lower quarters, about three-quarters of a mile back from the river." This was in Wilkinson County.—"The Cholera of 1849," in P. M. H. S., VII, 273. Also, De Bow's Review, VII, 381, mentioning the Dunbar plantations near Natchez.

In the parts of Mississippi where slaves were numerous about one cabin to four or five slaves was the average, if we can accept the returns in the census of 1860. A few statistics of typical plantations follow. In Wilkinson County George T. McGehee had only eleven houses for seventy-three slaves, but in contrast E. J. McGehee had twenty houses for forty-five slaves. There were 736 slaves in the county owned by members of the McGehee family and they were provided with 183 houses, about one house to every four negroes. William N. Mercer, one of the largest slaveholders in Adams County, had 104 houses for his 452 slaves. In Warren County, William L. Sharkey, formerly chief justice and later provisional governor of Mississippi, had twenty-five slave houses for his sixty-five negroes. In the same county Jefferson Davis, soon to become president of the Confederacy, had twenty-eight houses for the 113 slaves at "Brierfield"; his brother Joseph E. Davis had seventy-six houses for his 355 slaves.[106]

The cleanliness of the negro cabins depended on the negro as well as the owner or overseer. Some cabins were described as "the very picture of misery and filth," [107] others were carefully white-washed inside and out, and all trash cleared from under and around the structure and burned.[108] It is most improbable that the management of an estate ever objected to clean cabins. Plain business sense compelled the owner of negroes to command a modicum of cleanliness about the quarters, and rules and regulations were laid down to secure this.

Furniture inside the cabins was of the simplest, consisting generally of beds, chairs, and boxes. Most of this was home-made. The beds were frequently bunks built into the wall, with bottoms solid, slatted, or corded. In the latter type, holes were made in the sides of the beds, and heavy cord, or rope, was woven back and forth through the holes. Over this base was thrown a mattress, a home-made covering stuffed with corn shucks or hay.[109] In the older regions, the household belongings of the negroes were less rude, and included high post bedsteads, with mosquito netting, china ware, looking-

[106] Eighth Census (1860) of the United States, MS. slave schedules for Mississippi. Adams County returns are in vol. 1 and Warren and Wilkinson County returns are in vol. 5.

[107] *Memoir of S. S. Prentiss*, I, 74–75.

[108] "The Cholera in 1849," in *P. M. H. S.*, VII, 273. *Southwest by a Yankee*, II, 109. *De Bow's Review*, III, 419.

[109] *American Slavery As It Is*, pp. 99 ff.

glasses, trunks and chests for clothing, and much more besides.[110]

Now and then slaves were quartered away from their cabins. An epidemic such as cholera might force the master to move his slaves to a location that was considered more healthful,[111] and there a camp would be made and temporary sheds erected. Or in the course of ordinary plantation life, when several days labor was necessary at a distance from the regular quarters, a temporary camp was sometimes set up.[112]

Other sleeping quarters were sometimes provided. In one instance the negro cook slept in the kitchen, and this seemingly was the permanent arrangement.[113] Even more foreign to common practice was the arrangement in the household of a doctor, who with his wife and children occupied a one-room house. In this same room lived the only slave that the family possessed, a negro girl. The experience of this family would not recommend the practice. One night the negress murdered the whole family. She was convicted on circumstantial evidence and was presumably hanged.[114]

There were no provisions in the laws of Mississippi to protect the slave against too scanty shelter at the hands of his master. Slave-housing was noticed only in certain police regulations for the protection of the white population. Slaves could not be quartered in any incorporated town or city except on the usual residential lot of the owner.[115] The corresponding rule for the country was that not over six slaves could be quartered beyond a mile from the owner's residence unless there were a white male overseer with them.[116]

[110] De Bow's Review, VII, 381. Southwest by a Yankee, II, 242–243.
[111] "The Cholera in 1849," in P. M. H. S., VII, 276.
[112] Woodville Republican, Jan. 26, 1832.
[113] McCoy v. McKowen, 26 Miss. 487.
[114] Cicely, a slave, v. The State, 21 Miss. 202.
[115] Hutchinson's Code, p. 539. For a case arising under this law, see, Tifft v. The State, 23 Miss. 567.
[116] Hutchinson's Code, p. 539.

CHAPTER III

PHYSICAL AND SOCIAL CARE

The manager of a plantation, whether overseer or planter, had to profess some knowledge of many crafts. Not least of these was that of medicine, for physicians were sometimes at a distance, and their fees were always to be avoided if possible. In the contract between owner and overseer care of the sick was frequently included among the duties of the overseer.[1]

Common business prudence instructed the manager not to force a sick slave to go to the field. By the same token, the slave should not be allowed to loaf behind the screen of pretended sickness. A knowledge of diseases and a knowledge of the individual slave were the deciding factors; and the latter was probably the one chiefly relied on. The following instance was doubtless typical. An overseer, observed by Olmsted, dealt severely with a negro who was simulating sickness and ordered him to the field in spite of his protests; but the same day, this overseer was kind and sympathetic in prescribing for a slave who he believed was really sick.[2]

In another connection, the record of the Wheeless plantation during the cotton-picking season of 1858 has been given. During the nineteen weeks when this main crop was being gathered, 1,429 days of potential slave labor were accounted for. Of this number, 179 were lost on account of sickness. It is evident that the slaves on the Wheeless plantation missed an average about one day out of every eight. It should be further noted that this was in the season when hands could be least spared from the field, that sickness was recorded only for working days, and that there seem to have been no cases of

---

[1] Riley, "Diary of a Miss. Planter," in *P. M. H. S.*, X, 457. *De Bow's Review*, X, 626.

"If any of the negroes have been reported sick, be prompt to see what ails them and that proper medicine and attention be given them. Use good judgment and discretion in turning out those who are getting well."—Phillips, *Plantation and Frontier*, I, 114.

[2] Olmsted, *Back Country*, pp. 77-78.

protracted sickness. No deaths were reported, and there is no indication of an epidemic.[3]

In the daily entries in the Bowles plantation accounts appear the names of the slaves who were sick. A digest of these notations, which were all in the year 1851, gives the following number of days lost on account of sickness each month:

January	17, one of which was on a Sunday
February	18
March	16
April	11½
May	18 " " " " " " "
June	9
July	11
August	16, three of which were on Sundays
September	21
October	17
November	5
December	0

159½. If sickness on Sundays be excluded, the number of days lost from work on account of sickness were 154½.

On this plantation there were twenty-three working hands, eleven men and twelve women. The women missed over twice as many days as men on account of sickness.[4] A little less than seven days' work per slave were lost during the year, and, omitting Sundays and the four holidays at Christmas, sickness kept the slaves from working slightly over 2 per cent of the year. Every slave on the plantation was sick at least one working day. From the standpoint of the owner the slave, Tabby, had the worst record, having lost thirty-three days because of sickness.[5]

On the Leigh estate, the owner himself tabulated and commented on statistics of sickness. His monthly record for the year 1853 follows:

January	10	July	47½
February	13	August	41½
March	22	September	60
April	15½	October	32
May	65	November	22
June	69½	December	

[3] Wheeless MS.
[4] Men, 46½; women, 113.
[5] Bowles MS.

At the end of the year, he wrote, "There have been to the 24th of December 398 days of sickness to [among] 30 persons all of which occurred in the first 11 months." Earlier, toward the latter part of June, he had written:

"Good deal of sickness. Have thus far managed it myself. Have lossed by sickness this year 195 working days—besides 24 days of a woman who had an infant, in all 219 days lossed by 31 head or persons in the field, an average of over 1⅛ persons always. During May & June lossed 158½ days including the woman mentioned, or an average of over 3 persons always in the house, or rather less, on an average of 2½ days.

"The loss in work at a low calculation has been equal to the hoeing of 60 acres of cotton twice over & nearly 40 of corn once, or equal to the cultivating of 66 acres of cotton once—hoeing & ploughing." [6]

A few comments may be added. Twenty-five of the Leigh slaves were sick one or more days during the year. A few, but not many, more days were lost by the women than by the men. Finally, an examination of the monthly records of this plantation by one familiar with cotton farming shows that there was most sickness when there was most work to be done. As will be mentioned later, slaves were more likely to run away during the months of spring plowing and of fall gathering of the crops.

The large loss of time because of sickness might suggest that slaves were overworked. However, the records of work done by the slaves do not warrant this conclusion; and any sensible planter could realize, as did Mr. Leigh, that a day's sickness meant that a day's work was left undone. Therefore, work extorted by too great pressure might be more than balanced by illness. For this reason a planter usually gave the slave who claimed to be sick the benefit of the doubt, nor did he order him back to the field until danger of a relapse was clearly past. A planter who habitually exercised care along this line boasted that he had not lost a hand, except one killed by accident, in over five years and that his medical bill did not average fifty dollars a year.[7] If mortality rates are a fair index to health, slaves were sick only a little more than white people of ante-bellum Mississippi.[8]

[6] Leigh MSS.
There was also a great deal of sickness at times on Dr. M. W. Philip's plantation. Philips once wrote in his diary: "For first time in 2 months all hands out. God grant it may be healthy from this out."—"Diary of a Miss. Planter," in *P. M. H. S.*, X, 334.
[7] *De Bow's Review*, X, 624–625.
[8] Charles S. Sydnor, "Life Span of Mississippi Slaves," in *American Historical Review*, XXXV, 573.

From time to time healthy slaves enjoyed an extra day of rest with no other penalty than the discomfort resulting from the medical ministrations of the overseer or owner. To this view we are led by the rather large amount of sickness for which no satisfactory explanation was given in the plantation records, by the prevalence of sickness when there was a large amount of work to be done, and by entries in plantation records. Occasionally, instead of naming the disease which kept the slave from the field, the planter wrote "nothing" or "complaining." In one case a planter was able to verify such an opinion, for the entry in the account book was: "Nothing I believe, Right." [9] Another planter confided to his diary: "Eliza sick two days; more lazy and mad than sick." And a little later: "Nanny sick; same old sick." [10]

The most common ailments were chills, colds, and diseases of the intestinal tract, including worms and "bile." A relatively small amount of time was lost because of injuries of an accidental nature.

The slaves themselves had their own notions of how to cure various ailments.

"The medicines of the slaves were made of—'Yarbs,' as they called them. The most common of these were: boneset, blackroot (a root found on the creek banks and used as a substitute for calomel), witch hazel bark (for poultices), and tar water (made by burning the fat from fat pine and soaking it in water). This water was then given the negroes for colds and sore throats. Poultices of all kinds made of leaves and bark were favorite remedies. The more drawing power, so to speak, the better the result, according to the popular idea. Mustard was an old reliable; soft soap mixed with sugar was used as a poultice for boils, risings and suppurations as it would "draw it to a head." Moistened clay and chewing tobacco were used on insect bites and stings. The blood, after the heavy winter diet, was supposed to be thinned. This thinning was accomplished by the drinking of root or bark teas. Sassafras tea was the outstanding one. The roots of the sassafras tree were chipped or cut into small pieces, boiling water was poured over them, and they were allowed to steep until the water was a reddish pink. This blood thinning prevented spring ailments. A mixture of sulphur and molasses was also used for this purpose." [11]

Some of these very remedies were prescribed by planters, and doubtless not a little of their medical lore originated in the mind of

[9] Leigh MSS.
[10] "Diary of a Miss. Planter," in *P. M. H. S.*, X, 342, 346.
[11] Mrs. E. R. Jobe, "Social History of Ante-Bellum Mississippi," pp. 44–45. MS.

the black man. Among other sources of medical knowledge, newspapers gave free advice, usually by describing some treatment that in actual practice had been found efficient.[12] The medical problems of the plantation were also discussed in such magazines as *De Bow's Review*. Experience was possibly the greatest teacher. A planter should have developed some proficiency in curing chills after treating thirty or forty cases a year.

Some novel modes of treatment were occasionally evolved by plantation owners. At one time Mr. Thomas Dabney was faced by an epidemic of black tongue that affected forty of his slaves. Negroes under the care of doctors were dying on neighboring plantations. Dabney decided he could do no worse, so he gave his slaves what seemed to him a simple and sensible treatment, and lost not a single hand. The treatment consisted in a liberal use of port wine and mutton chops![13]

Planters exercised unusual care in time of epidemics. From costly experience they concluded that during a wave of cholera clean cistern water was much safer than well, spring, river, or bayou water. Of course, the cistern must not have been flooded by high water.[14] Regardless of cholera, intelligent planters preferred cistern water to any other kind, particularly in valley regions, and its use was common.[15]

Negro mid-wives from the same or neighboring plantations ruled over maternity cases.[16] Managers of slaves thought that negro women needed very little care at such times, which may partly account for the high rate of infant mortality. The care of the mother varied widely. On the Dabney estate another slave was directed to do all the mother's cooking, washing, and housework for a month, and, during the rest of the year, the mother did little more than care for her baby.[17] However, on most plantations, women were allowed only a month's cessation from field labor before and after confinement, and on some nothing but actual confinement released them from work.[18] According to the records of one estate a slave mother lost only twenty-

---

[12] The *Woodville Republican*, Nov. 9, 1824, contains two columns by a South Carolina planter telling how to treat bilious fever.

[13] Smedes, *Southern Planter*, pp. 66.

[14] Jenkins, "The Cholera in 1849," in *P. M. H. S.*, VII, 277.

[15] *De Bow's Review*, X, 623; III, 420. "Diary of a Miss. Planter," in *P. M. H. S.*, X, 337–338. *Back Country*, p. 49.

[16] *Back Country*, p. 47. Bassett, *Plantation Overseer*, p. 141.

[17] *Southern Planter*, p. 78.

[18] [Ingraham], *Southwest by a Yankee*, II, 125.

four working days at the time of child bearing.[19] In another instance, the overseer wrote the owner that as one of the slaves was expecting a child in four or five weeks, he did not propose to send her to the field until after the birth of the child.[20]

Newspapers frequently advertised extended and awesome lists of drugs that could be purchased from local establishments. While these were kept in stock for either white or black persons, an occasional advertisement such as the following one appeared.

"TO PLANTERS
Castor oil by the gallon for plantation use just received and for sale by,
H. J. BASS & CO." [21]

"A large medicine chest and several books on medical and surgical subjects" were part of the stock in trade of a good overseer [22] and, on most estates, a room or part of a room was converted into a small apothecary's shop.[23] The kinds of medicines purchased by those in control of negroes are shown by numerous entries in plantation account books. A few notations, taken at random from one of these, are here set forth.

1 lb Salts	.12½
1 oz. Calomel	.25
blue Mass	.25
one bottle Castor Oyl	.50
five bottles of Vurmifuge	1.25
one box strong pills	.25
one bottle brags linament	1.00
blister oyntment	.85
2 box of pain extractor	.50
Coppers sulphor & blue stone	.45
one bottle paregoreck	.50
Calomel and Turpentine	1.25 [24]

Whiskey was also used, particularly as a preventive of chills, being allowed to slaves who had worked in the rain, or who had been performing heavy tasks.[25]

[19] Leigh MSS.
[20] *Plantation Overseer,* p. 142.
[21] *Woodville Republican,* Dec. 24, 1836.
[22] *Back Country,* pp. 45–46. Van Buren, *Sojourn in the South,* p. 151.
[23] *Southwest by a Yankee,* II, 120–124.
[24] From Bowles MS. Many of these items, especially salts, are repeated many times.
[25] *Southern Planter,* pp. 83–84.

The following diary entries show how a planter, who was also a physician, thought diseases should be treated.

"Jane sick since Tuesday, fever; an emetic yesterday, oil this morning, now a hard chill.

"Jack and Eliza had a chill and fever today—ipecac, rhubarb and cream of tartar;

"Milly sick—Cr. Tartar and rhubarb, yesterday, calomel and ipecac, 4 doses of 5 grs. calomel and 1 ipecac today. Complains of head, some fever, but skin moist.

"Louisa sick (chill with fever following), calomel, 20 grs., ipecac 2 grs., opium ½ gr." [26]

On some of the larger estates there was a separate hospital building,[27] sometimes with a small room attached to serve as the home or office of the slave nurse.[28] Where there was no plantation hospital sick negroes who needed careful and skilful attention were sometimes brought into the home of the owner.[29] In an epidemic, the home of the planter might become the plantation hospital.[30]

Slaves who were dangerously ill remained in the plantation hospital or in their cabins and were daily visited by the owner or the overseer or a slave nurse. Those whose illness was slight, or who were convalescent, daily reported in person to the "big house." Prescribed medicine was taken in the presence of the planter, otherwise the slave would probably throw it away and rely on the African lore of the old women of the quarters. This dislike for medicine was at times capitalized by those who wished to break slaves from shamming sickness, and in such cases particularly disagreeable doses were prescribed.[31]

Slaves, particularly those who were aged or especially favored, received their food, while they were sick, from the table of the master.[32] The latter realized that the sick negro needed better food than the well, and this was generally provided. On one plantation, the nurse was supplied with sugar, coffee, molasses, rice, flour, and tea. The owner of this estate decreed that a patient should not touch

[26] "Diary of a Miss. Planter," in *P. M. H. S.*, X, 332, 334, 335, 359.
[27] *De Bow's Review*, VII, 382. *Southwest by a Yankee*, II, 120–124.
[28] *De Bow's Review*, X, 624.
[29] James v. Herring, 20 Miss. 336. Otts v. Alderson, 18 Miss. 476. Shewalter v. Ford, 34 Miss. 417.
[30] "The Cholera in 1849," in *P. M. H. S.*, VII, 275.
[31] *Southwest by a Yankee*, II, 120–124.
[32] *Ibid.*, II, 122. *Southern Planter*, p. 84.

vegetables or meat until restored to health, for he believed that many ate imprudently while convalescent.[33]

Mild illness and that of a common type was treated by the planter or overseer. The manager of an estate so large as to require at least four overseers stated that he rarely had occasion to employ a physician.[34] Moreover, quite a few Mississippi planters were themselves physicians. As a cotton plantation seems to have been the aim of most residents of the State, medicine and other professions were frequently stepping-stones to this end. Ingraham observed that "medico-planters are now numerous, far out numbering the regular practitioners . . ."[35] These gentlemen were, of course, able to assume charge of cases that were beyond the skill of overseers. On a few of the larger estates, where there were several hundred slaves, a physician was employed to care for them, or, as a variation, a physician was sometimes employed jointly by several neighboring planters.[36] In most cases, however, the physicians who prescribed for slaves were the selfsame persons who prescribed for masters, and it was said that the physicians of Natchez derived a considerable part of their income from services to the surrounding plantations.[37]

It is possible that the independent physician was more frequently employed by the small planter than by the large. No small planter could afford a physician on the staff of his plantation, nor would he or his overseer be so likely to have as wide a medical experience as the manager of a large estate. The normal planter generally sent for the neighboring physician when his slaves suffered from such diseases as consumption, rheumatism, spasms, or pneumonia.[38] Fees charged for attending slaves were often large. Dr. B. D. Knapp presented a bill for over $75.00 for attending Edgerton, a slave, for three or four weeks.[39] Dr. J. J. Pugh, the family physician of Mr. W. P. Perkins, of Madison County, charged $100.00 for attending Lucinda, a slave.[40]

A slave-owner living near Natchez might prefer to send a negro in need of medical or surgical attention to a hospital. Dr. C. S. Ma-

[33] De Bow's Review, X, 624. Plantation Overseer, p. 90.
[34] Back Country, p. 78.
[35] Southwest by a Yankee, II, 86.
[36] F. R. Ray, Greenwood Leflore, pp. 40–42. Southwest by a Yankee, II, 121.
[37] Ibid., II, 121.
[38] Plantation Overseer, pp. 109, 115, 139, 141, 142, 168, 199, 200.
[39] James v. Herring, 20 Miss. 336.
[40] Munn v. Perkins, 9 Miss. 412.

goun conducted the Mississippi State Hospital, where first-class patients were charged $3.00 per day and servants $1.00.[41] A rival institution operated by L. P. Blackburn and A. H. Brenham cared only for negroes. The following is a copy of part of its advertisement.

"NEW INFIRMARY OPENED FOR BLACKS
"The subscribers respectfully inform the planters of Louisiana, Southern Mississippi, Steamboat Captains, and all gentlemen engaged in slave traffic, that they have opened, about one mile from the Natchez Court House, on the old Court House Road, in the House that belonged to the late Mrs. Rulon, a most commodious
INFIRMARY FOR THE CURE OF ALL DISEASES OF COLORED PERSONS.
(Small Pox alone excepted.) Surgical operations, of whatever descriptions, will be carefully performed.
Terms—One Dollar per day will be charged for all services, including medical attention, board and lodging." [42]

As early as 1831 there were hospitals in Mississippi for the care of slaves, though it appears from the following bill that in this earlier time the cost was greater.

"Natchez, June 10, 1831.

"Estate of Archibald Terrell
"To James Bradley, Dr.
"Taking care of negro woman named Lucy at the Hospital from 10th of May—1831 to 10th—of June following at $2.50 per day $75
"By $7. received from Asa Kinne 7
_____
$68." [43]

"Knowledge and slavery are incompatible," wrote a citizen of Mississippi in 1832.[44] The laws of the State indicate that this was the view of the majority of the ruling class, for embedded in the code was the declaration that under no condition could slaves be taught to read and write.[45] This desire to keep slaves ignorant was doubtless the reason they could not be employed, except as menials, in printing establishments.[46]

The enforcement of laws was too frequently not uniform and a

[41] Natchez Mississippi Free Trade, Jan. 24, 1852.
[42] Ibid., Jan. 24, 1852.
[43] J. F. H. Claiborne MSS., vol. I, no. 39217, Library of Congress. For other cases of medical fees for attending slaves, see, Shewalter v. Ford, 34 Miss. 417: Stamps v. Green, 33 Miss. 546.
[44] Woodville Republican, Dec. 22, 1832, letter to the editor, signed "Citizen."
[45] Biographical and Historical Memoirs of Mississippi, II, 96.
[46] Hutchinson's Code, p. 948.

wealthy planter could do with impunity what a lesser person could not. On the one hand, T. Washington Jones, of Washington, Miss., advertised his embryonic school for negro children through the columns of the weekly press.[47] He offered to teach reading for two dollars a month; writing, two and a half; and arithmetic, three; with an evening school for grown people. Whether he planned to educate slaves or free negroes or both is not clear, but, if the free negro could not be educated, certainly the slaves could not. The plan met with opposition. In the next issue of the paper,[48] the attention of T. Washington Jones was called to the fact that, if he taught negro children, he would be liable to a fine of $30.00 or ten days' imprisonment and thirty-nine lashes. The pupil might suffer a similar penalty. It is not likely that this teacher persevered in his plans. An insignificant person could not teach reading and writing to slaves.

In spite of legal restrictions, many slaves learned their letters.[49] A slave-owner in North Mississippi said that all of his twenty slaves could read, having learned, he supposed, from one of the number who had acquired the art before he was purchased. The owner did not object, and the slaves bought their own books from peddlers, preferring religious stories.[50] This man did not even know that there was a law against allowing slaves to be taught to read!

A number of domestic servants throughout the State could read and write.[51] There were planters who stated, after the antislavery agitation was under way, that they would gladly have every slave able to read the Bible, but that they were deterred by the fanaticism of the age.[52] Some of the domestics, it appears, were taught by the children of the master's family, who enjoyed the transposition from the status of pupil to that of teacher. Such lessons were occasionally interspersed with attempts to teach poetry to a big field hand, or by thrashings administered by the small teacher.[53]

Slaves who performed the skilled work of the plantation, or who

[47] Natchez *Mississippi Republican*, May 28, 1818.

[48] *Ibid.*, June 4, 1818.

[49] There is a moderately literate letter to President Polk from Harry, a blacksmith, in *Plantation Overseer*, pp. 161–162.

An intelligent valet of President Taylor's son taught himself to read.—Lady Emmeline Stuart Wortley, *Travels in the United States*, p. 119.

[50] *Back Country*, pp. 143–144.

[51] *Southwest by a Yankee*, II, 247.

[52] *De Bow's Review*, X, 625.

[53] *Southern Planter*, pp. 79–80, 313. Five slaves, from among those who sat at the feet of such a teacher, later became preachers.

had positions of responsibility, were sometimes called upon to exercise their memories or reasoning powers. Their ability was sometimes great, as is shown in the following incident. On the Dabney estate,

"The cotton was weighed three times a day, and the number of pounds picked by each servant set down opposite to his or her name on a slate. Quite a remarkable feat of memory was exhibited by one of the negro men one day in connection with this. His duty was to help the overseer to weigh the cotton. One day the slate was caught in a rain and the figures were obliterated. This man came that night to the master's desk and gave from memory every record on the slate, the morning, mid-day, and evening weights of each picker. The negroes stood near enough to hear if he had made a mistake in any man's figures. It was the more remarkable as he could not have expected to be called on to do this." [54]

Though reading and writing were seldom taught to the slaves, there was much of manual training. Certainly, most of this was planned for the good of the owner rather than for any benefit the slave might secure. However, slaves were better equipped for the life of free men, when freedom finally came, because of their forced training in agricultural and domestic sciences in ante-bellum time.

Though secular education was denied the slaves, religious training was not. There were a few legal limitations on their religious life, but these were designed to keep the forms of worship from being used as a cloak for fanaticism or conspiracy.[55] The chief restrictions were that no free negro could exercise the functions of a minister of the Gospel, under a penalty of thirty lashes,[56] and slaves were as a rule also excluded. However, a master could permit one of his own negroes to preach on his plantation, though no outside slaves could attend the meeting.[57] It was further ordered that, in all convocations of slaves, at least two reputable white persons must be present.

Public opinion was not adverse to the religious training of negroes. Slaves were given religious instruction on many of the plantations. George Poindexter was defeated for Congress in 1822 partly because of a rumor that he was endeavoring to hinder the religious training of slaves. Though the rumor was untrue, it cost him votes. He had, in-

[54] *Ibid.*, p. 70.
[55] *Vicksburg Sentinel*, Jan. 26, 1841.
[56] *Hutchinson's Code*, p. 534.
[57] *Journal of the General Assembly of Mississippi*, 1831, Sen. Jour., pp. 190, 217.

deed, sought to strengthen police regulations about the assemblage of slaves, but his only aim was to preserve order.[58]

A number of slaveholders displayed commendable interest in the spiritual welfare of their negroes. One of them expressed his obligation and his purpose in the following paragraphs.

"Christianity, humanity and order elevate all—injure none—whilst infidelity, selfishness and disorder curse some—delude others and degrade all. I therefore want all of my people encouraged to cultivate religious feeling and morality, and punished for inhumanity to their children or stock—for profanity, lying and stealing. . . .

"I would that every human being have the gospel preached to them in its original purity and simplicity; it therefore devolves upon me to have these dependants properly instructed in all that pertains to the salvation of their souls; to this end whenever the services of a suitable person can be secured, have them instructed in these things—in view of the fanaticism of the age it behooves the Master or Overseer to be present on all such occasions. They should be instructed on Sundays in the day time if practicable, if not then on Sunday night." [59]

Many plantation slaves were permitted to attend church services in a nearby town, and Ingraham estimated that two thirds of the negroes in Natchez on Sunday were on the way to church. Most of the black churchgoers were women, the men preferring to gossip on the street corners.[60] Negroes often attended the same services as their masters, and on the minute books of many of the churches appear the names of slaves who were faithful and devout members.[61] Negroes were generally seated separately, either in galleries at the back of the church, or, in less pretentious structures, in a group of seats set apart in the main body of the church.[62] Occasionally a partition several feet high separated masters and servants.[63]

Though slaves and masters often worshipped together, there were

---

[58] Claiborne, *Mississippi*, pp. 384–385.
[59] Phillips, *Plantation and Frontier*, I, 114–115.
[60] *Southwest by a Yankee*, II, 55–56.
[61] *Southern Planter*, p. 106 and minute books of almost any of the older churches.
[62] *Southwest by a Yankee*, II, 55, 64.
In many of the old structures, the gallery yet remains. In the College Hill Church, in Lafayette County, the gallery has been removed, but the doors are still evident through which access was gained. In this church, as in many others, the steps were so placed as to lead from the church yard into the gallery so that the slaves did not enter the body of the church.
For another seating arrangement see, *Sojourn in the South*, p. 208.
[63] Thomas Battle Carroll, *Historical Sketches of Oktibbeha County* (*Mississippi*), p. 88.

a few congregations, particularly in the towns, that were composed wholly of the former. For a time the basement of the Methodist Church of Grenada served as a place of worship for slaves on Sunday afternoons. The Sunday school of the white members had been conducted in this same place a few hours earlier in the day. A few years later a separate church was provided for the negroes, services being conducted by a slaveholder.[64]

Allowing the slaves to visit town on Sunday had some disadvantages, for instead of attending services many used the freedom of the town for marketing or for dissipation.[65] This weekly tide of slaves created serious problems for town governments, and planters suffered from the demoralization of their negroes. For this reason, many slaveholders kept their negroes at home on Sunday and provided local religious services, as was also the practice on estates that were far distant from any town. Solon Robinson gave the following description of such an arrangement. "Upon one plantation I visited in Mississippi, I found a most beautiful little Gothic church, and a clergyman furnished with a house, provisions and servants, and a salary of $1,500 a year, to preach to master and slaves." [66]

To create such a condition as has just been described, a union of wealth and religious interest was required. Where these were not so evident, the plantation hospital or some other building was used to house the Sunday congregation. The preaching was frequently done by a white minister. A number of the planters were retired clergymen; for some of these, as well as many physicians and lawyers, deserted their profession and became planters. However, after the transition, many of them preached from time to time in destitute churches, or regularly officiated over congregations of their own slaves.[67] On a few of the large estates, a minister was employed to devote all of his time to religious work on the plantation.[68] As most planters had neither the means nor the inclination to do this, other arrangements were made. One such plan was described in a letter written by a Presbyterian minister to General Quitman.

[64] Rebecca Stokes, "History of Grenada," MS., citing *The Grenada Methodist Church* (pub. 1916).

[65] *Southwest by a Yankee*, II, 128.

[66] *De Bow's Review*, VII, 221. See also, *Southwest by a Yankee*, II, 67, 256–258.

[67] *Southwest by a Yankee*, II, 67, 125.

[68] For instance, Greenwood Leflore employed a minister to preach to his 400 slaves each Sunday.—Ray, *Leflore*, pp. 40–42. *De Bow's Review*, VII, 221; X, 625.

"Pine Ridge, Sept. 4th, 1831.

"Gen. J. A. Quitman—

"Honored and Dear Sir: I doubt not you will excuse me for trespassing upon your attention for a few moments—especially when you learn the occasion. The Church of Pine Ridge, within whose bounds you have a plantation, is now making an effort to give the gospel to every rational being under its care—the *young* as well as the *old*—the *bond* as well as the *free*.

"In order to do this effectually, it is necessary to adopt the system of *plantation* preaching which is now acknowledged to possess more advantages than any other. It requires, however, a greater number of preachers, than where all can be assembled in one place.

"One minister can take charge of about nine plantations, giving them instruction, *preaching* and *catechising* every second or third Sabbath; preaching during the week when desired, celebrating marriages, visiting the sick and burying the dead.

"There are already two such assistants employed in my parish, and thus far the plan has succeeded admirably.

"Nearly all the planters here feel their responsibility for their servants, so deeply, that they have united to provide *regular* and *frequent religious* instruction for them by good and competent teachers. In this way the servants are made accountable for themselves and the master is relieved from his most solemn responsibility in this respect.

"Nearly every plantation has adopted the plan, and by uniting, the expense is very trifling, about one dollar per head, for all over four years of age. The services of an *educated man,* (and none others are so well suited to the work,) cannot be obtained for a salary less than five or six hundred dollars.

"Some of the smaller plantations, in order to have as frequent service as the others, give rather more than a dollar apiece.

"As a church, we are laboring and praying for the conversion of the whole world, and we deem it but reasonable that the good work should commence at home. And masters, when they remember their accountability, and that they are to meet their servants at the judgment bar of God, readily concur with us. They acknowledge their obligation to provide for the *spiritual* as well as temporal wants of those whom God has entrusted to their care.

"I would further add, that the teachers employed will be under the constant supervision of the session of the Church, some of which are themselves planters in this neighborhood.

"Hoping to hear from you as soon as convenient, and to learn your views and feelings, as regards the subject in general, and also in reference to your own place in particular, I remain,

"Yours most respectfully and truly,

"B. W. Williams." [69]

[69] *Mississippi*, pp. 387–388.

Whether General Quitman favored this plan is not known, but it is evident from the letter that some other planters were using it. Ingraham tells of several neighboring planters who jointly employed a Presbyterian minister, a former missionary among the Choctaw Indians, to preach to their slaves.[70] A visitor to Mississippi, about 1856, found at Natchez three Presbyterian ministers, all born in the North and all well educated, who preached solely to negroes. One of the three preached across the river in Louisiana. Another preached on Sunday nights to a large negro congregation in Natchez and on Sunday mornings and afternoons he preached on neighboring plantations. The third preached regularly on several plantations within a radius of ten or fifteen miles of that town. One of these ministers stated that each of the plantations on which he preached paid him $250 a year.[71]

In some places there were entire circuits of the Methodist church composed of congregations of slaves and it was stated, in 1845, that the Methodist Episcopal Church had seven missions to the negroes in Mississippi.[72]

Among the questions yearly considered by the Mississippi Baptist State Convention was this: How may we improve the spiritual condition of the colored population? Slaveholders were censured for allowing their negroes to buy and sell on the Sabbath and for failing to realize their great responsibility for the spiritual welfare of the slaves. It was suggested to the Convention that missionaries be appointed to devote their entire time to slaves, and that, so far as practicable, slaves be formed into congregations separate from white people. By so doing, slaves could be given a larger share in their own services, and the preaching could be better fitted to their intelligence.[73]

In addition to formal preaching by ordained clergymen, there were other forms of religious worship and among these were Sunday schools taught by some member of the planter's family or by the planter himself.[74] The Rev. James Smylie, one of the earliest Presbyterian ministers to settle permanently in Mississippi and for many years stated clerk of the Presbytery of Mississippi, devoted his entire

[70] *Southwest by a Yankee*, II, 127–128.
[71] *African Repository*, XXXII, 268.
[72] *Ibid*. Also *Proceedings of the Meeting in Charleston, S. C., May 13–15, 1845, on the Religious Instruction of the Negroes, etc.*, p. 69.
[73] *Proceedings of the Mississippi Baptist State Convention*, 1856, p. 23; 1857, p. 26; 1858, p. 38; 1859, p. 40; 1860, p. 32.
[74] *Southwest by a Yankee*, II, 127, 256–258. *Back Country*, p. 182.

time in the latter part of his life (he died in 1853) to the religious instruction of negroes. Out of his experiences he prepared a
catechism for slaves which was approved by the Synod of Mississippi
and which was extensively used.[75] A planter who had managed an
estate for twenty years and who had accumulated nearly one hundred
slaves wrote a simplified catechism for the edification of his own
negroes. Although every question had been made leading, after many
years of effort he was discouraged at the results. Well he might have
been, for one of the negroes, when asked "In whose image were you
made?" answered, "In the image of de debil, master." [76] However,
other masters were more successful. Some of the slaves of William
Montgomery attended family prayers in his home and frequently led
in prayer themselves.[77]

On many plantations slaves were encouraged, but not ordered, to
attend the services that were provided. Other planters felt it their
duty to force the slaves to be present, and one issued an order that
before coming, "every negro is expected to wash himself, comb his
head, and put on clean clothes." [78] M. W. Philips had a rule "requiring
negroes, one and all, to attend preaching." His overseer was a conscientious objector, believing that "it is a sin to *make negroes* attend,
and against his conscience." [79]

It should not be thought that all slave-owners in Mississippi were
equally interested in the spiritual interests of their property. To many
it was a matter of little consequence,[80] and some rather actively opposed any form of religious service for their slaves. The manager of a
large estate declared that negro preachers were considered the worst
characters on the place. Although white ministers had preached there
from time to time—apparently voluntarily—he did not expect to
allow this any more. It excited the negroes too much, and interfered
with subordination and order.[81]

There was a wide difference of opinion as to the effects of religion
on the negro. Among the white people there was a rather general dis-

[75] T. L. Haman, "Beginnings of Presbyterianism in Mississippi," in
P.M.H.S., X, 214.
[76] *Southwest by a Yankee*, II, 256–258.
[77] "Diary of a Miss. Planter," in *P.M.H.S.*, X, 474.
[78] *De Bow's Review*, X, 626.
[79] "Diary of a Miss. Planter," in *P.M.H.S.*, X, 453. See also, *Back Country*,
p. 182. *Southern Planter*, p. 198.
[80] *Back Country*, p. 145.
[81] *Ibid.*, pp. 92–93.

like for negro preachers, so much so that in the parts of the State where slaves were most to be found, preaching by negroes became generally prohibited.[82] Instead, slaves were assigned minor rôles in services conducted by white persons.[83] But in other sections, slave-holders seem to have had no objection to negro preachers.[84] The character of the negro, as well as that of the master, had much to do with the custom on any given plantation.

Some of the negroes were decidedly.changed for the better by a religious reformation and forswore dancing, swearing, and other habits or amusements. All who were associated with them noted their improvement.[85] It was, however, the opinion of many slaveholders that religious negroes were the worst characters on the plantation. By this they meant that often the slave who displayed the greatest religious fervor in meetings was exceedingly lax in his daily life and behavior.[86] Doubtless the slave was not unique in this great discrepancy between profession and daily life. But the emotionalism of the negro made his religious profession so unmistakable that perhaps more was expected than should have been. The balance is pretty well shown by the statement of one slaveholder that there was no difference in the market value of sinners and saints.

Few records of the superstitions of Mississippi slaves have been found. Whether the negro brought the following belief from Africa is not known; it may have been borrowed from the whites, for cases of this superstition can be found in European folklore. John, a slave, was accused of having committed murder in Hinds county. During the trial it was stated that he and another slave, Willis, together watched a crowd of people going toward the body of the murdered negro. Willis told John that a jury was being formed and that all the negroes who had been working near the scene of the crime would have to file past the body, each in turn placing his hands on it, and that blood would flow from the wounds as soon as the murderer touched the body. On hearing this John at once jumped the fence behind the place where he had been talking to Willis and started running away from the scene.[87]

[82] *Southwest by a Yankee*, II, 263–265. *Back Country*, p. 92.
[83] *De Bow's Review*, X, 625.
[84] *Back Country*, p. 145.
[85] *Ibid.*, p. 145. *Southern Planter*, p. 161.
[86] *Back Country*, pp. 92, 186–187.
[87] John *v.* The State, 24 Miss. 569.

The State required the presence of white persons at religious meet-ings of slaves as a safeguard against disorder or the teaching of in-surrectionary doctrines. However, there must have been a certain honesty of purpose on the part of those planters who attended or they would have avoided this task. Though the negroes may have failed to develop as they should, through too much oversight and direction in religious matters, they doubtless received more intelligent instruction and participated in a more orderly form of worship under the tutelage of the white people.

The owner of an estate frequently preferred that his negroes choose their mates from their fellows on the same plantation, and on many of the larger estates this would be the natural order of things, for it was the rule on some of these that the social life of the negroes be restricted to the plantation, with no exchanging of visits to neigh-boring estates.[88] Captain Isaac Ross, a highly successful and humane master, kept his slaves in a separate social unit.[89] In case a slave in-sisted on marrying elsewhere, one or the other of the owners was likely, by purchase, to unite the couple on the same plantation. If this was not feasible, the husband was given a pass from time to time to visit his wife. On one plantation, such slaves left an hour before sun-set Saturday afternoon, except one negro whose wife lived twenty miles away. He left at noon Saturday, and returned at noon Mon-day.[90] There were planters, however, who forbade any marriage what-ever by one of their negroes to a slave of another estate, and punished severely any who broke this rule.[91]

Plantation marriages were often the occasion of celebrations, with holidays and barbecues, and sometimes the house of the master was the scene of the festivities.[92] The ceremony was performed either by

---

[88] This would work little hardship when 200 slaves were owned by one man, and another 300 were under his administrative control on neighboring estates.— *Southern Planter*, p. 77.

[89] *A Brief History of the Ross Slaves*, p. 11.

[90] *Back Country*, p. 154.

Mr. John Townes Leigh of Yalobusha County wrote: "Two of my men have wives on President Polk's plantation which adjoins mine, and whom they are free to visit every Saturday night and remain with till Monday morning."—*De Bow's Review*, VII, 381.

[91] For instance, Mr. Hinson, who resided near Clinton, Miss.—Henry S. Foote, *Bench and Bar of the South and Southwest*, p. 98.

[92] Bowles MS. *Southern Planter*, pp. 55, 78.

a white clergyman,[93] a negro preacher, [94] the master.[95] or some member of the latter's family.[96]

But many planters took little or no interest in the marital affairs of their slaves. According to Henry Stuart Foote,[97] Daniel, a negro overseer or driver, was allowed two wives, though he was later deprived of his favorite after incurring the displeasure of his master. Likewise, in sales of slaves, many planters showed but little interest in keeping married couples together. Though some of the slaves were soon able to console themselves after separation from their mates, this, of course, did not excuse the callousness of the masters.[98]

Planters commonly agreed that a chaste negro slave was rare and that immorality among slaves, both before and after marriage, was almost universal. Some slaveholders struggled to better conditions, "by preaching virtue and decency, encouraging marriages, and by punishing, with some severity, departures from marital obligations; but it was all in vain." [99] Others left the negroes to their own sins, made no attempt to teach morality, took cognizance of conditions only when quarrels or disturbances broke out, and then warned or flogged all participants.[100]

Regardless of the views of individual planters, the laws of Mississippi gave no sanction to slave marriages. The attorney for the slave, George, charged with violating a slave girl under ten years of age, told the supreme court that such a crime "does not exist in this State

[93] Leflore, p. 40.
[94] Back Country, pp. 153–154.
[95] "Diary of a Miss. Planter," in P. M. H. S., X, 439.
[96] Southern Planter, p. 78. See also, Southwest by a Yankee, II, 128–129.
An unusual account of her own marriage ceremony has been told by an old negro woman, who was a slave at the time of her marriage. She and her suitor were taken to the field by the owner, and there the ceremony was read, the negroes standing between the handles of a plow. The negress knew no reason for the use of the plow in the ceremony.
[97] Henry S. Foote, Casket of Reminiscences, pp. 201–210.
[98] For instance, Southern Planter, p. 77.
One of the unusual cases of the kind was recorded in Foote, Bench and Bar, pp. 98–102. An attempt was made at Clinton, Miss., to punish a negro man for his common-law marriage to a mulatto slave of the town. The owner refused to sanction this marriage off the plantation, and in attempting to punish the slave the master was murdered. The slave was tried, and at the trial the negress seemed in such deep agony that she drew forth the sympathy of some of the lawyers at the court. A few weeks later the man was hung. In the crowd that witnessed the execution was the negress, gaily garbed, and attended by one who was soon to become her next husband.
[99] De Bow's Review, X, 623. Back Country, pp. 153–154.
[100] Back Country, p. 89.

between African slaves. Our laws recognize no marital rights as between slaves"; and such iniquity could be dealt with only by their owners. The court virtually agreed![101]

There was never much agitation in favor of giving legal sanction to slave marriages. Such a law might have caused complications when slaves were placed on the auction block. At one time a newspaper noted with mild approval a proposal made in North Carolina to legalize marriages between slaves, to preserve sacred relations between parents and young children, and to permit the education of slaves. The Port Gibson *Reveille* stated: "The main features of the movement have been adopted in practice, or at least approved in theory, by nearly all our planters, so far as circumstances would allow." The paper argued that the enactment of such laws for Mississippi might have advantages, for by such legislation "the enemies of the institution will be robbed of their most fruitful and plausible excuses for agitation and complaint."[102] It is certainly true that the failure to respect marriages between slaves, particularly when they were sold, was much criticized and rightly so.

Negro women were too valuable in the field to be allowed much time to care for their children. A month or so after the birth of a child, the mother returned to her task. Thereafter the child was cared for during the day by the plantation nurse, who was generally a woman too old for work.[103] On larger plantations a house was set apart as the nursery for the children. On the Bowles estate this was a double size cabin with a fireplace in each end, and to this nursery the children were brought each morning before the mothers went to the field. There were sometimes low cradles, with the rockers cut from a solid plank. The mothers returned to the nursery three or four times each day, which of course cut down their field work about one half, depending largely on the distance from the field where work was in progress to the quarters.[104] To save this lost time, in good weather the

---

[101] George *v.* The State, 36 Miss. 316. In the interest of brevity, the term supreme court will be employed throughout this work, though this court was officially designated as the High Court of Errors and Appeals under the Constitution of 1832, and use of the shorter term was not resumed until 1869.

[102] *De Bow's Review,* XIX, 130.

[103] *The Cultivator,* n. s., II, 272. "Diary of a Miss. Planter," in *P.M.H.S.,* X, 465.

[104] *Back Country,* p. 47. *De Bow's Review,* X, 624. *The Cultivator,* n. s., II, 272.

flock of infants might be brought to the field and cared for by the plantation nurse under one of the weather sheds.[105]

When the children were able to walk, they still remained about the quarters, supervised by the nurse and consuming a variety of food. On the bill of fare of various plantations there was for the negro children, sweet milk, buttermilk, corn meal mush, turnip greens, "pot-licker," hominy, "meat gravy, and small pieces of meat, thickened with broken corn bread and boiled hominy, seasoned with salt and lard, to which [was] occasionally added molasses." [106]

The care of slave children was often a matter of considerable concern to planters. Colonel Dunbar, who resided near Natchez, collected to the plantation on which he resided most of the aged and the infants from his other plantation, so they would be under his immediate direction. This policy he carried so far that there were scarcely fifty hands among the hundred and fifty negroes on the home place.[107]

During the first five or six years of their lives, negro children were useless in plantation work, but at the end of this time they began to help with cotton picking.[108]

As they got beyond the discipline of the plantation nurse, they were sent to the field to keep them out of trouble, or to punish them for mischief already committed. This is illustrated by the verbal testimony of one who had a share in the following juvenile crime. The small son of a slave-owner and some five or six negro playmates amused themselves by pulling green apples from the trees in the orchard. When the mischief was detected, the negroes were ordered to the field to pick cotton for the rest of the day.[109]

A task that was often assigned to young negroes who were just beginning full time work was that of "water-toter" for the hoe and plow gangs.[110] From that they graduated to scattering cotton-seed, knocking down old cotton stalks, helping to put up fences, hauling, and so on, to full field work.

Practically no African names were retained by slaves. Classical and Biblical names supplemented the names that were in common use by

[105] *Southwest by a Yankee,* II, 125–126. Ingraham, ed., *Sunny South,* p. 59.
[106] *De Bow's Review,* VII, 281–282. *Leflore,* p. 40. *Southern Planter,* p. 58. Also statements of ex-slaves.
[107] *De Bow's Review,* VII, 381.
[108] *Southwest by a Yankee,* II, 126.
[109] See also "Diary of a Miss. Planter," in *P. M. H. S.,* X, 465.
[110] *Back Country,* p. 48.

the white population. Each slave generally had but one name. To avoid confusion they were differentiated, when two slaves on the same place had identical names, as Big Martha and Little Martha, or less commonly Jim's Martha and Sam's Martha. The white people of the State seldom used the word slave when speaking or writing of this class. Instead, they employed such terms as servants, field hands, force, hands, people or negroes. Specific negroes were addressed as boy or woman, and the term boy was used until the negro was in the thirties. Old slaves were ordinarily addressed as uncle, aunty, granny, or old lady.[111]

As slaves grew old, their tasks were lightened in proportion to their failing strength. On most of the larger plantations there were negroes who either did no work or not enough to compensate for their food, clothing and shelter. No instance has been found of a master's failing to care for such slaves and they generally seem to have been treated as well as able-bodied field hands.[112]

[111] *Southwest by a Yankee,* II, 254, and contemporary writings in general.

[112] A large part of the will of Elizabeth Green, dated October 29, 1833, is made up of provisions to secure kindly treatment for slaves who had been faithful for a number of years. The following sentences will serve as a sample. "It is also my will and desire that my son Abner shall have my negro man Lem, provided he will give to my daughter Louisa Perryman his negro man George in lieu thereof, and also not to put Lem under the control of an overseer . . . as I have several old and faithful servants who have been good, dutiful, and obedient to me through life and whom I am extremely anxious shall not serve as slaves after my death, I shall therefore dispose of them as follows. It is my will and desire that my negro man Tom and his wife Lear shall not serve as slaves after my death, and that my son Abner shall act as their guardian and protecter, and see that they are paid a reasonable compensation for their services in whatever capacity they may see proper to serve. It is also my wish that Tom and Lear shall live with some one of my children and that her two children shall live with her until the youngest shall arrive at the age of ten years. At that time they are to be sold to whichever of my children will give the best price for them, and the money arising from the same to be equally distributed among my grand-children." Similar provisions were made for seven other slaves.—Will of Elizabeth Green, MS.

A similar bequest, and one that came before the courts, is Weathersby *et al. v.* Weathersby, 21 Miss. 685.

CHAPTER IV

PLANTATION AND POLICE CONTROL OF SLAVES

According to the census of 1860 there were 3,552 plantations in Mississippi of thirty or more slaves and there were 3,941 persons in the State who gave their occupation as overseer.[1] Allowing for those who were unemployed and for a few plantations large enough to need several overseers, it appears that the average slaveholder employed an overseer soon after his slaves exceeded thirty in number;[2] and there is doubtless some connection between this and the tendency to call a slaveholder a planter, if he owned over thirty slaves, and a farmer, if he owned less than that number.[3] One overseer to fifty

---

[1] *Census of 1860 (Population)*, p. 273.

[2] The following examples support this view. James K. Polk's Mississippi plantation was managed by an overseer from its establishment in 1834. On it were thirty-seven slaves and the proportion of active hands must have been small for by 1839 only 271 acres were in cultivation.—Bassett, *Plantation Overseer*, pp. 262, 267–268.

Overseers managed the Bowles and Wheeless plantations which could muster at most during the picking season twenty-three and fifteen hands respectively.—Bowles MS. and Wheeless MS.

Judge Carroll estimated that in Oktibbeha County most of the owners of thirty or more slaves had overseers.—Carroll, *Historical Sketches of Oktibbeha County (Mississippi)*, p. 86.

[3] A comparison of the occupations of the members of the Mississippi Convention of 1861 with their holdings in slaves as shown in the MS. slave schedules of the census of 1860 shows that the ownership of about thirty slaves was the dividing line between farmer and planter.—P. L. Rainwater, "Mississippi—Storm Center of Secession, 1856–1861," chapter IX, MS.

Also, this view is upheld by a comparison of the number of persons listed as planters (3,098) with the number of persons owning thirty or more slaves (3,552) in this census.—*Census of 1860 (Population)*, p. 273.

On the other hand, an examination of the MS. slave schedules of the census shows that the local census-takers had widely different opinions as to the meanings of the words planter and farmer, and any calculation made on the basis of their figures can have little exactness. There is a possibility that those who compiled the census tables adopted a uniform rule for determining the numbers of planters by using the figures submitted by the census-takers without using their divergent opinions as to the difference between these two occupational classifications.

Olmsted's opinion as to the difference between farmers and planters was as

negroes was considered by some to be an ideal arrangement, with 100 as the maximum. If the slaves exceeded the latter number, they were usually divided into two forces and another overseer was employed.[4] If the planting venture continued to succeed, plantation management became even more complex. At the opposite extreme from the farmer, toiling in the field with one or two slaves, was the vast plantation with its several ranks of authority.[5]

A large estate, located on a tributary of the Mississippi River and almost isolated from the rest of the world, had the following form of government. As the owner was non-resident, the highest local source of authority was a manager, a man of some refinement and education. The approximately five hundred slaves were divided into four groups with quarters some distance apart. Over each was an overseer who was assisted by negro drivers, usually two, one for the plow gang and one for the hoe gang. The slaves were thus controlled by one manager, four overseers, and eight or so negro drivers.[6]

A brief description of overseer, driver, and slaves returning from the field illustrates the functioning of this kind of plantation government.

"First came, led by an old driver carrying a whip, forty of the largest and strongest women I ever saw together; they were all in a simple uniform dress of a bluish check stuff, the skirts reaching a little below the knee; their legs and feet bare; they carried themselves loftily, each having a hoe over the shoulder, and walking with a free, powerful swing, like *chasseurs* on the march. Behind them came the cavalry, thirty strong, mostly men, but a few of them women, two of whom rode astride on the plow mules. A lean and vigilant white overseer, on a brisk pony, brought up the rear." [7]

follows. "When the largest share of the labor is not intended to be applied to the cotton crop, but is divided among various crops, as is usually the case where less than four hundred acres are held in possession by the proprietor, I term the enterprise a farm in distinction from a plantation."—*Back Country*, p. 160 note.

Olmsted's method of distinguishing between planters and farmers supplements rather than contradicts the view that the difference between the classes lay in the number of slaves owned.

[4] *Back Country*, pp. 27–29, 81. Van Buren, *Sojourn in the South*, p. 136.

[5] Even on estates sufficiently large to warrant employing an overseer, he or the owner might rarely, when there was a great pressure of work, labor in the field with the negroes.—Riley, "Diary of a Mississippi Planter," in *P. M. H. S.*, X, 348.

[6] *Back Country*, pp. 72–74.

[7] *Ibid.*, pp. 14–15.

Assuming that an overseer was ordinarily employed before the slaves on a plantation exceeded forty, approximately half of the slaves in Mississippi were controlled by overseers.[8] The rest worked mainly as domestic servants in the towns, as assistants to white laborers, and, chiefly, as field hands of small farmers who could not afford to hire overseers. Farmers with only a few slaves often worked in the field with them. Under such circumstances masters and slaves were generally on amicable, informal terms,[9] punishment was less frequent,[10] and the life of the slave more nearly approximated that of a free man. As discipline was lax, negroes were likely to be less prompt in service, though, on the other hand, they more often suffered from petulant and undignified treatment.[11]

Slaves generally fared worse when they were supervised by overseers instead of by their owners, especially if the latter were non-resident, as was true on about half of the plantations of over fifty slaves in the cotton districts bordering the Mississippi River.[12] One reason overseers were hard taskmasters was that they had no permanent interest in the slaves, either as persons or as property. Even more important was the plantation owners' demands for large cotton crops. Since "The future of the overseer depends altogether on the quantity of cotton he is able to make for the market,"[13] his prospects were excellent, if he could, for instance, show that "He made 140 Bales of Cotton last year for Mrs. Luckett with 19 hands."[14] Not only was his reëmployment dependent on the cotton crop, but even his current wages were often in proportion to the number of bales produced. Consider the following contract made between Murden Hariston, of Lowndes County, and his overseer, Robert D. Sale. The latter was to receive $500 for the year 1839, which would be increased to $600, if the plantation produced 180 bales, A further bonus of $25 was offered, if 200 bales were made.[15] Under such a contract, there was ample incentive for the overseer to force the slaves to work hard.

[8] *Census of 1860* (*Agriculture*), p. 232.
[9] [Ingraham], *Southwest by a Yankee*, II, 26.
[10] *Back Country*, pp. 140–157, 160, 183.
[11] *Ibid.*, pp. 146–165, 173–175.
[12] *Ibid.*, pp. 61, 119, 202.
[13] *Ibid.*, p. 61.
[14] Wailes, Diary, MS., XIX, 12.
[15] Hariston *v.* Sale, 14 Miss. 634. For other bonus contracts see "Diary of a Miss. Planter," in *P. M. H. S.*, X, 452, 456–457, 461; Wailes, Diary, MS., XIX, 63–64.

On the other hand, the master expected his slaves to be well treated, for damage to them might easily offset the proceeds from a large crop. The overseer thus faced a dilemma: he must treat the slaves well and he must produce as much cotton as possible. Since his wages depended in many cases on the latter, he could hardly be expected to deal gently with the negroes.

A brutal overseer, however, was seldom in demand. While the chief *desideratum* of the planter was an overseer who could make the slaves work, "some overseers had the art of managing slaves without punishment." [16] There was no necessary contradiction between humane care of the working force and the production of a good crop. Some plantation managers attained this dual end by a system of rewards or by the judicious use of praise.[17] Success, when it was realized, was not so much the result of any peculiar system as it was the creation of an unusually able man. Some persons, without resorting to punishment, can command obedience; some cannot—which was as true of overseers as of "school ma'ams." Overseers with determination but without "the art" forced obedience with the whip or with handcuffs.[18] The lot of their slaves, unless the negroes were utterly spiritless, was sore.[19] While most planters did not desire harsh overseers for their own slaves, many of them occasionally sent an incorrigible negro to be subdued by a neighboring overseer who had a reputation for the strictest sort of discipline. The very existence of such an overseer in the country had a quieting effect on slaves, and the reputation of a few plantation tyrants is remembered by some ex-slaves to this day.[20]

A change of overseers was a momentous matter to slaves; the new régime might be either more or less severe than the old. If they had been under lax discipline, a struggle frequently ensued to determine the limits of the new overseer's authority. A strict disciplinarian generally had trouble when he followed an easy, slack manager.[21]

[16] *Plantation Overseer*, p. 92.
[17] *Ibid.*, p. 111.
[18] *Back Country*, p. 45.
[19] *Plantation Overseer*, p. 92.
[20] An old negro was asked if he had ever heard of a notorious overseer of Jacob Thompson.
"Yassar, he was a mean man. He carried his spade with him."
"Why did he carry a spade?"
"To bury de niggers after he killed 'em! Mostly he whipped 'em and den rubbed in salt and pepper."
[21] *Back Country*, pp. 82–83.

There are stories of slaves worsting new overseers and actually running them off the plantation. After such an episode, another man had to be employed. Following a change in management on a certain estate, Alfred, a powerful and unruly slave, refused to obey his new *de facto* master. The overseer had either to leave or to subdue Alfred. He chose to fight. By defeating Alfred he established his authority, and there was no further insubordination.[22]

The authority of the overseer, whose insignia of office was a whip, was practically without limit.[23] If the planter was resident, some cases might be appealed to him, but in most cases the life of the negro was in the hands of the overseer. By horn or bell he roused the slaves in the morning; by the same signal he ordered them to their cabins in the evening, and then made an inspection to see that they were there.[24] During the day, all work was according to his orders, and much of it was done while he watched every movement. Even the physical cleanliness of the negroes was under his supervision.[25] It was his duty to care for as well as to drive the slaves, and he might be held to account for the sickness or death of his charges.[26]

To fill properly the post of overseer, an understanding of many things was needful. One should know how to cultivate the staple and food crops of the day; how to care for the livestock of the plantation; how to operate the gin and mill; how to make bricks; how to fell timber and prepare it for building; how to erect the various houses and shelters of a plantation; and, above all else, how to make the slaves work. Though a plantation might be well directed by an overseer with little or no education—of which, in fact, most of them were destitute—wide experience and considerable intelligence were indispensable.

A master rarely found an overseer who could meet all the requirements of excellence in his profession. Among the various complaints against overseers, the following may be singled out for what it tells of overseers—and masters. "Overseers are not interested in raising negro children, or meat, in improving land, or improving productive qualities of seed or animals. Many of them do not care whether

---

[22] Related by Capt. Jack Townes, of Yalobusha County, Miss. The story was recorded in the plantation books of his father, but the books have been burned.
[23] Van Buren, *Sojourn in the South*, pp. 151–152.
[24] *Back Country*, p. 50. *De Bow's Review*, X, 626.
[25] *Back Country*, p. 80.
[26] "Diary of a Miss. Planter," in *P. M. H. S.*, X, 469.

property has depreciated or improved, so they have made a crop to boast of." [27]

For economic reasons, planters at the very least wanted their slaves so treated as not to endanger health or life. Some were actuated by more humane motives, and one cranky slave-owner forbade his overseers to have pockets in their trousers, because he once had one who "stood around with his hands in his pockets and cussed the niggers." Absentee planters sometimes gauged the success of an overseer by finding out how the slaves liked him, especially as this was shown by the number of runaways during his period of management.[28]

The slave was, by the very nature of slavery, engaged in continual warfare with the overseer. Occasionally this was physical. Generally it was an attempt to escape work, as by cheating the overseer in the apparent amount of work that was done. Though the latter could administer punishment, the slave could practice sabotage or could run away. These activities were always troublesome for the overseer; sometimes they brought down upon his head the wrath of the plantation owner; more rarely, as a result, the slave would draw a new overseer, for better or for worse.

The general course of an overseer was guided by the directions and advice of the master. While these were largely verbal, occasionally they were committed to writing. An excellent and wise set of rules were written, in 1857, by J. W. Fowler, of Coahoma County, for the guidance of his overseers.[29] Parts of this document will be quoted elsewhere. Another set of rules was published in a newspaper, in 1840, under the heading, "Useful Rules of an Old Overseer." Although it is most unlikely that any such smug and self-righteous overseer ever existed, these rules doubtless express some of the desires of the planters of the community. The parts that deal with the control of the negroes are as follows:

"2. I shall rise early, and never let the negroes catch me in bed of a morning, but see that they are all put regularly to work.

"3. After rising I shall not idle about, but go directly at the business of my employer. I shall see that the negroes are at their work—that the horses have been fed, the cattle attended to, etc. etc. If any of the negroes

[27] *Back Country,* p. 59, quoting the opinion of Dr. M. W. Philips, of Mississippi.
[28] *Ibid.,* p. 125, and *passim.*
[29] Phillips, *Plantation and Frontier,* I, 112–115.
Judge William L. Sharkey prepared a written "agreement" for the guidance of his overseer during the year 1842.—F. G. Davenport, ed., "Judge Sharkey Papers," in *Mississippi Valley Historical Review,* XX, 76–77.

have been reported as sick, I shall without a moment's delay see what ails them, and if they be really sick, I shall at once see that proper medicine and attendance are given them.

"4. Wherever the negroes are working, I shall consider it my duty to be frequently with them, in order that I might see how they get along. I shall not content myself with doing this once a day, but I shall do so repeatedly, observing every time what they are doing, and how they do it. I shall never permit them to do any work wrong, if it take them the whole day to do it right.

"5. I shall see that the negroes are regularly fed, and that they shall keep themselves clean. Once a week, at least, I shall go into each of their houses, and see that they have been swept out and cleaned. I shall examine their blankets, etc. and see that they have been well aired, and their clothes have been mended; and that everything has been attended to which conduces to their comfort and happiness." [30]

The immediate control of the negro in the field was frequently by another slave, generally known as the driver. Sometimes, though rarely, the black foreman was called an overseer.[31] There was a great difference in the powers and functions of overseers and drivers. In general, the former had general management of all the affairs of the plantation. The driver's chief duty was to stand over the gangs of field hands and constantly by voice and whip urge the toilers to their task.

The function of the driver may be better understood by observing him at work. Olmsted saw thirty or forty hoe hands, mostly women, at work in one field. A negro driver, armed with a whip which he often cracked at his fellow slaves, walked back and forth among them. Sometimes he allowed the lash to fall lightly on their shoulders and constantly urged them with his voice, calling out in a surly manner, "Shove your hoe, there! Shove your hoe!" [32]

The driver of the hoe gang constantly drove the laboring force and did not himself work. Though this was sometimes true of the plow gang, in this branch of plantation work the driver was more frequently a foreman who plowed with the rest and struck a fast pace which the others were expected to follow. At the end of the day the driver had the power and the duty of reporting to the overseer or master.[33]

[30] *Woodville Republican*, Feb. 8, 1840.
[31] *Emigrants from New Orleans*, p. 4. (See Bibliography.) It was said that among the black immigrants to Africa were several overseers.
[32] *Back Country*, pp. 48, 81–82.
[33] *Ibid.*, p. 47.

In addition to keeping the force of hands hard at work, on some estates each driver was personally responsible for all equipment used by his gang. This included almost all implements on the estate except the tools issued to the carpenters and blacksmiths.[34] Drivers sometimes had alternate charge of the quarters at night to keep order and quiet.[35]

A combination of virtues, seldom found in one man, were essential for a good driver. Among these were good judgment, impartiality, the power to command respect, and considerable physical strength. Realizing the imperfections of their drivers and of a system that gave one slave control over another, masters curtailed their power, particularly in regard to punishing. They either prohibited drivers from flogging other slaves or limited the number of lashes or allowed punishment only under the immediate supervision of the overseer.[36]

An occasional negro foreman was very superior. Pemberton, the slave of Jefferson Davis, was doubtless more able than most of the white overseers in the State. He was in virtual control of "Brierfield" a large part of the time.[37] Frequently a slave without title or any special privilege enjoyed the confidence of the master or mistress. Such a servant would inform the master of any serious trouble brewing among the slaves or would present their plea for some unaccustomed privilege, and so he might be considered the prime minister of the plantation.[38]

The position of driver would naturally please most slaves. In addition to relief from laborious field work it carried honor and material advantages. Christmas presents and other bounty were likely to come

[34] Leigh MSS.
[35] De Bow's Review, X, 626. Back Country, p. 47.
[36] De Bow's Review, X, 626. "Diary of a Miss. Planter," in P. M. H. S., X, 468.
Cuming in 1808 observed that corporal punishment was inflicted by overseers, from which he drew an interesting conclusion. "And here I will remark that the overseers of plantations in this whole territory, are for the most part a rough, unpolished, uncouth class of people, which perhaps proceeds from their being made use of literally as negro drivers, to keep those unfortunate wretches to their work in the field, and to correct them for all real or supposed offences. . . . They do this with their own hands, and not as in the sugar colonies, by one of the slaves themselves, appointed for that purpose and called the driver. This renders them callous to every thing like sentiment or feeling, and gives them a roughness and abruptness in their manners, which is extremely disagreeable and disgusting."—Cuming's Tour to the Western Country, 1807–1809, in Reuben Gold Thwaites, ed., Early Western Travels (1748–1846), IV, 328.
[37] W. L. Fleming, "Jefferson Davis, the Negroes and the Negro Problem," in Sewanee Review, XVI, 407–427.
[38] Smedes, Southern Planter, p. 75.

to the driver in larger amounts than to the common hands.[39] One driver was allowed to have two wives. Another enjoyed the distinction of wearing, while on duty in the field, "a splendid uniform coat of an officer of the flying artillery," which his master had probably bought in New Orleans after the Mexican War.[40]

On the other hand, the driver must generally have been unpopular among the other slaves. If he were severe and were too devoted to the interests of the master, hatred of him might even become so bitter as to endanger his personal safety. Ely was the driver on the plantation of W. M. Pickett, where, incidentally, there was also a white overseer. One Sunday afternoon Ely was ambushed and murdered by some of the slaves on the place. No motive can be ascribed unless it was that he had made himself hated by the exercising of his power.[41]

The responsibility of the planter did not stop with the control of his own slaves. Visiting slaves could, and occasionally did, cause trouble. A brief story will best illustrate this problem of plantation management.

Solomon, a slave of a Mr. Simmons, visited the plantation of a Mr. Leggett. The latter, with more generosity than wisdom, twice gave a dram of spirits to Solomon and to one of his own slaves, Mose. Some time later, Leggett was aroused from sleep by a clamor among the negroes. Taking his gun with him, he quieted the negroes and then returned to bed. The performance was repeated. This time Mose and Solomon were struggling together; later Solomon chased Mose around a tree, threatening him with a knife. The trouble subsided and Leggett again went to sleep. When morning came, Solomon was dead, having been stabbed. His owner subsequently sued Leggett for the value of the murdered negro.[42]

It is evident that, at least in theory, the slave was fully governed on the plantation. When the plantation manager went visiting, attended a barbecue, or went to town on business, a driver was generally left in charge. If not, the cotton brought in for weighing at the end of the day, or the amount of land plowed, was a fairly good index of what the slaves had been doing. Even if the slave were on a visit to another plantation, he was still subject to authority.

[39] Leigh MSS.
[40] Daniel, mentioned in Foote, *Casket of Reminiscences*, pp. 201–210.
[41] Ned and Taylor, *v.* The State, 33 Miss. 364.
[42] Leggett *v.* Simmons, 15 Miss. 348. See also, Newell *v.* Cowan *et ux.*, 30 Miss. 492.

Some planters, particularly the small ones, who were mainly outside of the southwestern part of the State, cared little about what system was used to extort work provided the end was accomplished. But on the great estates something like a military organization was effected, and a more detailed routine was established. A former naval officer might inject a little naval discipline into plantation management, or a newcomer from the North might fear the slaves and be unnecessarily severe. On the other hand, a native-born planter might be able to obtain as much work as either with less harshness and less formality. In all cases more rules were needed on the large plantation than on the small.[48]

A very few planters experimented with schemes of self-government in disputes and disturbances between slaves. Jefferson Davis and his older brother Joseph tried such a system with good results. Slaves who were accused of injuring their fellow slaves were tried before a jury of their fellows, with other slaves filling the rôles of the various officers of the court.[44] A. S. Morehead, of Copiah County, also gave his slaves a trial before a jury of their peers before whipping them. He was a lawyer and probably developed the plan without having heard of the experiments of the Davis brothers.

Slaves, it was generally agreed, had their own notions of propriety and of right conduct. These could frequently be used by an intelligent master to improve conditions on the plantation, particularly in the relations of the slaves with each other.[45] At the same time, it was the current belief that the slave did not work unless he was supervised or, more precisely, unless he knew the whip was constantly raised over his head. Olmsted tells of passing two gangs of negroes working within half a mile of each other. With one there was an overseer; not a slave raised his eyes to gaze on the traveler riding by. With the the other, a small gang of plowmen, there was no overseer; they all stopped their plows to gaze on the horseman slowly passing down the road.[46]

Though it was commonly assumed that the slave would spend his time on his master's plantation subject to the control of his master or, by delegated authority, to that of the white overseer or the negro driver, as a plain matter of fact, he was often at other places. A writ-

[48] *Back Country*, pp. 144–145. *Southwest by a Yankee*, II, 92–93, 113, 256.
[44] "Jefferson Davis," in *Sewanee Review*, XVI, 410–411.
[45] *Southern Planter*, p. 77.
[46] *Back Country*, p. 176.

ten pass to visit his wife on another plantation or to journey to town on an errand for his master granted a temporary legal escape from the estate. Illegally, he sometimes departed either in a break for permanent freedom or, more frequently, on a visit by night to his friends on a neighboring plantation or to enjoy the sights of town on a holiday, with the sincere hope that his brief taste of freedom would not be detected and punished. Travelers in the State frequently met negroes on the highways, traveling alone and not under the supervision of any white man.[47]

As the slave was out of his master's sight and beyond the reach of the overseer's whip at more or less frequent intervals, the State as well as local units of government entered the field of slave control, partly to aid slave-owners and partly to protect society in general. Laws for the control of slaves when off the plantation were enacted by the State. Local units of government supplemented these laws and were chiefly responsible for their enforcement.

According to the laws of Mississippi, a slave could not leave the domain of his master without a written pass.[48] Neither could a master allow his slave to go at large and live as a free man, which would amount to a perpetual pass. To be more exact, an owner could not permit his own slaves to be absent over four hours without a pass, nor permit strange slaves to remain on his premises.[49] Thus the State, while penalizing the slave who wandered too freely, insisted that the owner was responsible for the action of his own negroes and the negroes of others, if they came upon his plantation. One offense might result in two punishments—the whipping of the slave and the fining of the owner.

The following are examples of passes given to negroes:

"Oakland — June — 18—
"Pass J—— to Natchez and back again by sunset."
"E—— has permission to visit his wife on Mr. C——'s plantation, to be absent till 9 o'clock." [50]

Any person who discovered a slave off the premises of his master without a pass was obligated under the law to take him before a

[47] *Ibid.*, p. 43, and *passim.*
[48] *Hutchinson's Code*, pp. 513–514.
[49] *Ibid.*, pp. 516, 526.
[50] *Southwest by a Yankee*, II, 129.

justice of the peace.[51] Naturally, such a broad distribution of responsibility did not result in efficient enforcement and, therefore, a patrol was created to enforce laws concerning vagrant slaves.

Every slave-owner and all other persons subject to militia duty and below the rank of captain were subject to patrol duty. The captains were responsible for the regulation of patrols in their districts. At each company muster, it was their duty to make a list of patrol detachments, each of which consisted of a leader and three other members. These groups of four were arranged in order. Each was expected to serve once in two weeks or oftener, if so ordered by the captain. However, any member of the patrol was allowed to provide a substitute.[52]

The structure of the patrol was thus but an adaptation of the militia to the control of slaves. This arrangement was evidently not satisfactory for changes were soon made. In 1831, incorporated towns were authorized to control the patrol system within their own boundaries, thus limiting the authority of militia captains to the rural parts of the State.[53] Two years later the remaining power of militia captains was transferred to the boards of county police,[54] each member of which was authorized to appoint patrol leaders, who then summoned patrol detachments of five or more persons. By these changes the system was decentralized and made subject to the local units of civil government. This was a wise move for the problem of roving slaves was essentially local.

The primary duty of the patrol was to apprehend any negro who was not in his proper place, namely, on his master's plantation, and so to suppress all restless wandering. It was its duty to visit slave quarters or any other places where assemblies of slaves or disorderly free persons were suspected. Three classes of negroes might be caught. If the negro were free but in an illegal assembly, he should be delivered to a justice of the peace. If he were a runaway slave, the same procedure was followed, and the patrol received six dollars. Finally, if the slave were away from home and without a pass, but was apparently not a runaway, the law required the patrol to administer fifteen lashes.[55] A distinction was thus made between the

[51] *Hutchinson's Code*, pp. 513–514.
[52] *Ibid.*, pp. 527–528.
[53] *Ibid.*, p. 535.
[54] These bodies are to-day known as county boards of supervisors.
[55] *Hutchinson's Code*, p. 527.

slave caught visiting the next plantation without a pass and the bona fide runaway.

The patrol was not expected to capture runaways unless they were found during the routine of inspections or unless they became a nuisance to the general public. The latter was provided for in a law with the following singular preamble: "Whereas many times slaves run away, and lie out hid, and lurking in swamps, woods, and other obscure places, killing hogs, and committing other injuries to the inhabitants of this state. . . ." This Mississippi law was evidently copied from a North Carolina colonial statute of 1741, which was introduced by precisely the same preamble. The provisions of the Mississippi law were that, if a band of fugitives became a public nuisance, any justice of the peace could order a patrol leader to collect the necessary force, search for and seize the slaves, and commit them to jail. As this was not an ordinary patrol duty, its members were entitled to a reward of thirty dollars for each slave captured. Although this sum was to be paid out of the State treasury, three fourths of it was later to be collected from the owner of the fugitive by the State.[56]

In general, the patrol was a drafted group of men, forced to make the rounds and see that slaves were not out of their places. In spite of legal penalties both for its leader and members for non-performance of duty,[57] the patrol seems to have been no more efficient than the medieval town watch.[58] The laxity of patrols and the resulting disorders among the slave population are illustrated by conditions that existed in Woodville.

In the newspaper published in this town there was printed, in 1825, the following letter.

"Mr. Printer;
    "An inquiry is frequently made, what is the existing law upon the subject of PATROLS? The power of ordering out Patrols is delegated to the Commissioners of Roads . . . and in case of default or neglect on their part, the Captains of the revenue Beat Companies may exercise the same power. Our black population is kept in no kind of discipline, . . . and our village is crowded with them on every Sunday. . . . It is hoped that for

[56] *Ibid.*, pp. 518–519. *A Collection of All the Public Acts of Assembly of the Province of North-Carolina: Now in Force and Use*, etc. (1752), p. 171.
[57] *Hutchinson's Code*, pp. 529–530.
[58] *Southwest by a Yankee*, II, 258–259.

the security and property, and the lives perhaps of the people, that the Patrols will be ordered out.

"A Slave Holder." [59]

The editor printed this communication, adding his own plea for better enforcement of the patrol laws.

PATROLS

"We would earnestly call the attention of those whose duty it is to the communication which appears in our paper today upon the subject of Patrols. The many depredations which have of late been committed upon property of our citizens by runaways predict the immediate necessity of keeping up a rigid patrol." [60]

In 1832, another citizen who objected to the amount of freedom slaves enjoyed published a letter in the *Republican*. He disliked the custom of allowing slaves to wander about the country at Christmas, many of them more or less drunk, and he reminded the readers of the paper that, shortly before, it had been necessary to guard a religious service with a band of armed men. After this incident a meeting of citizens had appointed a "committee of vigilance to aid in keeping down meetings of slaves in the corporation." He therefore advised slaveholders to "keep them at home as much as possible, that they may know nothing else but their master's farm." It would be better, he added, to send them to the field Christmas day, if no other way could be discovered to keep them at home, and grant holidays at different times, so that all slaves would not be free to roam unrestrained on the same day.[61] Ingraham stated that slaves were seldom drunk except at Christmas, when the sober ones were more easily counted than the drunk.[62]

The corporation of Woodville enacted a law, in 1836, prohibiting slaves from visiting town on Sunday unless accompanied by a white person, or from attending church without written permission. Any slave, whether resident of town or country, if found loitering about the streets, shops, or public buildings, should be seized by the patrol or the town constable and punished by lashes, not exceeding twenty.

[59] The person who wrote this letter was either mistaken as to the authority for ordering out the patrols or he was describing a practice that may have been widespread, namely, of the power being delegated by local arrangements to some authority other than the militia captains, who were at this time the legal rulers of patrols.

[60] *Woodville Republican*, Sept. 17, 1825.

[61] *Ibid.*, Dec. 22, 1832.

[62] *Southwest by a Yankee*, II, 56.

At the same time, the town council did not approve Sunday work as a means of keeping slaves at home, for owners would be fined for this unless it were a work of necessity.[63]

This law either did not better conditions or, if so, only for a season, for three years later it was reënacted. The only difference was a slight increase in penalties and an attempt to force slave-owners to coöperate. They would be fined, if their slaves were caught in town contrary to the law.[64]

Two years later, in 1841, the problem continued to be troublesome. As the previous attempts to keep the slaves out of town, especially on Sundays, were apparently not successful, a change was made in the enforcement of the law. The town constable was made responsible for seizing slaves, and he was given power to summon as many as four citizens to serve not over twelve hours on patrol duty. Refusal to obey the summons of the constable was punishable by a twenty dollar fine.[65]

In 1845, the town council attacked the evil again. Having tried all the expedients they knew to keep slaves from congregating in Woodville, they could only call attention to the laws in force and make a plea for their observance. They were anxious to be lenient, but "they are also determined to rid the community of the intolerable pest of having our streets filled up with trading carts and noisy and drunken negroes on the Sabbath." [66]

The council then lapsed into a subdued quiet on the subject, which seems, however, to have been the result of defeat and not of victory. Two years later under the heading "Our Village!" there appeared in the newspaper a description of, and protest against, conditions in Woodville. The following is a synopsis of the letter to the paper:

> The streets of the town were crowded with gambling negroes on the Sabbath day, and at night they could be seen at all hours prowling about with pilfered truck. A Jewish wedding was celebrated one Tuesday night, and a number of vagrants assembled with every kind of noise-maker to *chevauxris* the married couple. The crowd then moved on to the home of one of the oldest and most respectable citizens of the town and at midnight disturbed this gentleman and his family. The writer stated most emphatically that two thirds of the band were negroes, and asked, "why tax ourselves to keep up the patrol as it seems to be of no value?" [67]

[63] *Woodville Republican*, Apr. 23, 1836.
[64] *Ibid.*, Oct. 12 through Dec. 9, 1839.
[65] *Ibid.*, Mar. 27, 1841.
[66] *Ibid.*, June 28, 1845.
[67] *Ibid.*, Sept. 18, 1847.

Woodville's struggle with the problem of controlling slaves seems to have been an example of local conditions through the State.

Natchez also had its troubles. As early as 1798 Governor Sargent wrote: "*Natchez,* from the the perverseness of some of the people, and the ebriety of the negroes and Indians on Sundays, has become a most abominable place." [68] The historian, Claiborne, did not deny this but explained that it was a result of French and Spanish influence, for in those days the Sabbath, after mass, was devoted to picnics, visiting, and the like. The trouble continued through the years. Though the Sabbath calm of the upper city was not disturbed by the slaves going to and from church or loitering on the street corners, the stores in the infamous "Natchez under the Hill" were open all day and were filled with negro slaves and boatmen. The former were buying luxuries with money secured by the sale of their garden produce.[69]

To clear Natchez of slaves who did not belong there, the courthouse bell was rung at four o'clock on Sunday afternoons.

"Then commences a ludicrous scene of hurrying and scampering, from the four corners of the town; for woe be to the unlucky straggler, who is found after a limited period within the forbidden bounds! The penalty of forty lashes, save one, is speedily inflicted, by way of a lesson in the science of discretion." After the bell, slaves were "soon seen following their noses, with all commendable speed, along the diverging highways, keeping time to the tune of 'over the hills and far away,' to their respective plantations." [70]

Grenada also found it necessary to supplement the State laws for the police control of slaves. Upon the constable was imposed the task of ringing a bell at nine in the evening, as a signal for all slaves to be in their proper places. It was also the duty of the patrol in Grenada to whip every slave found away from home, unless on business of his master, and this had to be evidenced by a written pass.[71]

Slaves seem to have enjoyed more freedom of movement than is generally recognized. Many of them in the towns or on nearby plantations evidently moved here and there as they pleased except during working hours. Indeed, the supposedly dominant race was

[68] Claiborne, *Mississippi*, p. 208.
[69] *Southwest by a Yankee*, II, 54–56.
[70] *Ibid.*, II, 72–73.
[71] Stokes, "History of Grenada," MS., citing, the MS. Record of meetings of Grenada Selectmen, covering the period, Aug. 9, 1836 to May 2, 1856.

often on the defensive not against insurrection but against annoy-
ance. This laxity in dealing with slaves when they were away from
their plantations explains in part the remark of Ingraham that restrictions over negroes were very rigorous in law, but not in fact.[72]
Alexander M. Clayton, an eminent jurist of the State, after sum-
marizing the slave laws of Mississippi in 1850, added this conclusion:

> "The police regulations, in reference to slaves are strict. In practice,
> however, they are much neglected, and the discipline is lax. In general,
> they are a contented race, and a resort to law for their punishment un-
> necessary." [73]

Both in the mode and the kind of punishment there were several
differences between the treatment of slaves and white persons. Slaves
were seldom sent to jail; they would not feel greatly disgraced
thereby, and they would escape plantation labor even though they
might have to work while imprisoned. The owner would, therefore,
be penalized more than the slave. The punishments of slaves by the
State were of three other kinds. The whip was used on those convicted of either petit or grand larceny, with a maximum of thirty-
nine lashes "well laid on," according to the language of the laws.[74]
At the other extreme, the death penalty was imposed for the commission of certain felonies, and it is noticeable that some felonies
were punishable by death, if the criminal were a slave, but by lesser
penalties, if he were a free white person.[75] Finally, if a slave was
convicted of a felony that was not capital, the law directed that he
or she be burnt in the hand by the sheriff in open court and given
such other corporal punishment as the court ordered. The penalty
for a second offense was death.[76]

Practically all slaves accused of crimes other than felonies were
tried before a justice of the peace who was, in most cases, required

---

[72] *Southwest by a Yankee*, II, 258.

[73] *De Bow's Review*, VIII, 22–23.

[74] Poindexter, *Revised Code of the Laws of Mississippi* (1824), pp. 381–383.
Revised Code of the Statute Laws of Mississippi (1857), p. 247.

[75] Among the offenses that were in the early days of the State punishable by
death, if committed by a slave, were these: assault and battery on a white person
with attempt to kill; mixing or administering medicine with intent to kill;
maiming a free white person; attempt to commit a rape on a free white woman
or female child under the age of 12 years; attempt to commit any capital crime;
being voluntarily accessory before or after the fact in any capital offense; man-
slaughter of any free person; burning a dwelling house, store, cotton-house, gin,
outhouse, barn or stable.—*Poindexter's Code*, p. 381.

[76] *Ibid.*, p. 381.

to associate with himself another justice of the peace or several local slaveholders or both. As the years went by there was an increasing tendency to require the justice of the peace to call in advisors in the trial of slaves charged with lesser crimes.[77]

Jury trial was granted all slaves charged with felonies. Twenty-four men were called, at least twelve of whom had to be slaveholders. Both parties had the right to challenge jurors for cause according to the rules of law, and in capital cases a peremptory challenge to the number of six was granted the prisoner.[78]

The slave was not placed on oath in the limited types of cases in which he was allowed to testify.[79] Instead, he was warned by the court that, if his testimony proved false, he would "be ordered by the said court, to have one ear nailed to the pillory, and there to stand for the space of one hour, and then the said ear to be cut off, and thereafter the other ear nailed in like manner, and cut off at the expiration of one other hour, and moreover to receive thirty-nine lashes on his or her bare back, well laid on, at the public whipping post, or such other punishment as the court shall think proper, not extending to life or limb." [80]

Such an injunction, backed with the dignity of the court, would probably incline most slaves to truthfulness, and this was doubtless the purpose of the law. No case has been observed where the penalties of this act were imposed, though the punishment remained in the code of the State until 1857, limited in later years to false witness in capital cases only. In cases of lesser crimes, false testimony from a slave was punished by the lash.[81]

The following cases show that in one respect slaves occupied a favored position before the courts:

Peter, a slave, in 1837, murdered a white man. Immediately after the crime, he was seized by a party of white men and told that he would be hanged unless he confessed. When they began to make preparations for the execution, Peter admitted his guilt. He was then taken before a justice of the peace and in the presence of his captors the confession was repeated and recorded. On the basis of this confession, for this seems to have been the chief evidence, Peter was

[77] *Ibid.*, pp. 372, 382, 383, and the section on slaves *passim. Revised Code of 1857,* p. 250.
[78] *Poindexter's Code,* p. 383.
[79] *Hutchinson's Code,* p. 515.
[80] *Poindexter's Code,* p. 382.
[81] *Revised Code of 1857,* p. 249.

convicted. An appeal was taken to the supreme court, which held that the confession, even though it had been made before the justice of the peace, was not admissible evidence. "Being a slave, he must be presumed to have been ignorant of the protection from sudden violence, which the presence of the justice of the peace afforded him, and he saw himself surrounded by some of those before whom he had recently made a confession." [82]

Several years later the hired slave, Van Buren, who had stolen two jugs of whiskey and two loaves of sugar, was sentenced to be branded in the hand and to receive twenty-five lashes a day for four successive days. He had confessed after being whipped and threatened with further whipping. Following an appeal, the supreme court reversed the judgment of the lower court and granted a new trial on the ground that the part of the confession that had been made under threats and punishment should not have gone to the jury.[83]

In 1853, Theophilus Pritchard, of Yazoo County, was choked to death in his own bed by three slaves. The next day two of the negroes confessed to a number of white neighbors who had assembled. Though the negroes were evidently not punished or threatened, their attorneys sought to exclude their confession from the jury on the ground that their servile condition necessarily operated on their minds. For a white man to tell a slave to confess was almost equivalent to using duress. "Perpetual slavery and free will are incompatible." [84]

The laws of Mississippi in several instances established severer penalties for slaves than for white persons who had committed the same crime. Within the limits of the law, however, the accused slave seems to have received fair treatment by the courts, and there was some attempt to keep the scales of justice balanced by making allowance for the effect of slavery on his character. Furthermore, financial considerations prompted slave-owners to defend their negroes. The supreme court stated: "Constant experience shows masters diligent and just in reasonable defense of accused slaves." [85]

[82] Peter v. The State, 12 Miss. 31.
[83] Van Buren v. The State, 24 Miss. 512.
[84] Dick, Aleck and Henry v. The State, 30 Miss. 593. See also, Green v. The State, 23 Miss. 509.
[85] Sam v. The State, 33 Miss. 347.

CHAPTER V

PUNISHMENTS AND REWARDS

Since the ordinary incentives to labor which operate on free men were lacking in slavery, various punishments and rewards were used to force or persuade slaves to labor. Considering these separately, we will first list some examples showing why slaves were punished.

One negro was disciplined because his overseer could not find him in the field where he had been told to work.[1] On another estate the negroes understood that punishment would be meted out to a plow hand who did not feed his mules when the horn was blown at sunset.[2] A fugitive was usually punished when he was returned to the estate.[3] A cook who failed to arise in time to prepare breakfast by the usual hour was whipped.[4] Olmsted observed an overseer reproving negro mechanics for not getting on faster with their work, and one was threatened with a whipping for not paying attention to directions that had been given him.[5] On this same plantation field hands were threatened with whippings "If you don't work faster."[6] Slaves were punished for bringing spirits on the plantation, for drinking,[7] for not

[1] Young v. Thompson, 11 Miss. 129.
[2] Ned and Taylor v. The State, 33 Miss. 364.
[3] The following notations in the manuscript diary of Spooner Forbes speak for themselves:
July 11, 1859. "Jake & Harrison ran away. Harrison came to Town & took his whipping & went back. Jake not heard from."
July 20, 1859. "Jake come home again & got a good whipping."
June 28, 1860. "Jake ran away at dinner time."
July 15, 1860. "Jake came in this morning."
July 16, 1860. "Whiped Jake today for going in Town."
Mar. 18, 1862. "Jake ran away sent to Jo Willis & got his dogs but did not catch him."
Mar. 20, 1862. "Jake came in at ½ past 4 o'clock & took his whipping and acknowledged his stealing."
For a similar case, see Bowles MS.
[4] McCoy v. McKowen, 26 Miss. 487.
[5] Olmsted, Back Country, p. 78.
[6] Ibid., p. 82.
[7] De Bow's Review, X, 624. Leigh MSS.

respecting their own marriages, or for stealing.[8] A negro man who cooked for the other slaves was threatened with a dozen lashes if he sent poorly baked bread to the hands in the field. His master thus appears to have been more interested in the health of the field hands than in the ruining of the bread.[9]

From this list it is evident that failure to do a given amount of work was not as often the cause of punishment as the doing of work badly or the infraction of some plantation rule or special order. Nevertheless, failure to hoe enough corn or to pick enough cotton also led to punishment, as we are told by Dr. J. W. Monette. He stated that after the cotton was weighed at the close of the day:

". . . those who are found to have brought in less than their usual quantity, unless for good reasons, are called in order of their names: the individual advances, and if his reasons are insufficient, he is ordered to lie down upon his face, with his back exposed; when he receives ten, twenty, or fifty stripes with the whip, according to his deserts. In this way the overseer goes over the list, punishing only those who have idled away their time."[10]

A large amount of whipping indicated a poorly run plantation, and any planter would envy the one who could write that on his estate there were "as few sour looks and as little whipping as on almost any other place of the same size."[11]

In the effort to curtail the amount of punishment, overseers were frequently instructed to punish only after deliberation, and the power of the negro driver was strictly limited. This was covered in the following rule that was part of the code of a plantation in Mississippi. "Whipping, when necessary, shall be in moderation, and never done in a passion; and the driver shall in no instance inflict punishment, except in the presence of the overseer, and when, from sickness, he is unable to do it himself."[12]

The usual mode of punishing negroes was with the whip, and this was so severely applied that permanent marks were sometimes left on their bodies. Fancy whips to be used on black backs were for sale at stores within the State, and the purchasers could find "Spurr's

[8] De Bow's Review, X, 623–624.
[9] Ibid., VII, 382.
[10] [Ingraham], Southwest by a Yankee, II, 286–287.
[11] De Bow's Review, X, 625.
[12] Ibid., X, 626.

Ivory handled Planters Whips, Overseers do., ivory handled Twigs." [13]

A citizen of Mississippi gave, in the 1830's, the following description of the flogging of slaves:

"Whipping is generally performed with as much care and humanity as the nature of the case will permit. A person standing at the distance of two hundred yards, being unacquainted with the mode, and hearing the loud sharp crack of the whip upon the naked skin, would almost tremble for the life of the poor sufferer. But what would be his surprise, after hearing fifty or one hundred stripes thus laid on, to go up and examine the poor fellow, and find the skin not broken, and not a drop of blood drawn from him! Yet this is the way in which the whip is generally used here upon the slaves: very few planters would permit them to be whipped on the bare back with a rawhide, or cow-skin, as it is generally called. Though, as in everything else, there is a great difference in the degree of severity exercised by different masters: yet we must take the general rule, as applicable to the great class of planters. The common overseer's whip consists of a stout flexible stalk, large at the handle, tapering rapidly to the distance of about eighteen inches, and thence continued with cord or leather; the whole is covered with a leather plat, which continues tapering into, and forms the lash—the whole together being about three feet and a half long. To the end of the lash is attached a soft, dry, buckskin cracker, about three eighths of an inch wide and ten or twelve inches long, which is the only part allowed to strike, in whipping on the bare skin. So soft is the cracker, that a person who has not the sleight of using the whip, could scarcely hurt a child with it. When it is used by an experienced hand it makes a very loud report, and stings, or 'burns' the skin smartly, but does not bruise it. One hundred stripes well laid on with it, would not injure the skin as much as ten moderate stripes with a cow-skin." [14]

Paul, the headwaiter in the hotel at Grenada, was suspected of complicity in the escape of several fugitives who had left neighboring plantations and fled to the North. Slaves were found concealed in the

---

[13] *Woodville Republican*, Aug. 8, 1835; Sept. 5, 1835.

[14] *Southwest by a Yankee*, II, 287-288, from an appendix written by Dr. J. W. Monette, of Mississippi. One of the less exaggerated of the abolitionist descriptions of whipping negroes was given by Mr. A. A. Stone, who wrote from Natchez in 1835 that on a plantation of fifty slaves, during the cotton picking season, it was the rule to have a negro whipped every night, often two or three, and occasionally fourteen or fifteen.

"They always lie down and receive it on their bare back and buttock. If they are uneasy they are sometimes tied; the hands and feet being stretched out to a stake driven for the purpose. But they are usually held by other negroes. In a bad case one takes hold of each hand and each foot, and another sits on his head. If they don't hold him well, give them a cut or two with the whip, and I warrant you they will hold him still enough if they have to take their teeth."—*Liberty* (an anti-slavery pamphlet, pub. 1837), pp. 140-144.

garret of the hotel and, as one of them was the father of Paul's wife, this strengthened the suspicion. Paul was, therefore, taken to a shed near the edge of the town, bound, and beaten with a raw-hide, which was applied only when a very severe punishment was desired. As this extorted no confession, resort was had to what was called the "hot paddle." This was a thin piece of wood with holes bored through it, and it was applied to the naked flesh; but Paul never confessed. As a result of his punishment he was confined to his bed in the hotel for over a week.[15]

While whipping was by far the most usual mode of coercion, negroes were sometimes branded on the chest or face, or had an iron clog or band attached to the ankle. These more severe punishments were usually reserved for habitual runaways.

Punishment was not always physical. Most of the planters simply wanted the slaves to perform their tasks and they took no delight in the lash. Ingenuity was sometimes shown in devising ways of controlling slaves. Jim frequently slipped away from his estate in north Mississippi to enjoy a vacation of a few days in the river bottoms. His master was very anxious to break this habit, and finally tried an unusual expedient. The next time Jim tried to escape, he ducked into the wrong door of the gin house and fell into a room full of lint. Covered with cotton, he was hauled out, and the master ordered him brought to the "big house." It was time for the evening meal, and Jim was commanded to sit down at the table with the white family. This overthrow of all tradition and custom was too much for Jim. The meal was evidently the most miserable one in his career, for he never ran away again.

Practically every master could have made the lot of his slaves more disagreeable without resorting to corporal punishment. For instance, a slave could be disciplined by refusing to give him the usual pass on Saturday night to visit relatives on the next plantation, by stopping his allowance of tobacco, or by assigning to him harder tasks. There is one instance of displeasure being shown by taking from a negro one of his two wives.[16]

To some slaves there was held out the hope of eventual emancipation. Captain Isaac Ross proposed to send his negroes to Africa and there free them. This he provided for in his will. A few slaves, how-

[15] W. H. Venable, "Down South before the War," in *Ohio Archæological and Historical Quarterly,* II, 501–502.
[16] Foote, *Casket of Reminiscences,* pp. 201–210.

ever, were excepted by name.[17] While Ross excluded these negroes because he believed they would hinder the colonization venture, this action also operated as a punishment for their general course of life.

Although slaves were more frequently disciplined by their own masters or overseers, they sometimes suffered at the hands of officers of the State or of neighboring planters. A plantation owner could not legally permit over five strange slaves on his plantation at any one time,[18] and he was at liberty to give as many as ten stripes to a strange slave that came on his estate.[19]

Some planters were disturbed by the lax régime of their neighbors. The laws that have been cited served, therefore, to keep the slaves on a well-ordered estate from being corrupted or disturbed by disorderly visitors. One planter, James Newell, made a standing order that any outside slave who caused trouble on his estate should be seized by the home slaves and brought before him. This order once brought disastrous results. A neighboring negro, who had created some disturbance on the Newell plantation, would not submit to seizure. He struck out across the fields with the other slaves after him in full cry. When he reached the bayou, he jumped in and started swimming. The chase seems to have called out the savagery of the pursuers, for they began hurling brickbats from the bank at the human quarry in the water. The negro was drowned, though it was not proved that he was actually struck by one of the missiles.[20]

Some punishment was necessary in a system of slavery. However, chastisement was not always kept to a minimum, and there were a few cases of terrific punishment that were almost past believing. Some of these will be cited though they should not be taken as normal.

A hired negro slave started to run away. The temporary master forced the negro at the point of a pistol to return and then stabbed him with a knife.[21] A negro woman, who was with child, threatened to run away. Because of this threat, she was whipped in a cruel and unusual manner.[22] A negro fugitive was placed in jail, clad only in a gingham dress, although he was a man. The unusual costume was probably occasioned by the slave's lacerated skin, for even the hard-

[17] Claiborne, *Mississippi*, p. 389.
[18] *Hutchinson's Code*, p. 526.
[19] *Ibid.*, pp. 513–514.
[20] Newell *v.* Cowan *et al.*, 30 Miss. 492. See also, Leggett *v.* Simmons, 15 Miss. 348.
[21] Young *v.* Thompson, 11 Miss. 129.
[22] Trotter *v.* McCall, 26 Miss. 410.

ened jailer wrote that "he has been lately most inhumanly whipped from his neck down to his feet." [23] A negro near Port Gibson was tarred and feathered.[24]

Olmsted wrote that the most severe punishment he witnessed anywhere in the South was on a Mississippi plantation. The offender was a negro girl who had slipped away from her work in the field and was hiding in a gully nearby. When discovered, the overseer ordered her to kneel and struck her thirty or forty times across the shoulders with his raw-hide whip. She was then made to lie on her face, and the whipping was continued with great force on her bare legs and back.[25]

Some of the outrages perpetrated on negroes can hardly be classed as punishments. Governor Foote narrates the trial of a man who charged a negro of good character with theft, dragged him from his bed, and inflicted more than a thousand stripes on his bare back. It was found that the negro, "in the intenseness of his agony . . . had bitten his tongue in two." [26] The same writer also tells of a blacksmith who was twice tried for murder, one of the victims being "a negro fellow, whom he had actually held upon the burning coals until the fire found its way to his vitals." [27] The Supreme Court of Mississippi once had to pass on a case arising from the murder of Jack by his master and the latter's friend, both of whom were drunk.[28] In Oktibbeha County a grand jury indicted a man for whipping a slave to death.[29] The subjection of one race to another, coupled with the inability of the subordinate race to testify against the dominant race, made brutal punishments possible. However, these revolting extremes were rare.

There was always a chance that the power of the State would be felt by the aggressor. The drunken murderers of Jack were sentenced to seven years' imprisonment apiece, the court holding that, if a slave was killed while his master or overseer was inflicting corporal punishment, the rules of the common law upon the subject of murder would regulate the character of the offense.[30] By State law, a master

[23] *Woodville Republican,* Sept. 11, 1830.
[24] Spooner Forbes, Diary, MS., Mar. 19, 1859.
[25] *Back Country,* pp. 83-87.
[26] Foote, *Bench and Bar of the South and Southwest,* pp. 72-73.
[27] *Casket of Reminiscences,* pp. 203-204.
[28] Kelly and Little *v.* The State, 11 Miss. 518.
[29] Carroll, *Oktibbeha County,* p. 86.
[30] Kelly and Little *v.* The State, 11 Miss. 518.

was subject to indictment for cruel or unusual punishment inflicted by him, the offense being classed as battery upon his own slave. The decision as to what constituted cruel or unusual punishment was a matter to be decided by the jury. This law was not a dead letter; at least one case arose to the supreme court in which an overseer was convicted of inflicting cruel punishment on a slave who was under his authority.[31] One of the first cases appealed to the Supreme Court of Mississippi grew out of the murder of a slave by a white man. Though it was questioned by the defense whether it was a crime for a white man to kill a slave, the court held that the act did constitute murder, for "Has the slave no rights, because he is deprived of his freedom?" The murderer was sentenced to be hanged July 27, 1821.[32]

It is difficult to make a close estimate of the extent to which slaves were punished in the regular course of plantation management. One index, which has to be used carefully, lies in the description of fugitive negroes. In the files of the *Woodville Republican*, between the years of 1823 and 1848, a total of five hundred and fifty fugitive slaves were described. Of this number, fifty-eight bore on their bodies permanent marks of punishment. Eleven had been branded, usually on the forehead, cheek, or breast. Forty-one had scars of whippings, some of them severe and not merely temporary marks. In describing such scars, the jailer usually wrote that the negro was "much marked with the whip." One fugitive claimed that his scars were "caused from severe whipping with a cow skin, at the time of the South-Hampton insurrection." [33] In many cases there were old scars under the fresh lacerations of the most recent flogging. One of the fugitives had an iron collar around his neck, and six of them had iron bands about their legs. A chain four or five feet long was attached to one of these bands, and to another a ball and chain.[34] The wearer of the latter had recently escaped from the chain gang in Natchez. These iron bands were sometimes inscribed with the initials of the owner. One, for instance, bore the letters: "A. Bird & B. Rouge." [35] On one negro was the imprint of the branding wires as well as the marks of the whip.

These facts concerning evidences of punishment on the bodies of runaway slaves need some explanation. In the first place, the average

[31] Scott *v.* The State, 31 Miss. 473.
[32] The State *v.* Isaac Jones, 1 Miss. 83.
[33] *Woodville Republican*, June 1, 1839.
[34] *Ibid.*, Sept. 16, 1837.
[35] *Ibid.*, July 10, 1841.

fugitive was undoubtedly more recalcitrant than the average slave. He was, therefore, more likely to bear marks of punishment. In the second place, the newspaper examined was published close to the Louisiana State boundary line. Many of the slaves advertised in the *Woodville Republican* had escaped from Louisiana plantations. Of the fifty-eight fugitives who bore marks of corporal punishment, eight claimed the county where the newspaper was published as their home. Of this eight, six had been whipped and two had been branded. In neither of the latter cases were the letters of the brand the same as the initials of the current owners of the slaves. Another ten of the marked slaves claimed other parts of Mississippi as their homes. Over half of the fifty-eight said they had run away from Louisiana, and a few were from other States.

In plantation diaries and account books, punishments, whether with the whip or otherwise, were seldom recorded. The overseer of the Bowles plantation wrote in the plantation book that Frank "got himself whooped" after running away.[36] Though the overseer seemed, therefore, to have had no objection to recording "whoopings," this is the only mention of punishment on the estate during the year. In the diary of Spooner Forbes, whippings were mentioned with moderate frequency. The account books of the Leigh plantation intimate that slaves were occasionally punished, but in the twenty or more years that M. W. Philips kept a diary of events on his estate, punishment is mentioned but once. Cyrus, a particularly unruly slave, had run away. He told his captors that he had fled to escape five hundred lashes the overseer had threatened to give him because his carelessness in erecting certain gate posts had displeased Dr. Philips. The latter confided to his diary that Cyrus's story was a lie. In the Wheeless record book and in the account of "Burleigh" written by Susan Dabney Smedes punishments are rarely mentioned.

Olmsted tells of one man, in most respects a very kind master, who boasted that on his plantation of seventeen slaves there had scarcely been a hundred strokes of the whip in the past year.[37]

On another small plantation the owner said that he had not whipped a slave in five years " 'cept maybe sprouting some of the young ones sometimes."[38] On President Polk's Mississippi plantation, however, whippings were frequently administered, particularly to returned

[36] Bowles MS.
[37] *Back Country*, p. 183.
[38] *Ibid.*, p. 143.

fugitives. Sometimes the punishment was severe.[39] There was, apparently, more punishment in the regions where there were large plantations. A stricter discipline seemed necessary in view of the large slave population. Furthermore, a larger per cent of the masters of large estates were absentee, and, as a result, overseers and negro drivers had control of the slaves.

In discussing physical punishment of slaves, two points should be borne in mind. In the first place, the penological practice of the age was not adverse to this kind of punishment. Even white criminals were branded in Mississippi in the early part of the nineteenth century.[40] In the second place, as has been pointed out in the previous chapter, slaves were rarely jailed except when they were fugitives from service or were awaiting trial for a serious crime. The population of the State penitentiary was white, with the addition of an occasional free negro,[41] and hardly any negro slaves. It suited the economic needs of the owners to have negroes flogged and returned to work as soon as possible.

The effect of punishment varied with its amount and the nature of the slave. In a few instances, several of which have been mentioned, the brutality of the punishment resulted in the death of the victim. In other cases, the slave became desperate and violent under the lash. Ike, a slave, attempted to kill his overseer, and did indeed stab him, because the overseer tried to punish him.[42] At the other extreme, a few slaves attempted to kill themselves. Cyrus, who was mentioned above, cut his own throat, though not fatally, to avoid return after having run away. Another slave, who had burned his master's gin house, stated that he had committed this crime because he wanted to be hanged.[43] These are extremes. The vast majority seem to have accepted an occasional whipping as a matter of course, and were not greatly affected. There was a little closer attention to work for a time, and there was doubtless a slight breaking of the slave's spirit, which resulted in the appearance so frequently mentioned in old descriptions of fugitive slaves, a "downward" or a "down cast look." [44]

[39] Bassett, *Plantation Overseer*, *passim*.
[40] Dunbar Rowland, ed., *Official Letter Books of W. C. C. Claiborne, 1801–1816*, I, 242.
[41] *Jour. Gen. Assem. of Miss.*, 1840–1841, Sen. Jour., p. 207.
[42] Ike *v.* The State, 23 Miss. 525. *Woodville Republican*, Jan. 30, 1836; Jan. 24, 1846.
[43] Sam *v.* The State, 33 Miss. 347. *Woodville Republican*, Oct. 21, 1828.
[44] *Woodville Republican*, Jan. 30, 1836.

Owners of negroes, in attempting to encourage them to labor diligently, had recourse to rewards as well as to punishments. Some of these were designed to encourage general good behavior and contentment among the negroes; others were allotted to those who had done a specific task well. Gratuities and tips, while not rewards in one sense of the word, were frequently given to slaves. House servants and those who served in hotels were more likely to receive small presents of money than other classes of laborers, and it might be added that the donors were usually guests and were not the owners of the slaves who were the recipients.[45]

As a compensation for some unusual deed in the interest of the owner or of the State or for faithful service over a number of years, a slave was sometimes set free. With this purpose in mind, a master incorporated the following sentence in his will. "The very faithful and meritorious service of my negro boy Jim, I cannot consent to pass unrewarded; my will, therefore, is that for said meritorious services, the said Jim shall be forever set free . . ."[46] Another slave-owner and his wife, Daniel and Jane Clark, signed the following deed in January, 1800.

"Jupiter Dowda an African, who was our first slave, and truly a man of probity, died in Philadelphia and is buried in the potter's field at that place. He served us twenty years during which period we never knew that Jupiter did a base thing, told a falsehood, got intoxicated or swore an oath. In consideration of his uncommon fidelity to us we emancipated him and his wife Nancy, Jonathan his son and Isabella his daughter, and we now manumit his daughter Susana, and we do hereby warrant unto her her freedom against our heirs and administrators and all others forever."[47]

These freed negroes might be sent to Africa or to a free State, or they might be allowed to remain in Mississippi, though in the latter instance, after 1822, a special act of the legislature was a prerequisite.[48] Emancipation may, therefore, be considered as a reward for unusual or long-continued good service.

A number of miscellaneous practices followed on the various

[45] Smedes, *Southern Planter,* pp. 97, 106. Leigh MSS.
[46] Shattuck, Executor, *v.* Young & wife, 10 Miss. 30.
[47] MS. Adams County (Miss.), Records. Deed Book B, p. 9.
In addition to emancipating John, Israel P. Smith bequeathed to him $500 and further provided that his executors purchase and set free John's wife.—Adams County, Will Book number 2, p. 431.
Other instances of manumissions as rewards for faithfulness may be found in Luckey *et al. v.* Dykes *et al.,* 10 Miss. 60; Mahoner *v.* Hooe *et al.,* 17 Miss. 247.
[48] *Hutchinson's Code,* p. 523.

plantations of the State served to lighten or give interest to the life of the negroes. On one estate the entire force was several times allowed an afternoon or a whole day in which to go fishing.[49] On another the negroes were allowed to trap game, chiefly rabbits, turkeys, and racoons.[50] One planter had among his slaves a good fiddler, who was kept well supplied with catgut, and it was his duty to play for the negroes every Saturday night until twelve o'clock. He was accompanied by Ihurod on the triangle, with Sam thrown in for good measure to "pat." [51]

Another bright spot in the life of slaves was the distribution of presents or luxuries, especially at Christmas. This was the custom on a number of estates [52] and amounted in one instance to a thousand or fifteen hundred dollars' worth of molasses, coffee, tobacco, calico, and "Sunday Tricks," which averaged about eight or ten dollars a slave.[53] Tobacco, which was usually distributed at shorter intervals at the rate of one pound a month to the negro,[54] was generally bought by the hogshead.[55] It was frequently of a somewhat inferior grade, designated in the market as "negro tobacco." [56]

Permission was sometimes accorded the slaves to work for wages after the routine work of the plantation was done. For instance, one planter paid some of his slaves for extra work they did in making shingles, and made the following dignified notation of the transaction: "Credit Frank & Co. $6.40 for shingles; John & Co., $1.20; Jacob, $1.20." [57] On another plantation, some of the slaves went to the swamps on Saturdays and Sundays and made puncheons, which were rough boards split from logs. One workman realized $50 in one year from this source.[58]

During the cotton-picking season, prizes were often given to stimulate the negroes to do good work. On the Dabney estate, prizes were awarded each week during this season. They ranged between a dollar and a picayune, a small Mexican coin valued at 6½ cents. Nelly, a young negro woman who was the best picker on the estate,

[49] Riley, "Diary of a Miss. Planter," in *P. M. H. S.*, X, 368, 433.
[50] *Back Country*, p. 75.
[51] *De Bow's Review*, X, 625.
[52] *Southern Planter*, 68–69. *Southwest by a Yankee*, II, 243.
[53] *Back Country*, p. 51.
[54] *Ibid.*, p. 75.
[55] *Southwest by a Yankee*, II, 242.
[56] *Woodville Republican*, July 18, 1840.
[57] "Diary of a Miss. Planter," in *P. M. H. S.*, X, 449, 453.
[58] *Back Country*, p. 51.

received over $17.00 at Christmas as her share of the prize money.[59]

Another privilege granted slaves was permission to visit neighboring towns or plantations for the purpose of attending church, marketing, or visiting friends and relatives. Doubtless the passes authorizing the trip were given mainly to those who were in good standing. Many slaves were allowed to cultivate their own small garden patches, or to raise a few chickens or pigs. It was illegal for an owner to allow his slaves to keep horses, mules, cows, or dogs, or to cultivate cotton for their own use.[60] However, this, like many of the laws relating to slavery, was not strictly enforced, for private patches of cotton were cultivated by slaves on some estates.[61] In the season of 1849, on the Polk estate, the servants' crop was about 8,400 pounds of seed cotton, which would amount to about seven bales of an average weight of 400 pounds, which was the weight of the standard bale of that day.[62] Five years earlier M. W. Philips's negroes were raising their own cotton in small quantities and having it ginned by their master for the usual toll of 10 per cent.[63]

Private patches of cotton cultivated by the negroes were likely to be troublesome to the master. The danger was that the slave would add to his private supply by stealing from his master and, therefore, slaves were prohibited by law from raising cotton for their own use. Indeed, the slave had no legal right to own anything. Though he, in effect, possessed the clothes issued to him and enjoyed practical ownership of such produce as he raised in spare times, all this was legally the property of his master. The supreme court once heard it stated that a slave "has no more political capacity, no more right to purchase, hold or transfer property, than the mule in his plough. . . . He is himself but a chattel . . ."[64]

In the Bowles plantation book are a number of entries concerning negroes' corn sold at Christmas and concerning money spent by the slaves. One of these is an itemized statement of twenty-three dollars that were distributed to the negroes. Some of them drew on the money to their credit at different times during the year, receiving from

[59] *Southern Planter*, pp. 68–69.

[60] *Laws of Miss.*, 1817, pp. 168–169. *Hutchinson's Code*, p. 519.

[61] *De Bow's Review*, VII, 381.

[62] In this season Mrs. Polk's poorer grades of cotton sold at 7 and 7½ cents a pound, the better at 10¾ and 11½ cents.—*Plantation Overseer*, p. 187.

[63] Nov. 22, 1844. "Ginned for Daniel, 256 lbs., toll 25 lbs.; Charlotte, 201 lbs., toll 20 lbs.; Bob 230 lbs., toll 23 lbs.; Bill, 107 lbs., toll 10."—"Diary of a Miss. Planter," in *P. M. H. S.*, X, 395.

[64] Hinds *et al. v.* Brazealle *et al.*, 3 Miss. 837.

twenty cents to three dollars at a time. The total receipts of several of the slaves amounted to as much as five dollars. This seems to have been the money due the negro for the corn he had raised in his spare time and paid as he asked for it after the grain had been bought or sold through the agency of the plantation manager.[65]

On a much larger number of estates slaves cultivated their own vegetable gardens or kept their own chickens.[66] Masters sometimes included among the instructions to the overseer an approval of this practice. For instance, J. W. Fowler instructed his overseers to allow such slaves "as may desire it a piece of ground to raise potatoes, tobacco. They may raise chickens also with privileges of marketing same at suitable leisure times." [67]

The slaves considered marketing their garden and hen-house products the most important part of the whole transaction. This was often simply accomplished by selling it to the plantation owner. A visitor in Mississippi observed a son of President Taylor pay to an aged negro $1.67½ for chickens. The price was set by the slave and was paid by the master without debate, though he commented to the English visitor that the slave "invariably charges the very highest prices for them." [68]

According to the laws of Mississippi, a slave had to secure a written permit from his master before buying or selling any goods.[69] Either the masters granted this willingly, or the law was disregarded, for slaves bought and sold freely. The money gained was usually spent for trinkets, food, whiskey—which was prohibited by State law and generally by plantation orders—or clothing of better grade than was usually issued to slaves.[70]

Planters were not adverse to slaves using plantation corn to fatten their private chickens, but there were objections to any system which allowed negroes to buy and sell and to handle money. As one master summed it up, these private economic ventures led the negroes to "acquiring habits of trading in farm produce, which invariably leads

[65] Bowles MS.
[66] *Southwest by a Yankee*, II, 54. *Back Country*, pp. 74, 75, 182. *De Bow's Review*, X, 624. *Mississippi*, p. 144.
[67] Phillips, *Plantation and Frontier*, I, 114.
[68] Wortley, *Travels in the United States*, p. 119. Leigh MSS.
[69] *Hutchinson's Code*, p. 514.
[70] *Back Country*, pp. 75, 182. See also, The State *v*. Borroum *et al.*, 23 Miss. 477.

to stealing, followed by whipping, trouble to the master, and discontent on the part of the slave." [71]

Another objection was voiced by municipalities. Their complaint was that on Sundays the streets were crowded with negroes trading their garden produce for the wares of the village. [72]

These evils of the trade between slaves and the outside world caused planters much concern. One of the latter reached the following solution. He continued to allow to each slave a separate garden plot, but he strictly prohibited the sale of its products. It then followed that, if the slaves gardened, it would be only for home consumption. In lieu of the old trading privileges, five dollars was given each Christmas to the head of every family on the estate. [73]

On the Polk plantation was another instance of the substitution of money payments for the older practice of allowing the slaves to manage their own private gardens or patches. It was pointed out above that, in 1849, the negroes on this place produced about seven bales of cotton in their own interests. Several years later we find that about $200 in cash was being distributed to the negroes at some kind of regular intervals, probably yearly. No mention was made at this later date of private cotton patches. The money payment was probably a compensation for the withdrawal of this privilege. [74]

It is likely that this change on the Polk plantation was suggested by certain interesting experiments on the neighboring Leigh estate. John Townes Leigh, an intelligent planter, who sometimes gave helpful advice to the overseers on the Polk place, allowed his slaves to cultivate their own private cotton patches. From the sale of their crops, several of the negroes saved as much as fifty or one hundred dollars. [75]

Following the death of J. T. Leigh in January, 1850, the management of the estate was assumed by his son, P. Randolph Leigh. He soon adopted a plan which allowed the negroes what might be termed rudimentary salaries. It was about this time that money payments were first made to the slaves on the Polk estate. P. R. Leigh

[71] De Bow's Review, X, 624.
[72] Woodville Republican, June 28, 1848.
[73] De Bow's Review, X, 624.
[74] Plantation Overseer, pp. 203, 210–211. The money given these slaves seems mainly to have been secured from the hiring to other planters of Harry, a blacksmith belonging to the Polks.
[75] De Bow's Review, VII, 381.

notified his slaves that each could count on a definite allowance. When, from the plantation supplies, the slaves drew articles that were not necessities, they were charged for them. Fines were imposed for various forms of misbehavior. On the days of the settlement, which usually came six months apart, the charges for luxuries and the fines were subtracted from the allowance, and the remainder was given to the negro in cash.

Bearing in mind that there were forty-nine slaves on this estate in 1852, counting children, it will be of interest to list some of the aggregate sums of money paid to the slaves, and to enumerate some of the charges made against them.

On April 16, 1851, there is this entry: "To cash to negroes for their portion for year 1850,. part paid in Dec. 128.10." Over against this is the entry: "By cash of negroes for shoes, 22.40." Through each year in which accounts are extant, such entries occur. There are in addition numerous small items such as "to servant, .15," or "To little negroes, .5," as well as an occasional entry like that of November 17, 1850, "Pd. for best cotton picking during my absence on a trip to Virginia 1.00." In other words, tips and occasional special rewards were used. But, above all this, each negro could count on a definite sum of money at a set time, if he behaved himself, kept his needs to a minimum, and did his work well. The slaves did not have to work overtime on their private plots to secure these sums. The idea of P. R. Leigh is evident in two of his entries during 1860. On February 25, he noted in his books $109.50 "To gratuity to negroes for year 1859." He then entered against the negroes $93.20 "By articles furnished negroes from supplies purchased (Not *necessary* articles of support)."

An idea of the detailed workings of the system may be secured by reading copies of the accounts of three of the slaves.

EPES		Dr.	Cr.
1852			
April 20th	Good judgement in hauling from Grenada		
21st	Neglect in making Jeff get the tumbril cart in time, causing a loss of time in going back	1.00	
May 6th	Very mean scraping of cotton and but little work 2d days scraping		
Octo	1 pr shoes for wife	1.00	

1853		Shoes given up. Having been engaged in buying whiskey and receiving stolen whiskey as well as having it stolen, instead of $12.50 will receive nothing	

BARNEY

1852

Apr	21st	1 pr shoes	1.00

A portion of the year not so careful with his mules as he ought to be, his general conduct good, but cannot be classed as first rate his highest run might have been $9.00 is allowed 8

ELLEN

1853

Sept	1st	By dues 1st May	1.00	
Oct	4	To cash	1.00	[76]

Finally, in considering the rewards given to slaves, it should be remembered that the larger plantations were worlds in themselves. There was room for honor and disgrace, for easy tasks or hard, and so there was room for advancement or for demotion in the labor system of the plantation. There were more subtle ways of punishing slaves than with a whip, and money prizes were far from being the only kinds of rewards. Doubtless a slave would prefer to drive a wagon load of cotton to Memphis, with a dollar and ninety cents to spend for food and lodging—or in any other preferred way—than to labor with the hoe gang in the field.[77]

[76] Leigh MSS.
[77] Bowles MS. *Southern Planter*, p. 83.

CHAPTER VI

FUGITIVES

In days of old, names were frequently conferred because of some personal trait, habit, or occupation. An example of this was observed on an extensive river-bottom plantation in Mississippi where there was a negro man who answered to the name of Swamp. There was a fast-fading recollection that he had in his early youth borne the name of Abraham. His newer name was given because he spent a large part of his time in the swamps that fringed the plantation, going without permission and contrary to plantation rules. Swamp, the worst runaway on the estate, personified one of the most annoying problems that faced slaveholders.[1]

The escape of a negro, if permanent, was a large financial loss to the planter. Even if the negro was regained, there was some disruption of work and more or less breakdown in the morale of the working force, which made the escape of slaves an economic problem of considerable proportions. Society as a whole, even the non-slaveholding class, was affected by runaway slaves. The depredations of fugitives and the local and interstate troubles that runaway slaves caused were of concern to all people in the South.

In Mississippi a slave was considered a runaway, if he was eight miles or farther from home without a pass or if he had absented himself from his master's service for two days.[2] Incidentally, this implies that a slave who did not have his master's permission could make a short and brief excursion without being classed under the State law as a runaway slave.

One of the most important questions in connection with runaway slaves is that of why slaves fled from their masters. This serves as the natural approach to the whole subject of fugitives. Further, it brings to the surface many of the evils of slavery, for running away was one of the few ways by which a slave could protest against un-

[1] Olmsted, *Back Country*, p. 88.
[2] *Hutchinson's Code*, p. 528.

pleasant conditions on the plantation. It is evident that in studying fugitive negroes one is probing the evil side of slavery.

It is probable that slaves absconded most frequently for the purpose of rejoining severed ties of family or of friendship. To illustrate, at the close of an advertisement for Isaac, a fugitive, it was stated: "Isaac will probably go to the neighborhood of Woodville or Natchez, where he formerly lived." [3] It was said of another that he might be lurking about Laurel Hill, for his wife lived in that neighborhood.[4] It was thought that Jack had gone toward Kentucky, from whence he had been imported,[5] and Charles was suspected of having started toward Tennessee, either to see his wife or his mother.[6]

A large number of negroes escaped soon after they were sold to new masters. A still larger number escaped from slave-traders,[7] which further seems to indicate that a breaking of home ties, coupled with an uncertain future, sent many slaves to the lost and found columns. There was a negro carpenter who ran away, paradoxical as it may seem, to avoid leaving his home and friends. His master was planning to ship him north, so the negro fled that he might stay near home.[8] Even more unusual was the situation of Eliza, a negress, who was confined as a fugitive in the jail of Yalobusha County. According to her story, she had been deserted by her master, a half-breed Indian who had moved west. The story seems probable for it was told in 1836, and there had been a large westward migration of Indians just before this time.[9]

Through the hot summer months most of the slaves were at work in the cotton fields, and the labor required was greatest in September and June. It is noticeable that more slaves were missing from April

[3] *Woodville Republican*, June 15, 1824.
[4] *Ibid.*, Aug. 21, 1830.
[5] Natchez *Weekly Chronicle*, Nov. 2, 1808.
[6] Bassett, *Plantation Overseer*, pp. 129, 132, 134, 216. To illustrate the form in which such suspicions were often cast, the following advertisement is given:
"70 Dollars Reward!
"Absconded from the Forest Plantation of the late William Dunbar, on Sunday the 7th instant, a very handsome Mulattress called Harriet, about 13 years old, with straight dark hair and black eyes. This girl was lately in New Orleans, and is known to have seen there a man whom she claims as her father and who does now or did lately live on the Mississippi, a little above the mouth of the Caffalaya. It is highly probable some plan has been conserted for the girl's escape. . . ."— *Washington Republican and Natchez Intelligencer*, April 10, 1816.
[7] For instance, Natchez *Mississippi Republican*, Nov. 6, 1821.
[8] *Woodville Republican*, Apr. 28, 1838.
[9] Grenada *Bulletin*, May 5, 1836.

to October than in other months. The largest number of flights occurred in September and June. Coupling these facts with human nature, it may be supposed that another reason why slaves left home
was to avoid the times of greatest work. Certain it is that cold
weather was not looked on with special favor by a prospective runaway. Sleeping in the woods and traveling by night is pleasanter in
warm weather.[10]

Owners of slaves sometimes ventured a guess at the motive of
escape. If we may assume that the majority of them were correct,
many slaves were enticed away from home, sometimes by white
men [11] and sometimes by negroes. Now and then in a dispute over
the ownership of slaves one party acted on the assumption that possession was nine tenths of the law and, to make assurance doubly
sure, he removed the property in question to parts unknown.[12] Most
of those who suspected that their slaves had been stolen simply stated
this belief, and announced the reward offered for the conviction of
the thief. It occasionally appeared that a slave had been stolen so that
his services could be used by the thief.[13] But in most cases the motive for escape was clouded with uncertainty and the owner listed
several causes for leaving, among which robbery was sometimes suggested. This is illustrated in the advertisement of one embittered
master who stated that his slaves, Freeman and Jim, had probably
been seduced "by some rascally white man," and, if not, they were
probably attempting to pass as free negroes as "no doubt there are
individuals who would not hesitate to give them free passes." [14] Another planter believed that a slave who had run away was either under
the protection of a white man or was trying to make his way to a
free State.[15]

A third master believed that both statements could be made of the
same slave. He suspected that his slave was trying to gain permanent liberty, and that he was traveling north in company with the

[10] Dr. J. W. Monette's description of cotton culture in [Ingraham], *Southwest
by a Yankee*, II, 281–291, makes it plain that in the latter part of May and early
June cotton was scraped, and this constituted the first "rush" of the season. In
September and October there was a second period of great pressure when cotton
was being picked. August and January were probably the months of lightest
work.
[11] Natchez *Weekly Chronicle*, Nov. 2, 1808.
[12] *Woodville Republican*, Nov. 26, 1825.
[13] Randall *v.* The State, 12 Miss. 349.
[14] *Woodville Republican*, May 15, 1830.
[15] Vicksburg *Sentinel and Expositor*, Feb. 20, 1844.

abolitionist who had encouraged him to leave home.[16] But the white seducer was not always well disposed toward his fugitive companion. Jim and John were stolen in Petersburg, Georgia, by a man named Green. Six months later they were placed in the Woodville jail, after having left Green in Alabama. They both showed the marks of severe whipping, probably administered by Green.[17]

On March 12, 1856, Warner, a slave of John A. McGill, was given a pass permitting him to go by steamer from McGill's Adams County plantation to St. Joseph, Louisiana. Warner left the plantation, but he did not go to St. Joseph. Instead he went down the river in a skiff, accompanied by George Hamilton, a white clerk who had been working for McGill. The pair traveled to New Orleans, then turned east to Mobile, and eventually reached Richmond, Va. A considerable sum of money that had been intrusted to Warner sufficed to meet their traveling expenses. In Richmond they were captured. It was thought at the time that Hamilton had promised the slave to take him north and there set him free, but that his real scheme was to use Warner and the latter's stolen money until they had reached the Richmond markets, and there fatten his purse by delivering Warner to the slave-traders.[18]

In 1842, the readers of the *Vicksburg Sentinel* were informed that an abolitionist had been captured in the very act of aiding Mississippi slaves to escape. The abolitionist was L. R. Lawrence, alias John Smith, who had been in Vicksburg several weeks, posing as a preacher from Connecticut. Mr. Potterfield, of the firm of Potterfield and Company, found him smuggling three slaves on board a boat bound for Cincinnati. Two of the slaves belonged to Governor Lynch, and the other to Mr. Randolph. When the discovery was noised through Vicksburg the people were highly incensed, but Lawrence was placed safely in jail. His bond was set at $10,000.[19]

Negro-stealing was one of the most serious offenses that could be committed in Mississippi and was punishable with a maximum fine of $300 per slave and a penitentiary sentence of from three to twenty years.[20] Many of the inmates of the State penitentiary had been

<hr>

[16] *Woodville Republican*, June 1, 1839.
[17] *Ibid.*, Oct. 6, 1832.
[18] Hamilton *v.* The State, 35 Miss. 214.
[19] *Woodville Republican*, Feb. 19, 1842, citing the *Vicksburg Sentinel*.
Another case of a white abolitionist endeavoring to aid in the escape of Mississippi slaves is mentioned in William Still, *The Underground Rail Road*, p. 27.
[20] *Revised Code of 1857*, p. 240.

convicted of this crime. Of the twenty-eight persons in the penitentiary in 1841, two had been sentenced for negro-stealing, and each was serving a sentence of ten years. The figures for some other years were as follows: In 1846 there were eighty-nine convicts, eleven of them convicted of negro-stealing; in 1849, the numbers were eighty-six and seventeen respectively; in 1853, 104 and eleven; in 1859, 163 and fifteen.[21]

Apostles of freedom were sometimes black as well as white. Iris, a negro woman, left her master for the probable reason that she could not resist the persuasions of Drew, a fugitive from a neighboring estate.[22] Planters and overseers dreaded a slave with a reputation for running away, not only because of the danger of his escape, but even more because he might persuade others to go with him. By boasting of his exploits he could easily spread discontentment among slaves who were ordinarily satisfied.[23]

In spite of the fact that the majority of slave-owners were men of conscience, there were undoubtedly some who were brutal in dealing with their slaves. And there were just as certainly some slaves who were not only intractable but even dangerous and savage. For one or another of these reasons—and it is seldom possible to distinguish between them—slaves were now and then severely disciplined. In most cases all that is known is that the fugitives bore the marks of the whip, which had sometimes been severely applied.[24] A whipping, or the mere threat of this or another form of punishment, frequently sent the negro to the woods. Rarely, the flight was preceded by a desperate attempt to resist.[25]

One overseer ungrammatically, but graphically, related to the master the circumstances under which several of the slaves ran away.

"Henery had become so indiferent about his duty I was compeld to corect him, he resisted and fought mee I awdred charls to take hold of him being the nearest but refused to dwo so. after Henry and myself had been combatting some time he got loose from mee and got into the swamp wile I was pursuing him, Gilbert, Charls, and Perry was running the other wey.

[21] *Jour. Gen. Assem. of Miss.*, 1848, Sen. Jour. p. 269; *ibid.*, 1853, Sen. Jour., p. 68. *Report of the Mississippi Penitentiary for the Year 1859*, p. 39.

[22] *Woodville Republican*, Feb. 21, 1835.

[23] *Plantation Overseer*, pp. 147, 204, 217.

[24] *Woodville Republican*, Sept. 11, 1830.

[25] The overseer "was whipping the fellow, when he turned and tried to stab him—then broke from him and ran away."—*Back Country*, pp. 47, 79, 83.

the only reason was because they did not take holt of the other boy when awdred." [26]

It is evident that a fugitive slave was the natural product of any friction in plantation management. One negro left home because he had been given twenty-five lashes for pretended sickness.[27] A team of mules got away from another, so the negro ran away because he feared punishment.[28] Gilbert had been stealing, and Addison had killed one of the plantation shoats. Believing that punishment was imminent, they fled.[29] Moses ran away from the plantation of his owner, Mr. Abram N. Scott, immediately after striking the latter's overseer a severe blow with a saw.[30] The culprit took a considerable supply of clothing with him, some of which was probably stolen. A Louisiana slave departed after breaking open a trunk and stealing four hundred dollars in specie together with a considerable amount of clothing, and he added to this offense by taking a good horse to assist in his departure.[31]

For a short time after a strict overseer took charge of a plantation, especially when his predecessor had been lax, there were likely to be a number of runaway slaves. If this condition continued, it was reasonable proof that the overseer was incompetent and could not command his charges without being unmerciful in his punishments.[32] It therefore follows that many of the runaways were caused by the discipline of the plantation. Sometimes the slave deserved punishment, sometimes not, but there were certainly a number of instances of both kinds.

From time to time slaves fled to escape punishment for crimes more serious than assault or theft. In two newspaper notices, the fugitive negro was charged with murder. One was Sampson, who had killed John M. Netterville with a horn-handled dirk-knife.[33] Another negro who was jailed in Woodville gave his name as William, but later admitted that his name was Dave, and that he was the murderer of his master, Charles Carson, in East Feliciana, Louisiana. The jailer added, "there is but little doubt he is the murderer that is

---

[26] *Plantation Overseer*, pp. 146–147.
[27] William Chambers, *American Slavery and Colour*, appendix, p. 202.
[28] Riley, "Diary of a Miss. Planter," in *P. M. H. S.*, X, 442.
[29] *Plantation Overseer*, pp. 113–114, 154.
[30] *Woodville Republican*, Nov. 5, 1825.
[31] *Ibid.*, Apr. 17, 1847.
[32] *Plantation Overseer*, pp. 125, 154.
[33] *Woodville Republican*, Jan. 30, 1836.

advertised in the St. Francisville paper of May 24th." [34] On the day that Dave was apprehended, Lucy was placed in the same jail. She had run away with Dave but does not seem to have been an accomplice in the murder.

Something of the desperate nature of some of the runaways may be gleaned from the following newspaper account. About sundown on an October afternoon, in 1845, Mr. John Lindsey, overseer on the plantation of Mr. A. C. Dunbar, saw a strange negro entering one of the houses in the slave quarters. The overseer stationed two negroes at the door and entered the cabin. Not finding the burglar, he climbed a ladder to a small garret room, saw the fugitive and commanded him to stand still. The slave rushed Lindsey, effectively kept him from using his pistol, and stabbed him above the heart. Lindsey staggered out of the house, directed the servants to pursue the fugitive, and then fell, dying in a few minutes. The newspaper stated that, "the negroes on the plantation could with difficulty be restrained from burning the murderer upon the spot. This shows in what estimation they held Mr. Lindsey." Jim, the murderer, was later hanged. [35]

At least two other causes for absconding remain to be named. A few slaves departed with the direct purpose of gaining their freedom, and these fugitives were especially anxious to cover as much distance as possible before their absence was detected. For this reason they sometimes delayed their start until they had procured a pass authorizing a journey to a neighboring plantation.

If a slave left home with the determination to reach a free State, few avenues of escape were better than the boats that regularly engaged in the river trade. The advantage of boat travel was that the runaway could cover long distances without being seen by many people. Eyes that had read newspaper descriptions of the fugitive would rarely see the negro. In a large number of advertisements threats such as this may be found: "Steamboat captains are hereby forewarned from taking him, as I will enforce the rigor of the law." [36] The constant repetition of such threats in almost all cases where it was thought that the slave was making a break for liberty, [37] and the large fines provided for masters of river craft who gave

[34] Ibid., May 27, 1828.
[35] Ibid., Jan. 10, 1846.
[36] Ibid., Dec. 22, 1838.
[37] For instance, see Natchez Weekly Chronicle, Apr. 23, 1810.

harbor to fugitives,[38] clearly proves the reality of this danger. The fear that the slave was trying to ride to freedom on a steamboat was increased, if the negro was known to have worked on the river,[39] for example, if he had been employed as a cook on a river boat.[40]

Planters frequently thought that permanent freedom was the goal of a slave who was endued with the following characteristics and attainments: intelligence,[41] skill in some trade such as carpentering,[42] superior geographical knowledge,[43] supply of good clothes,[44] and money,[45] the ability to read and write,[46] and a light skin.[47]

The usual objective of a Mississippi slave with freedom as his aim was one of the northern States,[48] particularly Ohio.[49] However, there were other destinations. A place of refuge might be sought in an Indian tribe.[50] New Orleans, with its large number of free negroes, was a cave of Adullam. For a time, in the 'twenties and 'thirties, Texas and Mexico had some attractions. There was an account in the *Republican* of a gang of men who were regularly engaged in smuggling slaves across the Sabine River into Mexico. It was reported that an organization, extending as far as Alabama, conveyed slaves to the grand depot on the Sabine.[51] One man, John Hayes, was killed in Louisiana while conducting toward Mexico three slaves whom he had stolen in Concordia Parish.[52]

It sometimes happened that a fugitive would not try to leave the State, but would attempt to establish his identity as a free negro and remain in the South. His success in doing this usually depended

[38] *Hutchinson's Code*, p. 533.
[39] *Woodville Republican*, June 11, 1831.
[40] *Ibid.*, Sept. 5, 1840.
[41] *Ibid.*, May 11, 1824; July 8, 1826; June 11, 1831.
[42] *Ibid.*, May 26, 1829; June 11, 1831.
[43] *Ibid.*, Dec. 29, 1838.
[44] *Ibid.*, June 11, 1831; May 26, 1829; July 7, 1832.
[45] *Ibid.*, Dec. 29, 1838.
[46] *Ibid.*, Mar. 17, 1842; Aug. 10, 1833; May 26, 1829; July 24, 1841.
[47] *Washington Republican and Natchez Intelligencer*, April 16, 1816. *Woodville Republican*, Dec. 22, 1827; April 4, 1829; July 7, 1832; June 22, 1844.
[48] *Plantation Overseer*, p. 147.
[49] For an instance of a Mississippi slave who reached Ohio, and ultimately Canada, see *American Slavery and Colour*, appendix, p. 202.
[50] For instance, the Cherokees.—Vicksburg *Sentinel and Expositor*, Feb. 20, 1844. The State law requiring Indian agents to assist in the rendition of fugitive slaves also implies that slaves had sometimes found refuge among the Indians. *Laws of Miss.*, 1819, pp. 70–71.
[51] *Woodville Republican*, Nov. 5, 1825.
[52] *Ibid.*, Sept. 15, 1832.

on the acquisition of a free pass and on avoidance of any one who might recognize him. Since the procurement of a pass or certificate of freedom was attended with certain conditions that a runaway could not fulfill, this document could only be secured in some illegal way. A literate slave might try his hand at writing one himself, as a negro bricklayer once did.[53] Another fugitive, Allen, was suspected of having a free pass for he had run away before and when captured had a pass in his possession. Possibly Allen could manufacture a certificate of freedom for he could read imperfectly, could make a short calculation correctly, and could write a few words.[54] On the other hand the need might be filled in the way feared by Matthew N. Brandon, who announced the escape of his slave William, and stated that he might claim to be free and "get some person to write him a free pass, as he is a very bright mulatto." [55] If no better avenue were open, the fugitive might steal the papers of a *bona fide* free negro, a procedure followed by a fugitive from Aaron Burr's friend, Harman Blennerhassett.[56]

The troubles of the fugitive were far from over when the certificate was secured. One negro secured, we know not how, a certificate of freedom. But he could not read and either forgot or had never been informed of the name that was written on the paper in his possession. When he was challenged he gave his own name, which did not tally with the name written on the certificate. He was, of course, taken to jail.[57]

There was an interesting newspaper story of a Mississippi slave who sought to change his status from slavery to freedom and yet remain in the State. A Mr. Rogers, of Madison County, journeyed to the neighboring town of Manchester on business, and there he happened to find a slave who had recently escaped from his brother. When he apprehended the negro, the latter presented his certificate of freedom which was in good form in every particular with one glaring exception. The whole thing was printed, including the name of the slave, his description, and the date. It was, therefore, very

[53] *Ibid.*, Aug. 27, 1836.
[54] Harriet Beecher Stowe, *The Key to Uncle Tom's Cabin*, p. 359, citing Natchez *Free Trader*, Nov. 6, 1852.
[55] *Woodville Republican*, Apr. 4, 1829.
[56] *Washington Republican and Natchez Intelligencer*, April 17, 1816. An earlier notice of the escape of slaves from "La Cache" appeared in the Natchez *Weekly Chronicle*, April 23, 1810.
[57] *Woodville Republican*, Mar. 5, 1836.

clearly a forgery. Several months later the father of the two brothers, one of whom was the owner and the other the finder of the slave, was riding in the canebrake near his home looking for some cattle. He chanced upon a pile of blankets lying on the ground. Upon investigating he also discovered a copy of the Mississippi *Digest* and a tin box of type. In this box was the very form from which had been printed the pass that was in the possession of this fugitive negro. The writer of the newspaper article ventured the guess that the miniature press was operated by a negro.[58]

Many, possibly most, of the runaway slaves left for no outstanding reason. As one overseer expressed it, Alfonso "toke a notion to ran away a few days ago."[59] The irksomeness of regular and compulsory work, coupled with the call of the road, created a temptation that was occasionally irresistible. In spite of almost certain capture, followed by very probable punishment, running away was a regular part of the life of some slaves. Planters looked upon it almost as though it were a disease. If a slave established a reputation as a fugitive, his market value would greatly decrease. This is illustrated by the few facts known concerning the career of Jacob. He escaped from his master in Texas and made his way to Mississippi before he was taken up as a runaway. After being in jail for six months without being claimed, he was sold at public auction as the law required. Within four days he escaped from his purchaser. Some months later Jacob's former Texas owner made his appearance. Though his negro had been sold and was again a fugitive, he received, as provided by law, the money secured at the auction of the slave, after first deducting jail and other fees. The county treasurer delivered to him $186.91. It is difficult to account for such a small price for a young and able-bodied slave except on the ground that he had already had quite a career as a runaway.[60]

A few of the negroes who were jailed as runaway slaves claimed to be free. Whether they stated the truth we cannot, in most cases,

[58] *Ibid.*, May 30, 1835.
[59] *Plantation Overseer*, p. 218.
[60] *Woodville Republican*, Mar. 14, Oct. 17, Nov. 21, 1840; April 3, 1841.
In the *Laws of Miss.*, 1828, p. 96, there is mentioned a fugitive slave who was sold for $113.97, plus the costs of his stay in jail and the bill for advertising the negro. A negro boy was sold in Mississippi for $1,000. He had been imported and sold because he was a runaway; when the latter fact was known his value decreased to $500 or $600.—Noel *et al. v.* Wheatly, 30 Miss. 181.

tell at this late date. They may easily have been slaves who boldly claimed freedom, hoping that the story would be believed. An additional advantage was gained by such a bluff; the slave would not have to state the name of his master, and the latter would, therefore, have more difficulty in tracing and regaining his servant. But sometimes the slave broke down, possibly under pressure, and gave the name of his owner.[61] A *bona fide* free negro was, of course, liable to arrest unless he had with him at all times his certificate of freedom, and the presumption was that a negro without the certificate was a slave. A free negro was occasionally arrested, either without the certificate or because of the suspicion that the paper was forged or stolen. There may have been cases where this resulted in the permanent enslavement of the captive. There was certainly one free negro who was jailed as a fugitive and sold into slavery, but he afterward recovered his freedom by a judgment given by the county circuit court, and the purchaser of the negro was presumably refunded the purchase price.[62]

There was no unanimity of aim among the fugitives in regard to the locality they were trying to reach. Many were endeavoring to return to their old homes, but usually the only purpose was to avoid places where they would be recognized and apprehended. There were men near the river who made their living cutting wood to be burned on the steamboats. These men were sometimes willing to give refuge and employment to a runaway in return for the work he would do with an ax. An owner who had at least heard of this situation, if he had not indeed suffered from it himself, appended to an advertisement of a runaway slave a warning to captains of steamboats and other river craft not to harbor or assist this negro to escape. The warning was addressed "particularly to wood-choppers, who unfortunately for slaveholders," often helped and employed this class.[68] Another planter stated that one of his slaves had been employed for two months by a wood-chopper who was located on the bank of the Mississippi about five miles below Fort Adams.[64] Many of the wood-cutters were North-country men, particularly from the western part

[61] *Woodville Republican*, June 23, 1832.
[62] *Laws of Miss.*, 1828, p. 96.
   For other instances of the arrest of negroes who claimed to be free see, *Woodville Republican*, Sept. 22, 1827; Dec. 22, 1838; Sept. 19, 1835.
[68] *Woodville Republican*, June 11, 1831.
[64] *Ibid.*, July 23, 1836.

of Michigan.[65] They had no interest in or sympathy for slavery, and so did not feel constrained to assist in returning fugitives to their masters.

The average runaway seems to have taken nothing with him in his excursion into the broad world except the clothes on his back. Though an occasional negro had a small reserve, as Celia, who had a bundle containing a calico dress and a blanket,[66] there were just as many who were not adequately clad for the weather. In fact the jailer of a fugitive who was apprehended in February stated that the negro "had on scarcely any clothing at all, but rags." [67] Of another negro, named George, the following statement was made. He has a "small spot on the left side of his face that is blacker than the other skin, but he may be called right black, . . . he may be said to be almost naked, so much so that I can't describe his dress." [68] On the other hand, the worthy jailer was well insured against blushes by the superabundant clothing of a good number of runaways. One young slave by the name of William had his six-foot frame clad in two shirts, two pair of trousers, and a coat.[69] Ordinarily, an unusually plentiful supply of clothing in the possession of a fugitive signified one of two things: Either the negro had been doing a grade of work somewhat higher than that of a field hand, such as laboring as a tanner,[70] a carriage-driver, or a mechanic; or else his stock of clothes had been suddenly and illegally increased before departing by purloining some of the garments of his master. The resulting array was at times very impressive. One would hardly expect a fugitive to travel in a black fur hat, blue dress coat, and white trousers, but this was the clothing of one runaway who was reported traveling at night.[71] This outfit was mild though when compared with that of Isaac, who was "an arch cunning fellow." He left his master, in 1824, with the following collection of clothing and accouterments. On the eve of his departure he wore a fur hat, an old ruffled shirt, a snuff-colored surtout coat, a red and white striped marseilles vest, a pair

[65] Phillips, *Life and Labor in the Old South*, p. 339, citing, Tyrone Power, *Impressions of America*, II, 118.
[66] *Woodville Republican*, Dec. 1, 1838.
[67] *Ibid.*, Feb. 5, 1841.
[68] *Ibid.*, July 21, 1829.
[69] *Ibid.*, Sept. 10, 1825.
[70] *Ibid.*, Sept. 28, 1833.
[71] *Ibid.*, July 14, 1832.

of yellow nankeen pantaloons, and a pair of new boots with brass heels. As a reserve, Isaac carried certain possessions of his master, namely: a pair of white jean pantaloons, a silk handkerchief, a French gold watch, a double-barrelled pistol of brass, a dirk with a red morocco scabbard (silver mounted), a pocket book containing a five and a twenty dollar bill on the Mississippi Bank, and $3.37½ in cash, together with a parcel of notes, accounts and such things to the amount of four or five hundred dollars.[72]

A somewhat less imposing array of stolen property was taken by John and Warriner who escaped from a Hinds County plantation. What they lacked in the splendor of their outfit was more than equaled by the desperate way in which they burned their bridges behind them. Just before departing they robbed the United States mail while the mail-rider was eating his supper. The culprits escaped on two stolen horses, both fully equipped with saddles, saddle-bags, and bridles. They also took a frock coat, two cloaks, two or three close-bodied vests, two new white beaver hats, a valuable silver patent lever Liverpool watch with a steel chain, and a gold key and seal. Both negroes were able to read and write.[73]

A small number of runaways left home on stolen horses, and a good many took stolen clothing, but the large majority had nothing except the garments in which they were clothed. It is probable that many carried with them some food, but this is only a surmise. There was little point in describing the food in the possession of a runaway, since it would not be valuable in establishing his identity. It would soon be eaten and the stock replenished in devious ways. At any rate, the only mention of food in these musty advertisements is the statement that a fugitive named Peter had a wallet with nothing in it but some provisions.[74] Several runaways carried firearms with them,[75] and one, for some unknown reason, unless in anticipation of a long period of freedom, took a mosquito bar.[76] He absconded in March. Another "had also a spelling book with him, and says he can read."[77] One dark-skinned troubadour carried his violin to cheer his journey and had an audience with him in the person of Nancy, also

---

[72] Ibid., June 29, 1824.
[73] Ibid., Nov. 17, 1827.
[74] Ibid., July 9, 1831.
[75] Ibid., Nov. 1, 1845.
[76] Ibid., Mar. 27, 1847.
[77] Ibid., Apr. 6, 1844.

a runaway, who was some ten years his senior.[78] Several other fugitives were identified by their ability to play on the violin. One of these was left-handed.[79] This means of identification, by the way, suggests that the fugitive's life in jail was not always unpleasant for these advertisements were written by the sheriff. We might well imagine that the custodians of the county jail would regret having a good musician taken from their care.

Very little was said in old newspaper notices of the life of a runaway while he was at large. Neither was there any comment on the relationship between fugitives and slaves who were still at their places. In a few cases, the time the slave was at large was indicated. Several times this amounted to six months and once to a whole year.[80] There was a notice of one fugitive by the name of Henry, who climbed a thorn tree, possibly to spend the night there, and in falling out lacerated his neck badly. The wounds healed, but the scars were evident when he was jailed some time later.[81]

From sources other than newspaper files some information can be assembled on the life of fugitives. A few were, of course, making the best time they were able, on foot or by any other means of transportation, toward friends in other places or in the direction in which freedom was thought to reside. Most of the runaways, however, stayed close to the plantation. At night they often slipped back to the quarters to receive food from their fellow slaves, and occasionally they spent the night in their own cabins. Most of the time they were in the woods or swamps close to the plantation. Doubtless they frequently watched their fellows toiling while they lolled in the shade near the edge of the forest.[82] It was best to stay near friends for the fugitive could expect no help from strangers. Whether slave or free negro, Indian or white man, any person who harbored a fugitive slave was liable to severe punishment.[83]

According to the overseers of the time, most of the runaways were back at work within two weeks after the time they left. They were, of course, welcomed by a whipping.[84] Experienced managers of slaves

[78] *Ibid.*, June 23, 1838.
[79] *Ibid.*, Mar. 19, 1831.
[80] *Ibid.*, July 21, 1829. Also, Randall *v.* The State, 12 Miss. 349.
[81] *Woodville Republican*, Apr. 28, 1832.
[82] *Back Country*, pp. 48, 79.
[83] *Hutchinson's Code*, p. 537.
[84] *Back Country*, pp. 79, 87.

were accustomed to runaways, were usually confident that they were in the neighborhood, and used various means to regain control over them. One overseer stated that, if many negroes escaped or if they stayed out too long, he could always bring them in by putting pressure on those who were at work. By cutting off their privileges or increasing their work, he would compel them to stop giving food to the runaways who would then soon come in;[85] or he would watch for tracks about the quarters and so get a fresh trail for the dogs to follow.[86]

It is very probable that a runaway could venture into a town on certain days with little risk of detection. At any rate, the constant repetition of laws prohibiting slaves from coming to town on Sunday and of articles protesting against "the intolerable pest of having our streets filled up with trading carts and noisy and drunken negroes on the Sabbath," suggests that on Sundays and holidays there was scarcely any enforcement of the regulations against negroes frequenting the town on those days. It may be that runaways could mingle in the large numbers of slaves with comparatively little danger of being recognized.

In their wanderings, runaway slaves sometimes traveled and camped in gangs, usually small. The fact that occasional groups of four or five ran away together would indicate this, and a patrol was once or twice notified that a camp of fugitives was located at a certain spot. One such group had two horses in their possession.[87] However, no instance has been found of a large number of slaves taking flight together, or later forming a large group to travel together. In 1830, there was a rumor of a proposed slave insurrection, particularly in Jefferson County, to be followed by a migration of all the slaves eastward to the sea coast, from whence they hoped somehow to get passage to Africa.[88] There was a slight increase in the number of runaways about this time, but generally speaking, there seems to have been no attempt of a large number of slaves to escape together. Fugitives usually departed alone and the largest group that has been noted contained only six runaways.[89]

The technique of advertising and capturing runaway slaves deserves some attention. Only twice were bloodhounds mentioned in

[85] *Ibid.*, p. 88.
[86] *Ibid.*, p. 48.
[87] *Woodville Republican*, Apr. 18, 1840; Oct. 6, 1829.
[88] *Ibid.*, Dec. 25, 1830.
[89] *Ibid.*, Dec. 15, 1827.

the *Republican* in the course of twenty-five years, though, of course, this does not prove that they were rarely used. In one of the instances mentioned a slave who had murdered his overseer escaped. He was pursued with dogs and captured.[90] The other mention of dogs is in the following advertisement. "A situation wanted, as overseer and manager of plantation affairs by a young man capable every way of managing the same, and who has a pack of negro dogs well trained, and is enabled thereby to keep negroes at their places." [91] It might be remarked that this advertisement was regularly printed from December until the end of the following April, and it does not seem probable that the applicant found a position, since most overseers were employed before the first of the year.

There was little reason to mention bloodhounds in the newspapers. On the other hand, several of the overseers interviewed by Olmsted mentioned in a matter-of-fact way that dogs were successfully used in trailing fugitives. Sometimes, however, an experienced fugitive outwitted the hounds, and rain obliterated the trail.[92] Professional slave-catchers with specially trained dogs could be found in different parts of the State.[93] A slave-owner, who lived near Port Gibson, made the following entries in his diary:

August 28, 1861, "Alick run away last night, tracked him to Center Creek & would have caught him with the Dogs if a very heavy rain had not followed, thereby making it difficult for them to trail."

April 19, 1862, "J. Willis, J. W. Andrews & myself with Mack Mitchell & his dogs spent all day hunting Willis' Negro Henderson, but did not succeed in catching him."

April 7, 1863, "Started before day with Ritchers dogs in hunt of negroes, staying out until one o'clock, but did not catch any one." [94]

Several runaway slaves were found in trees. Though dogs were not on their trails at these times, it may be that earlier experiences had taught them the advantage of climbing a tree when capture seemed imminent.[95]

[90] *Ibid.*, Jan. 24, 1846.
[91] *Ibid.*, Dec. 19, 1846.
[92] *Back Country*, pp. 47–48. "Diary of a Miss. Planter," in *P. M. H. S.*, X, 433.
[93] Venable, "Down South before the War," in *Ohio Archæological and Historical Quarterly*, II, 502. *Woodville Republican*, Jan. 24, 1846. Carroll, *Oktibbeha County*, p. 87.
[94] Diary of Spooner Forbes, MS.
[95] Randall *v.* The State, 12 Miss. 349. *Back Country*, pp. 186–187. *American Slavery and Colour*, appendix, p. 202.

Ordinarily, the owner of a fugitive who had been at large for some time placed an advertisement in the newspapers. On the basis of such a description the runaway was sometimes recognized and taken into custody. However, there were many whose names were never printed. Bloodhounds and newspaper advertisements aided in capturing only part of the fugitives. Many were apprehended by private citizens and some by the patrols. It was the duty of the latter to seize fugitives found in the course of its duties, though it was not ordinarily expected to go in search of them. Those serving on a patrol were legally obligated but little more than any other citizen to seize fugitives, for any person was legally empowered to do this,[96] and either commit them to jail or send them to the owner. While the laws of the State gave all persons this power, the supreme court in 1845 indicated that this law went further than the mere bestowal of a privilege, for the court stated: "It is the duty of every good citizen, who finds a slave at large, without a permit from his owner, . . . to deliver him to the nearest justice of the peace, for commitment." [97]

As large areas of the State were for many years possessed by the Indians, Indian agents were required to act as jailers of any fugitive slaves captured in their territory. The owner was required to pay the agent $30 to redeem each, one half to be given as a reward to the person who seized the slave, the other half to be used by the agent in building a jail, purchasing irons, or securing other equipment useful in guarding runaway slaves.[98] Keepers of ferries and toll bridges also were ordered not to let slaves pass without written permission,[99] and the fact that these men sometimes had stocks for holding prisoners indicates that they expected to do their duty.[100]

No general rules can be given that will cover the ways most of the runaways were taken. The brains of the white population and of the loyal blacks were matched against the cunning of the fugitives, and examples will best show how runaways were captured.

A negro boy, Charles, ran away from the Mississippi plantation of President Polk. The overseer and others who desired his return communicated with each other and hurriedly reconstructed the past life of the negro: the places where he had lived, to whom he had been hired, where his relatives labored, and other facts that might afford

[96] *Hutchinson's Code*, pp. 517–518.
[97] Randall *v.* The State, 12 Miss. 349. Thompson *v.* Young, 30 Miss. 17.
[98] *Laws of Miss.*, 1819, pp. 70–71.
[99] *Hutchinson's Code*, p. 519.
[100] *Back Country*, pp. 29–30.

reasonable guesses as to where the boy had gone. Letters were written, or trips made, to these places, and a net was thus spread to secure his return.[101]

Henry, Perry, and two other negroes fled at another time from the same estate. They left hurriedly, after disobeying the overseer, who thereupon tried to fathom the probable moves they would make. "I concluded that henry wold try to get his cloths while I was weying cotton at night got a cople of men to watch for him while watching for him Perry was slipping up and was awderd to stand but he broke and he shot him in the legs with smawl shot sow I got him, and he is at work." [102]

A planter met a slave with a jug in his hand riding horseback toward Natchez. Suspecting the negro of being a runaway, he demanded his pass. The slave, after a brief search, said he had lost it. On being asked the name of his master, he made a ready answer. Just at that moment the questioner recognized the brand on the horse and exclaimed, "You are a runaway, boy—you belong to Mr. D——." The slave leaped from his horse, cleared the fence, and fled through the woods toward home. The questioner sent the horse, deserted by the runaway, home by one of his own servants. The master of the runaway, as soon as he was appraised of the matter, at once assembled his slaves. All were there, the fugitive having already returned to his place. After trying for some time to make the guilty one confess, he ordered the entire force to march with him over to the home of his neighbor who could single out the runaway. After a short distance had been covered, he stopped the line of slaves and told them that their long walk was caused by the runaway who refused to confess, and that when he was pointed out, he would let them help punish the culprit. Shortly after the march was resumed the runaway stepped forward and admitted his guilt.[103]

After a runaway was captured, there still remained the problem of taking him to jail or to the owner. Sometimes he went docilely enough; sometimes he fled as was told in the last paragraph. Frequently he was put in irons.[104]

Another man, traveling toward Natchez, overtook a runaway whom he ordered to come with him as he went toward the city. This

---

[101] *Plantation Overseer*, pp. 131–132.
[102] *Ibid.*, pp. 146–147.
[103] *Southwest by a Yankee*, II, 130–131.
[104] *Back Country*, p. 48. *Plantation Overseer*, p. 215.

the negro did. But when they came to a thicket about six miles from Natchez, he refused to go farther. The white man threatened to shoot the slave but evidently showed no gun. The negro bolted into the thicket and escaped, doubtless proud of having outwitted the white man, who should not have given such good evidence that he was not armed.[105]

North of Woodville the public road followed a ridge beneath which were low lands extending to the Mississippi River. The place used to be notorious for the robberies that had been committed there, and it was well suited for lawless work, since escape was easy and pursuit was difficult. North of this spot Mr. Allen once caught a runaway,

". . . and started to take him to Woodville to the jail. He put him in irons and carried him along in his waggin. The nigger was peaceable and submissive till they got along onto that yer ridge place. When they got thar, all of a sudden he gin a whop like and over he went twenty foot plum down the side of the ridge. 'Fore Allen could stop his hoss he'd tumbled and rolled himself 'way out of sight. He started right away arter him, but he never cotched a sight on him agin." [106]

Several runaways were apprehended by negroes. In the notice of the commitment to jail of Davey is the brief statement that he was delivered by Stephen Johnson, a negro man. A fuller account is given of the capture of Jim, who had escaped from a negro-trader. Jim came to Colonel Wade Hampton's negroes where they were camped not far from the Louisiana line. A negro driver, who was in charge of the camp of slaves, had Jim seized and brought to jail.[107] Ingraham tells several anecdotes of the capture of fugitives by other slaves. From these stories one gathers that the capture was generally made under the special order of a white person or by a negro who was in a responsible position.[108]

A few attempts to capture runaways ended in tragedies. One of these is briefly recorded in a newspaper notice.

[105] *Back Country*, pp. 30–31.
[106] *Ibid.*, p. 18.
[107] *Woodville Republican*, Jan. 26, 1832.
    In Newell *v.* Cowan *et ux.*, 30 Miss. 492, the story is told of the attempted capture of a slave by the negroes of a neighboring estate on which the slave had trespassed.
[108] *Southwest by a Yankee*, II, 261–263. Ingraham, ed., *Sunny South*, pp. 86–87.

"INFORMATION"

"On Monday night last, the patrol for this beat received information that there was a gang of runaway negroes encamped about two miles from the village of Pinkneyville. They immediately went in search of them, and in attempting to secure them, one negro fellow was shot and mortally wounded —he stated that his name was John Williams, and that he belonged to a Mr. Cormic, or Comic, who lives with a Mr. Williams, residing about fifty miles above New Orleans. The negro is since dead—he is supposed to have been 25 or 28 years old; 5 feet 7 or 8 inches high; spoke the French and English languages, and had a scar on his shoulder, supposed to have been made by a gun shot wound." [109]

The Supreme Court of Mississippi heard the story of the killing of another fugitive slave. One night a Mr. Thompson discovered a runaway prowling about his premises. He attempted to arrest the slave, who was armed with a large knife and club. When the fugitive refused to surrender, Thompson shot and killed him. The owner of the slave brought suit and the courts ordered Thompson to pay for the slave. In giving its decision, the supreme court held that it was illegal to kill a fugitive who was trying to escape, unless he menaced the life of the captor. It was not proved to the satisfaction of the court that Thompson was in this danger.[110]

Although captured runaways were ordinarily placed in jail, a few were retained by those who found them. Four cases of this kind were mentioned in the *Woodville Republican*.[111] In two of these no explanation was given. One negro was in private hands because there was no jail in the county.[112] Another was too sick to be sent to jail.[113] The latter slave, by the way, had been stolen near Nashville, Tennessee, brought to Natchez on a flatboat, and was there left to shift for himself, presumably because his sickness made him a burden to his new and dishonest owner. None of these fugitives who remained in private hands seem to have been kept under any duress. One man stated that the negro temporarily in his care was being

[109] *Woodville Republican*, Oct. 6, 1829.
[110] Thompson v. Young, 30 Miss. 17.
[111] *Woodville Republican*, Nov. 12, 1825; June 24, 1826; July 21, 1827; Oct. 3, 1835.
[112] *Ibid.*, Nov. 12, 1825.
[113] *Ibid.*, Oct. 3, 1835.

allowed to run at large, and another of the four announced that, if the negro, John, was not claimed in six weeks or two months, he would be placed in the county jail for safe keeping.

Another case of a slave's not being sent at once to jail is recounted by Olmsted. A man in southwest Mississippi apprehended a runaway, but, on the advice of a physician, he did not send the slave to jail because yellow fever was raging there. The negro soon escaped but was later recaptured. His owner, learning of the first capture and escape, was very angry. He informed this person that he should have obeyed the law and not followed his judgment, and sternly counseled him always to send fugitives to jail regardless of the probable consequences.[114] This was a correct view of the law, for the captor of a runaway must deliver him at once either to his owner or to a justice of the peace who would commit him to jail.[115]

Little can be written about the immediate delivery of slaves to their owners. Doubtless they usually suffered at the hands of the law of the plantation, but the laws of the State had no further application. On the other hand, there was yet much to be done after a justice of the peace committed a fugitive to jail.[116] After confining the negro, the jailer prepared for the newspapers an advertisement containing such information as would enable the owner to recognize his slave.[117] Also, it was the jailer's duty to elicit from the fugitive the name of his master and then to write to this individual. If the outcome of this attempt to communicate with the owner indicated that the negro had not been truthful, he was given twenty-five lashes. This would presumably extort another name and address to which the jailer would send another letter. Letters and floggings alternated until the owner was located, or until six months had elapsed. At the end of six months, the law required that the slave be sold at public auction, proper notice of the time and place having previously been given through the papers. With some exceptions,[118] funds secured from the sale of unclaimed fugitives reverted to the county treasurer, after all costs, such as jail fees and printer's bills for advertising, had been

---

[114] *Back Country*, pp. 29–30.
[115] *Hutchinson's Code*, pp. 517–518. *Laws of Miss.*, 1850, p. 229.
[116] *Hutchinson's Code*, pp. 517–518.
[117] Some years later it became the duty of the sheriff to forward notices of runaway slaves to the public printers of the State.—*Ibid.*, p. 537, law of Feb. 16, 1839.
[118] Shelton *v.* Baldwin *et al.*, 26 Miss. 439.

deducted.[119] If the owner later appeared and proved his claims, he was reimbursed.[120]

Jails were also used by slave-owners, if a slave was suspected of scheming to escape. The following entries copied from the diary of a master need no comment. The dates, except for the last, were in March, 1860.

11. first discovery of Ellicks design to run away; could not find him at night.
12. Come to the conclusion to put Ellick in Jail for safe Keeping & sell him the first chance.
13. Got him & put him in Jail.
14. gave Ellick a severe whipping, but only learned from him his design to run away.
15. did not visit Ellick today & I find he has not told me the truth in any particular.
16. came in at 5 o'clock visited Ellick & whipped him, learned nothing further from him.
20. Come to the conclusion to try Ellick again.
21. Took Ellick out of Jail & sent him out to Place. Am afraid he will run away at last.

On May 8, 1863, there is the following:

Jake & Ellick both gone off with the Yankees. expect to see them again when we whip the Yankees at Vicksburg(?) [121]

Occasionally a slave escaped from one of the jails in the State, which was in some cases not a difficult feat. After describing a fugitive, a sheriff once added that the negro was in the "Jail of Wilkinson County, Mississippi, which is very insecure, and the owner is requested to call for said negro, as the building is unfit to receive negroes as a Public Jail, and I cannot be responsible for an escape." [122]

While most of the runaways were held in county jails, a few were kept in the State penitentiary. In the fiscal year ending November 27, 1843, this institution earned for the state $102.60 by keeping runaway slaves.[123] Also, runaway slaves in the incorporated

[119] The total printer's bill for advertising James, an unclaimed fugitive, sold in Amite County, in 1831, was $34.00.—*Woodville Republican*, Apr. 30, 1831.
[120] *Hutchinson's Code*, pp. 517–518, 530. *Laws of Miss.*, 1828, p. 96. This is briefly summarized in *Southwest by a Yankee*, II, 189–190.
[121] Diary of Spooner Forbes, MS.
[122] *Woodville Republican*, Aug. 27, 1836.
[123] *Jour. Gen. Assem. of Miss.*, 1842–1843, Sen. Jour., p. 271.

towns of the State could be removed from jail and used on public works. In 1829, five years after the passage of the law permitting this, it was enacted that a ball and chain should be attached to the fugitive being used on public works or that some other device be used which would best unite security and humanity.[124] The law was further amended, in 1846, by the specific statement that runaway slaves must not be used on any private work.[125] We are told by a person of that time that, while riding through Natchez,

". . . a sudden clanking of chains, startled our horses, and the next instant a gang of negroes, in straggling procession, followed by an ordinary looking white man armed with a whip, emerged from one of the streets. Each negro carried slung over his shoulder a polished iron ball, apparently a twenty-four pounder, suspended by a heavy ox chain five or six feet in length and secured to the right ancle by a massive ring." [126]

Some of the officers of the law owned farms or small cotton plantations. When work was behind in their fields, they must have looked with longing eyes at the runaway slaves who were loafing their hours away in jail, waiting for the owner to come and claim them. A deputy sheriff in Madison County found the temptation too great. Almost a dozen negroes were in jail. The sheriff did not expect them to be taken out for nearly a year, for in this instance the negroes were not runaways, but were being held pending the settlement of a suit. The deputy concluded that the jail was a bad and unsafe place to keep slaves. All of them might die there. Humanity and self-interest were both served, so the deputy reasoned, by placing the prisoners in the field with his own slaves to cultivate his cotton and corn.[127]

One noticeable feature of advertisements concerning fugitive negroes was the heedless attitude of the average owner toward the escape of one of his slaves. Often the negro was at large several months before a notice was placed in the paper. Sometimes a planter waited until several of his negroes ran away before using the lost and found column. The reward for the return of the slaves was comparatively low. The rates, on the average, were as follows: For the capture and commitment of a runaway to the nearest jail, or for

[124] *Hutchinson's Code,* p. 531.
[125] *Ibid.,* p. 541.
[126] *Southwest by a Yankee,* II, 185–190.
[127] Garrett *v.* Hamblin, 19 Miss. 219.

holding him until the owner could send for him, ten dollars was the reward. Usually fifteen or twenty dollars was offered for the return of a fugitive to the owner, thereby saving the expense of going after or sending for the negro and of paying jail fees. It was customary to offer more for the apprehension of a slave who had fled a long distance, especially if he had entered another State. There was some increase in the reward, if the slave was unusually well qualified to make a successful attempt to gain his freedom. Likewise, the reward often amounted to several hundred dollars, if the fugitive was accused of theft or murder, if he was supposed to be traveling under the protection of a white man,[128] or if he had escaped from a trustee.[129] These things seem to show that flight of slaves did not greatly disturb the equanimity of most owners. In only a few cases did their anxiety break through the crust of advertising formality.

Newspaper advertisements constitute one of the chief sources of information concerning fugitive slaves. Though these notices were usually of scant length and leave untold much that we would like to know, they have one great asset as historical material. They are not biased. Here was no case of attacking or defending the institution of slavery. If your slave took French leave, several hundred dollars' worth of your property was gone. The owner would, therefore, write as accurate a description as possible and publish it. Likewise, when a runaway was apprehended and placed in the hands of the sheriff, as has been pointed out, it was the officer's legal duty to publish such information as would lead the owner to recognize his property. And so we have dispassionate statements concerning motives for escape, clothing, punishments, and other things pertaining to fugitive slaves, and, withal, uncolored by any attempt to extol or attack the system of slavery. There was no incentive to paint conditions in bright colors, for whatever was written was primarily for the eyes of other slave-owners.

So far as newspaper material is concerned, chief reliance has been placed on the *Woodville Republican*. Though other newspapers of the State were consulted, it seemed best to make an exhaustive study of at least one file, in order that a few statistical results could be marshaled. The *Republican* was chosen because it was available in a file that is reasonably complete over a period of twenty-five years.[130]

[128] Natchez *Weekly Chronicle*, Nov. 2, 1808.
[129] Vicksburg *Sentinel and Expositor*, Feb. 20, 1844.
[130] The *Woodville Republican* is the second oldest newspaper in the State of

Advertisements for runaway negroes in the *Woodville Republican* were usually accompanied by a small cut of a slave in the process of absconding. A stock of six cuts, three of men and three of women, was added to the equipment of the paper about eighteen months after its establishment.[181] These were used with great punctiliousness in practically all announcements concerning fugitives, and to some extent in notices concerning sales of slaves. Now and then an advertisement of a runaway negro man was accompanied by a cut representing a negro woman, but this never happened unless there were not enough cuts of men to go around. Since very many more men absconded than women, the paper soon purchased engravings of two more runaway men. Finally, in 1831,[182] four new cuts of men were added. These four were all alike and represented a rather portly and prosperous slave executing a dignified departure.

In the advertisements that were placed in the paper by either the loser or the finder of the slave, it was essential to give information that would lead to the return of the slave to his owner. In practically all cases there was a description of the slave's clothes, height, weight, age, and the name of the master. A number of captured slaves concealed their owners' names and gave fictitious ones instead. In several instances an advertisement that had appeared regularly for some time was changed by having a different name inserted as that of the owner. Once or twice the jailer commented that the change was made after the fugitive had been whipped.[183] Occasionally a slave preferred the floggings of the jailer to divulging the name of his owner. This was true of Dennis. After he had been unclaimed for six months the sheriff gave notice that he would be sold at public auction, for "No other information respecting his owner can be got from him by chastisement or otherwise." [184]

In descriptions of fugitives, any individual peculiarities were noted. Most of these can be grouped under the heads of general appearance, scars, iron rings attached to the body of the slave, man-

Mississippi, beginning its life in December, 1823. From this date the paper was examined through the year 1848 with the exception of the file for 1834. Woodville is the county seat of Wilkinson County, which is situated in the extreme southwestern corner of the State.

[181] *Woodville Republican*, May 21, 1825.

[182] *Ibid.*, Jan. 8, 1831.

[183] This can be observed by tracing the advertisements concerning Lewis, appearing in *ibid.* from June 10 through Dec. 9, 1836.

[184] *Ibid.*, Apr. 22, 1826.

nerisms in talking, and the ability to speak any other language than
English.

To illustrate a few of these points, the jailer said that one fugitive
had a "mulattoish complexion." [185] He remarked that another was
equipped "with mustache on chin." [186] The youngest recorded runaway was fourteen years old. As a distinguishing trait it was said
that he "appears to be easily frightened or scared." [187] If the slave
was unusually handsome or "remarkably ugly" [188] the fact was usually
stated. One runaway had "remarkable large blue eyes." [189] In 1805,
Mr. Thomas M. Green stated that his fugitive negro, Moses, was "of
a rusty black complection, spare made, knock-kneed, lanthorn-jawed,
large scattered eyebrows, weak voice, . . ." He added that Moses
"probably will show to a stranger a pleasant countenance"! [140] Some
years later the reader of Mississippi newspapers was asked to be on
the watch for Daniel, a "well set, hardy villain" who was bow-legged,
sparrow-toed, and minus a small piece from the end of his thumb.[141]
A number of fugitives were identified by scars and several by having had their ears pierced for rings.[142] While many of the scars were
the results of accidents, a number were the permanent markings of
more or less remote punishments.

Peculiarities in speech furnished another clew to the identity of a
runaway. It was reported that Eliza Ann talked politely and freely,
often using the word "well." [143] Henry "speaks long when talking,
with a whine to his voice," [144] while Tom was a handsome negro, a
"great talker and loud, with a little mouth." [145] Far removed from the
fluency of Tom was the stuttering of another who "stomps on the
ground when the word is hard to get out." [146]

A few fugitives were described as Africans, the term being used to
designate the land of their birth. This conclusion was apparently
reached because of the way the negro talked. It was said that a cer-

---

[185] *Ibid.*, Sept. 6, 1828.
[186] *Ibid.*, Sept. 6, 1848.
[187] *Ibid.*, Sept. 27, 1828.
[188] *Ibid.*, Nov. 17, 1829.
[189] *Ibid.*, July 21, 1829.
[140] Natchez *Mississippi Messenger*, Sept. 6, 1805.
[141] *Woodville Republican*, Aug. 10, 1833.
[142] *Ibid.*, Jan. 12, 1833.
[143] *Ibid.*, June 13, 1835.
[144] Vicksburg *Sentinel and Expositor*, Feb. 20, 1844.
[145] *Woodville Republican*, June 12, 1830.
[146] *Ibid.*, Nov. 20, 1841.

tain fugitive was "an African, or speaks much like one." [147] Some negroes, particularly those from Louisiana plantations, could speak French as well as English. The fugitive, William, was able to add Spanish to his list of linguistic accomplishments.[148] Another, who had lived in the Choctaw country for a number of years, had a good command of the language of that tribe.[149]

Close scrutiny shows that many fugitives were advertised for several consecutive months. As required by law, the sheriff advertised each fugitive until he was claimed or until six months elapsed. If the latter, there was then a month's notice of the approaching sale of the unclaimed negro. Sometimes as many as thirty consecutive notices were concerned with the same fugitive.

In a period of twenty-five years 165 fugitive negroes were advertised by their owners, and 385 by the sheriff, in the *Woodville Republican*. This total of 550 should be slightly lowered because of one or two duplications. The average number of runaways advertised in this paper each year was about twenty-two. There were doubtless many others whose names were never printed. On the other hand, a number of fugitives advertised in the *Woodville Republican* neither escaped from Wilkinson County nor came into that region, for a master sometimes placed advertisements in the papers of several neighboring towns. In reality the slave might never get to any of them.

In most cases each slave was separately advertised by the jailer or sheriff even though there were other slaves in jail at the same time. However, there appeared in a Natchez paper, in 1821, one notice that included seven slaves in the Wilkinson County jail. Each of the seven had a different owner, if we may believe the slaves. Two had fled from Natchez, a like number from Louisiana, one from Tennessee, the sixth had not given the name of his home, and the seventh had escaped from slave-traders, Messrs. Bearly and Robert.

In November, 1848, the *Woodville Republican,* united with the Concordia (La.) *Intelligencer* in preparing a "Runaway Register" to be published each week. These papers planned to include a brief description of every slave in jail within the States of Mississippi, Louisiana, Arkansas, and Illinois. A total of forty-four runaways were reported in the first issue of this register. Fourteen of these

[147] *Ibid.,* Sept. 3, 1831. Natchez *Mississippi Republican,* Nov. 6, 1821.
[148] *Woodville Republican,* Jan. 22, 1831.
[149] Natchez *Weekly Chronicle,* Mar. 29, 1809.

were in Mississippi jails and twenty-seven in Louisiana. Eight of the forty-four runaways stated that they had fled from Mississippi masters. The register is an interesting attempt to afford better facilities to the planters for tracing their fugitive slaves and also is indicative of the total number of runaways in the jails of a section of the South at one time.[150]

The facts stated about the "Runaway Register," and about the number of fugitives advertised in the *Woodville Republican* might suggest that running away was a rare vice. This does not follow. As many slaves escaped and were recaptured without the mediation of newspapers, no exact estimate can be made of the total number of runaways. It is probable that the newspapers advertised the bolder and more successful. Even if they were caught, they were at least able to remain at large long enough to excite uncertainty about their ultimate return.

A runaway slave's career might terminate in any of the following ways. The large majority of those whose names appeared in advertisements were doubtless regained by their legal owners. It is reasonably certain that a captured fugitive was secured by his owner, if the newspaper notice disappeared before six months elapsed. This is subject to the exception of a few who escaped from jail.[151] If the notice placed in the paper by a planter was seen only once or twice, this also indicates the recovery of the fugitive.

A few Mississippi slaves succeeded in acquiring their freedom. Newspaper advertisements give no clew to the number of these. It is probable that De Bow was referring to these successful runaways when he listed forty-one fugitives from Mississippi in 1850, out of a total of 1,011 fugitives from fifteen States.[152] Without giving exact figures, the *Census of 1860* announced that Mississippi was one of the States that had suffered a considerable increase of fugitive slaves. This conclusion was evidently drawn from the returns in the sixth column in the manuscript slave schedule of this census which was headed: "Fugitives from the State." Obviously, returns under this head could not be precise for in many, probably in most, cases the owner did not know where his fugitive was.[153]

[150] *Woodville Republican*, Nov. 21, 1848.
[151] *Ibid.*, Apr. 30, 1836.
[152] J. D. B. De Bow, *Industrial Resources of the Southern and Western States*, III, 426.
[153] *Census of 1860* (*Population*), p. xv. MS. slave schedules of this census.

In a very few instances the career of a runaway slave was ended when he was killed in the attempt to arrest him.

Finally, a few fugitives were sold to new owners at the end of the jail term of six months. The fugitives who gave fictitious names of owners evidently believed that any change was better than returning to the former master. At any rate, of the 385 negroes who were placed in the Wilkinson County jail as runaways, twenty-nine were sold at public auction because they had not been claimed within the six months provided by law.

CHAPTER VII

Buying, Selling, and Hiring

When the Choctaw Indians crossed the Mississippi River after selling their lands to the United States in 1830, their chief, Greenwood Leflore, remained behind. This half-breed, who had already proved his ability to govern the Indian braves, now began to take an important part in the affairs of the white race. In one respect he surpassed most white men, for his slaves eventually numbered close to four hundred. A sheaf of yellowed bills of sale tells part of the story of the growth of his black army.[1]

In addition to these purchases, Leflore's slaves increased by births. Before 1860 there had been ample time for rearing some of his field hands, for the first recorded purchases were in the 1820's.

Many of Leflore's purchases were local transactions. A number of slaves were bought from neighbors. A few, such as Mary and her child Rachael, were secured from other members of the Leflore family. Indeed, some of the slaves doubtless continued to cultivate the same soil which they had tilled for their former master, for Leflore was adding to his holdings in land as well as in negroes.

In December, 1857, Leflore purchased from Theodore Johnston, of New Orleans, Fanny, a mulatto girl about eighteen years old. The price was $1,800. This was a large sum, but Fanny was a present for Mrs. Leflore, and she was well trained to serve as the personal maid of the mistress of a large estate.[2] Though a few other bills of sale were dated in New Orleans, a number of slaves were bought from other States, and several vendors are recognized as professional slave-traders. In both 1824 and 1825, Leflore bought negroes from Isaac Franklin, of Tennessee. In 1829 and the following year, transactions were completed with another Tennesseean, Benjamin Stanley. In 1830, ten negroes were secured for the sum of $4,200 from James F. Taliferro, of Amelia County, Va. This Indian chief was evidently

[1] These bills of sale are part of the collection of Greenwood Leflore MSS. in the possession of Miss Florence Ray, Memphis, Tenn.

[2] The record of this transaction is the only paper in the collection in which a printed bill of sale was used by filling in the proper blanks. The other papers are informal documents, frequently only four or five lines in length.

known as a large purchaser of slaves. J. P. Medly, of Greensboro, Miss., added the following postscript to a letter addressed to Leflore: "I have a valuable house girl for sale if you know of any one who wishes to purchase inform them. I have one 16. and one boy 23. boy 7. & a good seemstress."

Only one record of a sale by Leflore is preserved among his papers. This, however, included two negroes. The sale was handled, in 1841, by the New Orleans firm of Halsey and Bell, who disposed of Martha through an agent for $650. Sarah was not so salable. After some delay she brought $410 at public auction. Leflore did not receive the full price for the sum of $119.20 was subtracted to cover the cost of boarding the slaves in New Orleans, for auctioneer's charges and other commissions, and for new clothes to show the slaves off to best advantage in the market.[3]

Leflore is said to have made it a rule never to separate families nor to sell negroes unless they were unruly.[4] The latter was doubtless true for he was succeeding and was constantly buying rather than selling slaves. He therefore had no reason to part families by selling husband, wife, and children to different masters. But his records show that he generally bought negroes singly or in twos, and most of them were young. A number of these must have been separated from relatives.

His largest purchase was a lot of one hundred slaves who ranged in age from a few months up to eighty-six years. They were secured on June 1, 1839, from the estate of S. D. Miller, deceased. The purchase price does not appear on the bill of sale, but it must have been a sum that few persons of the State could have raised. The slaves were fortunate in not being divided among a number of buyers.

Most of the bills of sale, recording Greenwood Leflore's purchases, include a statement of the amounts paid for the slaves, and in these, two periods of peak prices are evident, one in the middle of the 1830's and the other in the last few years before the Civil War.

Leflore's relation to the slave-trade was no closer than that of many Mississippi planters, for most of the capital of the Old South was invested in slaves and land. The average prosperous planter occasionally bought both of these commodities. On the other hand, just as buildings and stocks of goods to-day go under the hammer to expiate the poor judgment, misfortune, or rascality of their owner, so in

---

[3] The disposal of another Mississippi slave in the New Orleans market is described in Phillips, *Life and Labor in the Old South*, pp. 156-157.

[4] Ray, *Leflore*, p. 40.

former days slaves marched to the auction block. Steady and unvarying success was necessary, if a planter avoided selling negroes. Reverse was attended by a mortgage, and most planters were in debt a large part of the time. Further reverses compelled the planter to sell slaves. A good crop and a high price the next year might restore his credit and allow him to purchase new slaves. This is why most planters bought and sold from time to time.

On the whole, Mississippi planters purchased more frequently than they sold. Thomas Dabney sold only four slaves, three for serious faults and one because the negro requested it.[5] There is no record of his purchases. Leflore sold little and bought much, but he, like Dabney, was prospering and had no reason to sell except to rid the plantation of an occasional undesirable negro. On the other hand, William Dunbar, M. W. Philips, and James K. Polk sold as well as bought frequently.[6]

In Mississippi the supply of slaves seldom equaled the demand, and it therefore follows that most of the Mississippi slaves who were sold passed into the hands of other citizens of the same State. Most Mississippi planters participated in this local trade and both bought and sold to neighbors and others who were close at hand. In contrast to this, Mississippians bought many slaves from other States but exported relatively few. Mississippi's relation to the interstate slave-trade was, therefore, in the main, one-sided. Finally, few Mississippians were ever directly concerned in the importation of negroes from outside the United States.

Before discussing Mississippi's relation to the interstate and the foreign phases of the trade, local or short-range transactions will be described, and at the same time some things that were also common to longer-range dealings will be presented.

An examination of old Southern newspapers shows that enormous numbers of negroes were sold by sheriffs and trustees to satisfy debts, particularly in periods of business depression, such as the panic of 1837. In addition to such involuntary sales forced upon the owner by legal process, economic pressure exerted in other ways compelled many masters to sell negroes. In announcing sales, slaveholders fre-

[5] Smedes, *Southern Planter*, pp. 103–104.
[6] Eron Rowland, *Life, Letters and Papers of William Dunbar*, pp. 23–57, 351–352. Riley, "Diary of a Miss. Planter," in *P. M. H. S.*, X, 332, 339, 352, 408, 442. Bassett, *Plantation Overseer*, pp. 100, 119, 197.

quently stated that such a course was forced on them by business reverses. Doubtless they hoped this would keep the public from thinking that the negro was being sold for a fault, for such a suspicion
would lower his market value. Though this was often rank hypoc-
risy, some advertisers seem to have sincerely regretted that they
were compelled to sell a particular slave. In advertising the sale of a
negro house servant and her two children, their owner stated: "The
woman Sarah is well known in Woodville, and nothing would induce
me to part with her but the want of money, which cannot be had in
any other way." [7]

The death of a planter was often followed by a public sale of his
property, including, of course, the negroes.[8] Though the slaves were
sometimes divided among the heirs, at other times they were sold to
pay the debts of the deceased.[9] Moreover, it was often impossible equi-
tably to divide an estate of slaves, especially if they were few in
number. Therefore they were sold and the proceeds of the sale distributed in money. Business, health, or similar causes forced a few
slave-owners to leave the country. Their departure was often preceded by a sale of their slaves.[10] Another and rather unusual kind of
forced sale resulted when a runaway slave remained in jail for six
months without being claimed by his master. The purchaser at such
a sale needed to be wary, for the slave might be an habitual runaway;
he might even have left home to escape punishment for some crime.
Naturally, the price of unclaimed runaways was rather depressed.

In a large proportion of local sales the negroes were sold by the
sheriff or a trustee rather than by the owner. After ample notice had
been given through the local press, the sale was conducted at the
courthouse, though another place was sometimes substituted. In
the town of Woodville many slaves met their new masters under the
"Royal Oak," a massive tree that shaded most of one side of the
square on which was the business section of the town.[11] Particularly
in executors' sales, the home plantation of the slaves was apt to be
the scene of the auction. Executors sometimes showed a desire to sell

[7] *Woodville Republican*, Apr. 15, 1837. For similar instances of economic
pressure see, *ibid.*, Jan. 14, 1843, and Dec. 12, 1827.

[8] J. F. H. Claiborne, *Life and Correspondence of John A. Quitman*, I, 86.
Woodville Republican, Aug. 18, 1824. Pearson *et al. v.* Moreland *et ux.*, 15
Miss. 609.

[9] *Woodville Republican*, Aug. 27, 1825.

[10] *Ibid.*, Sept. 17, 1825.

[11] *Ibid.*, May 16, 1835; Jan. 2, 1836; Apr. 15, 1837.

plantation and negroes together.[12] A sale of this kind, somewhat reminiscent of serfdom, would possibly not effect any great change in the life of the slaves. The new owner might be more severe than the former one, but the converse was also often the case. In either event the physical surroundings and conditions of life remained approximately the same, and ties of family and friendship were unbroken.

In the local slave-trade, many transactions were conducted along the simplest lines. Sometimes a planter privately bargained with his next-door neighbor for a slave. He might need a blacksmith and the neighbor might have an extra one. Again, many planters were disturbed by having slaves visiting their wives on adjacent estates. To avoid this, the wife could be purchased or the husband sold. Such a sale served both economics and humanity. For similar reasons, many slaves were privately sold. These local sales relieved stresses in the social fabric of slavery. The slave, remaining in the same neighborhood, could still see his old friends, and the change of hands might even give a temporary relief to the monotony of bondage.

Two additional phases of the local slave-trade merit attention. Some slaves were sold without suffering any separation from family or accustomed surroundings; other slaves experienced great changes though their ownership remained the same. The former might occur when a slave was sold by one member of a family to another or when a man bought a slave he had been hiring for some time.[13] On the other hand, two slave-owners, possibly relatives, might unite their forces on a single plantation. Years later, after the slaves had intermarried, the masters might sever their business connections and thereby destroy the family unions among the slaves.[14]

Regardless of fluctuations in the average price of slaves from year to year, there were certain factors that a purchaser always needed to consider when he entered the market.[15] To have any value at all, a

[12] In *ibid.*, Jan. 26, 1832, there was advertised for sale a plantation of 650 arpents and equipment, including 10 hands, 5 men and 5 women, all to be sold together. There were four other slaves that might be bought with the plantation, if the purchaser desired. A few of the similar cases may be found in *ibid.*, Dec. 4, Nov. 13, 1830; Feb. 18, 1837; May 4, 1839; Jan. 11, 1840; Jan. 16, 1841.

[13] *Plantation Overseer*, p. 100.

[14] "Diary of a Miss. Planter," in *P. M. H. S.*, X, 476. *Plantation Overseer*, p. 197.

[15] Naturally, the price of slaves in Mississippi varied with the price of cotton. —[Ingraham], *Southwest by a Yankee*, II, 244. According to tradition, the following rule was approximately correct during the 1850's: when cotton sold for ten cents a pound, a prime field hand was worth $1,000; with cotton at twelve cents,

slave should certainly be sane in mind and healthy in body.[16] Good
character was an important consideration. This was more easily determined, if the slave had an established reputation in the neighborhood.[17] Slaves who had been reared in the locality, or who had at
least been there long enough to be acclimated, were more valuable
than recently imported slaves, which is proved by the many advertisements in which negro property was so described.[18] If native-born
or acclimated slaves could not be procured, negroes from Virginia
seem to have been preferred in the Mississippi market.

The age of the slave was important for, as he advanced in years,
his capacity for work decreased. The shrewd buyer refused to purchase a slave whose age kept him from doing more work than the
cost of his upkeep. Neither would he buy a slave who was within a
few years of such an age. After a slave reached this period he became
with each passing year more of a liability to his master.[19] An aged
negress of good reputation might be sold to a family seeking a nurse
for children,[20] or to the owner of a rooming-house,[21] or an old negro
man who was skilled in some craft might find a market,[22] but as a
rule the demand for slaves advanced in years was small. A negress
forty-five years old sold under an execution at public auction for only
two dollars. Though there may have been other factors, a number of
persons thought her worth little or nothing because of her age.[23] The
average purchaser preferred slaves in the neighborhood of twenty
years old.

An added value in the case of a young negro woman was her
capability to bear children. It might be added that the sole ownership
of a negro child was vested in the owner of the mother. Strange to
relate, one of the clearest contemporary statements of the value of a

the value of the negro rose to $1,200. Ordinary slaves were worth less, but their
cost varied in proportion. Trader William H. Fitzgerald reported on Jan. 10,
1833, that he had sold thirty slaves for $15,200, the prices ranging from $300 to
$1,000. A few years later these prices would have been much higher.—A MS.
catalogued in G 170, Department of Archives and History, Jackson, Miss.
Examples of advanced prices in later years can be found in Frederic Bancroft,
Slave-Trading in the Old South, pp. 308–309.

[16] Simmons v. Cutreer, 20 Miss. 584. Kinley v. Fitzpatrick, 5 Miss. 59.
[17] *Woodville Republican,* Apr. 15, 1837.
[18] *Ibid.,* July 20, 1833; Nov. 25, 1826; Dec. 12, 1829.
[19] Brown v. Forbes, 16 Miss. 498.
[20] *Woodville Republican,* Apr. 22, 1837.
[21] *Southwest by a Yankee,* II, 60.
[22] *Woodville Republican,* Oct. 20, 1827.
[23] Brown v. Forbes, 16 Miss. 498.

prolific negro woman is found in a *Defense of African Slavery* that
was prepared by W. B. Trotter of Mississippi. He wrote:

"On all large farms there are frequently a large portion of the slave
women, and some one or more of them in a state of pregnancy all the
while, and this class of slaves, if properly taken care of, are the most
profitable to their owners of any others, and if not properly taken care of,
are altogether valueless. It is remarkable the number of slaves which may
be raised from one woman in the course of forty or fifty years with the
proper kind of attention." [24]

The price of negroes was based on calculations of probable increase
as well as on estimates of the amount of work they could do. One of
the most valuable gifts or legacies that could be made to a young
person was one or more young negro women. With good fortune the
children and grandchildren of the gift should in time create an estate
of considerable size. [25]

Though opinions varied as to the relative value of mulatto and
black slaves, [26] there does not seem to have been a great difference
between their market price. However, if the mulatto was very white,
he was not very salable as a slave. The courts were once informed
that this was so in the case of a light mulatto girl. [27]

One more question to be considered in acquiring a slave was:
"What can he do?" As work in the field was the usual lot of a slave,
the necessary strength and experience for this were considered. The
price of a slave was enhanced, if he had been trained to do work that
required more skill. The value of a negro woman was greater if she
was a good cook, ironer, washer, [28] or seamstress. [29] Certain negro
men advertised for sale were higher priced because they were skilled
either as shoemaker, [30] teamster, [31] ox-driver, carpenter, [32] mechanic, [33]
engineer, or blacksmith. [34]

[24] William B. Trotter, *History and Defense of African Slavery*, p. 181.
   In an advertisement in the Natchez *Mississippi Free Trader*, Jan. 24, 1852,
Henry I. Peck boasted: "I have raised as many negroes on that plantation in
proportion to the number of women as can be found elsewhere."
   [25] Newell v. Newell, 17 Miss. 56. Kilpatrick v. Bush et ux., 23 Miss. 199. Ferguson v. Applenhite, 18 Miss. 304.
   [26] Olmsted, *Back Country*, pp. 90–92, 155.
   [27] Munn v. Perkins, 9 Miss. 412.
   [28] *Woodville Republican*, July 20, 1833; Jan. 16, 1836.
   [29] *Ibid.*, Sept. 14, 1833.
   [30] *Ibid.*, Mar. 28, 1828; Mar. 28, 1829.
   [31] *Ibid.*, Apr. 3, 1830.
   [32] *Ibid.*, Dec. 27, 1831.
   [33] *Ibid.*, Apr. 13, 1833.
   [34] *Ibid.*, Mar. 10, 1832.

Most litigation over the title to slaves was very similar to suits involving other kinds of property. However, slaves were sometimes considered a unique species of property. The court once held that, "a court of chancery will not interfere to prevent the sale of personal property, unless it be of some peculiar character, as slaves, or have some peculiar value, by reason of which damages might not afford adequate compensation for its loss." [35] In another case it was stated before the court that slaves are a peculiar kind of property "especially a favorite or family slave." [36] A number of cases hinged upon warrants or guarantees made at the time of the sale. In private sales within the State the vendor gave a warrant of mental and physical soundness as well as of good title, though the former could be waived by written agreement. In one case there was also a guarantee that the slave in question was not a runaway. This slave had been imported from Louisiana, where such a guarantee was customary.[37]

Warrants of soundness in body and mind must have caused the gentlemen on the bench many a puzzled moment. The following is a typical case. A negress was bought in Virginia in September, 1855, and on the fifth of the following January was sold in Mississippi to a Mr. Ford. There was a guarantee of soundness although she had a cough at the time. Twenty-one days later she was sick in bed at the purchaser's house, in comfortable quarters and attended by a regular physician. On the first day of February she died of pneumonia. Though the weather was bad and there was much sickness in the neighborhood, this was the only case of pneumonia. Ford sought to recover the $1,050 he had paid for the woman, basing his plea upon the warrant that she was sound in body.[38] There was a similar case of a negro woman who, though she seemed to have a bad cold at the time she was sold, was warranted sound. She died soon after of consumption. This case was complicated by the fact that the purchaser chose the negress himself.[39]

Mental troubles were also aired in court. A man bought a negro

---

[35] Beatty et al. v. Smith et al., 10 Miss. 567. *Revised Code of 1857*, p. 529.

[36] Murphy v. Clark, 9 Miss. 221. See also, Morris et al. v. Dillard et ux., 12 Miss. 636. ". . . no constable shall be authorized to levy on any negro, unless there is no other personal estate sufficient to satisfy the debt . . . ,"—*Hutchinson's Code*, p. 701.

[37] James v. Kirk, 29 Miss. 206. *Laws of Louisiana*, 1833–1834, p. 7.

[38] Shewalter v. Ford, 34 Miss. 417. See also, Kinley v. Fitzpatrick, 5 Miss. 59. Houston v. Burney, 10 Miss. 583. Lindsey v. Lindsey, 34 Miss. 432.

[39] Munn v. Perkins, 9 Miss. 412.

woman, warranted sound in mind and body. He soon discovered that she was subject to fits and was often taken "all of a sudden, in a strange way." The vendor claimed that it was all pretense on the part of the woman, and the court was called on to untangle the affair.[40]

When a slave above fifteen years of age was imported from another State, an additional guarantee of good character was required.[41] On the other hand, if a slave was sold under a court order by the sheriff, there was only a title warrant. The purchaser had to decide for himself whether the negro was mentally, physically, and morally sound.[42]

It is evident that all these guarantees or agreements at the time of sale benefited one or the other of the two parties to the contract, but not the negro. Only two exceptions have been found in the reports of the Supreme Court of Mississippi. Both of these arose from sales made outside the State. The cases are similar, and only one will be described. In 1830, a negro slave was sold by Anderson of Missouri to Duncan of the same State, with the provision that the negro remain in servitude fifteen years and then be set free. The negro was resold to Chamberlain who brought him to Mississippi. There, at the expiration of the fifteen years, the negro sued for his freedom.[43]

Though there was, ordinarily, nothing in Mississippi bills of sale to to safeguard the interests or wishes of the negro, there were some slaveholders who endeavored to sell only in family lots. Ingraham, writing of the slave auction at Natchez, noted: "It is a rule seldom deviated from, to sell families and relations together, if practicable, and if not, at least to masters residing in the neighborhood of each other. A negro trader, in my presence, refused to sell a negro girl for whom a planter offered a high price because he would not also purchase her sister." [44] Cornelius Vanhouten wrote his last will in October 9, 1850, and directed his executors to sell all his slaves except Joe, "but in no event to separate families." [45] Though Caleb Stowers' will contained no pronouncement against breaking slave families, he tried to prevent this by bequeathing his slaves in family lots to his various heirs. He did not expect any of his negroes to be sold

[40] Patterson v. Kirkland, 34 Miss. 423. See also Simmons v. Cutreer, 20 Miss. 584.
[41] Statutes of the Mississippi Territory, pp. 386–387.
[42] Hutchins et al. v. Brooks, 31 Miss. 430.
[43] Roach v. Anderson, 28 Miss. 234. See also Sam v. Fore, 20 Miss. 413.
[44] Southwest by a Yankee, II, 203.
[45] Will of Cornelius Vanhouten, MS.

upon his death.[46] Philander Smith, whose will was made in Adams
County, in 1824, also arranged by name for the distribution of his
slaves taking considerable pains "not to part the said Sterling and
Annie from their youngest child, even for a short time" and to avoid
other family separations.[47] With the same purpose in view, Sally Hoggatt included the following sentences in her will:

"I give unto my two sons Nathaniel and Phillip Hoggatt forty nine
slaves, to be equally divided between them within six months after my
death, to wit," [the names of the slaves appear in the original will but are
here omitted].

"Several of the above named slaves are connected in families with those
belonging to my son Philip, and it is my will and wish that they, my sons,
Nathaniel and Phillip may so divide them as to avoid as much as possible the
separation of families, and it is my sincere wish that my two sons may be
able to divide the before named forty nine slaves in an amicable and friendly
manner." [48]

A planter, advertising the sale of his estate of 1,500 acres, gave
notice that he wished to sell also "30 or 40 Negroes, or perhaps more,
(that I can not say at present, disliking to separate families)." [49] The
practice, occasionally followed, of selling land and the negroes upon
it together would, of course, keep family ties intact. The wording of
some advertisements suggests that there was a desire to sell the slaves
in family lots.[50]

On the other hand, many advertisements listed together the mothers
and each of their children by name, but the fathers' names were in a
distant part of the advertisement. When the title to one slave was in
six different hands between 1835 and 1841, it is difficult to see how
family ties could have been respected.[51] A fair cross-section of the
policy that was generally followed at slave-sales in regard to family
ties can be found in a single advertisement. A citizen of Vicksburg
announced that he wanted to dispose of a family of slaves consisting

---

[46] Will of Caleb Stowers, MS.
[47] Will of Philander Smith, MS., Adams Co., Will Book 1, p. 330.
[48] Will of Sally Hoggatt, MS., Adams Co., Will Book 2, p. 253.
[49] *Woodville Republican*, Oct. 22, 1836; Jan. 14, 1843.
[50] A sheriff's sale to satisfy claims and costs arising from certain suits against
John W. Gildart, advertised to take place on the first Monday in March, 1835,
included the "following slaves,—Congo and his wife, Sukey and her four children
John, William, George and Thomas, Juba and his wife, Cynthia and Sam."—
Ibid., Feb. 28, 1835; Nov. 2, 1839; Nov. 14, 1840.
[51] Taylor *v.* Stone, 21 Miss. 652.

of a man, a woman, and their six-year-old child. At the same time he wanted to procure a good boy ten or twelve years old. Supposing that he accomplished his purpose, his sale may have kept a family intact, but his purchase almost certainly destroyed one.[52]

Mississippi was not one of the chief participants in the foreign slave-trade. When the importation of slaves from outside the United States was first prohibited by federal law (1808), Mississippi lacked nine years of becoming a State. Her slave population was at that time small and, therefore, few Mississippi negroes could have been legally imported from abroad. To aid in the enforcement of the federal prohibition, the Mississippi-Alabama territory, in 1815, ordered the seizure and public auction of slaves imported from outside the United States. Half of the money secured was to be placed in the public treasury; the other half could be claimed by the collector of customs or private informer responsible for the capture.[53]

Shortly before the federal prohibition of the trade became effective, William Dunbar, a prominent planter of the Natchez region, decided to replenish his supply by purchasing newly imported Africans. He signified this desire in a letter dated February 1, 1807, to Thomas Tunno and John Price, of Charleston, S. C. They were directed to procure for him slaves from Africa to the amount of 3,000 pounds sterling under the following specifications: The negroes should be between twelve and twenty-one years old; well formed and robust; three or four times as many men as women; and from the Niger River region. He stated that the negroes of the "Iboa" nation were disliked in the Mississippi region and should, therefore, be excluded from the order. Preference was expressed for Africans of the Bornon, Houssa, Zanfara, Zegzeg, Kapina, and Tombootoo tribes. Should the slaves be procured, Dunbar preferred their being sent by water from Charleston to New Orleans.[54]

Mississippi's slight participation in the foreign slave-trade was chiefly the buying of alien slaves who had landed in another State.

[52] *Vicksburg Sentinel*, Apr. 17, 1844.
An account of the separation in an auction sale of a negro boy from his aged mother is described in Joseph B. Cobb, *Mississippi Scenes*, pp. 81 ff.
[53] W. E. B. Du Bois, *Suppression of the Slave Trade*, p. 109, citing Toulmin, *Digest of the Laws of Alabama*, p. 637.
[54] Eron Rowland, *William Dunbar*, pp. 351–353. Claiborne, *Mississippi*, pp. 105–106.

Slaves imported into Texas, especially before her incorporation into
the United States, were often brought to New Orleans or other dis-
tributing centers.[55] Mississippi planters constantly bought slaves in
the New Orleans market; some foreign-born negroes were probably
brought into Mississippi from that city. A slave-smuggler, finding it
difficult to introduce his cargo into New Orleans, might bring the
negroes up the river and sell more directly to planters. A newspaper
in the southwestern corner of Mississippi gave its readers the following warning, though some planters may have construed this as a
sly suggestion that a bargain in slaves might be had, if the importer
could be found: "The New Orleans papers have published a note of
J. W. Smith, U. S. District Attorney, warning the planters and other
citizens of La., from purchasing or concealing a number of negroes
who were recently brought into the Mississippi, by an American vessel
from Havana, as all persons thus transgressing, will be liable to a
penalty of from $1,000 to $10,000, and an imprisonment of from
three to seven years." [56]

Stephen A. Douglas said that "he had seen, with his own eyes,
three hundred of these recently-imported, miserable beings, in a slave-
pen in Vicksburg, Miss., and also large numbers at Memphis,
Tenn." [57] Such a statement is difficult to credit, for foreign-born
negroes, particularly native Africans, were rarely to be found. However, newspapers reported that four negroes from the cargo of the
"Wanderer" were brought to Mississippi and disposed of in Marshall
County. It was rumored that others of the same cargo were in a
neighboring county.[58]

The "Wanderer" landed its smuggled cargo shortly before the
Civil War. At this time the high price of slaves caused considerable
agitation in the South in favor of reopening the foreign slave-trade.
A number of persons in Mississippi desired this, which doubtless accounts for the pious remark of the papers that the "Wanderer" slaves
in Marshall County seemed docile, industrious, and well pleased
with their new homes and improved condition.[59]

Mississippi's interest in the foreign slave-trade was evident in the
Vicksburg Commercial Convention (1859). Though the question had

[55] *Suppression of the Slave Trade,* pp. 112–113, 161.
[56] *Woodville Republican,* Aug. 13, 1825.
[57] *Suppression of the Slave Trade,* pp. 181–182.
[58] Phillips, *Plantation and Frontier,* II, 54–55.
[59] *Ibid.*

been discussed in the Knoxville Convention in 1857,[60] much stronger feeling was shown at Vicksburg, where there was a clear demand that the trade be legalized.[61] In the same year as the Vicksburg Convention, Congressman William Barksdale and Senator A. G. Brown, of Mississippi, condemned a resolution against the foreign slave-trade.[62] Even Jefferson Davis, soon to become president of the Confederate States, denied "any coincidence of opinion with those who prate of the inhumanity and sinfulness of the trade. The interest of Mississippi, not of the African dictates my conclusion." He opposed the immediate reopening of the trade, fearing a paralyzing influx of negroes, but added: "This conclusion, in regard to Mississippi, is based upon my view of her *present* condition, *not* upon any *general theory.*" [63]

As the reopening of the foreign slave-trade seemed highly improbable, it was suggested that more slave labor might be supplied to Mississippi, and the penalties of the federal law avoided, by importing Africans as indentured servants, bound to labor for a number of years and then to be liberated.[64] To say the least, the legality of such a scheme was questionable. The results of the plan would certainly have been baneful, even for slave-owners. For years there had been in the State a great antagonism to any increase in the number of free negroes. The importation of indentured negroes would have rapidly increased this class and planters would have soon protested against this intolerable situation.

The illegal importation of outright slaves was much less dangerous for the institution, though the individual importer was, of course, liable to severe punishment. An unusual attempt to break the federal law, or else to play a joke on society, appeared as an advertisement in a Mississippi paper. The notice was addressed to shipowners and masters of the merchant marine. William S. Price and seventeen others offered to "pay three hundred dollars per head for one thousand native Africans, between the ages of fourteen and twenty years (of sexes equal), likely, sound, and healthy, to be delivered within

[60] *De Bow's Review*, XXIII, 298–320.
[61] Herbert Wender, *Southern Commercial Conventions, 1837–1859*, pp. 230–235. Foote, *Bench and Bar*, p. 69.
[62] *Suppression of the Slave Trade*, p. 175.
[63] *Ibid.*, p. 176.
[64] Natchez *Daily Free Trader*, Feb. 13, 1858.

twelve months from this date, at some point accessible by land, between Pensacola, Fla., and Galveston, Texas; the contractors giving thirty days' notice as to time and place of delivery." [65]

Although few foreign-born slaves entered Mississippi, census reports show that the increase of the black population of Mississippi was too rapid to be accounted for by excess of births over deaths. A large part of the increase was by importation from one or another of the older slave States. Some slaves came with their immigrant masters; others were transferred by professional traders; still others were bought by established Mississippi planters. This steady stream of incoming slaves was an outstanding feature of the institution in Mississippi. Few, if any, southern States received as many slaves and exported as few.

An example of the immigrant master who brought his slaves with him was Leonard Covington, who came from Maryland to Mississippi toward the end of 1809. He had already attained prominence as a member of Congress and as an Indian fighter. The union of political and military prestige was partially responsible for his move, for he secured an appointment as lieutenant colonel of dragoons, and his duties necessitated his presence in the Mississippi Territory. There was another motive which was common to most emigrants from Maryland and Virginia. This was the hope that, by exchanging old land for new and by cultivating cotton instead of tobacco, wealth could be more easily obtained. Covington was fortunate in having in the new region a brother as well as several friends to whom he could write for advice and assistance in matters pertaining to his removal. It is fortunate for the historian that this was the case, for his letters reveal clearly the questions that were uppermost in the mind of a slave-owner meditating a change to the distant Mississippi region. The following is part of a letter he wrote in August, 1808:

"You have never been circumstantial as to the manner and terms of hiring your people. It would certainly be material to the owner of slaves, whether their treatment in many respects was such as would be desirable, and in what manner the payments for hirelings were made; if in advance, or punctually at the month's end. Whether the slaves were well fed; and only compelled to work from 'sun to sun.' It is possible that so much labor may be required of hirelings and so little regard may be had for their constitu-

[65] *Suppression of the Slave Trade*, p. 182 note, citing Enterprise (Miss.) *Weekly News*, Apr. 14, 1859, quoted in *26 Report of the Am. Anti-slavery Soc.*, pp. 41–42.

tions as to render them in a few years, not only unprofitable, but expensive. In your case, who pays the doctor, abides the loss from death or running away? Do the negroes in that country generally look as happy and contented as with us, and do they as universally take husbands and wives and as easily rear their young as in Maryland? Are they satisfied with the change and with their treatment? Is the culture of cotton much easier, and a more certain crop than our tobacco? Is there any probability that you will have any better market for your cotton than we shall have for our tobacco should our differences with Europe terminate in a war? Will this not depend upon the progress of manufactures in this country? Is the expense of making a cotton crop, where a man has hands of his own, considerable? What seems to be the current price of horses, cattle, etc., etc. The expense of clothing must be less than in a more northern climate. On lands of the U. S. such as you would like to purchase, what would be the probable expense of rough buildings and clearing for a small crop, say for ten or twelve hands? What time would such a preparation take? Fruit— is it abundant and well flavored, etc. etc. What seems to be the usual fare or allowance for working negroes, where a planter has a good many, from 10 to 20, for example? Have you any sudden or great changes from heat to cold, and do you suffer as much from droughts or violent falls of rains as with us? I have a thousand more questions in my head, but pushed for time just now, must hope that you will say everything that I could ask, not forgetting politics, the state of religion, if there be much amongst you." [66]

Intelligent answers to these queries would be valuable to all who are interested in the status of slaves, but the questions alone, by showing the viewpoint of the owner, suggest the treatment and care Covington gave to his slaves.

Five or six of the slaves, doubtless the house staff, traveled to Mississippi with Covington and his family, who came in some state, with "a close carriage (Jersey Stage) a Gig and horse Cart, the damnedest cavalcade that ever man was burdened with." The main working force had made the journey some months earlier under the care of three white men. Though Covington journeyed in the early winter, most of his servants were transferred in the summer, a season that slave-traders later avoided. Being unable to dispose of his Aquasco plantation in Maryland, Covington divided his slaves. Twenty-five were left under an overseer to cultivate that estate and thirty-one were taken to Mississippi. It is worthy of note that those brought to the new country were, on an average, five years younger than those left behind.

[66] Nellie W. Brandon and W. M. Drake, eds., *Memoir of Leonard Covington by B. L. C. Wailes*, pp. 51–52. Some of the material in this *Memoir* was first printed in *Plantation and Frontier*, II, 201–208. Phillips also reproduces two papers that were omitted from the *Memoir*.

Naturally, the removal of a group of slaves belonging to one master caused comparatively few broken ties of family or friendship. But even the Covington exodus caused some disturbance. Alexander Covington, already in Mississippi, had left a negro, Sam, in Maryland. His brother Leonard, the emigrant, endeavored to make an arrangement suitable to both Sam and his master. This was difficult because "Sam himself maintains a sullen silence on the subject and neither yields consent to accompany my [Leonard's] people, or to be sold or exchanged." Among other expedients, Leonard suggested that his brother have some of the slaves in Mississippi write to those still in Maryland "a few fine flourishes touching the good things and matters of Natchez . . . which Sam has lost by not going." This subtle scheme to persuade Sam to travel willingly to Natchez failed. He was left in Maryland, after being exchanged for Dick. The latter was brought to Mississippi.

In addition to bringing Dick, a thirteen-year-old negro girl, Ally, was brought by Leonard as a profitable investment for his brother Alexander, and she, most probably, was separated from her family. Finally, it appears that Watt, a slave of Leonard Covington, had a free negro wife, Rachael. She and her two children decided to accompany the slave husband and father to the new territory. As they had no way of meeting the expense of the journey, Covington advanced the money, with the understanding that the free negroes should repay it by laboring either for him or for other persons after the trip was over.

Some years after the Covingtons' arrival in Mississippi, President James K. Polk established a plantation in the north central part of that State. His venture was under the immediate control of a succession of overseers, whose reports to the owner appear in J. S. Bassett's *The Plantation Overseer as Revealed in His Letters*. They describe the movement of a body of slaves from the old plantation in Tennessee to the new establishment in Mississippi; the attempts of some of these negroes to return to their friends or relatives; the shifting of slaves from Mississippi to Tennessee, or the reverse, under the orders of the owner; the discussion of buying more negroes in a neighboring town; and the coming and going of negroes that belonged to other members of the Polk family.[67]

The importations of the Covington and Polk slaves illustrate how

[67] *Plantation Overseer, passim.*

a large number of the slaves who were brought to Mississippi came with their owners or were sent under the care of overseers.[68] Many other negroes came to the State when established Mississippi planters purchased directly from distant markets. Some went in person; others sent special agents [69] to select slaves in Washington, Richmond, or other markets. As much as fifty thousand dollars was sometimes in the hands of one of these masters going in search of more slaves.[70]

An immigrant to Mississippi could hardly find a more lucrative investment for surplus funds than to purchase extra slaves, bring them with him to Mississippi, and there sell them at the advanced prices which generally prevailed in the Southwest. This plan was evidently followed by William Rochel who published the following advertisement in 1810: "I have upwards of twenty likely Virginia born slaves now in a flat bottomed boat lying in the river at Natchez, for sale cheaper than has been sold here in years. Part of said negroes I wish to barter for a small farm. My boat may be known by a large cane standing on deck." [71]

There is no way of knowing with accuracy the per cent of slaves brought to Mississippi by immigrant masters; or, on the other hand, the per cent who were imported through the trade in slaves, either by regular traders, or by masters or agents who traveled to other States and there purchased slaves. Dr. Frederic Bancroft "supposes that, in the 'fifties, when the extreme prejudice against the interstate traders had abated and their inadequate supplies were eagerly purchased, fully 70 per cent of the slaves removed from the Atlantic and the border States to the Southwest were taken after purchase or with a view to sale, that is, were objects of slave-trading." [72] This leaves only 30 per cent as the part brought by immigrant owners. Of the slaves who were not brought such a distance and were imported into Mississippi from an adjoining State, a larger share, probably 50 per cent, were brought by their masters.[73]

Almost no slaves were introduced into Mississippi from the West.

---

[68] The migration of another planter, Col. T. S. G. Dabney, to Mississippi is recorded in *Southern Planter* and is summarized in Phillips, *American Negro Slavery*, p. 179.

[69] *Woodville Republican*, Nov. 5, 1825.

[70] *Southwest by a Yankee*, II, 244.

[71] *American Negro Slavery*, pp. 189–190, citing Natchez *Weekly Chronicle*, April 2, 1810.

[72] *Slave-Trading*, p. 398.

[73] *Ibid.*, p. 400.

While many were brought up the Mississippi River from New Orleans to the south, most of these were merely distributed from that city, having been reared in other States.[74] The regions to the east and north supplied Mississippi with the majority of her slaves, and it appears that Virginia, Tennessee, Kentucky, and South Carolina furnished more than other States. From these sources negroes were brought, some by water and others by land routes. It is doubtful if slaves being transported to Mississippi by professional traders fared much better or worse than if they were being brought by their masters. Both found it to their interest to convey their slaves as economically as possible without endangering life or health, though the negroes of a few benevolent masters fared better than the average.[75]

A description of how slaves were transported down the Mississippi River and how they were prepared for the market, as well as a few glimpses of some practices of the trade, was recorded by William W. Brown. This slave was for a time hired by Walker, of St. Louis, as an assistant in his slave-trading operations. According to Brown, Walker fed his slaves well with bacon and corn-bread on the way down the river. To keep the slaves from escaping, especially when the boat tied up to take on wood, they were chained in pairs. To continue the story of the negro assistant:

"On our way down, and before we reached Rodney, the place where we made our first stop, I had to prepare the old slaves for market. I was ordered to have the old men's whiskers shaved off, and the grey hairs plucked out, where they were not too numerous, in which case he had a preparation of blacking to color it, and with a blacking brush we would put it on. This was new business to me, and was performed in a room where the passengers could not see us. These slaves were also taught how old they were by Mr. Walker, and after going through the blacking process, they looked ten years younger; and I am sure that some of those who purchased slaves of Mr. Walker, were dreadfully cheated, especially in the ages of the slaves which they bought.

"We landed at Rodney, and the slaves were driven to the pen in the back part of the village. Several were sold in this place, during our stay of four or five days, when we proceeded to Natchez. There we landed at night, and the gang were put in the warehouse until morning, when they were driven to the pen. As soon as the slaves are put in the pens, swarms of planters may be seen in and about them. They knew when Walker was expected, as he always had the time advertised beforehand when he would be in Rodney, Natchez, and New Orleans. These were the principal places where he offered his slaves for sale." [76]

Walker transported his slaves down the Mississippi River on steam-boats, some of which had regular quarters for negro passengers.[77] Others brought their slaves on the various river craft of the times, including the plebeian flatboats.[78] In 1826, a flatboat was drifting down the river, loaded with five white men and about seventy-five slaves, lately purchased in Maryland. About a hundred miles below Louisville, Kentucky, the negroes revolted. All the white men were killed and the slaves sought safety and freedom in flight. Most of them headed north, but fifty-six of their number were captured in Indiana, and some others were probably located later.[79]

Most of the slaves were brought to Mississippi on foot, covering possibly twenty-five miles a day and consuming seven or eight weeks on the road from Virginia.[80] Traders preferred to bring their gangs through in the autumn. The change of climate was generally less injurious at that time; moreover, the slaves reached Mississippi at the conclusion of the planting season, when the plantation owners were more able to purchase, having the funds or credit of the recently gathered crop of cotton.[81]

On the journey south, slaves were well fed and not pushed too fast. They were usually in better condition when they reached Natchez than they were when they left Virginia. A supply of food was conveyed in the caravan, and this was supplemented by purchases along the way. A small planter in north Mississippi usually disposed of his surplus pork and corn to the slave-traders, of whom, it may be added, he had a better opinion than was generally current in the State. Some of the traders to whom this farmer sold had as many as two hundred negroes in one coffle.[82] On the other hand, negroes on the march were not as well clothed as fed. As there was no economy in providing new

[76] *Narrative of William W. Brown, a Fugitive Slave*, written by himself, pp. 40, 43 ff.

[77] *Woodville Republican*, Mar. 16, 1839.

[78] *Ibid.*, Dec. 12, 1835; June 15, 1839; July, 17, 1841.

[79] *Ibid.*, Oct. 14, 1826.

[80] James *v.* Herring, 20 Miss. 336.

[81] In June, 1852, trader Thomas G. James made a special effort to dispose of forty-five negroes. "All of whom he will sell at a small profit for cash, or acceptances on approved commission houses in New Orleans, as he wishes to close out and go on to Virginia after a large lot for the fall trade. Call and see." —Natchez *Mississippi Free Trader*, June 26, 1852.

[82] *Back Country*, pp. 152–153.

clothes for the journey through the forests, negroes generally reached the market in rags. However, before being put on the auction block new clothes were provided. Though most of the slaves walked, there were wagons, carts, or other vehicles to convey the infants, aged, or those who became sick along the road. The slaves, particularly the men, were chained. In general, they were more closely guarded in the early part of the journey, lest they try to get back home to loved ones. As the country became stranger there was less vigilance. Nevertheless, a rather large per cent of fugitive slaves claimed to have escaped from the coffles or the slave pens of traders.[83]

On reaching Mississippi, traders distributed their slaves to the planters by several methods. Some had fixed headquarters. A short distance out of Natchez in the angle of two roads were several low, rough, wooden buildings, that partially enclosed a narrow courtyard. This was an important market.[84] In front of it were usually found the saddle-horses of planters or of the traders; inside were the negroes awaiting sale. They were dressed in the "usual uniform of slaves, when in market, consisting of a fashionably shaped, black fur hat, roundabout and trowsers of coarse corduroy velvet . . . good vests, strong shoes, and white cotton shirts. . . ." When not on display before a prospective purchaser the slaves seemed in excellent spirits and had no difficulty in amusing themselves in various ways. The entrance of a planter was the signal for the negroes to line up, the men on one side and the women on the other, in approximate order of size. They were examined and questioned but not as minutely as one might expect, for the slave-dealers of the Forks of the Roads were permanently established and guaranteed their sales. In the line of men was sometimes a husband, and in the opposite line his wife. In a sale described by Ingraham, the purchaser of a man agreed to take the wife also, with the understanding that she should be returned, if the feminine members of the family were not satisfied with her.[85]

Though, in addition to Natchez, there were more or less permanent markets in Vicksburg, Woodville, Aberdeen, Crystal Springs, and

[83] In general, *Southwest by a Yankee,* II, 234–241, serves as the basis of this brief sketch of the overland trade. See also, *Slave-Trading,* pp. 282–293. There is a brief description of the equipment of the overland trader in Collins *v.* McCargo, 14 Miss. 128.

[84] In early times the place was called Niggerville, for which the more euphonious name of Forks of the Road was later substituted.—*Slave-Trading,* p. 301.

[85] *Southwest by a Yankee,* II, 192–197.

other towns, most of the traders seem to have stayed only a short while in any one place. The business required at least yearly journeys to the slave-producing States. After displaying negroes a short time in a Mississippi market, traders who found business dull very naturally moved elsewhere, thus earning for themselves the description of transient or itinerant traders.[86] The statement made in reference to a certain McCargo, that he was "often seen in Natchez" [87] is probably applicable, with various towns substituted for Natchez, to a large number of the slave-traders. This same McCargo, though he frequently bought and sold negroes in Natchez, seems not to have had any permanent building for this purpose. On one occasion he rented a house near the race track to accommodate the lot of negroes just brought from Virginia.

The trader who moved from place to place found advertising peculiarly desirable. Though he came frequently to a given town and had, so to speak, a regular clientele, it was necessary to give due notice of his return. Walker, of St. Louis, sent notices to the places at which he expected to stop on his trips down the river. Frequently, a trader's advent was advertised in the newspapers of the neighboring towns, as well as in the town where he proposed to establish himself, as is seen by a careful examination of the following advertisement of the well-known Austin Woolfolk. His headquarters was in Natchez, but the advertisement appeared in a Woodville paper.

"NEGROES FOR SALE. The subscriber has on hand *seventy-five* likely young Virginia born Negroes, of various descriptions, which he offers to sell low for cash, or good acceptance; any person wishing to purchase would do well to call and suit themselves.—I will have a constant supply through the season.—I can be found at Purnell's Tavern.
Natchez, December 1st, 1826.   "Austin Woolfolk." [88]

Though a trader's regular business might be based on purchases in Virginia and sales in Natchez, he seldom hesitated to buy and sell along the road, if this could be done with advantage. Slaves were bought in Mississippi and resold in the same State by men whose chief occupation was long-distance trading.[89]

[86] James v. Elder, 23 Miss. 134.
[87] Collins v. McCargo, 14 Miss. 128.
[88] *Woodville Republican*, Dec. 2, 1826. This notice appeared each week for three months.
[89] Wells v. Treadwell, 28 Miss. 717.

The closest approach to a complete list of those who sold in the Natchez market at any one time is to be found in a manuscript preserved in the State Department of Archives and History of Mississippi. A copy of this follows:

Amount rec'd by Robert Bradley late Tax Collector of Adams County from Vendors of Slaves [for part of the year 1833]

Paul Pascal	$ 157.26
Thomas McCargo	79.43
Benjamin Hansford	43.88
Grigsby & Oldham	168.15
John W. Anderson	113.75
Samuel Wakefield	200.00
Levin D. Collier	40.50
Warren Offutt	65.00
John Clark	2.20
Harris Williams & Co.	80.93
Isaac Franklin	200.00
Stephen R. Chinworth	41.75
Michael Hughes	54.92
Prince Griffen	67.47
Robert & Nelson Tindal	18.00
Landon Harrison	13.00
Woolfolk & McDaniel	52.41
William Lee	2.90
William G. Clay	43.74
Obediah Gordon	45.85
William G. Skillman	57.70
William W. Eldridge	70.00
Merrit Williams	66.00
Joel White	96.25
R. A. Puryear	93.80
Moses Singleton	40.50
A. R. Wynn	60.80
Thomas Henningway	10.50
Samuel Wakefield	182.70
George Redman	47.75
O. G. Cates & G. C. Taylor	35.50
James Polk	135.27
	$2387.93 [90]

The individual returns of most of these men have also been preserved. That of the first trader in the list is as follows:

[90] MS. in Department of Archives and History, Jackson, Miss., catalogued as G 170.

"State of Mississippi Adams County I Paul Pascal have sold slave[s] to the amount of fifteen thousand seven hundred and twenty six dollars up to this date May 30th 1833

P. Pascal

"State of Mississippi Adams County I Paul Pascal do solemly swear that the above is a trew [sic] and perfect account of all sales of merchandize or sales of slaves made by me since the preceding Return or collection of Taxes so help me God.

P. Pascal

"Sworn to before me the 30th day of May 1833
Robert Bradley T[ax] C[ollector], A[dams] C[ounty]." [91]

These taxes were imposed under a law of 1826 which levied a tax of 1 per cent on the gross sales of all auctioneers, "as well as transient merchants and vendors of merchandise and slaves." [92] One might suppose that some of these tax payments were made on sales of commodities other than slaves because of the smallness of several of the amounts and because of the words of the law, that the tax should be levied on "transient merchants and vendors of merchandise and slaves." On the other hand, at the head of the list is the clear statement that these payments were received from "Vendors of Slaves," and a close examination of the law shows that small taxes were to be expected from some of those from whom the tax was to be collected. This might be true of a commission merchant who acted as auctioneer only on rare occasions, or it might be true of a transient trader who entered the county and after selling one or two slaves moved on to other markets. It should be noted that this tax was collectable only from auctioneers and from transient merchants. Traders who had permanent headquarters—and these did the largest business—were not subject to this tax. [93] Therefore, the total amount of tax collected, according to this return of the collector, will not indicate the total sales in the Natchez market during the year 1833 or even for any part of that year.

Further, the tax here recorded as paid by each trader is by no means indicative of his total sales for the year. A statement of the method of collecting the tax will make this clear. If a transient slave-trader entered any county in Mississippi, it was the duty of the tax collector of the county to place him under a $200 bond. The bond was conditioned upon the trader giving on oath a true report of all

[91] *Ibid.*
[92] *Laws of Miss.*, 1824–1838, p. 89.
[93] Newman *v.* Elam, 26 Miss. 474.

his sales and paying the 1 per cent tax thereon before leaving the county, or within two months. This explains the appearance of the name of Samuel Wakefield twice in the same list. Evidently, he brought slaves into Adams County, made the $200 bond and began selling. As soon as his sales amounted to $20,000 the tax had equaled the bond, so the tax was paid and a new bond entered. When he was ready to leave the county, he had sold an additional number of slaves whose value amounted to $18,270, and it was necessary for him to pay a second tax of 1 per cent of these sales.

As has just been stated, the list of persons who paid taxes to Robert Bradley in proportion to their sales of slaves does not comprise all who sold in Adams County in 1833. Moreover, there were others who traded before or after that year. It is, therefore, necessary to supplement Bradley's list with additional traders whose names were gleaned from such sources as their newspaper advertisements, references to them in court records, notices of fugitive slaves, contemporary letters, and books of travel.

In addition to Austin Woolfolk, whose name frequently appears in Mississippi newspapers between 1826 and 1847, and who is too famous to require comment,[94] Rowan and Harris imported a number of slaves for the Mississippi market between 1833 and 1847.[95] There are also meager contemporary references to Tedence Lane, who introduced slaves in the fall of 1835;[96] to a trader by the name of Winfield;[97] to Townshend and Lewis;[98] and to A. C. Omohundro and Company.[99]

Among the traders who were referred to either as residents of or importers from Virginia was Thomas McCargo, who has already been mentioned.[100] Cochran and John D. James purchased a boy in Richmond and sent him south in a gang that reached Natchez in 1845.[101] In 1855, and for several years earlier, John W. Mallory was engaged in the slave-trade between Virginia and Mississippi, selling largely in the eastern counties of the latter State.[102] William Price imported

[94] Woodville Republican, July 1, Dec. 2, 1826; June 16, 1832; Jan. 23, 1847.
[95] Adams et al. v. Rowan et al., 16 Miss. 624.
[96] Thomas et al. v. Phillips, 12 Miss. 358.
[97] Woodville Republican, Dec. 3, 1831.
[98] Ibid., Oct. 6, 1832.
[99] Natchez Mississippi Free Trader, Jan. 24, 1852.
[100] Collins et al. v. McCargo, 14 Miss. 128.
[101] James v. Herring, 20 Miss. 336. Lyell, Second Visit to the United States, II, 126.
[102] Holman et al. v. Murdock, 34 Miss. 275.

negroes from Cumberland County, Va.,[103] and Thomas Sanders brought slaves from Washington County.[104] From that same great source of slaves came Arthur Mosely,[105] Barrum,[106] and Martin [107] to sell in Mississippi markets.

Among the Tennessee traders whose operations extended into Mississippi were Bradford and Crafford [108] and probably Leigh, Maddox, and Company.[109] At any rate, the second member of this firm was spoken of as a negro speculator of Tennessee.[110]

Kentucky furnished James Kelly,[111] William Ford,[112] and probably Thomas Coot, who, in 1825, bought a negro in Kentucky and sold him in Natchez.[113] From North Carolina came Alexander Putney [114] and William Gillesbey.[115]

Traders with depots in New Orleans, but with business operations extending into Mississippi, were Franklin and Armfield,[116] T. Williams (?),[117] Slatter—doubtless the famous Hope H.—,[118] Dickson,[119] and John Robertson, whose headquarters was either in New Orleans or Mobile.[120] Some of these from time to time brought a part of their New Orleans stock in trade to Natchez. On the other hand Walter L. Campbell seems not to have invaded the Natchez market further than to advertise that he had an excellent supply of negroes on hand in a New Orleans depot.[121] This also seems to have been true of trader C. M. Rutherford whose negroes were kept at 159 Gravier street, New Orleans.[122]

A number of the New Orleans commission houses that handled the

[103] *Woodville Republican,* Nov. 17, 1827; July 10, 1830.
[104] *Ibid.,* Oct. 16, 1830.
[105] *Ibid.,* Aug. 7, 1847.
[106] *Ibid.,* May 21, 1836.
[107] *Ibid.,* Sept. 1, 1832; Dec. 12, 1835.
[108] *Ibid.,* Oct. 21, 1828.
[109] Fearn *et al. v.* Shirley *et ux.,* 31 Miss. 301.
[110] *Woodville Republican,* June 13, 1835.
[111] *Ibid.,* Feb. 4, 1832.
[112] *Ibid.,* May 27, 1828.
[113] *Ibid.,* Apr. 12, 1825.
[114] *Ibid.,* Jan. 26, 1832.
[115] *Ibid.,* July 7, 1829.
[116] *Ibid.,* Aug. 12, 1837.
[117] *Ibid.,* Mar. 19, 1842.
[118] *Ibid.,* May 14, 1842.
[119] *Ibid.,* Mar. 25, 1848.
[120] *Ibid.,* Dec. 12, 1848.
[121] Natchez *Daily Courier,* Nov. 1, 1859.
[122] Natchez *Mississippi Free Trader,* Jan. 24, 1852.

cotton crops of Mississippi planters also purchased for them plantation supplies, including slaves. Jefferson Davis received a letter dated Aug. 9, 1852, that illustrates a phase of this practice. Payne and Harrison, commission merchants of New Orleans, wrote Davis that they were sending him a negress who was an excellent washer and ironer as well as a first-rate cook. She was valued at $850 and had been purchased from a trader, but she could be returned within two weeks, if she proved unsatisfactory.[123]

At Natchez, the chief Mississippi slave market, there were a number of traders. In addition to several who have been mentioned, Blackwell, Murphy, and Ferguson, in the fall of 1859, had 150 negroes at the Forks of the Road, with fresh supplies expected through the season.[124] A competitor of this firm was P. Griffin [125] who may have been, a few years earlier, senior partner in the slave-trading firm of Griffin and Pullam.[126] Robert H. Elam also had a permanent depot in this city,[127] and another Natchez trader was Thomas G. James.[128]

For many years before 1837 a man by the name of Herring was a dealer in slaves near Vicksburg.[129] Netherland was engaged in local trading in the State [130] and soon after 1840 Richard Lindsey, trader in slaves, was stationed at Natchez.[131] James Elder was a transient slave-dealer in Mississippi sometime before 1851,[132] and some years earlier William H. Fitzgerald was engaged in the same business.[133]

Now and then restive and resourceful slaves escaped from traders. Advertisements of these fugitives give the names of additional slave-traders. In 1821, a slave in the Wilkinson County jail stated that he had escaped from Bearly and Robert.[134] Much later a slave ran away from trader John Mason at Natchez.[135] The firm of Cotton and Wake-

---

[123] Dunbar Rowland, ed., *Jefferson Davis, Constitutionalist, His Letters, Papers and Speeches*, II, 176–177.
[124] Natchez *Daily Courier*, Nov. 1, 1859.
[125] *Ibid.*, Nov. 3, 1859.
[126] Stowe, *Key to Uncle Tom's Cabin*, pp. 269–270, citing Natchez *Courier*, Nov. 20, 1852.
[127] Newman *v.* Elam, 26 Miss. 474.
[128] *Key to Uncle Tom's Cabin*, pp. 269–270, citing Natchez *Courier*, Nov. 20, 1852.
[129] *Bench and Bar*, pp. 40–43.
[130] Wells *v.* Treadwell, 28 Miss. 717.
[131] *Woodville Republican*, Apr. 23, 1842.
[132] James *v.* Elder, 23 Miss. 134.
[133] MS. catalogued G 170 in Department of Archives and History, Jackson, Miss.
[134] Natchez *Mississippi Republican*, Nov. 6, 1821.
[135] *Woodville Republican*, May 30, 1846.

field also lost, near the southern boundary of Mississippi, a slave they had bought in Fleming County, Ky.[136] John Freeman, a trader of New Orleans, lost a slave he was bringing up the Mississippi River.[137]

The number of names in this list, and there were doubtless others that have not been discovered, indicates the great extent of the slave-trade in Mississippi. It should be noted, however, that a number of these traders spent as much time in other regions as they did in Mississippi, and some had their headquarters elsewhere. A few are known to have been in this State but a small part of the time; it may be that several never personally entered the State but were represented there by agents. However, the list indicates those traders whose names were well known in Mississippi and whose operations extended into the State.

To the present day a certain odium clings to the term slave-trader. It may seem illogical that owners of slaves, who from time to time purchased from traders, would have scorned men in this business, but this seems to have been the case. It is debatable whether the disapproval of the trader in negroes was honest, or whether it was a convenient sentiment which made the slave-trader a scapegoat for much of the evil of slavery. Public opinion was against the trader, but it was even more against the trade. It may be that the current Southern tradition, which considers the slave-trader a social leper, has come from a fusion of two closely related attitudes of earlier times: some dislike for the trader and a greater dislike for certain aspects of the trade. The Supreme Court of Mississippi once listened to the following words:

"I can imagine a man who would hold slaves, who would think it perfectly right to own such property, and cultivate his cotton field by their labor, and yet scorn to make a business of buying and selling human beings for speculation; nay, who would abhor and detest both the speculator and the dealor, and who would shun his society. And I can imagine a community of such men. . . . I do not attempt argument before this court to prove the wide differences between a slave holder and a slave trader; such an attempt before this court, who are slave holders, I would consider in-

[136] *Ibid.*, Oct. 6, 1832.

[137] *Ibid.*, June 15, 1839; July 3, 1841.

Slave-Trading, pp. 309–310, 315, gives the names of the following additional traders whose operations extended into Mississippi: W. P. Davis, W. F. White and Co., M. N. Robertson and Co., Adams and Wicks, Saunders and Bradley, Bolton, Dickins and Co., McRae and Folkes, W. A. Shewalter, Thomas E. Mathews, and A. H. Forrest and Co., the leader of which was doubtless a brother of the better known N. B. Forrest.

sulting to their feelings. Mississippi, for some time [before 1832] had been peculiarly the theatre of the exhibitions of the unfeeling cruelties of the latter class of men, until all good men no doubt had become disgusted and possessed of a strong wish to exclude from the country this class of speculators, at least the spectacles which had offended their feeling, so often arising from this species of commerce." [138]

The court's opinion was in entire accord with this part of the argument, and was expressed in the following words:

"The [constitutional] convention [of 1832] deemed that the time had arrived, when the traffic in this species of property as 'merchandize,' should cease. They had seen and deplored the evils connected with it. The barbarities, the frauds, the scenes so shocking in many instances to our feelings of humanity and the sensibilities of our nature, which generally grew out of it, they, therefore, determined to prohibit in the future." [139]

The supreme court could well have a gloomy view of the slave-trade. The justices knew as well as the average citizen how the trade was conducted, and their experiences on the bench added a large fund of information concerning its seamy side, even though all phases of the evil did not come before their official gaze. No cases arose that were based solely on the inhuman treatment of slaves in the course of the trade. There was practically no way in which these could be brought into court; but the judges often heard of fraud and wrong practiced by one white man on another.

A frequent irregularity in this trade was the refusal, on purely technical grounds, to pay for slaves that had been purchased.[140] Another shadow that lay across the slave-trade is exemplified by the deaths of seven recently purchased slaves from diseases they presumably had at the time of the sale.[141]

A planter could usually detect a physical defect in a slave for sale. Other imperfections were less noticeable and yet might as seriously impair the value of the slave. For instance, a slave who frequently ran away had a depressed value, unless the habit could be concealed from the purchaser. Habitual runaways were, therefore, often sent to markets where they were not known, sometimes in a distant State.[142] It was

[138] This was part of the argument of Mr. Anderson in Green v. Robinson, 6 Miss. 80.
[139] Ibid.
[140] See below, cases arising under constitution of 1832.
[141] Adams et al. v. Rowan et al., 16 Miss. 625. Also, Merrill v. Melchior, 30 Miss. 516.
[142] James v. Kirk, 29 Miss. 206.

also customary to transport negroes who had been convicted of crime and they were frequently sent to Mississippi and Louisiana. Soon after the Southampton insurrection it was reported that fifteen or twenty negroes who had participated were brought to New Orleans in irons. The citizens of that city were so aroused that no attempt was made to land them. Instead, it was assumed, the traders took them up the coast and secretly disposed of them to Louisiana and Mississippi planters.[143] At another time the threatened importation of twelve Maryland slaves, all convicted of crime and pardoned on condition of transportation, agitated southwest Mississippi.[144] Evidently one of the duties of a patriotic newspaper was to warn the community of the approaching sale of criminal slaves, as is shown by this news item: "A gang of forty negroes from Fayetteville, N. C., for sale arrived in this city about a fortnight since. Do our readers recollect any *recent reports* from this place?" [145]

Though a few traders were men of notoriously bad character,[146] the average professional slave-trader could not afford to lose his reputation for conventional honesty. Nevertheless, negroes were from time to time stolen to be resold to a new master, and although this was rarely done by professional slave-traders, it constituted another blot on the trade. For instance, John Loflin was intrusted with three negroes, whom he was to transport to Augusta, Ga., and there deliver them to the purchaser. Instead, Loflin struck out in the direction of Mississippi or Louisiana, with the probable intention of selling the negroes there and pocketing the proceeds.[147] There is an account of another negro, who was stolen near Nashville, Tenn., and brought down the Mississippi River to Natchez.[148] Not only were there reports of particular instances of negro stealing,[149] but it was common for planters to suspect that fugitive negroes had been stolen.[150] The legislature once appropriated $150 to reimburse a private citizen for his expenses in appre-

[143] *Woodville Republican*, Nov. 19, 1831.
[144] *Ibid.*, Jan. 8, 1827.
[145] *Ibid.*, Nov. 26, 1831, citing Natchez *Gazette. Southwest by a Yankee*, II, 259.
[146] *Bench and Bar*, pp. 40–43.
[147] *Woodville Republican*, Sept. 25, 1830.
[148] *Ibid.*, Oct. 3, 1835.
[149] *Ibid.*, Feb. 13, 1841. *Laws of Miss.*, 1838, "An Act making certain appropriations," pp. 336–337; 1833, p. 111; 1857, p. 82.
[150] *Woodville Republican*, Mar. 20, Sept. 11, 1830; May 16, 1835; Mar. 14, 1840; Jan. 3, 1846.

hending a man who had stolen slaves.[151] Slave-stealing was severely punished, and the slave thief of the Old South was as greatly hated as the horse thief of the more recent West.

Several instances of negro-stealing merit more detailed attention. A coroner's jury once convened in Wilkinson County to investigate the death of a small negro girl, whose body had been found in a gully. It was supposed that she had been stolen by a white man.[152] Free negroes were occasionally reduced to slavery by unscrupulous persons. A Natchez newspaper, in 1809, published a warning that, if a yellow woman, Cloe, and a yellow man, Harry, were sold, the full penalties of the law would be imposed and the sale declared void, for they were both free. The mother of Cloe and Harry inserted the notice in the paper, but, in spite of her efforts, they were sold into West Florida which at this date was foreign territory.[153]

Strange to relate, a negro once attempted to enslave a fellow free negro. The facts are stated in the following notice:

"NOTICE TO THE PUBLIC, That there is a free man of color in the County of Pike, State of Mississippi, known by the name of *John*, and appears to be thirty-five to forty years of age; who came to this place from the State of South Carolina with one *William Pendarvis*, a free man of color:—the said John passed here for some time as a free man, but afterwards the said Pendarvis made a considerable effort to *enslave him*, The *said John*, and commenced suit in the Circuit Court against me, for the hire of John, as he termed it, during his stay with me as a free man—in defense of which suit, I obtained evidence from the State of South Carolina which is now in the possession of the Clerk, for Pike County, purporting the said John to have passed some time there as a Free man—and is hereby believed to be free by all conversant with the circumstances.

"R. T. Sparkman." [154]

A very peculiar perversion of the slave-trade was corrected by an act of the Mississippi Legislature of 1833:

"An act to emancipate Indiana Osborne. Whereas, it is represented to the Legislature that Samuel H. Osborne, of the county of Hinds, has recently purchased an infant child whom he believes to be the issue of white parents, who have procured child to be brought to this State and sold as a slave; whereas, also, the said Samuel H. Osborne has expresed to this body his desire to emancipate said slave, whom he calls Indiana Osborne, to educate her and restore her to her natural rights; whereas, the disposi-

[151] *Laws of Miss.*, 1858, pp. 156–157.
[152] *Woodville Republican*, Jan. 24, 1829.
[153] Natchez *Weekly Chronicle*, Mar. 29, 1809; July 1, 1809.
[154] *Woodville Republican*, Nov. 12, 1831.

tion of the said Samuel H. Osborne is philanthropic as a man, honorable as a citizen, and evidence of a sacred regard to liberty; and whereas, said child being presented to view of the Legislature, it is the sense and opinion of the Legislature that said child is the offspring of free white parents;

"Sec. 1. *Be it enacted by the Legislature of the State of Mississippi*, That the said Indiana Osborne be and she is hereby emancipated and set free from slavery, and she is invested with all the rights, privileges, and immunities of any other free white female in this State." [155]

While these unusual cases were far from being everyday events in the slave-trade in Mississippi, there was a tendency for the business to abound in unethical transactions. This might have been sufficient cause for restricting the trade, but there were other reasons. Most of the traders, being transients, had no permanent interest in the community. Also, there was apprehension arising from the rapid increase in the slave population. In each of the two decades preceding 1830, the negro population of the State was doubled. The white population was not keeping pace, though it also was increasing.[156] This created a potential danger, particularly in the southwestern and western parts of the State, where the negroes greatly outnumbered the whites. Fear of an uprising was fanned by rumors that a few of the recently imported negroes were either within or very close to the criminal class. The supreme court stated: "Another alarming evil grew out of it [*i. e.*, the interstate slave-trade], which was highly dangerous to the moral and orderly condition of our slaves, and that was the introduction of slaves from abroad of depraved character, which were imposed upon our unsuspecting citizens by the artful and too often unscrupulous negro trader." [157]

In 1828, Governor Brandon, one of the State's best chief executives, sent a message to the legislature which contained the following views of slavery and the slave-trade. In this able paper appears yet another reason for limiting the importation of slaves into Mississippi.

"The Southern States generally, having passed laws to prevent the importation of slaves for the purposes of traffic, has left Mississippi almost the only receptacle for the surplus black population of the Middle States, where their labor is not found so productive as in the South; the vast number annually imported into our State, has excited uneasiness in the minds of many of our fellow-citizens, and caused them to feel much solici-

---

[155] *Laws of Miss.*, 1833, pp. 169–170. This occurrence evoked some newspaper comment; see *Woodville Republican*, Dec. 14, 1833. For a somewhat similar case see *Laws of Miss.*, 1846, pp. 446–447.

[156] *Census of 1850*, p. 449.

[157] Green *v*. Robinson, 6 Miss. 80.

tude that we should adopt the policy of our neighboring States. Slavery is an evil at best, and has invariably operated oppressively on the poorer classes of every community, into which it has been introduced, by destroying that mutual dependence which would otherwise exist between the rich and the poor, and excludes from the State, in proportion to the number of slaves, a free white population, through the means of which alone, can we expect to take rank with our sister States. With these reflections I submit it to the wisdom of the General Assembly, to say whether the period has not arrived when Mississippi in her own defense, should as far as practicable prevent the further introduction of slaves for sale." [158]

Though there was never any objection to the direct purchase of slaves from other·States by Mississippi planters, there was evident much disapproval of the importation of slaves by traders. As a result, various restrictions were from time to time placed upon the interstate trade. Sometimes it was regulated; once it was entirely prohibited; and it was almost constantly taxed. Since all these restrictions were caused by the same set of objections, and since they were frequently imposed simultaneously, they will be discussed together.

In the year that congress closed the foreign slave-trade, the legislature of the Mississippi Territory decreed that no slave over fifteen years of age could be imported without a certificate of good character signed by two freeholders of the State or territory from which the slave was imported. However, the law neither applied to importations by residents of nor immigrants to Mississippi. Its application was therefore limited to professional slave-traders.[159]

In the constitution of 1817, which marked the birth of the State, the legislature was prohibited from restricting importations by immigrants. It was, however, given "full power to prevent slaves from being brought into this state as merchandise." [160] Under this authority the legislature, in 1822, reënacted the law of 1808 requiring a certificate of good character for slaves imported for purposes of sale. Proper machinery was provided for enforcing the law, and due penalties established for its infraction.[161]

Three years later the legislature began taxing the slave-trade. A law approved February 4, 1825, imposed a 2.5 per cent tax on the gross sales of all auctioneers, "as well as transient merchants and vendors of

[158] *Mississippi*, p. 386.
[159] *Statutes of the Mississippi Territory*, pp. 386–388. Law of Mar. 1, 1808.
[160] Constitution of 1817.
[161] *Hutchinson's Code*, p. 513. The law was not always observed.—Holman *et al. v.* Murdock, 34 Miss. 275.

merchandise and slaves." [162] Next year, on January thirtieth, the act was amended by reducing the tax from 2.5 per cent to 1 per cent.[163] This may have been designed as a nuisance tax, a supposition suggested by reading the tirades directed against the slave-trade. However, since transient traders—slave-peddlers they might be called—had no fixed place of business and were thus exempt from most State taxes, the purpose may have been to equalize the burden of taxation. For several years after its imposition the tax on the sales of wandering traders was apparently collected with regularity.

On the second Monday of September, 1832, at a time when there was much criticism of the interstate slave-trade, a convention met at Jackson to revise the State constitution. An amendment was soon proposed to strike out the words, the legislature "shall have power to prevent slaves from being brought into this state as merchandise," and in their place insert, "the introduction of slaves into this state, as merchandise, shall be prohibited after the — day of —, 18—." May 1, 1833, was proposed as the proper time. An amendment was offered, and lost, to change 1833 to 1899. However, another amendment was accepted which exempted actual immigrants from the effects of this prohibition.[164] In its final form, this part of the constitution of Mississippi of 1832 was as follows: "The introduction of slaves into this state as merchandize, or for sale, shall be prohibited from and after the first day of May, eighteen hundred and thirty-three: Provided, That the actual settler, or settlers, shall not be prohibited from purchasing slaves in any state in this Union, and bringing them into this state for their own individual use, until the year eighteen hundred and forty-five." [165]

Almost at once protests arose against this section of the constitution of 1832. On March 2, 1833, the legislature submitted to the people a constitutional amendment to annul it and substitute the provisions of the constitution of 1817 on this subject. This amendment was not approved by a majority of the voters and so was lost.[166] Before the next meeting of the legislature the question became something of a campaign issue and one candidate stated his strong opposition to any

[162] *Laws of Miss.*, 1824–1838, p. 82.
[163] *Ibid.*, p. 89.
[164] Groves *et al. v.* Slaughter, 15 Peters (U. S.) 453, from the argument of Mr. Gilpin.
[165] Section 2, constitution of Mississippi of 1832, *Hutchinson's Code*, pp. 50–51.
[166] Groves *et al. v.* Slaughter, 15 Peters 454, from argument of Mr. Gilpin.

legislation which might strengthen the constitutional prohibition.[167]

At the next meeting of the legislature, in the latter part of 1833, the senate again proposed a constitutional amendment reopening the trade, but the house refused to concur.[168] However, the two houses united in passing an act to tax the trade in slaves. This act, approved on December 23, 1833, was an amendment to the act of 1825. Its main features were: The bond for transient merchants was increased; the tax was again made 2.5 per cent; and citizens of the State were subjected to the tax, as well as aliens, if they imported slaves for sale or speculation, or indeed for any other purpose than for "agricultural or other laborious employment." [169] There was no further change until 1837, when the legislature finally imposed penalties on those who disregarded the constitutional prohibition of the importation of slaves for sale, and declared that all notes arising from this trade were void and not collectable.[170]

During the period from 1833 until 1837 an unusual situation existed. The importation of slaves for sale was prohibited by the constitution, but the legislature had not established any penalties. To the contrary, it seemed to countenance the trade by placing a tax upon it, though, as will appear, this was very poorly collected. During these four years a great boom in north Mississippi largely stimulated the demand for slaves. Approximately half of the land of the State was opened to white settlers following the dispossession of the Choctaw and Chickasaw Indians by the treaties of Dancing Rabbit (1830) and Pontotoc (1832). The whole State enjoyed a wave of prosperity. The demand for slaves was unprecedented and Mississippi newspapers frequently remarked on the increased importations and advanced prices of negroes. News items from the press of the supplying States were noted with interest, and the Richmond *Compiler's* comment on the unusually high prices being offered for young negroes in Jefferson County, Va., was copied in the *Woodville Republican*.[171] In the fall of 1835, Mississippi newspapers reported that a great emigration from Virginia was in progress. They had heard of a Virginia gentleman who

[167] This gentleman seems to have confused the question of State prohibition with the very different issue of Federal interference with the trade.—*Woodville Republican*, Oct. 19, 1833. Southern nerves were getting a little frazzled at this time.

[168] Groves *et al. v.* Slaughter, 15 Peters 454, from argument of Mr. Gilpin.

[169] *Laws of Miss.*, 1824–1838, pp. 523–525.

[170] *Ibid.*, pp. 758–760. This law was approved by the governor May 13, 1837.

[171] *Woodville Republican*, July 11, 1835.

estimated that 100,000 negroes would be brought to Mississippi in the winter of 1835–1836 by emigrating white planters alone. When the idea was ridiculed, this gentleman was said to have named over a hundred families from a single county who would bring 10,000 negroes.[172]

These and many other newspaper comments were unequal mixtures of fact and fancy, but they show that a boom was on in the middle 'thirties. Importations must have been tremendous, for the slave population of Mississippi increased a fraction over 197 per cent between 1830 and 1840, practically twice the increase of any other decade from 1820 to the Civil War.[173] Such an era of expansion could not last long, and prosperity was followed by deep depression in 1837.

An account of the panic and the flush times just preceding it was given in the Philadelphia *United States Gazette* under the title: "Mississippi,—Her Pecuniary Embarrassments." The *Gazette* stated, in substance, that the cause of Mississippi's troubles was reckless speculation in slaves. From September through December, 1833, several thousand slaves were brought into the State and sold with such success that the following fall the trade was tripled. Profits were fine. Slaves were sold for New Orleans bills at four months' time instead of cash which had previously been required. Traders from Kentucky, Virginia, Tennessee, North and South Carolina, Georgia, Missouri, and Maryland brought in great numbers of slaves in the fall of 1835, quadrupling any previous year. Prices advanced from $700 to $1,000 and at the close of the season the average was $1,200. Traders allowed twelve or fourteen months' time at 10 per cent interest. "The Fall of '36 is a time to be long remembered. All the public highways to Mississippi had become lined—yea literally crowded with slaves. When they arrived, the immense number (swelling the rise of 40,000) made the heart of every trader ache." They pitched their tents on every hill, but purchasers were slow in appearing. Finally, in the winter of 1837 they were sold at prices ranging from $1,200 to $1,800, the traders receiving one and two year New Orleans bills discounted 10 per cent. Most of the bills, in the fall of 1835 and the spring of 1836, were protested for non-acceptance. Negro speculators became alarmed. In February and March of 1837 they secured their debts in deeds of trust and mortgages on nearly the whole property of the State. "In the three years the slave population of Mississippi in-

---

[172] *Ibid.*, Nov. 14, 1835, copied from the Natchez *Daily Courier*.
[173] The white population also increased greatly in this decade. *Census of 1850*, p. 449. *Census of 1860 (Population)*, pp. 268–269.

creased from 70,000 to 160,000, at average cost of at least 1,000 each! making the debt for slaves alone in three years $90,000,000 !"

A Mississippi newspaper quoted without criticism this account from the Philadelphia *Gazette*, though the Whig editor could not let pass the opportunity to blame the panic on the Democratic administration rather than on speculation in slaves.[174] While some of the figures were exaggerated, this account of the period of expansion was essentially correct. Reputations as well as fortunes were impaired. Outraged public opinion caused the resignation of the United States Senator, John Black, whose strivings for lands and slaves influenced his political career, particularly his attitude toward the United States bank.[175] Robert J. Walker faced a debt of several hundred thousand dollars and avoided ruin by ways that, according to Claiborne, were not honest.[176]

At the time of greatest speculation, the importation of slaves for trade was unconstitutional but not illegal. This suggested a way for Mississippi planters to escape ruin. They refused to pay the notes given in purchase of slaves who had been imported contrary to the constitution of 1832. A number of suits arose. The courts of Mississippi decided that though the legislature had provided no penalties, yet the words of the constitution alone were a sufficient prohibition of the trade. Therefore, promissory notes given in purchase of slaves imported by traders after May 1, 1833, were *ultra vires* and not binding.[177] On the other hand, these courts upheld the legality of importations by Mississippi planters for their own personal use.[178]

To avoid the ruinous effects of these decisions, a slave-trader, on the ground of diverse citizenship, brought suit in the federal courts. This case, which came before the Supreme Court of the United States as Groves *et al. v.* Slaughter, was introduced first in the circuit court for the eastern district of Louisiana. Slaughter, a non-resident of Mississippi, had two notes, totaling slightly over $14,000, received in exchange for slaves sold to Mississippians. In 1841, the supreme court affirmed the decision of the circuit court, which was in favor of Slaughter.[179]

[174] *Woodville Republican*, Mar. 14, 1840.
[175] *Mississippi*, p. 431.
[176] *Ibid.*, p. 415.
[177] Green *v.* Robinson, 6 Miss. 80. Brien *v.* Williamson, 8 Miss. 14. Collins *v.* McCargo, 14 Miss. 128. Wooten *et al. v.* Miller, 15 Miss. 380. Adams, Runnells *et al. v.* Rowan and Harris, 16 Miss. 625. Glidwell *v.* Hite, 6 Miss. 110. Thomas *et al. v.* Phillips, 12 Miss. 358.
[178] Hope *v.* Evans, 12 Miss. 321. A somewhat analogous subject is considered in Planters' Bank of Tennessee *v.* Conger *et al.*, 20 Miss. 527.
[179] Groves *et al. v.* Slaughter, 15 Peters 449. In the course of his argument,

As one would expect, this opinion of the federal court met with little favor in Mississippi.[180]

In the case of Groves *et al. v.* Slaughter, the question decided was whether the constitutional prohibition of the trade constituted a prohibition *per se* or whether the trade was legitimate until the legislature imposed specific penalties. The decision avoided the question of whether there was a conflict between the constitution of Mississippi and that of the United States. Since this was so, the courts of Mississippi felt free to proceed on the interpretation they had already set forth. In Brien *v.* Williamson [181] the Supreme Court of Mississippi maintained its position, giving its reasons in great detail because it was opposing the decision of the Supreme Court of the United States.

Thus there were two decisions, one by the highest court of the State, the other by the highest court of the United States, concerning the validity of notes given in payment for slaves imported contrary to the prohibition in Mississippi's constitution of 1832. The validity of a given note then depended simply on whether the case could be brought before the federal courts, which was only possible on the ground of diverse citizenship. A Mississippian who had sold slaves to a fellow-citizen of the same State could not collect a note arising from the transaction; a citizen of any other State could collect from a Mississippian, for here federal precedent would operate. One of the fundamental objections to the slave-trade was the drain of specie from Mississippi, and in this no relief was given.

The litigation that has been discussed arose from sales that were made in the four years after May 1, 1833. In 1837, the legislature finally passed an act prohibiting the trade, placing penalties upon those who participated in it, and specifically stating that notes arising from the trade were void and of no effect.[182]

Clay stated that on the decision of this case depended more than three millions of dollars due by citizens of Mississippi to citizens of Virginia, Maryland, Kentucky and other slave States.—*Ibid.,* p. 481. It is interesting to note that Robert J. Walker, who had largely speculated in slaves, was an attorney in this case.

The Supreme Court of the United States acted with more caution in deciding Groves *et al. v.* Slaughter than it did sixteen years later in the Dred Scott case. Yet the former case presented questions equally as explosive as those in the latter. A good discussion of this phase of Groves *et al. v.* Slaughter is in Charles Warren, *The Supreme Court in United States History,* II, 341–347.

[180] *De Bow's Review,* VIII, 22–23.

[181] 8 Miss. 14.

[182] *Laws of Miss.,* 1824–1838, pp. 758–760. Approved May 13, 1837.

This law was passed after the days of speculation were over and after the panic had set in. It was a gloomy period in the State, and many a thoughtful citizen was ruing the effects of the slave-trade on his own private fortune as well as on that of the commonwealth. Indeed, the act was passed at a time when few people cared to purchase slaves and when any sensible trader would refuse to sell except for cash. Governor Lynch was just four years too late when he announced to this special session of the legislature: "The question which presents itself and which I submit for your deliberation is—whether the passage of an act prohibiting the introduction of slaves into this State as merchandise may not have a salutary effect in checking the drain of capital annually made upon us by the sale of this description of property." [188]

No good end was gained by either the constitutional or the legislative prohibition of the slave-trade into Mississippi. The trade flourished greatly during the years the first alone was in force, and there was no desire to trade while both were in effect. One result was to fill the courts with numerous cases, and there was possibly a poetic justice to the humble slave in having his masters engage in ruthless warfare over the collection of his sale price. Also, planters had long been at the mercy of the traders who sometimes sold them diseased, criminal, or even stolen negroes. The tables were now turned. Many planters who had purchased slaves on credit now refused to pay, nor did the Mississippi courts compel them to do so. It was a ruthless game. Planters and traders were no more merciful to each other than to the dark-skinned property involved.

Even at the height of the restrictions it was possible legally to procure slaves from outside the State. Both the constitutional and legal prohibitions specifically stated that a citizen of Mississippi could purchase slaves abroad for his own use. This allowed a loophole which was soon found and used. The year after Mississippi's prohibitory law was passed we find trader Newton Boley with seventy or eighty slaves at Vidalia, La.,[184] and Boley's advertisements were placed in the Natchez newspapers.[185] With comparatively little inconvenience, planters of

---

[188] W. H. Collins, *The Domestic Slave Trade of the Southern States*, p. 53, citing the *Mississippian*, Apr. 21, 1837. See also, Groves *et al. v.* Slaughter, 15 Peters 484.

[184] Vidalia was also a convenient field of honor for the settlement of quarrels which had begun in Natchez.—*Southwest by a Yankee*, II, 16.

[185] *Mississippi Free Trader and Natchez Gazette*, Dec. 20, 1838, cited in *Slave-Trading*, p. 274.

the Natchez region crossed the river, purchased negroes from the regular traders, and the laws of Mississippi were infracted only in spirit! Within a few years, the trip across the Mississippi was dispensed with, and John D. James, a Natchez trader, openly advertised that he had ninety slaves to sell and more would be procured later.[186] Though the sales were made in Mississippi, James took the precaution of dating the bills of sale as though they had been entered into at Vidalia, and here the law was broken in letter as well as in spirit! [187]

It was not long before Mississippi regretted her limitation of the interstate slave-trade. The fear of a servile insurrection wore off and the evils of the trade were forgotten as the demand grew for more slaves. Although many planters were glad to repudiate their debts to slave-traders, some of them found the scheme a boomerang. Very naturally, the slave-traders stopped selling except for cash or on the best of security. As the year 1845 approached, slave-trading in Mississippi faced a crisis, for after that year the constitution of 1832 prohibited the importation of slaves by any person for any purpose. There was a little newspaper discussion of the question [188] and, with no apparent opposition, the section of the constitution of 1832 that prohibited the trade was superseded by the amendment of 1844–1846, which read as follows: "The legislature shall have, and are hereby vested with power to pass such laws regulating or prohibiting the introduction of slaves into this state, as may be deemed proper and expedient." [189] With power in its hands, the legislature at once legalized the slave-trade, provided the negroes were born inside the bounds of the United States and were of good character.[190]

In the years following the first of May, 1833, there was more or less question of the legality of the introduction of slaves into Mississippi for sale. As a result, the tax on this trade lapsed. When the trade became again lawful, an attempt was made to collect the old taxes. The sheriff of Itawamba County collected, in 1848, $333.33 from James M. Elder, a transient slave-trader. The latter protested, and the supreme court of the State decided in his favor, holding that the tax was no longer in force, having lapsed when the word *slaves* was omitted

[186] *A Second Visit to the United States*, II, 126.
[187] James *v.* Herring, 20 Miss. 336.
[188] *Woodville Republican*, Feb. 15, 1845.
[189] *Hutchinson's Code*, p. 51.
[190] *Revised Code of 1857*, p. 241.

from the revenue acts taxing transient merchants.[191] Slaves were not mentioned in such acts after 1833.[192]

Doubtless as a result of this decision the legislature of 1850 specifically revived this form of revenue. After imposing "an ad valorem tax of one and one fourth per cent on all merchandize sold by an auctioneer or transient vendor of goods . . . ," it further provided, "that all vendors of slaves as merchandize, who shall carry the same from point to point within this State, offering the same for sale as such, shall be assessed with the sales thereof as merchandize sold by transient vendors, and such taxes shall be collected according to laws now in force relative thereto." [193] Acting under this law, Samuel B. Newman, sheriff of Adams County, sought, in 1852, to tax Robert H. Elam, a resident negro-trader of that county, who conducted his business at a permanent depot and did not take his slaves from place to place within the State, offering them for sale. The supreme court decided in favor of Elam, because the tax of 1850 was imposed only on itinerant slave-traders, and Elam was clearly not within that category.[194]

From 1846 until the Civil War, the interstate slave-trade was legal in Mississippi. It was subject to taxation after 1850, and probably would have been between 1846 and 1850 except for an oversight of the legislature. The tax varied slightly in amount, and the mode of collection was improved from time to time,[195] but there was no essential change before the Civil War.

Throughout the 1850's there were many who regretted the reopening of the slave-trade into Mississippi. In 1850 Judge Alexander M. Clayton wrote: "the public mind is fast verging toward a return" to the policy of forbidding the importation of slaves for sale.[196] In 1861, while the legislature and the secession convention were sitting, and while commissioners were being appointed to visit other Southern States to solicit their coöperation, the governor recommended the passage of an act to prohibit the trade. He feared that the border States, in view of the gathering war clouds, would sell their slaves to Missis-

[191] James v. Elder, 23 Miss. 134.
[192] Laws of Miss., 1824–1838, pp. 523–525.
[193] Laws of Miss., 1850, pp. 43 and 49. Approved Mar. 9, 1850.
[194] Newman v. Elam, 26 Miss. 474.
[195] Laws of Miss., 1856, pp. 36 and 60. Approved Feb. 2, 1857.
[196] De Bow's Review, VIII, 22–23.

sippi and other far Southern States. The legislature did not follow his suggestion.[197]

The number of slaves brought into Mississippi either by slave-traders or by immigrant masters cannot be precisely stated. The foremost authority on the domestic slave-trade has made certain estimates, using as a basis the federal census reports of growth of population and allowing for the natural increase among the slaves. The estimates for Mississippi are that between 1830 and 1840 102,394 slaves were imported, an average of 10,239 a year. The estimated importations of the decade from 1840 to 1850 were 58,375, and in the last ten years before the Civil War, 56,560 or a total during these thirty years of 217,329 imported negroes. The exportations were small; possibly 1,000 being sent from the State between 1830 and 1840, 3,000 in the next ten years, and 8,000 between 1850–1860.[198] Of course, the trade fluctuated largely from year to year. Especially was this so during the decade of 1830–1840 when many more slaves were brought in during the middle years than during the extremes of this period.

If 60 per cent of the slaves imported from other States after 1830 were purchased either through traders or directly by Mississippi planters [199] at an average price of $800, it follows that in this thirty years the people of Mississippi spent $104,317,600 for negroes who had been raised outside the State and paid that amount of money or pledged that part of their credit for their payment. This takes no account of the value of the slaves brought in by immigrant masters or of the great numbers of transactions between two or more citizens of Mississippi. It is simply an estimate of the amount of capital obligated by citizens of Mississippi to persons outside the State in return for imported negro slaves.[200]

[197] *Mississippi*, p. 473 note.
[198] *Slave-Trading*, p. 387, and chapter XVIII, *passim*.
[199] *Slave-Trading*, p. 405.
[200] Although the tax records of Mississippi do not provide sufficient information to determine the amount of the slave-trade of the State, a few reports have been discovered and some comment on them is in order:

Between Nov. 10, 1830, and Nov. 10, 1831, there was received into the State treasury "on account of slaves sold as merchandize" $3,131.23½.—*Jour. Gen. Assem. of Miss.*, 1831, House Jour., p. 37. *Woodville Republican*, Jan. 12, 1832. In the following twelve months there was received from this source $3,279.49.—*Woodville Republican*, Jan. 26, 1833. Subsequently, the following sums came from this tax, though it will be noted that the records were not kept for yearly periods:

In Mississippi, a number of slaves were hired or rented, although such transactions were probably not so numerous as in Virginia or Maryland. Several circumstances might persuade a person to hire a servant rather than make an outright purchase. A family without sufficient funds to buy a slave might afford a hired domestic servant.[201] To invest in a high-priced blacksmith and then use him the greater part of the time on common field labor was poor economy. Therefore, the owner of a small plantation arranged to hire a slave who could do such work when the need arose.[202] Again, a large amount of labor was required in constructing a railroad, but the task might not extend over a long enough time to warrant buying slaves, and the finances of the company might not permit this.[203] For these and similar reasons there was a constant demand for hired slaves, especially in the towns. Slaves who could serve as mechanics, cooks, waiters, nurses, porters, gardeners, or common laborers were most likely to be hired.[204]

Jan. 1, 1833–Mar. 3, 1833	$1,065.17
Mar. 4, 1833–Nov. 19, 1833	2,625.13½
Jan. 20, 1835–Feb. 28, 1835	20.00
Mar. 18, 1835–Jan. 4, 1836	166.40
Jan. 5, 1836–Feb. 29, 1836	68.50
Mar. 1, 1836–Jan. 4, 1837	82.00

From the separately published *Argument of Robert J. Walker, Esq., before the Supreme Court of the United States . . . in the case of Groves et al. v. Slaughter*. Walker's last item is verified in the *Woodville Republican*, Jan. 28, 1837.

These taxes, until the end of 1833, were collected under the act of 1826, which imposed a tax of 1 per cent on the gross sales of transient dealers, and after 1833, under the act of December, 1833, which raised the tax to 2.5 per cent. One might suppose that these tax returns could be used to ascertain the gross transactions in slaves. This is far from being true. This tax applied only to itinerant traders (Newman v. Elam, 26 Miss. 474), and was further limited by the statement that "nothing in this act shall authorize a tax to be collected on the sale of any slave or slaves, sold by one citizen of this state, to another citizen thereof." Furthermore, the mode of collecting the tax allowed much room for dishonest returns, for the amount of the tax depended on the gross sales sworn to by the trader.

The exceeding smallness of the returns from this tax after 1833 is explained by the constitutional prohibition of the introduction of slaves for sale after May first of that year. Though there was a tax on the statutes, a trader would hardly report his own infraction of the constitutional prohibition, particularly when such a report would only lead to his being taxed. The taxes that were paid after May 1, 1833, were doubtless on slaves that had been imported before that date but not sold until afterward, which indicates the length of time a trader sometimes held his stock of goods before being able to sell to advantage.

[201] *Woodville Republican*, May 26, 1829.

[202] "Diary of a Miss. Planter," in *P. M. H. S.*, X, 462.

[203] Leigh MSS.

[204] *Southwest by a Yankee*, II, 250. *Woodville Republican*, Oct. 7, 1828; May 26, 1829; May 29, 1830; Dec. 26, 1833; June 6, 1835; Jan. 14, 1837; Jan. 3, 1846.

For various reasons some slave-owners found it more advantageous to hire out their negroes than to work or to sell them. Sometimes a planter had a surplus of skilled and high priced slaves, who could not be used with economy at common labor. These house servants or mechanics were, therefore, hired in neighboring towns.[205] Not far from Natchez once lived a German farmer who owned four negro men in addition to a woman and several children. He found it more profitable to hire all the men as porters or servants in Natchez than to keep them at home, and, with the aid of a single white man, he cultivated his farm himself.[206]

Another object to be secured by hiring rather than by selling slaves is indicated in a newspaper advertisement. A guardian gave notice that on the first Monday in January five negroes would be hired for the next twelve months. Four negro children had to be cared for in addition to the five adults, and the hirer had to assume the payment of all taxes and provide good clothing. It is significant that the advertisement was placed in the newspaper by a guardian whose wards were being supported, at least in part, by the hire of the slaves. It is even more significant that four of the five adult negroes were women, for in addition to their hire, the probable birth of children was important. Such an investment produced a yearly dividend and increased in capital value as well.[207] Some slaveholding families in Mississippi did not own an acre of land, and were supported in whole or in part by the income from hiring out the slaves.[208]

Under various circumstances, some of which have been illustrated, a planter considered it more profitable to hire a slave out than to sell him. There were doubtless slaves who could not be sold but could be hired. A negro's owner was responsible for his upkeep, even when he became old and unable to work. The responsibility of the hirer ceased on a specific day, which was seldom more than a year in advance. One would hesitate to purchase an ancient blacksmith, even though he could still do a good day's work, but would gladly pay a fair price for his labor for the next six months or year. Part of the money received for the hire of a slave amounted to a premium on an old-age pension, with

[205] *Southwest by a Yankee*, II, 251.
[206] *Back Country*, p. 41.
[207] *Woodville Republican*, Dec. 9, 1826.
[208] *Southwest by a Yankee*, II, 251.
In the *Woodville Republican*, Jan. 8, 1848, is a notice that five slaves would be hired on a certain day. This was the third year this advertisement appeared at the beginning of the year.

the master acting as insurer. This partly explains why the annual hire of slaves was a surprisingly large per cent of their capital value.

On January 16, 1849, a Mississippi planter made the following notation in his diary: "Hired from Wm. Montgomery 2 negroes, Henry and Matilda, at $200 for 12 mos. I pay clothing taxes and doctor's bills. Began today." [209] This illustrates the essential features of a hiring contract, which specified the negroes, the length of time, and the price, as well as any other agreements that were made. The cost of clothing, medical attention, and taxes were ordinarily borne by the employer. [210] It was occasionally stipulated in the contract that certain hired slaves should not be removed from the neighborhood because they had families. [211] It was, of course, expected that the slave would be treated reasonably well in all particulars—which meant little more than that his ability to work must not be impaired by mistreatment. [212]

Hiring of slaves, especially in agricultural operations, was generally on a yearly basis, though payment was sometimes made each month, [213] and daily wages were occasionally mentioned. The cost of hiring slaves by the day for work in a cotton mill, or a shoe factory, was about seventy-five cents for a man, fifty cents for a woman, and forty cents for a boy. [214] Naturally, rates were a little higher in the towns than in the country. The thrifty German, who worked his own farm near Natchez and hired his four men to others, received thirty dollars a month as hire of one of these slaves. [215] An estimate reported by Solon Robinson was probably nearer the average. According to this, a common negro man was worth from $10 to $15 a month; a woman cook or good house servant the same; and a negro carpenter or blacksmith from $25 to $45 a month. [216]

The following appraisal, made by an overseer, gives both the value of each slave and the hire for a three months' period, January 14 to April 14, 1846. The ages of three of the negroes were also noted.

[209] "Diary of a Miss. Planter," in *P. M. H. S.*, X, 427.
[210] *Woodville Republican*, Dec. 9, 1826.
[211] *Ibid.*, Jan. 3, 1846.
[212] Trotter *v.* McCall, 26 Miss. 410.
[213] *Woodville Republican*, June 6, 1835.
[214] *De Bow's Review*, VII, 176, 456. *Southwest by a Yankee*, II, 252.
[215] *Back Country*, p. 41.
   In January, 1860, near Port Gibson the negro Bob Miranda was hired for $20 a month.—Spooner Forbes, Diary, MS.
[216] *The Cultivator*, n. s., II, 365.

	Value	Hire for 3 months	Age [217]
Amanda	$600	$27	
Sherrod	400	15	
Tom	250		
Stephen	200		
Bob	200		
Alley	300	20	47
Emily	425	16	13
Julius	350	8	
Jim	800	60	22
Maria	550	22	

A more valuable source of information about many phases of hiring has been preserved in an account book kept by S. M. Meek, a prominent lawyer of Columbus, Mississippi, who, as guardian, controlled the slaves of the estate of Henry E. Cannon from 1844 through 1852 inclusive. Cannon's estate, exclusive of land, was appraised on June 27, 1843, at $9,263, of which $8,376 was the value of his slaves and the remainder was the value of 12 horses and mules, 2 yoke of oxen, a few hogs, cows and calves, 1 ox-wagon, 2 guns, hoes, axes, plows, etc. The appraisers seem to have set too high a value in most cases, for when the farm animals and tools were sold at auction to various purchasers on January 4, 1844, they brought on the average about a fifth less than the appraised value.

The slaves of this estate were hired out by the year for the nine years beginning with 1844, and each year Meek listed the hirer of each slave with the amount paid. These lists have been combined into one table showing the appraised value of each slave in the summer of 1843 and the sum for which he was yearly hired. The names of the hirers have been omitted, but it should be stated that each year the negroes were scattered to almost as many hirers as there were slaves and that they were not usually hired by the same person any two years in succession. Considerably more than half of the slaves were hired by seven or more different persons. In some cases they were hired by members of the Cannon family.

As for the profitableness of the venture, it appears that in less than six years the income from hiring amounted to the appraised value of the slaves, which was nearly three times as much as money invested

[217] Kirby *et al. v.* Calhoun, 16 Miss. 462. See also, Prewett *v.* Dobbs, 21 Miss. 431. Trotter *v.* McCall, 26 Miss. 410.

Summary of part of the accounts kept by S. M. Meek as guardian of the estate of Henry E. Cannon. The number before the name of each slave indicates the number of persons to whom he was hired; the first number following a slave's name shows his appraised value on June 27, 1843; the remaining numbers show the amount for which each slave was hired for the years 1844 through 1852. The totals are copied from the original MS.

	Name	Value	1844	1845	1846	1847	1848	1849	1850	1851[a]	1852
5	Chloe	450	90.00	76.00	75.00	112.00	110.00	80.50	85.00	152.00	170.00
9	Cooper	675	100.00	116.00	131.00	166.00	156.00	129.00	140.00		
9	Hannah	500	92.00	75.00	76.00	87.00	111.00	91.00	66.00	86.00	51.00
5	Cretia	300	30.00	rtd.[b]	rtd.	rtd.	rtd.	79.00	81.00	90.50	51.00
6	Lucinda	225		13.50	21.00	31.00	51.00	50.00	60.00	84.00	106.00
0	Old Sam	1	spt.[c]	spt.	spt.	spt.	spt.	spt.	spt.	spt.	spt.
0	Old Kate	100									
9	Elsey	475	103.00[d]	60.00	55.00	110.00	103.00	82.50	66.00	73.50	51.00
9	Silla	475	73.00	61.00	64.00	107.00	92.00	83.00	51.00	101.00	75.00
9	Renta	475	55.00	45.00	55.50	115.00	106.00	92.50	100.00	133.00	144.00
7	Harriet & child Ja-nette	530	60.00	71.50	61.00	116.00	118.00	82.00	80.50	81.00	81.00
4	Judy	500	95.00	rtd.	rtd.	rtd.	rtd.	82.00	67.00	100.00	91.00
4	Mary	225	42.75	31.00	19.25	29.00	32.50	46.50	56.75	80.50	90.00
6	Caty	180	36.00	20.00	37.00	38.00	33.50	48.50	26.00	24.50	40.00
2	Old Caty	40			11.00	rtd.	rtd.	rtd.	rtd.		
7	Quash	375	120.50	105.50	86.00	94.00	35.00	60.00	41.00	62.00	80.00

No.	Name									
7	Old Amy[e]	125	50.00	45.50	48.00	77.00	54.00	34.50	30.50	rtd.	83.00
8	Harriet	325	36.00	42.00	46.50	81.00	98.50	90.50	81.00	65.00	100.75
8	Amanda	325	35.50	46.50	43.00	87.00	92.00	86.00	82.00	86.00	120.00
7	Jesse[e]	300		35.00	26.00	55.00	91.00	61.00	69.00	120.00	120.00
9	Sam	675	144.50	140.00	150.00	185.00	160.00	155.50	150.00	191.00	175.00
7	Rachel	500	96.00	79.00	86.00	153.00	127.00	116.00	86.00	105.00	107.00
8	Darcas & child Rosanna	600	100.00	60.00	90.00	100.00	104.00	92.50	79.50[f]	71.00	107.00
3	Little Caty							21.00	36.00	39.00	51.00
		8376	1359.25	1122.50	1181.25	1744.00	1694.50	1663.50	1533.25	1745.00	1774.75

[a] By Chloe's name in 1850 is the notation: "Chloe died at Carters 30th July and deduction made accordingly (pro rata) for five months—$35.44."

[b] The word *retained* appears on the original manuscript wherever the letters *rtd* are written above. The meaning is probably that on these years these slaves remained in the service of the widow, Mrs. A. M. Cannon, and were not hired out.

[c] Likewise, the word *support* has been abbreviated to *spt*. Presumably, Old Sam could not be hired and was spending his old age at Mrs. Cannon's.

[d] By Elsey's name in 1844 is the notation: "Sick. Sued & only a portion of the hire allowed by the court."

[e] Old Amy and Jesse were hired together in 1844 for $50. By Old Amy's name in 1852 are the words: "Taking care of little Negroes."

[f] In 1849 after the name of Darcas is the notation: "Had to take Darcas, & Recd. $38.25 for the time she remained, afterwards hired her to T. E. Cannon for $24. (Confined at my house) & had to find clothes blankets etc."

at 6 per cent interest would have produced. Further, the income was, on the average, becoming larger as the years passed. Though the owner had to take the risk of losses by death, old age, and accident, as a matter of fact young negroes seemed to be at least replacing the old. Even at the time when Meek took charge of the estate, Old Sam was valued at only $1, and through the following years was presumably supported by Mrs. A. M. Cannon, widow of Henry E. Cannon. Old Kate probably died very soon after her master; Chloe died in 1851; Old Caty could be hired for only three years; and one or two others were evidently declining in value by the end of the nine years. On the other hand, more were increasing in value, if we may judge by the amounts for which they were hired; Lucinda, Mary, and Little Caty became old enough to be hired out during these years; and there were "little negroes" being cared for who in all probability would more than replace future gaps in the working force.

In October, 1853, this same Columbus attorney gave bond as guardian for another estate, that of Robert Lowndes Cannon. Though the facts of this guardianship are very meager, they are presented because they are for a later period and show a decidedly higher average income in proportion to the number of slaves hired. These negroes also were hired to different persons.

Year	Number of slaves hired out	Total income for the year from this source [218]
1854	15	$2342
1855	15	2375
1856	15	2239
1857	16	2346
1858	16	2567

Naturally, a slave who was highly skilled could be hired for much more than the usual rates. President Polk's slave, Harry, was hired to planters as far as forty miles south of Polk's Mississippi plantation and from this work, in addition to some that he did on Polk's place, he earned for his master between $350 and $450 a year.[219] Another blacksmith in the southern part of the State was worth $600 a year to his master.[220]

The services of a skilled negro mechanic were not often needed

[218] Meek MS.
[219] *Plantation Overseer*, pp. 161–162. See also, *Southern Planter*, p. 104.
[220] *Woodville Republican*, Jan. 16, 1841.

by one man for a long period of time. Such slaves were, therefore, hired first to one person and then to another, and their masters frequently had to direct their movements over a large territory. To avoid this exertion, a master might allow the slave to manage his own business engagements, thus granting him virtual freedom; and the slave would agree to pay the master a yearly sum. For instance, Nejar Scott, slave of Charles Montgomery of Mississippi, paid his master $600 a year for his own time. He worked as a skilled carpenter in various places, and indeed was in Louisiana a large part of the time. It was a profitable arrangement for the owner. Nejar was allowed to retain any profit he could secure over and above the $600 a year, and he planned to purchase his own freedom, as his father before him had done.[221]

The common hired slave was liable to be driven hard. His employer had no permanent interest in his well-being, but was greatly concerned over the amount of labor he could extort for a limited period of time. The hireling could not expect, therefore, to be treated as well as he would have been by his own master, though life was probably not so bad for the skilled hired slave. The value and nature of his work probably saved him from being molested by the negro driver or even by the overseer. Better still was the life of the slave who hired his own time. He differed but little from a free laborer, except that a large share of his earnings he could not keep.

It was said that masters who were sufficiently indulgent to allow a slave to hire his own time were seldom exacting in the yearly sum they expected the slave to pay for the privilege. This permitted a few slaves to accumulate a sum toward purchasing their freedom.[222] However, there were masters who would not allow a steady slave to hire his own time. If ever there was a slave who deserved the good favor of his master that negro was President Polk's Harry. He wrote his master and asked to hire his own time, reminding Polk that he had "been faitheful over the anvill Block" for thirty-one years, and had given his master eleven children—a most valuable present. Polk evidently believed that the present arrangement was too satisfactory to be tampered with and turned a deaf ear to Harry.[223]

[221] "Diary of a Miss. Planter," in *P. M. H. S.,* X, 454, note.
For another case of a slave who had evidently purchased his own time, and had paid his master $600 toward his own freedom, see MS. petition catalogued I 94 in Department of Archives and History, Jackson, Miss.
[222] *Southwest by a Yankee,* II, 251.
[223] *Plantation Overseer,* pp. 161–162.

As one would expect, white mechanics bitterly opposed the granting of virtual freedom to skilled negro workmen. An intelligent white
artisan would not teach his trade to a slave, even though he was offered a generous compensation.[224] Protests were placed in the newspapers,[225] and municipal ordinances were passed to prohibit slaves
from hiring their own time, going at large, and working as free
men.[226] A vigilance committee was proposed in Natchez as the most
efficient means of suppressing this practice.[227] There was a poorly
enforced State law which prohibited slaves from hiring their own
time. Very properly, its penalties were directed against masters who
permitted the practice. However, the slave would lose his status of
semi-freedom, and, rarely, might be sold to a new master, if the old one
did not pay the fines imposed.[228]

[224] *Back Country*, p. 180.
[225] *Woodville Republican*, Sept. 18, 1847.
[226] *Ibid.*, Oct. 12, 1839.
[227] *American Negro Slavery*, p. 412.
[228] *Hutchinson's Code*, p. 516.
There was often an interchange of courtesies between neighboring planters
when one or the other was behind in cotton picking or badly "in the grass." The
entire field force of one planter would be sent to the fields of the other for several
days or a week, and, when need arose, the courtesy was repaid.—Bowles MS.
Such transactions partook to such a slight degree of the normal hiring of slaves
that they are not here considered as a phase of the subject.

CHAPTER VIII

PROFITABLENESS OF SLAVERY

At the time when the United States secured control over the Natchez region, cotton was displacing tobacco and indigo as the staple crop of that locality. One reason for this change can be found in the New Orleans "Prices Current" that were printed in a Natchez newspaper of September, 1802, in which the following stand in notable contrast. "Cotton, per cwt. 19 to 20 dols. *brisk*" and "Tobacco, per cwt. 3 dols. dull." [1] Two years earlier cotton had brought even higher prices according to a traveler who was then in the territory. He reported that the price was from twenty-two to twenty-three dollars a hundredweight at Natchez and from twenty-five to twenty-six at New Orleans. In addition to these prices, the advent of the gin to the region made cotton the favored crop and the same traveler who reported prices declared in 1800 that "cotton is now the staple commodity in the territory." [2]

In 1795, Daniel Clark, of the Natchez region, met a traveler from Georgia who had seen the recently invented cotton-gin of Eli Whitney. Realizing the advantage of such a machine, Clark placed the traveler's description and a rude drawing of Whitney's invention before his negro, Barclay, who was a skilled mechanic. With this meager information, Barclay was able to construct the first gin in Mississippi. [3] The following year David Greenleaf began making gins near Natchez, and, in 1801, Isaac Nerson entered this business at Pine Ridge. [4] It was stated in this year that "almost every farmer of considerable force has a horsegin on his farm." Those who lacked them could have their cotton ginned by neighbors at a toll of one pound out of ten. Though a few experimented with water-power, most of the gins were turned by horse-power and separated from 500 to 1,000 pounds of

---

[1] Natchez *Mississippi Herald*, Sept. 28, 1802.
[2] James Hall, "A Brief History of the Mississippi Territory," in *P. M. H. S.*, IX, 254, 262.
[3] Wailes, *Agriculture and Geology*, p. 167.
[4] Claiborne, *Mississippi*, p. 143.

clean lint a day.[5] The manufacture of cotton-gins increased; by 1860 Mississippi was leading all other States. Her three factories, employing seventy hands, produced an annual product worth $131,-900.[6]

Six years after the gin reached Mississippi, a screw press for baling cotton was made in Philadelphia for William Dunbar after a model sent by him two years before. He hoped to indemnify himself for the large cost, which was over $1,000, by extracting cotton-seed oil. The press soon came into general use for forcing the lint into bales, though many years passed before any value was discovered in cotton-seed.[7]

In 1795, when the slave mechanic was making the first Whitney gin in Mississippi, a little Sea Island cotton was being raised, the lint being separated from the seed by the old roller-gin. Another smooth-seeded variety, locally known as Upland, was also grown. This however, differed widely from varieties that have later been called by the same name. A serious objection to Upland cotton was the difficulty of picking it and, while it had a fine long staple, it is probable that the Whitney gin injured it. Furthermore, in 1811 a disease known as the "rot" appeared and within a few years became very destructive. Upland cotton was, therefore, not satisfactory and little was produced. In 1811, sixteen years after the Whitney gin reached Mississippi, it was estimated that less than 1,000 bales were produced annually.[8]

After the War of 1812, Mississippi began to produce cotton on an enlarged scale. The reasons for this increase were: her population nearly doubled in the decade following 1810; prices of cotton were high from 1815 through 1824, reaching nearly 34 cents a pound in 1817; and, about 1815, a new variety, known sometimes as Tennessee and sometimes as Cumberland, was introduced into Mississippi. The chief advantage of Tennessee cotton was its immunity to the "rot." These stimulants brought Mississippi's crop to approximately 20,000 bales in 1821.

[5] "Mississippi Territory," in *P. M. H. S.*, IX, 555.
[6] *Census of 1860 (Agriculture)*, p. xxvi. One of the largest of these was the factory of T. G. Atwood, located at Kosciusko.—Vicksburg *Weekly Sun*, Nov. 5, 1860.
[7] *Mississippi*, p. 144.
[8] This estimate is for 500 pound bales, which is also true for the estimates on the next few pages.

PRODUCTION AND PRICE OF COTTON

Year	PRODUCTION (EQUIVALENT 500-POUND BALES, GROSS WEIGHT) United States	Mississippi	AVERAGE EXPORT PRICE, FOR THE UNITED STATES	NEW ORLEANS PRICES, MIDDLING COTTON Highest	Lowest
1791	4,180	———	25.0 [?]	——	——
1801	100,313	———	22.0	——	——
1811	167,189	———	10.7	——	——
1813	156,740	———	15.1	——	——
1815	208,986	———	29.4	——	——
1817 :....	271,682	———	33.9	——	——
1819	349,007	———	17.4	——	——
1821	376,176	20,000	16.6	——	——
1822	438,871	———	11.8	——	——
1823	386,625	———	15.4	——	——
1824	449,321	———	20.9	——	——
1825	532,915	———	12.2	——	——
1826	731,452	———	10.0	——	——
1827	564,263	———	10.7	11.0	8.5
1828	679,206	———	10.0	10.5	8.5
1829	762,800	———	9.9	9.8	8.0
1830	731,452	100,000	9.1	10.8	7.3
1831	804,598	(average of	9.8	9.8	8.0
1832	815,047	1826 and 1833)	11.1	12.0	9.3
1833	929,990	———	12.9	18.0	9.0
1834	961,338	———	16.8	19.0	11.5
1835	1,060,711	———	16.8	17.0	13.0
1836	1,127,836	———	14.2	16.0	8.5
1837	1,426,891	———	10.3	10.0	8.0
1838	1,091,838	———	14.8	15.0	8.0
1839	1,651,995	386,803	8.6	10.8	6.0
1840	1,346,232	———	10.2	10.5	7.8
1841	1,396,821	———	8.1	8.8	6.0
1842	2,033,354	———	6.2	7.5	4.5
1843	1,748,231	———	8.1	9.1	5.8
1844	2,076,737	———	5.9	6.3	4.4
1845	1,804,223	———	7.8	7.6	6.1
1846	1,602,087	———	10.1	11.6	7.5
1847	2,126,208	———	7.6	10.9	4.8
1848	2,612,299	———	6.5	9.5	4.9
1849	2,064,028	387,434	11.3	12.8	8.8
1850	2,133,851	———	12.1	13.6	6.3
1851	2,796,365	———	8.0	9.8	6.5
1852	3,127,067	———	9.8	10.8	7.9
1853	2,763,304	———	9.5	11.0	7.3
1854	2,705,252	———	8.7	12.0	7.5
1855	3,217,417	———	9.5	11.0	7.9

PRODUCTION AND PRICE OF COTTON—(*Continued*)

Year	PRODUCTION (EQUIVALENT 500-POUND BALES, GROSS WEIGHT) United States	Mississippi	AVERAGE EXPORT PRICE, FOR THE UNITED STATES	NEW ORLEANS PRICES, MIDDLING COTTON Highest	Lowest
1856	2,870,678	——	12.6	15.3	11.0
1857	3,008,869	——	11.7	16.3	8.3
1858	3,754,346	——	11.6	12.4	10.8
1859	4,541,285	962,006	10.9	11.8	10.8
1860	3,837,402	——	11.1	13.0	9.3

Figures in the first three columes (production in the entire United States, in Mississippi, and average export price for United States) are taken from *Atlas of American Agriculture,* part V, section A (Advance Sheets, 4), pp. 16–18. New Orleans prices were supplied by Mr. Henry G. Hester, secretary of the New Orleans Cotton Exchange. To facilitate comparison, these latter prices were changed from common fractions to the nearest decimal fractions. According to a State census taken in 1837, 317,783 bales (weight not stated) were produced in Mississippi in 1836.—*Woodville Republican,* May 20, 1837.

Though Tennessee cotton was hardier than the older black-seeded varieties, it had two objectionable features. It could not be picked rapidly, and its fiber was short and coarse. Therefore, it was easily displaced by Mexican or Petit Gulf cotton, which came into general use soon after 1820. As this, and strains of various names that were bred from it, permanently displaced the earlier varieties, its characteristics will be stated. The seed of Mexican cotton, like that of Tennessee, was woolly, but larger and more nearly white. More important, it was as healthy as Tennessee; it was more prolific; and the lint was longer and finer. Best of all, its bolls opened wide when ripe, and a cotton-picker could with the same effort bring in two pounds of Mexican for every one he could have picked of Tennessee or the black-seeded varieties.[9]

[9] *Agriculture and Geology,* pp. 142–143. *Mississippi,* pp. 140–142. Phillips, *Life and Labor in the Old South,* pp. 91 ff. *De Bow's Review,* II, 133–142; III, 1–20.

The two names of this important variety of cotton, Mexican and Petit Gulf, outline the history of its importation and popularization. The following story is told of the introduction of this variety to Mississippi and the United States.

"The Mexican seed is believed to have been first introduced by the late Walter Burling, of Natchez.

"It is related by some of our oldest citizens, who were well acquainted with him and the facts, that, when in the city of Mexico, where he was sent by General Wilkerson, in 1806, on a mission connected with a threatened rupture between the two countries, in relation to our western boundary, he dined at the viceroy's table,

These decided advantages brought Mexican cotton into general use in Mississippi between 1821 and 1830, and a great increase in production resulted. Although the price dropped to ten cents a pound shortly before 1830, Mississippi's crop was approximately 100,000 bales in that year, which was five times larger than it had been nine years before.

The decade following 1830 is the most important in the history of cotton production in Mississippi. A slight cause of increased production was the use of steam to turn cotton-gins, which began in 1830.[10] More significant was the fact that shortly after this year the northern half of Mississippi was relinquished by the Indians and delivered to white planters. Also, between 1832 and 1838 the price of cotton was high. With these forces operating in the same direction, there is small cause for wonder that Mississippi almost quadrupled her crop, producing 386,803 bales in 1839, which was, for the first time, the largest cotton crop of any State in the Union.

From 1840 to 1855 there was a period of depression. The price remained low, seldom exceeding ten cents, and middling cotton frequently sold in New Orleans for less than five cents. In 1849 Mississippi produced only a few hundred bales more than in 1839. However, this comparison should be tempered by stating that the 1839 crop was above the average of the surrounding years, while the 1849 crop was below.

With 1856 a third period of prosperity began. In that year the average price advanced three cents a pound and continued well above ten cents until the Civil War. Though this price was good, it was by no means remarkable. In the late 'fifties, profits in cotton were due more to large crops than to high prices. Of particular importance was the

and in the course of conversation on the products of the country, he requested permission to import some of the Mexican cotton seed—a request which was not granted, on the ground that it was forbidden by the Spanish government. But the viceroy, over his wine, sportively accorded his free permission to take home with him as many *Mexican dolls* as he might fancy—a permission well understood, and which in the same vein was as freely accepted. The stuffing of these dolls is understood to have been cotton seed."—*Agriculture and Geology*, p. 143.

Near the town of Petit Gulf (later known as Rodney) was an unusually intelligent planter, Dr. Rush Nutt. He was the first to raise Mexican cotton extensively. For many years planters far and near preferred seed that had been produced near Petit Gulf, and thus Mexican cotton became known as Petit Gulf cotton. Dr. Nutt and his neighbors for some years enjoyed a considerable profit from the sale of cotton seed.—*Mississippi*, p. 141.

[10] *Ibid.*, p. 141. However, the gin horse was undisturbed on many plantations until some years later.

crop of 1859 which, for the entire United States, exceeded every year before 1878. In 1859, Mississippi produced 962,006 bales.

As one would expect, the importation of negroes from outside the State, as indicated by their increase in number, was in proportion to the profitableness of cotton. According to the federal census, in each of the four decades before 1840 the slave population of Mississippi more than doubled. Between 1830 and 1840 there was an enormous increase—197 per cent. During the depression following 1840 the rate of increase was relatively small, 59 per cent from 1840 to 1850, and 49 per cent from 1850 to 1860.[11]

Mississippians believed, especially in such flush times as the early 'thirties, that to become wealthy one needed but to raise cotton; the prerequisites were land and negroes. There are other proofs, in addition to census figures, that Mississippi wanted more slaves. One who declared at the time that cotton and negroes were the chief topics of conversation wrote the following account of the feverish scramble for them.

"A plantation well stocked with hands, is the *ne plus ultra* of every man's ambition who resides at the south. Young men who come to this country, 'to make money,' soon catch the mania, and nothing less than a broad plantation, waving with the snow white cotton bolls, can fill their mental vision, . . . Hence the great number of planters and the few professional men of long or ancient standing in their several professions. As soon as the young lawyer acquires sufficient to purchase a few hundred acres of the rich alluvial lands, and a few slaves, he quits his profession at once, though perhaps just rising into eminence, and turns cotton planter. . . .

"Physicians make money much more rapidly than lawyers, and sooner

[11]

Year	No. of whites	Per cent increase	No. of slaves	Per cent increase
1800	5,179	———	3,489	———
1810	23,024	344.56	17,088	389.76
1820	42,176	83.18	32,814	92.02
1830	70,443	67.02	65,659	100.09
1840	179,074	154.21	195,211	197.31
1850	295,718	65.13	309,878	58.74
1860	353,901	19.33	436,631	49.04

This table, with the exception of the last line, is from the *Compendium of the Census of 1850*, pp. 45, 47, 82, 84. The numbers of white persons and of slaves in 1860 are taken from the *Census of 1860 (Population)*, p. 270.

In 1817, the State of Mississippi was carved from the older Mississippi Territory, which had also included Alabama. The per cents of increase in 1820 are, therefore, too small for the 1820 statistics of population were of Mississippi alone; the 1810 figures were of the larger Mississippi-Alabama Territory.

retire from practice and assume the planter. They, however, retain their titles, so that medico-planters are now numerous, far out-numbering the regular practitioners, who have not yet climbed high enough up the wall to leap down into a cotton field on the other side. Ministers, who constitute the third item of the diploma'd triad, are not free from the universal mania, . . . The merchant moves onward floundering through invoices, ledgers, packages, and boxes. The gin wright and the overseer, also have an eye upon this Ultima Thule, while the more wealthy mechanics begin to form visions of cotton fields, and talk knowingly upon the 'staple.' Even Editors have an eye that way." [12]

Slave-owners who had sufficient credit to secure many negroes generally were able to purchase the good lands that lay along the rivers. Thus, if one charts on a map the parts of Mississippi to which slaves were chiefly brought, the influence of geography is at once apparent, for the slave population was densest in the fertile bottom lands. Another attraction of such locations was that the rivers afforded the only means of transporting cotton to market. Also, many of the early settlers of Mississippi had come by water, and they naturally established plantations, villages, and towns close to the rivers.[13] In these older regions there was a high proportion of slaves, for sufficient time had elapsed for the accumulation of means to purchase them or for the original stock of slaves to multiply.

A discussion of the geographical distribution of slaves over Mississippi will establish the generalizations in the last paragraph. This distribution is even more significant if the proportion of slaves to whites in the different parts of the State is noticed.

In 1850 the slave population and the white population of Mississippi were almost equal, 309,878 slaves and 295,718 whites.[14] However, by analyzing these populations county by county, it is found that great inequalities existed in the various sections of the State. The general rule was as follows. In all the counties bordering the Mississippi River, except De Soto and Coahoma, slaves constituted more than 65 per cent of the population. The same was the case in the counties along the lower part of the Yazoo and Big Black Rivers and in Nuxobee and Lowndes Counties on the eastern edge of the State in the valley of the Tombigbee River. These fifteen counties con-

---

[12] [Ingraham], *Southwest by a Yankee*, II, 84–86. See also pp. 67–68.
[13] Notably, Natchez and the neighboring towns in the southwestern part of the State, and Cotton Gin Port and Aberdeen to the northeast on the Tombigbee.
[14] *Compendium of the Census of 1850*, pp. 45, 82.

tained approximately one half of the slaves but only one fifth of the white people of Mississippi.[15]

The remaining forty-four counties, of course, contained four fifths of the white population of Mississippi, in 1850, and only half of the slaves. The proportion of slaves to whites in these remaining counties may be formulated in the following statement. The counties that adjoined those already discussed contained about equal numbers of slaves and white persons. In nearly all the remaining counties the latter considerably outnumbered the slaves.

There were two counties in Mississippi, in 1850, in which the slaves outnumbered the whites over ten to one. In Washington County there were 7,836 slaves and only 546 white persons, a proportion of 14.1. In Issaquena County the proportion was 11.2 to 1 (4,105 slaves to 366 whites). If the white families in these counties were of the same average size as in all Mississippi,[16] the average white family in Washington County held 81.7 slaves and in Issaquena 63.9.[17]

This was the situation in the year 1850, and this year serves the purpose well, for it came after the internal expansion of the State was about completed, and yet it is nearer the center of the age of slavery than 1860. A study of the censuses of 1840 and of 1860 shows no great variation from the relative number of these two classes in different parts of the State in 1850. One exception should be made in the case of the northern counties that bordered the Mississippi River, De Soto, Tunica, and Coahoma. There were more white persons than slaves in these counties in 1840. Twenty years later, the slaves were in the decided majority. And in Bolivar County, just below these three, the ratio of slaves to white persons had greatly increased. Further, the population of these counties was comparatively small in 1840, but it grew very rapidly in the following twenty years.[18]

The pioneers of this northwestern part of the State were evidently not owners of great numbers of slaves, and, therefore, the land was

[15] The map in the front of the book shows the distribution of slaves over Mississippi in 1850 and the relation of this to river valleys and soil areas.

[16] According to the *Census of 1850*, p. xli, the white families in Mississippi averaged about 5.7 persons.

[17] *Compendium of the Census of 1850*, p. 260.

[18] The number of slaves and white persons in the various counties of the State in 1840 and 1860 can, of course, be found in the respective censuses of the United States. The figures for 1840 are also listed in the *Compendium of the Census of 1850*, p. 260. The most convenient place for finding the number of slaves and white persons in Mississippi in 1800, 1810, 1820, and 1830 is in the excellent summary included in the *Fifth Census of the United States, 1830*.

not chiefly cleared by slave labor. After clearings were made some of the white pioneers prospered and became planters. Many, however, sold their land to slave-owners and then moved to the less fertile hill lands or to virgin regions in the West.[19]

How fared the fertile river-bottom lands that were mainly appropriated by the large planters? Ingraham, after commenting on the craze for cotton and negroes, ventured a pessimistic prophecy in the 1830's:

"Not till every acre is purchased and cultivated—not till Mississippi becomes one vast cotton field, will this mania, which has entered into the very marrow, bone and sinew of a Mississippian's system, pass away. And not then, till the lands become exhausted and wholly unfit for farther cultivation. The rich loam which forms the upland soil of this state is of a very slight depth—and after a few years is worn away by constant culture and the action of the winds and rain. The fields are then 'thrown out' as useless. Every plough-furrow becomes the bed of a riverlet after heavy rains—these uniting are increased into torrents, before which the impalpable soil dissolves like ice under a summer's sun. By degrees, acre after acre, of what was a few years previously undulating ground, waving with dark green, snow-crested cotton, presents a wild scene of frightful precipices, and yawning chasms, which are increased in depth and destructively enlarged after every rain . . . Natchez itself is nearly isolated by a deep ravine . . . The south-west portion of this state must within a century become waste, barren, and wild." [20]

This prediction proved partially true. Twenty years later, Olmsted "passed during the day four or five large plantations, the hill-sides gullied like ice bergs, stables and negro quarters abandoned, and given up to decay" along the road from Woodville to Natchez.[21]

In 1856, B. L. C. Wailes, of Washington, Mississippi, wanted more land. On August thirtieth he "started for the Yazoo by the Valley road" to examine Mr. Mason's plantation, which was for sale, but he was discouraged to learn from an acquaintance that it "was

[19] In establishing his plantation in Hinds County, Miss., Mr. T. S. G. Dabney "succeeded in purchasing four thousand acres from half a dozen small farmers." —Smedes, *Southern Planter,* p. 47. A plantation, once established, frequently expanded at the expense of the neighboring small farmers, and sometimes the holdings of as many as twenty were absorbed.—Olmsted, *Back Country,* p. 329. The planter often wanted to be rid of his poor white neighbors as much as he wanted their land.—*Ibid.,* p. 75. Olmsted also gives the views of a small farmer toward this process of selling to the planter and then moving west.—*Ibid.,* pp. 141-142.

[20] *Southwest by a Yankee,* II, 86–87.

[21] *Back Country,* p. 19. Van Buren, *Sojourn in the South,* p. 49.

broken hill land much worn & exhausted and of little value." However, to quote from his diary, he:

"Learned that the Hayes place Old Fort St. Peters (or St. Clouds) was for sale concluded to go & examine it. It is occupied by a Mrs. White who leases and cultivates all of it that can be done to advantage. Mrs. White & son treated me with much politeness and after dinner the latter rode with me over the place a large portion of the tract which embraces more than 2000 acres consists of very broken bluff or hill land literally worn out & washed into large gullies and is destitute of timber the front on the river at the foot of the bluffs is very narrow some of it not more than 100 yards wide is also very much worn & the cotton growing on it very small and indifferent. The tract in short such a one as I do not want. As they confirmed all that was told me before in disparagement of Mr. Mason's place which was some 6 or 7 miles further up the river I concluded it was useless to go to see it." [22]

In December of the same year, Wailes found that Dr. Duncan, of Natchez, wanted to sell a plantation. He therefore, to use his own words:

"Left home for Woodville passed through Natchez at 11 o'clock Saw Doct Duncan got note to his overseer at Homochitto plantation. Fell in with Doct Calhoun on his way to his plantation adjoining Doct D.'s & rode several miles in his company arrived at Plantation about 2 o'clock got a horse and rode with the overseer over the place which I find in the most worn out and ruinous condition and all the land worth anything protected by a long & precarious levee and thoroughly set with Coco grass. All the buildings in very decayed & ruinous condition. Place not worth having." [23]

While only a small part of the land of Mississippi was in this ruinous condition in 1860, the evil had spread and become worse each year, and much land that was still cultivated with profit was less productive than it once was. An occasional planter laid his furrows and ditches at right angles to the slopes of the hills; thus his fields washed but little and the rich top soil continued to produce good crops.[24] But this was rare. Olmsted estimated that from ten to twenty crops rendered many plantations of virgin soil absolute deserts. He added: "The time will probably come when the soil now washing

[22] Wailes, Diary, MS., XVI, 68–69.
[23] Ibid., XVI, 171–172.
[24] The Cultivator, n. s., II, 272–273. Mississippi, p. 141, note.

into the adjoining swamps will be brought back by our descendants, perhaps on their heads, in pots and baskets . . . to be relaid on the sunny slopes, to grow the luxurious cotton in." [25]

That, however, was in the distant future. In Olmsted's time and earlier, as soon as one plantation was exhausted new land was sought elsewhere. After most of the land in the Natchez area was either in cultivation or abandoned because exhausted, there was a general movement to the northern part of the State. This was in the 'thirties and 'forties.[26] In the late 'forties and the 'fifties the supply of good soil in Mississippi was not equal to the demand. Planters began to investigate Arkansas and Texas lands,[27] and it is significant that in the last decade of slavery the white population of Mississippi for the first time failed to show a rate of increase in keeping with at least a normal excess of births over deaths.

When B. L. C. Wailes was pricing land, in 1856, he could have bought any amount of it for $5 an acre in the older part of the State near the towns, but much of it was badly worn. Better land cost $10 and occasionally as high as $20 an acre.[28] About this same time Olmsted observed that improved plantation land along his route from Natchez toward Alabama was valued at from $5 to $10 an acre,[29] though a large land company was selling poor land to poor men at $2 and $3 an acre.[30]

Assuming that one acre of improved farm land was worth two acres of unimproved, improved farm land in Mississippi was worth on the average slightly under $8 an acre, according to the census of 1850.[31] Ten years later improved farm land was worth $18 an acre,

[25] *Back Country*, p. 20.
[26] "The tide of emigration is rapidly setting to the north and east portions of the state. [In the 1830's.] Planters, who have exhausted their old lands in this vicinity, are settling and removing to these new lands, which will soon become the richest cotton growing part of Mississippi. . . . The strength and sinew of Mississippi must be hereafter concentrated in this fresher and younger portion of her territory."—*Southwest by a Yankee*, II, 95.
The details of this shift in the population of Mississippi, which was particularly evident between 1830 and 1850, can be found by comparing the *Census Reports*.
[27] Wailes, Diary, MS., 1856 and 1857, *passim*. *Back Country*, p. 21.
[28] Wailes, Diary, MS., 1856, *passim*.
[29] *Back Country*, pp. 158–159.
[30] *Ibid.*, p. 328.
[31] Improved farm lands   3,444,358 acres.
Unimproved farm lands   7,046,061 acres.
Cash value of farms $54,738,634.
  Census of 1850, p. 456.

still supposing it to have been worth twice as much as unimproved.[32] While the price of land varied slightly with fluctuations in the price of cotton, from $5 to $12 an acre was the normal price until after 1850. The abundance of good land in Mississippi kept the price from advancing until late. The inflation of the 'thirties did not greatly influence land values because at its height the northern half of the State was for the first time placed on the market. It was not until the late 'fifties that land values began to rise, due to the preëmption of the best lands by the greatly increased population. Finally, during the whole period, land values were kept reasonably low by the general opinion that farther west, in Arkansas or in Texas, fresh land could be had for $1 an acre.[33]

The erosion of much of the best soil in Mississippi cannot be blamed entirely on slavery, for a careless and extravagant consumption of natural resources has been general in America. However, the introduction of a great army of slaves multiplied the planters' power to produce cotton by whatever farming methods they chose to follow. The high value set on each unit of slave labor and the low cost of land inclined planters to treat the soil as a cheap commodity. It did not pay to use an $800 slave in ditching, terracing, or manuring $8 an acre land, especially when more could be bought whenever it was exhausted. Further, there were many planters who never built homes for themselves on their plantations, thus lessening their economic and sentimental stakes in their enterprises. To the absentee owner, the plantation was not a home but an open-air factory where land and slave labor were combined to produce cotton. Rich soil was only a species of raw material to be exploited in the way that would yield the largest immediate returns in cotton.

To admit that slavery impaired one of the chief natural resources of Mississippi does not necessarily prove that slave-owners did not prosper. That question deserves separate attention, which will be preceded by a discussion of sizes of slaveholdings in Mississippi.

In 1860, 436,631 slaves were in bondage in Mississippi. There were in the State 353,901 white persons,[34] of whom 30,943 were slave-

---

[32] Improved farm lands   5,065,755 acres.
Unimproved farm lands   10,773,929 acres.
Cash value of farms $194,760,367.
 Census of 1860 (Agriculture), pp. 84-85.
[33] *Back Country*, p. 20.
[34] *Census of 1860 (Population)*, p. 270.

holders.[35] From this are evident two interesting facts. About 8.75 per cent of the white population of the State were slaveholders, and the average holding of each of these was 14.1 negroes. The second fact needs analysis, and the first must be qualified.

Although only 8.75 per cent of the white population were slave-owners, practically all of these should be classed as heads of families. Their dependents were members of slaveholding families, and it would, therefore, be fairer to divide the white population on some basis that would recognize this. If 5.7 persons be considered the average size of a family in this region and at this time, then 176,375 white persons in Mississippi either owned slaves outright or belonged to slaveholding families. Even on this basis, slightly less than half of the white population was concerned in the ownership of slaves.

Though the average holding in slaves of each owner was 14.1 negroes, the slave estates varied greatly in size. The accompanying table [36] shows in detail this distribution. A briefer statement, how-ever, follows: Of the actual slaveholders, 14,498 (46.9 per cent) possessed from one to five slaves. There were 8,493 (27.4 per cent) who owned from 6 to 14 negroes. Likewise 6,257 (20.2 per cent) owned between 15 and 49 slaves; 1,638 (5.3 per cent) owned from 50 to 199; and 37 (.12 per cent) owned over 200 negroes. Only one person in the State was reported as owning over 500 slaves.

As the census was taken by counties, a planter's holdings in two counties were separately reported as though he were two different persons. As a result, the census statistics, and these figures based on them, slightly exaggerate the number of slaveholders and minimize the size of their holdings. It should be further noted that the figures given in parentheses represent the per cent of slaveholders but not

[35] *Census of 1860 (Agriculture)*, p. 232.
[36] *Ibid.*, p. 232.

Number of slaves	Number of owners	Number of slaves	Number of owners
1	4,856	15 & under 20	2,057
2	3,201	20 & under 30	2,322
3	2,503	30 & under 40	1,143
4	2,129	40 & under 50	735
5	1,809	50 & under 70	814
6	1,585	70 & under 100	545
7	1,303	100 & under 200	279
8	1,149	200 & under 300	28
9	1,024	300 & under 500	8
10 & under 15	3,432	500 & under 1,000	1

the per cent of the total white population. To find the latter, each figure should be divided by a little less than twelve. For instance, while 5.3 per cent of the slave-owners had over fifty and less than 200 slaves, this was only .5 per cent of the whole white population.[87]

After what has been earlier said of the geographical distribution of slaves over the State, one is not surprised to find that in 1860 five sixths of the plantations of 200 or more negroes were located in river counties,[88] a condition which was observed by travelers through Mississippi.[39]

The bare fact that Mississippi imported tremendous numbers of slaves is perhaps sufficient proof that her citizens wanted slaves, believing that ownership of them would bring wealth. It was certainly the current belief that slave-owners were rich. Olmsted was told that the plantations adjacent to the road entering Natchez from the south were owned by men worth without exception from a hundred thousand to ten million dollars.[40] Ingraham thought that as a class Southern planters were perhaps wealthier than any other class of men in America.[41] He declared that in the southwestern part of Mississippi annual incomes of twenty thousand dollars were common and that several individuals received from forty to fifty thousand

[87] Statistics on sizes of slaveholdings in 1850 can be found in *Compendium of the Census of 1850*, p. 95.

[88] The *Census of 1860* (*Agriculture*), p. 232, gives for each county in Mississippi the number of estates of slaves of different sizes. Below is a table which shows the location of the larger of these holdings.

Name of county	200 & under 300 slaves	300 & under 500 slaves	500 & under 1,000 slaves
Adams	3	3	–
Bolivar	1	–	–
Carroll	1	–	–
Claiborne	3	–	–
Hinds	1	–	–
Issaquena	2	1	1
Jefferson	–	1	–
Lowndes	2	–	–
Marshall	1	–	–
Monroe	1	–	–
Tunica	1	–	–
Warren	1	1	–
Wayne	–	2	–
Wilkerson	7	–	–
Yazoo	4	–	–

[39] *Back Country*, p. 16, and *passim*.
[40] *Ibid.*, pp. 27–29.
[41] *Southwest by a Yankee*, II, 89.

dollars a year.[42] This is his description of the way these great estates were amassed:

"The southern farmer can make from fifteen to thirty per cent. by his farm. He works on his plantation a certain number of slaves, say thirty, which are to him what the sinewy arms of the Yankee farmer are to himself. Each slave ought to average from seven to eight bales of cotton during the season, especially on the new lands. An acre will generally average from one to two bales. Each bale averages four hundred pounds, at from twelve to fifteen cents a pound. This may not be an exact estimate, but it is not far from the true one. Deducting two thousand and five hundred dollars for the expenses of the plantation, there will remain the net income of eleven thousand dollars. Now suppose this plantation and slaves to have been purchased on a credit, paying at the rate of six hundred dollars apiece for his negroes the planter would be able to pay for nearly two-thirds of them the first year. The second year, he would pay for the remainder, and purchase ten or twelve more; and the third year, if he obtained his plantation on a credit of that length of time, he would pay for that also, and commence his fourth year with a valuable plantation, and thirty-five or forty slaves, all his own property, with an increased income for the ensuing year of some thousands of dollars. Henceforward, if prudent, he will rank as an opulent planter." [43]

Undoubtedly there were some planters in Mississippi who equaled or bettered the estimates of Ingraham. Consider the following figures taken from the federal census of 1860. In Issaquena County there were 5,193 slaves between ten and seventy years old. (Including infants and aged, the total was 7,244 slaves. There were only 587 white persons in the county.) These negroes produced 41,170 bales of cotton of an average weight of about 400 pounds. Without deducting cooks, house-servants, blacksmiths, carpenters, and others who did little field work, this was an average of eight bales for every negro over ten and under seventy. Valuing cotton at eleven cents a pound, the owners received about $350 per negro.[44]

Most planters, even in their best years, did not equal such high profits as these. The following records better represent the earnings of normal Mississippi plantations. In 1851, on the Bowles plantation in Lafayette County, approximately twenty-three working hands produced 122 bales, an average of about 5.5 bales of 400 pounds each to the hand.[45] In 1858, fifteen hands on the Wheeless plantation in

[42] Ibid., II, 91.
[43] Ibid., II, 90.
[44] Census of 1860 (Population), pp. 266–269. Ibid. (Agriculture), pp. 84–85.
[45] Bowles MS.

Yazoo County produced eighty-seven bales, or slightly over 5.8 bales each.[46] During the three years 1857, 1858, and 1859, an average of twenty-four hands on the McArn plantation in Jefferson County produced an average crop of six bales to the hand.[47] These plantations were in different cotton-producing sections of the State. The first two were under the management of overseers; the third may have been. In each case, the largest number of negroes who picked cotton on any day was taken as the number of hands on that estate. House-servants, infants, the aged, and others who did not pick cotton were not included.

On the basis of these and other figures, let us investigate the profitableness of raising cotton by slave labor in the 1850's on a plantation of fifty slaves.

The chief source of income would be from cotton. Probably thirty of the fifty negroes worked in the field.[48] If these produced 5¼ bales each,[49] there would be a total of 158 bales which, at ten cents a pound, would be worth . . .

The expenses of the plantation would be as follows: 50 negroes at $600 each (in the late 'fifties the price was higher) represented an investment of $30,000. Calculating interest at 6 per cent, this amounted to   1,800

At least an equal amount should be added for depreciation in slave property by accidents, deaths, old age, etc. . .   1,800

As the average hand worked about twelve acres, 600 acres would be ample for pastures and woodland as well as fields.[50] Allowing $10 an acre, the investment in land at 6 per cent interest involved a yearly carriage charge of . . .   360

and it ordinarily depreciated at the rate of at least 3 per cent a year in value   180

Annual hire of an overseer, at least   300

Purchases from New Orleans or elsewhere of negro clothing, miscellaneous plantation supplies, etc.,[51]   1,000

Without including various miscellaneous expenditures, such as the purchase of corn and pork, of which few

---

[46] Wheeless MS.

[47] In 1857, twenty negroes picked 115 bales; in 1858, twenty-five negroes picked 151 bales; and in 1859, twenty-six negroes picked 165 bales.—McArn MS.

[48] See above, pp. 18–20.

[49] In addition to the figures given for the Bowles, Wheeless, and McArn plantations, see above, pp. 13–14.

[50] See above, p. 14.

[51] On Mar. 13 and 29, 1852, P. R. Leigh paid a total of $1,095.82 for plantation supplies brought by the steamers "Grenada" and "Osceola."—Leigh MSS.

plantations produced enough, the total of the expenses
and interest charges was ....　　　$5,440

On the basis of these calculations, the planter received $880 profit, though he was, of course, free to spend the interest on his investment in negroes and land, and this was the item that caused the profits from Mississippi plantations to appear high. The $880 might be considered the wages of the planter for managing the enterprise.

If anything, the above statement is too optimistic. P. R. Leigh, a very intelligent planter, managed forty-nine slaves. From his detailed accounts it appears that the net profit of his plantation from July, 1851, to June, 1852, was $2,194.81. It is evident that he but slightly exceeded 6 per cent interest on his investment with no allowance for such items as depreciation and his own wages as director of the enterprise.[52]

In 1834, a year of prosperity and good prices, the Polk plantation was established in Yalobusha County. Eight hundred acres of land were purchased at $10 an acre, though only 271 acres were cleared five years later and 566 acres by 1851. Thirty-seven slaves valued at $16,000 were placed on the land. Considering the amount of cleared land and the value of the negroes, it is probable that there were less than twenty hands in the lot. The total investment was close to $25,000. In 1860, the plantation was sold for $30,000, though some of the slaves had been otherwise disposed of. In 1851, if we may judge by the amount of land in cultivation, there must have been considerably more slaves than in either 1834 or 1861.[53]

During the nine years from 1849 through 1857, the average net proceeds from the cotton crop was about $5,375.[54] This was the total receipts from cotton less the various costs of marketing it: fire and river insurance, shippers' charges, freight, charges for storage and weighing, and commission on sale.[55]

While $5,375 was the average annual net receipt from cotton, this was not the net profit from the plantation. The overseer was paid from $350 to $550 a year.[56] Plantation supplies must have cost at least $500 a year,[57] besides the expenses of recapturing fugitive slaves, costs of medicines and medical attention, and the other miscellaneous

[52] Leigh MSS.
[53] Bassett, *Plantation Overseer*, pp. 262, 267-268.
[54] *Ibid.*, pp. 221-259.
[55] *Ibid.*, pp. 235, 254.
[56] *Ibid.*, pp. 6, 178.
[57] *Ibid.*, pp. 250, 255-256.

needs of a plantation. This left an average annual income of less than $4,500 from property that sold for $30,000 after some of the slaves had been disposed of. Making allowance for the aging of the negroes, the return was by no means princely even though the commission merchant several times stated that the price of the Polk cotton bettered the general market price because of its mark.

Captain Isaac Ross died in 1836, leaving property worth $150,000, in addition to 165 negroes. The latter must have been worth $100,000. The estimated annual income of his estate was $20,000, which was 8 per cent of the investment. This was in 1836, when cotton sold for sixteen cents a pound.[58]

Such figures as these explain why few cotton planters were able to follow Ingraham's optimistic plan of buying negroes and land on credit and paying for them in three years. While many tried, few succeeded. More stayed in debt, with crops mortgaged several years in advance,[59] finally getting ahead with a good crop or in lean years losing part or all of their negroes. Even though successful, the planter was constantly tempted to enlarge his fields and increase his slave force on credit. Sheriffs' and trustees' sales, adverse balances on the books of New Orleans merchants, and debts to slave-traders were all evidence that cotton plantations were not sure roads to wealth.[60]

On the other hand, it must be remembered that the planter's life had attractions and obligations that kept many from deserting it, even though their investments showed an inadequate return. The plantation supplied its owner with many of the necessities of life, and the planter often had numerous house and yard servants to give a pleasurable distinction and dignity to his mode of life as well as to relieve him and his family from physical labor.

Cotton, however, was not the only source of profit. A planter who barely made expenses by the sale of cotton might find his estate yearly increasing in value by the rearing of young negroes. With a good price for cotton in 1836, Isaac Ross was making $20,000 a year with 165 slaves. With the drop in the price of cotton, he would probably not have made expenses in 1848. However, his slaves had in-

---

[58] See below, pp. 226–229.

[59] *Back Country*, p. 29. *Southwest by a Yankee*, II, 93.

[60] "The panic is to a great extent uncalled for in Mississippi & difficulty among Commission Houses proves that there has been more speculation going on among our planters than was supposed and it turns out that the growing cotton crop has been largely anticipated to buy River lands at most unwarranted prices & negroes at $1500."—Wailes, Diary, MS., Oct. 17, 1857.

creased without a single purchase to 235. Though Ross was not a speculator, for by his will he freed his negroes and returned them to Africa, their value had greatly increased in twelve years.[61] Without planning to sell a single negro, and without speculating on a rising market, the planter who gave reasonable attention to the care of negro children would have good reason to believe that he was building a valuable estate for his own children. But all were not so wise. Especially in the regions of large and productive plantations, many slave-owners, according to M. W. Philips, drove the negroes too hard in making large cotton crops and thereby diminished the normal natural increase of their slaves. As that Mississipian wrote, they "killed the goose for the golden egg," instead of having due regard for both sources of profit—cotton and negroes.[62]

Large plantations probably yielded a larger return in proportion to the investment than small farms. One overseer could superintend fifty negroes almost as well as five, and negroes on large plantations could be trained for more specialized tasks. Olmsted, who did not believe slavery was profitable in most sections of the South, made the following judicious generalizations concerning Mississippi:

"It is quite plain, notwithstanding all the drawbacks attending the employment of forced labor, and notwithstanding the high price of slaves, that slave labor is employed profitably by the large planters in Mississippi, and in certain other parts of the South, in the culture of cotton. . . .

"Nor do I think myself warranted in denying that the production of cotton per acre on many Mississippi plantations may not be as large as it can be economically made with land as low and slaves as high in price as is at present the case." [63]

In brief, many Mississippi planters prospered in spite of slavery because cotton was profitable and land cheap.

The average free laborer seldom receives in exchange for his work more than food, clothing, shelter, and medical attention for himself and his family, with a guarantee against unemployment and a modest old-age pension. The planter paid these directly to his slave. In addition he paid from $500 to $1,800 to a slave-trader. What did he receive in return for the latter? He secured a perpetual contract to the slave's labor which guaranteed him a steady labor supply undisturbed by capricious turnover or wholesale strikes. He also gained

[61] See below, pp. 224–229.
[62] *Back Country*, pp. 58–59, quoting part of an essay in *The Cotton Planter* written by Dr. Philips.
[63] *Ibid.*, pp. 294–296.

the right to use force, if necessary, to extort from the negro work which in most cases amounted to no more than a fair amount a day. However, as the planter was not vexed by having his laborers work one day and loaf the next, the slave probably did considerably more in a year, though little more in a day, than free-negro farm hands of the present time.[64]

The plantation of thirty working hands represented an investment for land and negroes of about $40,000. With free labor, this should not have exceeded $10,000. Slave labor greatly increased the capital investment and, therefore, the interest charges. On the venture was imposed the necessity of supporting an investment which added nothing to the productivity of the soil or to the betterment of the farm equipment. It is most improbable that the efficiency of the working force was increased enough to justify the enlarged investment of capital.

The Mississippi planter made more money as a slaveholder than he would have done by his own labors. It is probable that his income would have been even larger with free labor. Had neither slave nor free labor been available, the soil would have been conserved better for later generations; but as it was, profits were reinvested in slaves. This accelerated the transformation of rich soil into cotton and poor land. The larger the profits from cotton, the more numerous were the purchases of slaves and "after that, it was more negroes to work more land to the end of the chapter." [65] From an economic standpoint, it is very questionable whether slaves were a good investment year in and year out even in Mississippi. But whether the profits were large or small, they were invested mostly in negroes and the total, by 1860, was enormous. At $800 apiece, the 436,691 slaves in Mississippi, in 1860, were worth $349,344,800. According to the federal census of that year, the total cash value of all farm land, unimproved as well as improved, of farming implements and of all live-stock in the State was $241,478,571.[66]

It is impossible to say without qualification whether the conver-

[64] The sociological aspects of the relation of master to slave, especially of the virtual payment of wages in food, rent, clothes, medical attention, taxes, recreation, etc., was discussed by Henry Hughes, of Port Gibson, Miss., in the *Treatise on Sociology* which he published in 1854. This and other writings of Hughes are discussed in R. M. Guess, "Henry Hughes, Sociologist," MS. thesis in the Library of the University of Mississippi.

[65] Reuben Davis, *Recollections of Mississippi and Mississippians*, p. 156.

[66] *Census of 1860 (Agriculture)*, pp. 84–85.

sion of this share of the capital of the State into negro slaves was economically sound. Much of this capital, it must be remembered, had been created by the labor of these slaves; on the other hand, immigrant white farmers would have come eventually to till the soil. Viewed in the light of subsequent history, the question resolves itself chiefly into this: Would Mississippi be in better or worse condition to-day, if its negro population were replaced by whites? On the other hand, if one cares to speculate on the soundness of Mississippi's large investment in slaves had slavery continued for a much longer period than it did, the answer would depend on whether the price of slaves held up. Since a fall in price of two dollars a slave would cause a drop of nearly a million dollars in the capital value of the slaves in the State, the profitableness of the institution depended largely on the price of slaves.

Considering the prices of cotton, land, and negroes, there were three periods when Mississippi planters prospered. Immediately before 1820 little cotton was being produced but those who raised it must have reaped very large profits.[67] The per cent of profit was not quite so large in the middle 'thirties, but much more cotton was sold. In spite of higher prices for slaves and lower prices for cotton, better varieties of the latter allowed cheaper production and large profits remained. In the third period, the late 'fifties, cotton brought only a fair price and slaves were very high. The margin of profit was therefore small. However, the increased price of slaves was not felt by those who already had them and not many were imported during this period. The average planter, while making a little better profit from cotton, also found that his stock of slaves was more valuable than formerly. To have both income and investment increase was encouraging, even though the ratio of income to investment did not improve. Finally, in this last period cotton crops were large.

Considering the three periods of prosperity, the price of cotton was lower in each peak than in the previous one; the cost of slaves was higher; and the crop of cotton was larger.

It is easy to understand why the defense of slavery proved popular in the well-nigh statewide prosperity of the 'thirties. Why did the veneration of slavery continue during the depression from 1837 until 1855? Considering the price of slaves and of cotton, it was impossible

[67] In addition to the table of prices given near the beginning of this chapter, see *Southwest by a Yankee*, II, 191–192.

for a planter to make large profits and many of them lost heavily. Neither does the moderate prosperity of the late 'fifties seem to have been sufficient to justify renewed confidence in the economic soundness of slavery. By 1860 Mississippi had nearly as many slaves as it needed. With the natural increase in slave population the price must have declined unless a market for the surplus could be found. Texas for a time could buy from Mississippi as Mississippi had for years bought from Virginia, but when Texas and the rest of the new Southwest were supplied, slave prices would fall unless more territory suited to slave labor could be discovered. As there was little probability of finding this within the Union, economics demanded that the slave-owner be an expansionist, for without a market slave prices must soon have declined.[68]

[68] Chas. W. Ramsdell, "The Natural Limits of Slavery Expansion," in *Mississippi Valley Historical Review*, XVI, 151–171.

CHAPTER IX

The Mississippi Colonization Society

In 1830, the year before the founding of the Mississippi Colonization Society, there were 519 free negroes and mulattoes in Mississippi. It seems hardly reasonable that this small number should have caused any serious concern to the white people of the State, particularly as there were many more in several other slave States.[1] On the other hand, a large proportion of this class lived in the southwestern counties of Mississippi where the slaves greatly outnumbered the white population.[2] Slaveholders feared that the mere existence of free negroes among slaves might make the latter dissatisfied, and there was always a possibility that some of the free negroes might actively endeavor to create discontent. This anxiety was accentuated in 1830 and 1831 as rumors reached Mississippi of slave insurrections in Virginia and North Carolina.[3] The middle States were also suspected of trying to unload their slaves on the markets of the lower slave States as a step toward abolishing slavery.[4] Finally, the rapid growth of the slave population of Mississippi was considered alarming. For these reasons a strong and apparently unanimous desire arose to abolish the free negro class, with certain exceptions, and in 1831 a law was passed which required all adult free negroes to leave Mississippi.[5] It is significant that almost the whole of this agitation came from the southwestern corner of the State; the newspapers that were most vigorous in the crusade were in Wilkinson and Adams Counties; from the latter county came the petition which induced the legislature to require that free negroes be removed from the State;[6] and this

[1] *Compendium of the Census of 1850*, pp. 45, 63, 83.
[2] *Ibid.*, p. 260.
[3] Franklin L. Riley, "A Contribution to the History of the Colonization Movement in Mississippi," in *P. M. H. S.*, IX, 355. "Free Negroes, and their Influence and Danger among Slaves," is the title of one chapter in W. B. Trotter, *A History and Defense of African Slavery.*
[4] Mitchell *v.* Wells, 37 Miss. 235.
[5] *Hutchinson's Code*, p. 533.
[6] Sydnor, "Free Negro in Miss.," in *American Historical Review*, XXXII, 785.

law of 1831 was framed by a committee drawn almost entirely from representatives of southwestern counties.[7]

In addition to making laws to force free negroes to leave Mississippi, there was a slight interest in schemes to persuade them to leave voluntarily. In 1824, seven years before the Mississippi Colonization Society was created, Mississippi free negroes were informed that they could find good homes in Haiti. For twenty issues the *Woodville Republican* prominently displayed a large advertisement of the advantages to be gained by removing to that island.[8] There were also several news items telling of the rise and decline of the Haiti movement.[9]

Had there been no free negro class in Mississippi, the Mississippi Colonization Society would probably not have been created. The purpose of this organization, as officially and publicly expressed, was to remove free negroes from the State. Embedded in its constitution were the words: "The object to which the Mississippi Society shall be exclusively devoted, shall be to aid the Parental Institution at Washington, in the colonization of free people of color of the United States on the coast of Africa. . . ."[10] In the early speeches and writings of the Mississippi colonizers there was never a plea for colonizing slaves. Speaking before part of the society, Daniel Williams, of Wilkinson County, affirmed that its members proposed "to transport back to Africa the land of their fathers, such free persons of colour as may choose to emigrate—and with any other views that party or prejudice may blend with this object, they totally disclaim all connection."[11] While there was more freedom of expression in private correspondence, we find Dr. John Ker, a leader in the movement in Mississippi, writing to Major Isaac Thomas, of Louisiana, "You and I, and I think all men of sound judgement and sober reflection, will agree, that as to the *slaves,* neither the Society nor our Government can in the remotest degree meddle with them."[12] Clearly, it was the official opinion of the organization, and the private opinion of some of its leaders, that the removal of free negroes was the only concern of the society. With such an objective, the society could appeal to those planters who thought that free negroes had a harmful influence upon

[7] *Jour. Gen. Assem. of Miss.,* 1831, House Jour., pp. 3, 8, and Sen. Jour., pp. 3, 7.
[8] *Woodville Republican,* Sept. 21, 1824, through Feb. 9, 1825.
[9] *Ibid.,* Oct. 5, 1824, and occasional notices until the middle of 1825.
[10] *Ibid.,* Aug. 6, 1831.
[11] *Ibid.,* July 16, 1831.
[12] Riley, "Colonization Movement," in *P. M. H. S.,* IX, 349.

slaves and to humane persons who believed free negroes would be happier and more prosperous, if removed to regions where slavery did not exist.

Even with its purpose restricted to the transportation of free negroes alone, the colonization movement had some enemies. One of these declared that while he had no objection to the removal of free negroes, he was by no means sure that the methods and ultimate aims of the American Colonization Society were above reproach. He particularly objected to a proposed bill by which congress would appropriate money for returning free negroes to Africa, fearing that, if the competency of the national government to legislate in this field were once established, there might be a repetition of the fable of the camel that was allowed to put his nose in the tent. Congress might soon attempt to control the entire question of slavery.[13]

As early as 1827, citizens of Mississippi began to read of the work of the American Colonization Society, and, naturally, the thought presented itself that this organization might be useful in solving Mississippi's free negro problem. The newspaper controversy just mentioned was in 1827, and in this same year, so far as we know, occurred the first attempt to advance the work of the American Colonization Society in Mississippi. An inquiry was addressed to Rev. William Winans, a prominent Methodist minister of the State, asking whether it would be wise to have an agent work in Mississippi. Winans answered in the affirmative, but he warned the society that great care must be exercised in selecting this individual. In saying this, he probably had in mind the hostile attitude of some in the community.[14] In September, 1827, there appeared in the *Woodville Republican* a letter describing the good state of affairs in Liberia,[15] and less than a month later this paper gave two columns to an article on the same subject.[16] In December of the following year there was a lengthy discussion of the aims of the American Colonization Society.[17]

As early as July 4, 1826, Mississippians began to contribute to the colonization movement and by 1829 nearly $1,000 had been collected, largely through the zeal of Winans, from over seventy persons,

---

[13] *Woodville Republican*, July 14, Aug. 4, 11, and 18, 1827.
[14] E. L. Fox, *The American Colonization Society, 1817–1840*, p. 81, in *Johns Hopkins University Studies in Historical and Political Science*, XXXVII. *P. M. H. S.*, II, 171, 174.
[15] *Woodville Republican*, Sept. 22, 1827.
[16] *Ibid.*, Oct. 6, 1827.
[17] *Ibid.*, Dec. 16, 1828.

churches, and Masonic lodges.[18] Each of two Mississippians agreed, in 1829, to give $100 a year for ten years.[19] All this was contributed before a colonization society was founded in the State.

An attempt was made near Natchez, in the fall of 1828, to form a Mississippi Colonization Society, but it failed because the impression was gained by the slaves that its object was their immediate emancipation. It was, therefore, necessary to suspend activities for a time.[20]

The Mississippi Colonization Society was organized in June, 1831. Probably because of the false start in 1828, its birth seems not to have been preceded by any publicity through the press or in open meetings. Some of its leaders were also interested in the organization of the Louisiana society and, therefore, the procedures in these States were possibly similar. We know from a letter of Dr. Ker, who was vitally concerned in the creation of both societies, that the plan in Louisiana was to organize quietly and thereby avoid conflict with any opposition before the movement was well started. A constitution was prepared and the signatures of prominent persons were privately secured, with the result that the society, as it were, began life full grown. Ker also considered publishing a compilation of some of the articles that had appeared in the official publications of the American Colonization Society. He thought this might be valuable, if it were discreetly edited, for "the regular publications of the society, excellent as they are, contain some things which are calculated to jar upon the Southern prejudices." [21]

On the first day of June, 1831, there was a meeting in Natchez in which a constitution was adopted and a full set of officers elected. The text of the constitution was as follows:

"CONSTITUTION

"Of the Mississippi Colonization Society, adopted at a meeting of the citizens of the State, held at Natchez, on the 1st day of June, 1831.
"Art. 1st. This society shall be called the Colonization Society of the State of Mississippi, and shall be auxiliary to the American Colonization Society.
"2nd. The object to which it shall be exclusively devoted, shall be to aid the Parent Institution at Washington, in the colonization of free people of color of the United States, on the coast of Africa, and to do this not only

[18] *African Repository*, II, 324; III, 127, 233, 384; IV, 256.
[19] *Ibid.*, V, 182.
[20] *Ibid.*
[21] "Colonization Movement," in *P. M. H. S.*, IX, 344–348.

by the contribution of money, but by the exertion of its influence to promote the formation of other Societies.

"3rd. An annual subscription of one dollar or more, shall constitute an individual member of the Society, and the payment at any time of twenty dollars, a member for life.

"4th. The officers of this Society shall be a President, nine Vice Presidents, and twenty-three Managers: Secretary and Treasurer to be elected annually by the Society.

"5th. The Presidents, Secretary and Treasurer shall be (ex-officio) Members of the Board of Managers.

"6th. The Board of Managers shall meet on their own adjournment or by order of the President, to transact the business of the Society.

"7th. The Treasurer shall keep the accounts of the Society, as well as take charge of its funds, and hold them subject to an order of the Board of Managers.

"8th. The Secretary shall keep the records of the Society, and of the Board of Managers, and shall conduct under the direction of the Board of Managers, the correspondence of the Society with the Parent Society, and other Societies.

"9th. The annual meeting of the Society shall be held on the first Wednesday of March in each year, at which meeting the officers of the Society shall be elected, who shall hold their offices for one year thereafter, and until others are elected in their places.

"10th. Fifteen members at all meetings of the Society, and seven members at all meetings of the Board of Managers, shall constitute a quorum to proceed to business." [22]

Few organizations have existed in Mississippi that could claim a group of officers equal in character and influence to those of the Mississippi Colonization Society. There has been preserved a list of those chosen at the creation of the society in 1831, as well as another list of those elected in December, 1838. At both times, the president was Dr. Stephen Duncan, of Natchez, physician, successful planter, president of the Bank of Mississippi and one of the wealthiest men in the State.[23] Among the other officers was Gerard C. Brandon, Governor of Mississippi, and Cowles Mead, formerly Secretary and Acting-Governor of Mississippi Territory, who remained a leader in public

[22] *Woodville Republican,* Aug. 6, 1831. A "Form of a Constitution for an Auxiliary Society" was from time to time printed on the paper jackets of the *African Repository.* This "Form" evidently served as a basis for the drafting of the constitution of the Mississippi society.

In 1838 the constitution was amended in several particulars. Among other changes the number of vice-presidents was increased to twelve, and the number of managers was decreased to this same size.—"Colonization Movement," in *P. M. H. S.,* IX, 406–408.

[23] Claiborne, *Mississippi,* p. 409; J. D. Shields, *Life and Times of Seargent Smith Prentiss,* p. 13; Dunbar Rowland, *Mississippi,* I, 666.

affairs after the State was created. His home was near Clinton, in Hinds County.[24] James Railey owned a large plantation,[25] and David Hunt, another officer, was a man of considerable wealth.[26] Near Rodney lived Thomas Freeland, an affluent planter, who was a delegate to the Baltimore convention that nominated General Winfield Scott for president.[27] The Rev. William Winans has already been mentioned. This prominent Methodist preacher spent most of his life at Mount Pleasant, sixteen miles southeast of Woodville. Isaac R. Nicholson, a lawyer of Natchez, attained the speakership of the House of Representatives of Mississippi, and was later a member of the supreme court of the State.[28]

Two of the officers were Presbyterian ministers, Zebulon Butler, for many years pastor at Port Gibson,[29] and J. Chamberlain, for a long time president of Oakland College, located thirty-five miles north of Natchez.[30] Surveyor-General Levin Wailes, of Washington, Mississippi, and Natchez, was in the list of officers,[31] as was Edward McGehee of Wilkinson County. The latter was a wealthy planter, pioneer railroad builder, and philanthropist, who refused the secretaryship of the treasury offered him by President Taylor. He was one of the largest slaveholders of the State, owning possibly a thousand negroes.[32] The Rev. B. M. Drake, a prominent Methodist minister, was for a time president of Elizabeth Female Academy, located in Washington, Mississippi.[33] Three of the officers, Joseph, Robert T., and Dr. William Dunbar, bore a name that had been famous in southwestern Mississippi since William Dunbar attained prominence during the Spanish régime. John Henderson, a venerated and respected citizen of Natchez, controlled large plantations and numerous slaves in Louisiana as well as in Mississippi.[34] Dr. John Ker likewise had plantations on both sides of the great river, to which he gave most of his attention, though he was by profession a physician.[35]

[24] Rowland, *Mississippi*, II, 213–214.
[25] *American Colonization Society*, p. 198.
[26] Rowland, *Mississippi*, I, 908.
[27] *Memoirs of Mississippi*, I, 769.
[28] Rowland, *Mississippi*, II, 341.
[29] *Memoirs of Mississippi*, I, 475.
[30] Rowland, *Mississippi*, II, 349.
[31] *P. M. H. S.*, V, 261.
[32] Rowland, *Mississippi*, II, 186–187.
[33] *P. M. H. S.*, II, 172.
[34] Rowland, *Mississippi*, I, 858.
[35] "Colonization Movement," in *P. M. H. S.*, IX, 337–341.

The remaining officials of the Mississippi Colonization Society, as recorded in the lists of those elected in 1831 and in 1838, were: the Rev. D. C. Page, Alexander C. Henderson, James G. Carson, William Harris, J. Beaumont, the Rev. S. G. Winchester, William St. John Elliott, William C. Conner, the Rev. Benjamin Chase, William Bisland, Edward Turner, John L. Irwin, Joseph Johnson, the Rev. George Potts, William L. Chew, Joseph Sessions, the Rev. John C. Burruss, William B. Melvin, R. M. Gaines, John H. Magruder, William Lattimore, Dr. A. P. Merrill, John Perkins, Dr. Rush Nutt, Felix Huston, B. R. Grayson, Alvarez Fisk, and H. W. Huntington. There is not space to comment on each of these men, but the student of the history of Mississippi will recognize the names of many who were prominent.[36]

Several citizens of Mississippi were officers of the American Colonization Society. Among these were, Dr. Stephen Duncan, the Rev. William Winans, Dr. John Ker, James Railey, the Hon. Robert J. Walker, Edward McGehee, and the Rev. Robert Paine, who were vice-presidents, and Francis Griffin, who was a life director.[37]

It is evident that the officers of the Mississippi Colonization Society were prominent in educational and religious life as well as in business and politics. Several of them were known far beyond the boundaries of their own State. They were not malcontents, failures, or sentimentalists. Practically all were permanent residents of Mississippi, and many of them were owners of large plantations and of numerous slaves. Further, a majority of them were residents of the counties in southern Mississippi that border the Mississippi River, that is, the counties of Warren, Claiborne, Jefferson, Adams, and Wilkinson.

[36] The officers for 1831 were listed in the *Woodville Republican*, Aug. 6, 1831, and the list for 1838 appeared in the Natchez *Weekly Courier and Journal*, Dec. 28, 1838. The latter item was cited in Riley, "Colonization Movement," in *P. M. H. S.*, IX, 406–407.

Of the ten persons who made gifts in excess of $5,000 to Oakland College, half were officers of the Mississippi Colonization Society. John Ker gave that college $20,000 and David Hunt's munificence was so great that his name has been incorporated into that of the institution.—Edward Mayes, *History of Education in Mississippi*, pp. 66, 71.

[37] These persons appear among the lists of officers of the American Colonization Society that were printed in the following pamphlets: *Report of the Naval Committee to the House of Representatives, August, 1850, in Favor of the Establishment of a Line of Mail Steamships to the Western Coast of Africa. . . . Twenty-eighth Annual Report of the American Colonization Society.* C. K. Marshall, *The Exodus: Its Effect upon the People of the South.*

The heyday of the Mississippi Colonization Society was from its founding to about 1839 or 1840. We will first consider its activities during this period.

Three weeks after the creation of the society there was a meeting of the board of managers in the Methodist Church at Natchez. An address to the public was prepared in which the objectives of the organizations were stated. These were: to arouse interest in colonization, to persuade free negroes to return to Africa, and to raise money for this end. It was estimated, in an optimistic moment, that twenty dollars was sufficient to send a negro to Africa. Included in the address was a description of the Liberian colony as well as an account of the work of the American Colonization Society. After meeting a few of the criticisms that were being directed against the movement, a plea was made for the creation of local auxiliary societies.[38] At least four of these were formed: the Woodville and Wilkinson County, the Port Gibson and Claiborne County, the Vicksburg and Warren County, and the Clinton and Hinds County Societies.[39]

The Woodville and Wilkinson County Society functioned in 1831 and at least through the following year. Its activities were largely a microcosm of those of the Mississippi society. In addition to holding meetings, it collected funds, discussed through the press the evil conditions of free negroes and the advantages to them and to Mississippi of their removal to Africa, and defended the American Colonization Society and the colony in Liberia.[40]

In 1832 the Mississippi Colonization Society published its first annual report, which shows, so far as its published statements were concerned, that it was still interested exclusively in removing free negroes. This account also indicates that its work was in the formative period, for no negroes had been removed. The following is a part of this report:

"The Society is increasing in numbers, . . . some subscriptions have been obtained, and . . . this has had a happy effect; the free people of color in this neighborhood have become awakened to the subject, and the advantages held out to them by a removal from their degraded political position here, to the land of their ancestors, where they can enjoy the rights and privileges of freemen, have created a great desire on their part to be better informed on the subject. They have called a meeting among themselves, appointed two of their own color to visit Liberia, to examine

[38] *Woodville Republican*, Aug. 6, 1831.
[39] *African Repository*, VII, 207.
[40] *Woodville Republican*, July 9 and 16, Dec. 17, 1831; June 30, 1832.

the country, and, make a report of the state and condition of the colony.

"A fund nearly sufficient to defray the expenses of their agents, in going and returning, has been raised among them. It is expected that they will set out immediately under the care and direction of the Society, and will return as soon as the trip can be performed to make their report.

"Your Board of Managers have been informed that a vessel will be fitted out by the parent society, and will sail from New Orleans in the month of May next, for the purpose of conveying emigrants to Liberia : a number will come from some of the western States, and it is contemplated to take as many from this State as may be ready to go. And the Board are happy to say, that they have understood several are now making preparations, and intend to avail themselves of the first opportunity to leave the State for Africa." [41]

Though the removal of free negroes continued to be the only publicly avowed purpose of the Mississippi Colonization Society, its actual work soon veered toward the colonization of slaves. The justification for this enlargement of aims is well stated in a letter written by Dr. John Ker less than two months after the formation of the Mississippi society. After discussing the humaneness and expediency of returning free negroes, he added :

"All experience I think goes to show at least the great probability, that the spirit of emigration will spread, and that for a long time the *demand* for means will only *increase* with its *supply*. Laws will probably be made in the slave holding states to prevent emancipation, except on condition of immediate emigration to Liberia. Those who have been withheld from emancipation by the conviction that it would be prejudicial to society to do so, will no doubt gratify their wishes, when this objection shall no longer exist. But will this be cause of complaint or regret to others ? Will it not on the contrary benefit other slave holders, rather by removing some examples of loose and injuriously indulgent discipline, the effect of mistaken feelings of Humanity ? Will it not have the effect also, of enhancing the value of those who may be left ? Will not the hands of slavery be strengthened as to those who shall remain, except from the only ground of hope to the slave, the voluntary act of his master ? Will it not have the effect of lessening the evils of slavery, both with regard to the bond and their masters, by creating such a state of things as will enable the latter to relax the former unavoidable rigor of discipline ? It is manifest to every slave holder that many evils arise from the existence of the free colored people amongst the slaves : and it would be unnecessary to expatiate upon this point." [42]

Here are certain reasons for favoring colonization that did not appear in the formal reports of the society, for in these the suggestion

[41] *Ibid.*, Mar. 31, 1832.
[42] "Colonization Movement," in *P. M. H. S.*, IX, 350–351. *American Colonization Society*, p. 158.

that emancipated slaves might be returned to Liberia is nowhere to be found. In suggesting that the society transport emancipated slaves, it seems that Ker's idea was somewhat as follows: the majority of the people of Mississippi did not object to the manumission of a slave, if the negro were immediately removed to Africa. But, most of the people did fear the word *emancipation,* particularly when it was used in connection with the federal government or even a national society. Since the colonization society was asking the central government to aid in returning negroes, it was best not to mention slaves in this connection. In the mind of the public the fear would arise that the government, after returning the slaves of owners who willingly emancipated them, might attempt to go further and remove the slaves of unwilling owners.

In the vigorous period of the life of the Mississippi Colonization Society, that is from 1831 to 1840, a considerable amount of money was collected. R. R. Gurley, the efficient secretary of the parent society, estimated that between January, 1834, and January, 1838, the societies of "Mississippi and Louisiana spent probably not less than fifteen or twenty thousand dollars in founding the settlement at the mouth of the Sinou river." [43] Later he stated that this figure was probably much too small. The president of the Mississippi society, Dr. Duncan, promised to give $300 a year for five years, an amount which he subsequently augmented. [44] Eleven years later, in 1842, we find that Dr. Duncan had given $2,500, probably in addition to the first $1,500, and in the following year he promised to give another $1,500. [45]

The largest contribution in Mississippi for colonization during the early years of the movement was for colonizing the slaves of Judge James Green. In 1836 it was stated that $7,000 had already been spent by Green's executors for this purpose and that it had been determined to devote an additional $25,000 to completing the task. In the same year, Gurley wrote: "Without my personal application to a single individual, and with my detention hardly for a day," $2,000 was raised in Mississippi. [46]

James G. Birney collected $1,400 as a result of two meetings held the same Sunday in Natchez and was thereby moved to comment on

[43] R. R. Gurley, *Mission to England,* p. 261.
[44] "Colonization Movement," in *P. M. H. S.,* IX, 347.
[45] *Ibid.,* pp. 377, 380.
[46] *American Colonization Society,* pp. 171, 198.

the good spirit in all benevolent things in the older parts of Mississippi.[47] Another agent, H. B. Bascom, collected over $1,300 on a visit to Mississippi in 1831.[48] In the spring of 1832 friends of the movement about Natchez subscribed over $6,000.[49]

David Hunt, who lived near Rodney, contributed $500 and occasionally $1,000 a year from about 1850 to 1860 and in addition made two donations of $5,000 and one of $25,000.[50]

These and many small contributions [51] show that close to $100,000 was contributed to the colonization movement from Mississippi. Indeed, in 1833 the Mississippi society became the creditor of the parent society by lending it $3,000 from its surplus with the understanding that the latter should expend that amount in colonizing Mississippi negroes when requested to do so by the Mississippi society.[52] Two years later the Mississippi society met with little success in an endeavor to hold the American society to this agreement.[53] In 1836 the secretary of the latter society stated in his report that he considered Mississippi and Louisiana the best fields in the Union for securing both emigrants and money.[54]

Few points were more frequently reiterated in the letters from the parent society to the Mississippi society than the necessity of employing an agent to work in the State, possibly devoting part of his time to Louisiana.[55] Several citizens of these two States were suggested as agents, among them the Rev. William Winans, but there is no record of their having formally become agents of the society. However, Winans was appointed by the Methodist conference to solicit funds in Mississippi and Alabama for the colonization society. He was probably more valuable to the society than any of its paid agents in the Southwest.[56] Gurley himself visited Mississippi at least twice in the interests of the cause, once in 1836 and again in 1839.[57]

[47] William Birney, *James G. Birney and His Times*, pp. 122–123.
[48] *African Repository*, VII, 206.
[49] *Ibid.*, VIII, 61, 81, 93, 122.
[50] *Ibid.*, XXIX, 219; XXXII, 19–20; XXXIII, 151; XXXIV, 64, 82; XXXVI, 95; XXXVII, 160.
[51] Several free negroes, presumably not emigrants, contributed small sums to the cause.—*Ibid.*, XVIII, 47; XXX, 287.
[52] *Ibid.*, IX, 57.
[53] "Colonization Movement," in *P. M. H. S.*, IX, 365.
[54] *African Repository*, XII, 336.
[55] "Colonization Movement," in *P. M. H. S.*, IX, *passim*.
[56] *Ibid.*, p. 369. *African Repository*, V, 182; VI, 80.
[57] "Colonization Movement," in *P. M. H. S.*, IX, 408. *American Colonization Society*, p. 198.

Cresson, a representative who worked mainly in the North, must have been in the State at least once, and the Rev. J. B. Pinney was in Mississippi in 1845.[58] James G. Birney, the lawyer of Huntsville, Alabama, who changed from slaveholder to abolitionist, represented the society in Mississippi in 1833. Shortly after this visit several of his articles were reprinted in the Mississippi press.[59] Another minister, H. B. Bascom, who was in Mississippi in the summer of 1831, was an energetic agent who was especially active in forming local societies.[60] He was followed within a few months by Robert S. Finley who returned a number of times to the State where he made speeches, secured contributions, and superintended the embarkation of emigrants. Finley seems to have been better liked than any of the out-of-the-state agents who worked in Mississippi and when the Mississippi society separated for a time from the mother society, Finley was employed as agent of the Mississippi society.[61]

The success of the Mississippi Colonization Society in the middle of the 'thirties encouraged its leaders to independent action. The society was flourishing and was, indeed, a creditor of the American society. The flush of success and something of State rights feeling led to a decision to form a separate African colony for Mississippi emigrants. It is also probable that the leaders of the movement in Mississippi felt that it would be wiser, since there was some local animosity toward the American Colonization Society, to steer a fairly independent course. Accordingly, in 1836, land was secured 130 miles south of Monrovia. "Mississippi in Africa" was to be the name of the colony and "Greenville" was to be its capital, being so named in honor of Judge James Green of whom more will be told later. As has been stated, the Mississippi society employed R. S. Finley as its separate agent.[62] The executive committee of the Mississippi society estimated that $20,000 a year for five years would place their colony on a basis of permanent and progressive prosperity.[63]

As Maryland already had a separate African colony, and as Louisi-

[58] *Ibid.*, p. 188. *African Repository*, XXI, 160.
[59] *James G. Birney*, pp. 122–128. *Woodville Republican*, June 15, July 27, Aug. 17, 1833.
[60] *African Repository*, VII, 138–139, 206–207.
[61] *Ibid.*, VII, 345; VIII, 315; XI, 64, 250–252; XIII, 63–64. *American Colonization Society*, p. 101. "Colonization Movement," in *P. M. H. S.*, IX, 366, 369.
[62] *African Repository*, XIII, 63–64.
[63] *South-Western Journal, a Magazine of Science, Literature and Miscellany*, vol. I, no. ii (Dec. 30, 1837). Published semimonthly by the Jefferson College and Washington Lyceum.

ana was moving with Mississippi in its secession from the parent society, the officers of the latter sought to block this step. Acting with considerable artfulness they first sought to dampen the self-reliance of the Mississippi society by intimating that the land purchased was unsatisfactory and that a native of great power was hostile to the enterprise.[64] Also, Gurley came to Mississippi in June, 1839, to attempt to bring the Mississippi society back to the fold.[65]

In the meantime, a revision of the constitution of the American Colonization Society made his task more difficult. Under the new constitution the Mississippi society, along with the others of the South, suffered because the voting strength of each State was now made proportional to its contributions in money, no account being taken of the large value of emancipated slaves.[66] In spite of this handicap, Gurley succeeded in a prolonged conference with the Mississippi society in patching up a truce between the two organizations. Though there were attached to the agreement some provisos —designed to keep "Mississippi in Africa" a separate unit in Liberia—by the end of 1840 the Mississippi society was on good terms with the American society.[67]

It might also be remarked that by 1840 the Mississippi society was nearly defunct. By this time the initial steps had been taken to secure the colonization of most of the negroes who were transplanted from Mississippi to Africa, although the negotiations necessary to effect the freedom of many of them extended considerably past 1840. The apparent activities after 1840 were but the reapings of earlier sowings. The force of the movement was spent about ten years after its birth.

Two causes of the decline of the Mississippi society have been mentioned, the revision of the constitution of the American society and the partial failure of the ambitious "Mississippi in Africa" plan. A third cause of waning interest in Mississippi was an article in the *Repository* written by Gurley. In it were statements that were strongly disapproved by Dr. Duncan, a most valuable and liberal member of the Mississippi society and for many years its president. Though the writer explained his position and in a measure apologized, Dr. Duncan's active interest seems to have ceased.[68] The patched-up

[64] *African Repository*, XII, 36; XIII, 192. *Mission to England*, p. 240.
[65] *African Repository*, XV, 200–201.
[66] *American Colonization Society*, pp. 119–122.
[67] *African Repository*, XV, 200–201; XVII, 43, 158; XVIII, 59–60. "Colonization Movement," in *P. M. H. S.*, IX, 408–411.
[68] "Colonization Movement," in *P. M. H. S.*, IX, 383–384.

friendship of 1839 between the two societies was completely destroyed when the Rev. William McLain displaced Gurley as secretary of the parent society. Soon after this event, Ker, the last influential and active friend of colonization in the State, became hostile to the management of the American Colonization Society. The subject is best explained in a letter from Ker to McLain. A Mr. T. M. Whiteside, who sought the position of agent of the society in Mississippi, was referred by McLain to Ker, who thereupon wrote to McLain: "I had no knowledge of Whiteside whatever & . . . I am somewhat surprised at *such* a reference to me and from *yourself*. In the first place I am only a single individual without any authority. . . . Our society has been essentially defunct for some years. It has for many years existed only in an Ex. Committee of which I was a member." Ker declared that the individual zeal of the members of this committee has been nearly extinguished because of the disregard of their rights and claims by the Executive Committee of the American Colonization Society and by its secretary, McLain.

Ker further stated that he had a personal ground for complaint against McLain. After the article in the *Repository* that was so much disliked by Duncan, Ker made two attempts to effect a reconciliation. McLain did not even reply to these letters. As a result, Duncan struck from his will a bequest to the society, and his feelings on the subject were so strong that Ker could not even discuss the matter with him.

A final indictment that Ker brought against McLain was that of failure to coöperate in the emigration of a large shipment of Mississippi negroes with the unfortunate result that many of them died of cholera. Their exposure was in part due to McLain's hurried and cowardly flight from New Orleans when he found that cholera was there.[69]

There is small wonder, in view of all these things, that the Mississippi society should have lost interest in the cause. Local conditions also tended to diminish its influence. One was the increase in cotton production and a consequent decline of interest in anything that would remove the sinews of this business. Another factor was the growth of the abolitionist movement and the confusion, in the popular mind, of this cause with that of colonization.[70] By 1842 public opinion in

[69] *Ibid.*, pp. 358–361.
[70] Robert J. Walker stated in the United States senate that "among the unfortunate consequences which had been produced in Mississippi, owing to the

Mississippi was so stirred that a law was passed declaring that no slave could be set free by will, even if this was conditioned on his leaving the State forever.[71] This law, strictly enforced, would of course have greatly hampered the work of the colonization society. Indeed, as will be pointed out later, it was enacted for this very purpose.

After the death of the Mississippi Colonization Society, about the year 1840, a few of the leaders strove to complete tasks that had been begun. Occasional efforts were made to take new steps, but without success. For example, R. S. Finley, who worked in Mississippi over a month in the spring of 1847, was not able to collect enough money to meet his frugal expense account of fifty dollars. His failure is the more evident when we realize that he worked in the section of the State that had earlier been most interested in colonization, namely, at Natchez, Vicksburg, and Oakland College.[72] This fiasco is a fair index to the change of sentiment that had taken place in a very few years. Occasional newspaper references to colonization can be found after 1844, but in general they were brief and frequently hostile. For example, in 1852, a criticism of the idea of emancipating slaves for the purpose of returning them to Africa appeared in one of the State newspapers. A short time after, the same paper had in its columns a copy of a letter of Governor Collier of Alabama relative to the American Colonization Society. He favored returning free negroes to Africa but not slaves.[73]

Through its entire history there was a close connection between the colonization movement and the religious bodies in Mississippi. About one fifth of the officers of the Mississippi society were ministers. Furthermore, the only two meetings that have been noticed were held in the Presbyterian and Methodist churches of Natchez,[74] and these same churches were thrown open for colonization addresses by James G. Birney.[75] The Wilkinson County Colonization Society

movements of the Abolitionists was the unpopularity of the Colonization Society, which previously, on the contrary had been extremely popular. There were many individuals in the state who had been beneficent contributors to it but who now were opposed to it." Speech of Jan. 27, 1837. *Congressional Debates,* vol. XII, part I, p. 535.

[71] *Hutchinson's Code,* p. 539.
[72] "Colonization Movement," in *P. M. H. S.,* IX, 396–399.
[73] Natchez *Mississippi Free Trader,* Jan. 10 and 28, 1852.
[74] "Colonization Movement," in *P. M. H. S.,* IX, 406–411.
[75] *James G. Birney,* p. 122.

seems to have been always welcome in the local Methodist church.[76] Finally, resolutions endorsing the movement were passed by these two denominations. In 1833, the Presbytery of Mississippi expressed "unabated confidence" in the colonization society and the following year pledged itself to contribute $100 a year for ten years.[77] Fourteen years later this confidence seems to have continued unshaken, for R. S. Finley was allowed to address a meeting of this Presbytery in the interests of the movement.[78] Likewise, the Mississippi Annual Conference of 1835 of the Methodist Episcopal Church, though denouncing the abolitionists, declared its esteem for the American Colonization Society, which it considered truly friendly to the whole African race and not harmful to the white.[79] This body continued to approve the movement in 1845.[80] The missionary society of Oakland College planned to send a young white man as a missionary to "Mississippi in Africa," [81] and the Presbyterian Synod of Mississippi coöperated with that of Alabama in purchasing a negro man and his family for $2,500 to be sent as missionaries. The slave, Harrison Ellis, was an intelligent blacksmith who had studied Latin and Greek and had made some progress in Hebrew.[82]

Having discussed various phases of the genesis, life, and decline of the colonization movement in Mississippi, there remains the question of what it actually accomplished in settling Mississippi negroes in Africa.

A few Mississippi slaves emigrated to Africa before June 1, 1831, when the Mississippi society was formally organized. The most noted of these was a Natchez slave known as Prince who was discovered to have been a man of rank in Africa. His freedom was given to him so that he could return there. Before sailing he was able to raise sufficient money to purchase his slave wife, and in the spring of 1829 the aged couple departed from the United States in the "Harriet." A year and a half later his eight children and grandchildren, all recently freed from slavery, sailed from Norfolk in the "Carolinian." [83]

---

[76] Woodville Republican, July 9, Aug. 6, 1831; June 30, 1832.
[77] American Colonization Society, p. 94. African Repository, X, 29.
[78] "Colonization Movement," in P. M. H. S., IX, 397.
[79] Woodville Republican, Dec. 5, 1835.
[80] American Colonization Society, p. 165.
[81] African Repository, XVI, 216.
[82] Ibid., XXII, 356; XXIII, 46-48.
[83] Ibid., III, 364-367; IV, 77-81, 243-250; V, 94, 281; VI, 60, 187.

In August, 1831, eighteen slaves, set free by Mrs. Elizabeth Greenfield who lived near Natchez, embarked for Liberia.[84]

As the avowed purpose of the Mississippi society was to remove free negroes from the State, especial interest attaches itself to the next emigrants, Gloster Simpson and Archy Moore. Doubtless they were the men referred to in the first annual report of the Mississippi Colonization Society, which stated that some free negroes were interested in emigrating and that two of their number expected to go to Liberia and bring back a report of conditions there. The journey of these explorers, for so they might be called, was well described in 1835 by Simpson himself.

"For a long time I had desired to find a place of refuge, where I might enjoy liberty and such advantages as I could not here in the South—not that I was treated unkindly in Mississippi. I have many dear friends there. But it is not possible for colored people to enjoy among white men all the privileges and advantages of liberty. I heard a great deal about Liberia, and read a good deal. Good people told me a heap about it, and I wanted to see it. So did some of my friends. One said to another, 'Will you go and see it for us.' But all were too busy. They sent to me to know if I would go. I said yes. So did Archy Moore. We started. First we came to New Orleans, but the vessel we expected to go in had sailed. Then we had to go to an eastern port. We started for Washington City. Met with many discouragements. In Fredericktown a lady said to me, 'Where are you going?' To Africa. 'Where?' To *Africa*. 'What—you such a fool as to go to Africa? Don't you know that the niggers will kill you and eat you there?' [A laugh] So other persons tried to dishearten and dissuade us from going, till we found Mr. Gurley in Washington. He received us in a friendly manner—encouraged us to go on, and provided for us a passage from Norfolk. Our voyage was much pleasanter than I expected. I found many Christian friends among the emigrants in the ship. We arrived at Monrovia the last day of June." [85]

Thus the two colored emigrants reached Africa, in 1832, and returned the same year. Nearly three years later they went to Africa again, this time leading a company of seventy-one emigrants, who sailed on the brig "Rover" from New Orleans on March 4, 1835.[86]

[84] *Ibid.*, VII, 217. *American Colonization Society*, pp. 212–215.
Mrs. Greenfield, formerly Mrs. Roach, was the donor of the land and buildings at Washington, Miss., for that pioneer institution for the education of women, Elizabeth Female Academy.—*Education in Mississippi*, p. 38.
[85] *Emigrants from New Orleans*, p. 3.
[86] The supplies that emigrants needed were, in the opinion of Robert S. Finley, as follows: "Bacon, beef, flour, corn meal, leaf tobacco, salt, nails, hinges, pots, skillets and all kinds of hardware, house earthen ware, pound beans, coarse cottons, and callicoes, hemp, linen, etc. etc."—*Woodville Republican*, Nov. 6, 1831.

Simpson and Moore had been prevented from returning earlier because their families were in bondage. Although Robert Cochrane,[87] the owner of Simpson's wife and five children, had formally given them to Simpson, they were not able to migrate before 1834 because they had been hired out. Not only did Cochrane relinquish his title to these slaves, valued at $4,000, but he also bequeathed $100 to each of Simpson's five children. Simpson himself owned a farm of 150 acres and was of sufficient prominence to have been invited to deliver a farewell message at the close of the sermon in Bethel church, the church of the white people of his community.

Archy Moore was less fortunate, in that he was compelled to purchase his son for $1,000 and his daughter for $750. However, interested white persons contributed $1,100 for this purpose.[88]

Another emigrant was David Moore, brother of Archy. David had been set free about nine years before for meritorious services. Not only was he successful in managing his own farm of 280 acres, but in addition he received $450 a year for managing an adjoining plantation. He was accompanied to Africa by his wife, for whom he had paid $500, by a female slave purchased at the same price, and by his six children and three grandchildren, for whom he had paid $3,500. He took with him a cotton-gin, about $1,000 worth of agricultural and mechanical tools, provisions and trade goods to an equal value, and about $3,000 in specie. He was probably the wealthiest emigrant to go from Mississippi to Africa.

Also, there was the free negro, Preston Spottswood, who had been employed as second barkeeper in a hotel in Port Gibson. His wife and three children remained in the United States, for he proposed to examine Liberia himself before taking them there.

One other emigrant free negro family was that of Richard Saunders, mechanic and cotton-gin wright. After the death of his owner in 1827, the executor of the estate allowed him to hire his own time for $250 a year and to keep whatever he earned over that amount. At the end of four years he was able to purchase himself for $1,000 in addition to having paid his annual hire. A few days before leaving Mississippi he purchased his wife and son for $1,125, and he also took to Africa a good set of tools for his trade.[89]

[87] Cochrane donated the 250 acres of land on which Oakland College was built.—*Education in Mississippi*, p. 66.
[88] *African Repository*, XI, 153.
[89] *Ibid.*, XI, 154.

These were the chief free negroes on the "Rover." With them sailed a number of negroes who had been freed by their owners for the direct purpose of sending them to Africa. Among these were eleven who had belonged to a Mrs. Bullock of Claiborne County. She had also contributed $700 for their outfit.[90]

Twenty-six slaves were from the estate of Judge James Green, who had been a prominent citizen of Adams County. As executors and trustees he had named his two sisters, Eliza C. Wood and Maltilda S. Railey, and his brother-in-law, James Railey. After distinctly excluding all other heirs-at-law, particularly Cowles Mead and any of his descendants, he devised his personal and real property to the three executors, subject to certain exceptions which will be mentioned presently.

One negro man, Granger, was specifically set free, and the executors were enjoined to make ample provision for him, the sum of $3,000 being suggested as proper. To each of the three executors were devised a number of slaves, who were mentioned by name: to Eliza C. Wood, forty-seven; to Matilda S. Railey, seventeen; and to James Railey, nine. Toward the close of the codicil to the will is the following matter, which is particularly relevant to colonization.

". . . My desire and will is that my following named negro slaves, to-wit, Henry Rust and children Hampton and Nael and Misha if Rusts wife at the time together with any children she may have by him Henry Hubbard and his child Lawson Sam Delany and his wife Suckey and child Sally, Adam his wife Charlotte and their children Dave Bunch and his brother George Jack Armstrong and his Silla Old George and his wife Peg be liberated by my said Executors and trustees acting for the time being at such times as they shall think proper if in their opinion said negroes or any of them from their continued good conduct be entitled to their freedom according to my wishes.
And in the event of any or all of said negroes and their children being emancipated as aforesaid and removing to Liberia to reside my desire in that event is that my executors and trustees give each of them so removing a liberal provision and I suggest a sum not less than two hundred Dollars nor more than five hundred Dollars to each one over twelve years of age and also an outfit to each; and a liberal sum and outfit to each under twelve years of age; to be paid out of my estate by my said acting Executors and trustees. And in the event said negroes or any of them being emancipated and not going to Liberia then the provision out of my estate for any who do not go to be regulated and given by my Executors and trustees as aforesaid according to their best judgements.

[90] *Ibid.*, XI, 250–251.

I also will and Desire that my negro Charlotte Butler wife of my negro man Granger liberated in my will be set apart and allotted to said negro man Granger by my said Executors and trustees. And after all my bequests devises and dispositions of my Property and directions to my said Executors and trustees contained in my last will & testament in this codicil thereto or expressed in any writing or verbally to my said Executors and Trustees (who are to determine the same) shall have been carried into effect executed and complied with most fully and liberally in every respect according to my intentions and wishes which are fully understood by my said Executors and trustees I give and bequeath all the rest and residue of my Estate of any Description to my said acting Executors & Trustees as provided in my will to be appropriated to the purpose and aid of emancipating negroes in the state of Mississippi and in the event of that not being practicable then towards the establishing or aiding in the endowing of an academy or school or other charitable objects as my said Executors and trustees for the time being shall deem best and think proper leaving it to their discretion, they being fully apprized of my wishes upon this subject." [91]

Judge Green died shortly after he made this will on May 15, 1832, for it was admitted to record at the June term of court in the same year.[92] A few months later at least part of the estate was advertised for sale: "The Forest Plantation," about eight miles below Vidalia, Louisiana, comprising 1,080 acres; "The Point Plantation" of 280 acres, which was seven miles below the first tract of land; and "Boling Green" in Claiborne County, Mississippi, comprising 1,500 acres.[93]

The executors thus entered at once upon their duties. It should be remembered that they were themselves slaveholders and were also among the legal heirs of the testator. Even though the negroes would otherwise have become their own property, they faithfully executed the will of Judge Green. They contributed from the estate $1,000 toward chartering the "Rover," $1,600 in outfitting the twenty-six slaves of Judge Green who sailed on this vessel, and shipped $4,400 in specie to the Governor of Liberia with a memorandum showing how the money should be divided among these slaves.[94] It is probable that a

[91] From a certified copy of Last Will and Testament, and the codicil thereto, of James Green, deceased. Record of Wills Book 2, pages 8 to 12 inclusive, Chancery Court, Adams County, Mississippi.
[92] Letter from W. H. Hale, chancery clerk, Adams County, Miss.
[93] *Woodville Republican*, Nov. 24, 1832.
The legislature of Louisiana passed an act authorizing the executors of the estate of Judge Green to move the administration of the part of the property that was in Louisiana to Adams County, Mississippi.—*Laws of Louisiana*, 1836, p. 148.
[94] *African Repository*, XI, 251–252.

number of other slaves were sent subsequently from this estate.[95] A year later the executors advanced $2,500 toward defraying the expenses of the schooner "Swift," and the officers of the colonization society expected them to devote an additional $25,000 to the cause.[96]

The free negroes, the slaves of Mrs. Bullock and the slaves of Judge Green's estate, who composed most if not all of the passenger list of the "Rover," were in New Orleans several weeks before they sailed, and Mrs. Wood and Mr. Railey were there part of the time to superintend the embarkation of the twenty-six in whom they were interested. During the delay at New Orleans there were two interesting meetings, one on January seventeenth and the other on February twenty-third. The latter was a farewell meeting and was addressed by Simpson and Moore, the two free negroes who had already been to Africa; by Finley, agent of the American Colonization Society; by Zebulon Butler; and by others. The earlier meeting was the occasion of the formation of all the emigrants into a Temperance Society. The program was impressive; there were numerous testimonies of good character; the pledge was taken by all the emigrants; and all was properly set off by the story of one negro, a brother of one of the emigrants, who pleaded with tears to be allowed to go, but was rejected because he was a drunkard.[97]

It is probable that the next emigrants from Mississippi to Africa sailed on the "Swift" in April, 1836. William Foster, who died near Natchez in 1834, had provided in his will that four families, twenty-one negroes in all, should be separated from his slaves and sent to Liberia, the rest remaining in bondage. In the same vessel were an additional twenty-one slaves who had formerly been the property of a Mr. Randolph, who lived near Columbus, Mississippi. The question of how to finance the transportation of the Randolph negroes had been the subject of some communication between the Mississippi and the American societies in the previous year. The former sought to recover for this purpose a considerable sum earlier loaned to the American Colonization Society. The latter practically repudiated the debt and at least confessed its inability to return the money at that time. However, its secretary promised to write to the Kentucky and Tennessee societies and to urge them to coöperate in supplying means

[95] Claiborne, *Mississippi*, p. 388. *American Colonization Society*, p. 198.
[96] *African Repository*, XII, 236.
[97] *Ibid.*, XI, 123–127, 251–252. *Emigrants from New Orleans*, pp. 1–2.

and equipment for the expedition. If necessary, the American society would supply any deficit in funds, but its secretary devoutly hoped that the shortage would not be great. Mr. R. S. Finley was suggested as the best person available to manage the embarkation of the negroes at New Orleans and it is probable that he undertook the task.[98]

In March, 1836, James Leech of Wilkinson County, died, having provided in his will that his servant Delila and her four children should be set free and sent either to Indiana or to Liberia, whichever they chose. One lot in Woodville was willed separately to Delila, and the rest of the property was to be sold and divided equally between her and three of her children, Jack, Harriet, and Nancy. Certain relatives of Leech claimed that the law prohibiting emancipations within the State except with special permission of the legislature [99] was in conflict with this will for the executors were directed—notice the order of the words—"to set the slaves free and remove them to Liberia." The courts, however, held that the sense of the will was to send the slaves away from the State and then free them, a procedure that was not contrary to law. Thus the will was upheld and it is possible, though not certain, that Delila and her children were sent to Liberia either in 1838 or 1839.[100]

Thirty-seven colored emigrants from Mississippi sailed on the "Mail" from New Orleans in May, 1838. Among these was Robert Leiper, an aged free negro of Natchez. Though his children would not go with him, he was accompanied by his daughter-in-law and her two children. It is probable that the other thirty-three negroes were from the estate of Judge Green. These were the first negroes to go to the new town of Greenville, Liberia, so named in honor of Judge Green. The Mississippi emigrants who had sailed on the "Rover" three years before and who had settled near Monrovia were invited to move to this new town in "Mississippi in Africa" and some, including Gloster Simpson, did so.[101]

The largest number of slaves to go to Liberia from any one Mississippi estate were those of Captain Isaac Ross, a native and resident of Jefferson County. He died in January, 1836. The part of his will and the codicils attached that relate to colonization have been summarized as follows:

[98] *African Repository*, XI, 336. *American Colonization Society*, pp. 199, 212–215. "Colonization Movement," in *P. M. H. S.*, IX, 365–367.
[99] *Hutchinson's Code*, p. 523.
[100] Leech v. Cooley, 14 Miss. 93.
[101] *African Repository*, XIV, 93–94; XV, 71–88.

"1. To his grand-daughter Adelaide Wade, he gave his cook, a woman named Grace, and all her children living at the time of his demise, unless the said Grace should elect, of her own free will, to go to Africa, in which case she and her children were to be transported there with his other slaves as hereinafter provided for. And then the said Adelaide, in lieu thereof, was to have an additional $2,000 besides her other bequests.

"2. His aforesaid grand-daughter shall take charge of and maintain comfortably, during their natural lives, testator's negro man Hannibal, and his three sisters, and he gave to Hannibal $100, annually, for life, and to each of his sisters $50, annually. But should they elect to go to Africa, they shall be permitted to go with and on the same footing with the other slaves; and should he so elect he shall be paid when he embarks $500, in silver, in lieu of the aforesaid legacy.

"3. Enoch, wife and children were to be conveyed free of expense, in twelve months, to the free State they might prefer, there to be manumitted and receive $500, in coin, or to Africa if they chose, on the same footing with the others, and receive $500.

"4. Excepting Tom, William, Joe, Aleck and Henrietta, and Jeffers, (who are to be sold as hereinafter provided,) all the slaves aged twenty-one and upward, within ten days after the growing crop shall be gathered, shall be called together by the executors and the provisions of the will be fully explained. Those electing to go shall be sent to Africa under the authority of the American Colonization Society. And the remainder of his estate, real, personal and mixed, (excepting always the negroes whose names are mentioned above,) be offered for sale at public auction, one-half the purchase money to be paid in cash and the balance in twelve months. The proceeds of the sale, and any money on hand or due, after deducting enough for the aforesaid legacies, to be paid over to the A. C. S., provided it will consent to appropriate it as follows, to-wit: 1st. To pay the expense of transporting to Africa of such of my slaves as may elect to go. 2d. To expend the remainder for their support and maintenance while there.

"5. Should the slaves refuse to go there, they (except those that have been specially named) are to be sold, and the proceeds paid over to the A. C. S., to be invested at 6 per cent., the interest to be employed for 100 years, in maintaining an institution of learning in Liberia, in Africa. If there shall be no government in Liberia, the said fund to be transferred to the State of Mississippi for a similar institution.

"6. Daniel Vertner, James P. Parker, Dr. Elias Ogden, Isaac Ross Wade, and John B. Coleman were appointed executors without bond." [102]

This was the substance of the will of Isaac Ross, an officer in the American Revolutionary army and an eminent citizen of his State, who possessed at the time of his death about 160 or 170 slaves. However, their colonization was not to take place before the death of his

[102] Claiborne, *Mississippi*, pp. 389–390, thus condenses the part of the will dealing with colonization.

daughter, Mrs. Margaret A. Reed, widow of United States Senator Thomas Buck Reed.

Captain Ross combined unusual business acumen with kindness and benevolence. One who knew him wrote:

"The slaves who are the subjects of his bounty were kept disconnected from those on other plantations, and constitute one great family of *one hundred and seventy persons,* who have been treated more like children than slaves. They are represented to have no superiors among their cast in good morals, industry, and intelligence. To render them happy appears to have been a principal object of their owner. He was an excellent planter; yet for many years, instead of endeavoring to increase his estate, he developed and applied its great resources to increase the comforts of his people. Some conception of its extent may be formed from the statement that the crop on it for the present year will pay all the debts, and that it may hereafter accumulate at the rate of *twenty thousand* dollars per annum." [108]

"Prospect Hill," located nine miles from Port Gibson, was the center of the Ross estate. The value of the property, over and above that of the negroes, was estimated at $150,000 at the time of the owner's death. With an estate of such value, producing a net income of $20,000 a year, there should have been ample funds to carry out the desires of Captain Ross. Unfortunately, some years elapsed before the negroes set sail. During this period the value of the estate shrank almost to the vanishing point; the number of slaves largely increased.

The initial difficulty was that the executors with the single exception of Isaac Ross Wade, a grandson, failed to qualify; while he, with some of the other excluded heirs, laid plans to break the will although he took no legal action to that end. This was highly provoking to Mrs. Reed and Isaac Ross, junior, both of whom were in sympathy with the desires of their father. Indeed, they each made wills providing for the emancipation of at least part of their own slaves. Isaac Ross, junior, died in 1836. Slaves from his estate may have been among the seventy-seven Mississippi emigrants on the "Renown," which sailed in June, 1843, and was wrecked on the Cape Verde Islands where a supply of horses, jacks, and provisions was sought. No lives were lost, however, and with the assistance of the American

[108] *A Brief History of The Ross Slaves,* pp. 11–12.
Jefferson Davis, though opposed to colonization, was probably referring to the Ross emigrants when he stated that he knew and highly esteemed the slaves who had been sent to Africa by one master.—Rowland, *Jefferson Davis, Constitutionalist,* IV, 522–523.

consul another vessel was secured and the voyage to Liberia was completed.[104]

After witnessing the difficulties that were met in administering the will of her father, Captain Ross, Mrs. Reed, who died in 1838, willed her slaves, including those she inherited from her father, in fee simple to Zebulon Butler and Stephen Duncan. Both of these men, the former a Presbyterian minister of Port Gibson and the latter a wealthy resident of Natchez, favored colonization and understood the desire of Mrs. Reed. Though the slaves were given them outright by Mrs. Reed, they knew that she wanted them sent to Liberia. After a legal fight this was done, though it was "said that Dr. Duncan actually obtained his portion of the slaves by having them run away from the plantation and secreted on the banks of the Mississippi until a steamboat was hailed to take them on to Louisiana, whence he sent them to Liberia." [105]

The Reed negroes sent to Africa by Butler and Duncan composed all but twenty of the ninety-two Mississippi emigrants on the brig "Lime Rock," which sailed from New Orleans on March 10, 1844. The cost of returning the entire ninety-two, including provisions for the first six months in Africa, amounted to at least $5,394.80. The "Lime Rock" was two months on its journey, anchoring at Monrovia on May sixth. Two of the emigrants died at sea; nineteen settled at Monrovia; and the others, presumably the Reed negroes, went down to Sinoe and settled in the Mississippi colony in and about Greenville.[106] Other slaves from the estate of Mrs. Reed had sailed with an earlier expedition, either on the "Mail," in 1838, or the "Renown," in 1843, and had also settled at Greenville.[107]

We will not attempt to follow the intricate and extended litigation concerning the will of Captain Isaac Ross, senior. It is sufficient to state that in its December, 1840, term the State supreme court decided against the heirs. In referring to the law which prohibited the emancipation of slaves in Mississippi, except with the approval of the legislature in each instance,[108] the court concluded that though this "might seem to prohibit emancipation out of as well as within the State by a citizen, yet such a construction would be manifestly con-

---

[104] *African Repository*, XV, 71–88; XIX, 81–82.
[105] *A Brief History of The Ross Slaves*, p. 31.
[106] *Twenty-eighth Annual Report of the American Colonization Society* (1845).
[107] *African Repository*, XX, 284–286.
[108] *Hutchinson's Code*, p. 523.

trary to the spirit of the law. . . . The evil contemplated by the legislature was the increase of free negroes by emancipation. The removal of slaves belonging to citizens of the State, and their emancipation in parts beyond her territorial limits was no injury to her." [109]

Though it would seem, after this decision, that the will of Captain Ross could now be administered, there remained much trouble ahead. Wade and the other defeated heirs carried the fight into the legislative halls of the State. They even spread the rumor that, if the legislature did not block the emancipation of the Ross slaves, there were 500 armed men who had sworn to use force to keep the negroes from being colonized. In addition to bringing this pressure to bear on the legislature, the heirs also declared that Isaac Ross was not in sound mind when he made his will, but was under the influence of "the terrors of death and judgement, inspired by 'priests and fanatics.'" The measure that the heirs sought to force through the legislature would make illegal any bequests of slaves for purposes of emancipation, and would be retroactive over the will of Isaac Ross. It was chiefly due to Dr. John Ker, who was a member of the upper house, that the close lobby maintained by Wade was not entirely successful. Though a bill was finally passed, in 1842, that forbade any manumission of slaves by will, the law was not retroactive. In case a will was already probated, one year was allowed in which the slaves could be removed from the state. [110]

The last clause of this law made necessary the removal of the Ross emigrants from the State within twelve months. This could not be accomplished because of the further maneuvers of Wade, the administrator and manager of the estate. Ker had by this time accepted the position of agent and attorney of the American Colonization Society in this case. A bill was filed within the year in the name of the society to compel the executor to carry out the provisions of the will. As a result of this further litigation the supreme court held that the one-year clause of the act of 1842 would not apply here because "the acts of the executor constituted such a fraud, that neither he nor anyone claiming by virtue of his acts acquired any rights." [111]

---

[109] It is worthy of note that Seargent S. Prentiss was a counsel in this case, serving those who were endeavoring to fulfill the will of Isaac Ross.—*Seargent S. Prentiss*, p. 313.

[110] *Hutchinson's Code*, p. 539.

[111] "Prospect Hill," where Wade and his family lived, was burned in 1845. There is evidence to show that the negroes, who had become restive under the long delay, did this with the hope of destroying Wade whom they con-

Thus ended all legal obstacles to the return of the slaves. Great demands had been made on the time and patience of Dr. Ker and other friends of colonization. The expense of the litigation had been so great that the estate of Captain Ross was now found insufficient to meet the cost of transporting the negroes to Africa. The estate was further impoverished by the fees due Wade for his twelve-year executorship.[112] As the estate could not furnish sufficient money to send the negroes to Africa, other sources had to be discovered. Some funds were secured by contributions from the officers of the Mississippi society.[118] The American Colonization Society was also approached and presumably gave aid. A pamphlet of thirty-six pages was published by the New York Colonization Society, in 1848, giving a good account of the history of the Ross slaves and making a plea for at least $8,000, the amount necessary to consummate the will of Captain Isaac Ross.[114]

The way was finally cleared of all financial and legal obstacles and in January, 1848, thirty-four of the Ross slaves and an additional one from the estate of Mrs. Reed sailed on the "Nehemiah Rich."[115] A year later one hundred and forty-one Ross slaves and one Reed slave sailed on the "Laura" from New Orleans.[116] The total number of Ross emigrants was variously estimated at from 235 to 300. This wide lack of agreement may be accounted for in part by the natural increase of the slaves during the twelve years between the death of their benefactor and the time of their emigration and in part by the question of what slaves to count in making up to the total. In addition to the slaves under the executorship of Wade, there were the slaves bequeathed by Isaac Ross, senior, to Mrs. Reed and liberated by her; the slaves earlier owned by Mrs. Reed; and the slaves liberated by Isaac Ross, junior.

An unfortunate occurrence marred the departure of the "Laura." The Ross emigrants were sent on a river steamboat to New Orleans by Ker, who expected them to be met by McLain, secretary of the American Colonization Society. Cholera suddenly developed in New Orleans and McLain immediately departed without providing for

sidered the chief obstacle to their being freed.—Anna Mims Wright, *A Record of the Descendants of Isaac Ross and Jean Brown*, pp. 72–74.

[112] *Ibid.*, pp. 69–74. *A Brief History of the Ross Slaves*, p. 35.
[113] "Colonization Movement," in *P. M. H. S.*, IX, 377, 380.
[114] *A Brief History of The Ross Slaves.*
[115] *African Repository*, XXIV, 59–61, 77, 210–211.
[116] *Ibid.*, XXV, 118–121.

the safety of the slaves. For a time Ker feared that they would
be returned to him, which would probably have resulted in their
permanent enslavement under the law of 1842. He believed that,
if a ship had been ready, it would have been less dangerous to send
the slaves on than to retain them anywhere in Mississippi or
Louisiana. But McLain left without doing anything. Thus, the slaves
were exposed to the disease and, as a result, many deaths occurred
on the voyage to Liberia. Those of the Ross slaves who had sailed
about a year earlier seem to have suffered no casualties.[117]

After the sailing of the "Laura" there was no large group of
emigrants to leave Mississippi for Africa at any one time. Among
the twenty-one negroes on the "Clintonia Wright," which sailed from
New Orleans in April, 1849, two were from Mississippi. These were
Isaac and Cally Morris, both old and probably free negroes.[118]
Henry Boatner, who gave his occupation as musician, emigrated in
January, 1852. He had been emancipated by J. B. Byrne, of
Centerville who had also contributed $50 toward the passage
of this thirty-seven-year-old slave.[119] In May of the same year
Edward and Susan Bolles of Lafayette County sailed on the
brig "Ralph Cross" from Baltimore. Though both had been born
slaves, they had purchased their freedom. On the same boat were
Peter Adams and his son, Wesley, who had been set free by
Mrs. Land of Centerville.[120] G. J. Vick of Vicksburg freed eight of
his slaves and they sailed on the "Zebra" from New Orleans
in December, 1852.[121] A family of five slaves emancipated by
Mrs. Nancy Jennings of Kemper County sailed from Baltimore
in 1853.[122] On the "Elvira Owens" from Savannah in May, 1856,
sailed fourteen negroes liberated by Mrs. Elizabeth Holderness of
Columbus.[123] James West, who had been freed by C. C. West of

[117] The following sources supplied the material for the discussion of the
colonization of the Ross Slaves: Riley, "Colonization Movement," in
P. M. H. S., IX, 331–414; Claiborne, Mississippi, pp. 388–391; American Coloni-
zation Society, pp. 202–204; Ross et al. v. Vertner et al., 6 Miss. 305; Wade v.
American Colonization Society, 12 Miss. 670; Wade v. American Colonization
Society, 15 Miss. 663; African Repository, XV, XIX, XX, XXIV, XXV; A
Brief History of The Ross Slaves.

[118] African Repository, XXV, 218.

[119] Ibid., XXVII, 122; XXVIII, 128.

[120] Ibid., XXVII, 183.

[121] Ibid., XXIX, 70.

[122] Ibid., XXIX, 220.

[123] Ibid., XXXII, 253–254.

Woodville, sailed in December of the same year.[124] The last emigrants from Mississippi to Liberia before the Civil War were fifteen free negroes from Pontotoc who sailed in May, 1860. All bore the surname Manns, and all but two had been born free.[125]

The total number of negroes to go to Liberia from Mississippi was about 571, which was approximately one twentieth of all the emigrants sent from the United States by the American Colonization Society and its auxiliaries.[126] It is probable that at least 500 of these were slaves freed by their owners with the object of colonizing them.

Some Mississippi slave-owners failed in their attempts to free their slaves and send them to Liberia. In December, 1827, Silas Hamilton of Adams County requested the American Colonization Society to provide passage early in June for his twenty-three negroes. This was four years before the Mississippi society was formed. Hamilton hoped to supply agricultural implements and carpenters' tools but was unable to finance the transportation of his slaves. His letter to the society shows how strongly he felt slavery to be a moral and religious evil. In language that would have warmed the heart of the most ardent abolitionist he welcomed the creation of the American Colonization Society, which afforded the means whereby, "I may be enabled to wipe from my character the foulest stain with which it was ever tarnished and pluck from my bleeding conscience the most pungent sting." [127] But Hamilton was not to see his wish fulfilled so early. Three years later he was still writing to the society in regard to his slaves. No evidence of their return has been found.

Drury W. Brazeale, resident of Claiborne County, died in 1834,

[124] *Ibid.*, XXXIII, 25.
[125] *Ibid.*, XXXVI, 143.
[126] A tabulation of emigrants to the end of the year 1859 is given according to States in the *African Repository*, XXXVI, 115. In *ibid.*, XXXIII, 152–155 is a table which shows the number of emigrants each year from each State to the end of 1857. To the totals given in these tables I have added the fifteen free negroes who departed from Pontotoc in 1860, too late to be included in either table. I have also added Prince and his wife and the eighteen slaves freed by Mrs. Greenfield, who sailed in 1829 and 1831 respectively. Though there is ample evidence that these twenty emigrated to Africa, they were either omitted from the tables mentioned above or listed under some other State which was probably due to their having departed from Mississippi before the State colonization society was organized.
[127] *American Colonization Society*, p. 193.

after providing by will for freeing four families of negroes, supplying them with a suitable outfit, and sending them to Africa. In 1836, the American Colonization Society planned to transport them at an early date,[128] but, in 1839, the superior court of chancery of Mississippi enjoined the executors from carrying this part of the will into effect. It is, therefore, most improbable that the slaves of Brazeale were sent to Liberia.[129]

N. H. Hooe, of King George County, Virginia, provided in his will for the emancipation and colonization of over a hundred of his slaves in Mississippi as well as some in other States. He desired his estate to furnish means for transporting them and to give each one twenty-five dollars when he reached Africa. Gurley was made the executor of this will. The difficulty was that Hooe both made his will and died in the year 1844, two years after the passage of the law of Mississippi that prohibited such a bequest. When the will was brought before the courts of Mississippi, its defense was, of course, undertaken by the colonizationists, but the supreme court declared the will invalid so far as the emancipation of slaves domiciled in Mississippi was concerned.[130]

Another unsuccessful attempt to colonize Mississippi slaves appeared in the will of Robert Lusk, who gave all his slaves "to John H. B. Latrobe, Rev. Wm. McLean, and W. W. Seaton, in trust for the American Colonization Society," and also $3,500, presumably to be expended in removing the slaves to Liberia. These men were leaders in the colonization movement. The court declared the will of Robert Lusk invalid. Part of the decision in this case was in marked contrast to an opinion of the same body handed down just sixteen years before. In 1840, the court stated, in substance, that it was not against the policy of the State of Mississippi for an owner to send his slaves out of the State for the purpose of manumission.[131] In 1856, in referring to the American Colonization Society, the same court stated that "its operation was calculated strongly to promote emancipation, and it may, therefore, be regarded as founded on a principle not consistent with the growth and permanency of the institution of slavery."[132] It is evident that the court had changed

[128] *African Repository*, XI, 36; XII, 235.
[129] Clarke *v.* McCreary, 20 Miss. 347.
[130] Mahorner *v.* Hooe *et al.*, 17 Miss. 247. "Colonization Movement," in *P. M. H. S.*, IX, 398. *American Colonization Society*, p. 206.
[131] Ross *et al. v.* Vertner *et al.*, 6 Miss. 305.
[132] Lusk *v.* Lewis *et al.*, 32 Miss. 297.

its mind in regard to the policy of the State toward emancipating slaves.

Among the futile attempts to remove negroes from Mississippi to Africa was one that involved free negroes. In 1854, the board of police of Pike County was authorized by a special act of the State legislature to hire out annually at public auction all free negroes in the county with the surname *Lundy*. The money derived from the hiring of these negroes should be loaned at 8 per cent until the total reached $6,000. At that time, a contract should be made with some person or persons to transport the Lundy negroes to Liberia and provide comfortable lodging and board for twelve months.[133] No record has been found of whether the plan was put into operation, but it is almost certain that none of these free negroes were transported. The Lundy negroes were mulattoes with an evident scandal connected with their origin, and this may account for the desire to remove them from the State. They were a peaceful lot who were well behaved during the Civil War and took no part in the disturbances of reconstruction.[134]

These instances of unsuccessful attempts to colonize slaves cannot serve as an accurate measure of the desire of Mississippi planters to send their negroes to Africa. There were doubtless others who would have colonized their slaves, but who were deterred by the knowledge that it was impossible to accomplish this by will after the passage of the law of 1842. For instance, Edward McGehee, of Wilkinson County, an officer of the Mississippi Colonization Society and one of the largest slaveholders of the State, seriously considered planting a colony of his slaves on the coast of Liberia.[135]

As has already been stated, the land at the mouth of the Sinoe River, located about 130 miles southeast of Monrovia, was purchased by the Mississippi and Louisiana Colonization Societies. At the town of Greenville, laid out on this tract, Mississippi emigrants began to settle in 1838.[136] Just as Greenville was named in honor of the former master of the first large group of emigrants, so also other small

[133] *Laws of Miss.*, 1854, pp. 358-359.
[134] All Pike County Records were destroyed by fire in 1882. The above information was gained from old residents of the county.
[135] Rowland, *Mississippi*, II, 187.
[136] *Mission to England*, p. 240.
An early map of Liberia showing the location of Greenville and the neighboring villages of Rossville and Reedville can be found in *African Repository*, XXVII, 193.

neighboring settlements were given the names of other Mississippi and Louisiana benefactors of the colonists.

Several years before the founding of Greenville, Liberia, the land was viewed by two free negro men, Moore and Simpson, who have already been presented. Their description of the country is interesting both because of what they said and of the occasion on which they spoke; they were on the verge of conducting a number of their friends to that region. After some preliminary remarks, Moore stated to the assembled emigrants chiefly from the Green estate:

"As to the natural productions of the country, they exceed anything I ever saw in all my travels elsewhere. Besides such fruit as we have here, they have a great variety, that grows only there. They have fine grapes. I ate delicious English grapes there. The palm tree I had often heard of, and it is mentioned in the Bible. I saw it growing. It is a singular tree. I saw some two or three feet over. They grow very high, without a single branch or limb. Right on the top is a cabbage, or what looks so much like a cabbage you couldn't tell the difference a little way off. The leaves they use for covering their houses, from the trunk they get a juice, that makes wine, and an oil, that is used for butter and lard. I ate of it, and found it very good. The fibre they used instead of flax and hemp. [Of this fibre he exhibited a specimen—also a piece of the cam wood, a valuable dye wood, of a beautiful red color.] This wood is worth sixty dollars a ton, is abundant and easily obtained. It is as good as gold and silver to trade with.

"As to the style of living among the Colonists, it was quite superior to what I expected to see. Many houses, where I visited, look like those of respectable white families, and had I not seen the occupants, would have supposed them inhabited by white people. One Sabbath we were invited by Mr. Devany to dine with him. We went home with him. He introduced us into his sitting room. It was well furnished with carpet, chairs, two elegant sofas, two handsome mirrors, etc. In a little while the folding doors, separating the parlor from the dining room, were thrown open, and we were invited to take seats at the table there, richly set and well supplied with every good thing to eat. Now, some may think because I have lived in the country in Mississippi, I have never seen good style. But I have lived in the first families of the country. I lived many years with Governor Claiborne of your State. Twenty years ago, I know, the furniture in the best houses in the western country, was not better than what I saw in common use in Liberia. I go willingly. I have got a living here in slavery; and now that I am free, if I can't, with health, get a living there, then let me suffer. There is no winter there. I believe I can live easier and better there than I can here." [137]

[137] *Emigrants from New Orleans*, p. 4.
Devany, whom Moore met in Liberia, was doubtless Francis Devany, formerly of Philadelphia, who was in 1830 high sheriff of the colony of Liberia. —*African Repository*, III, 250; VI, pp. 97 ff.

There was something affecting in this description of Africa by one who had just visited it, and who was encouraging a number of his fellows as they set forth for the land of their ancestors. The occasion was well likened, by an interested spectator, to the report of the spies whom the Israelites had sent into the land of Canaan. And so they returned, and Greenville was founded. Several interesting letters came back from this town, one of which will serve as a fair sample. This communication was addressed to Dr. John Ker.

"Greenville Sinoe, October 12th, '49.

"Respected Sir—As an opportunity occurs by the Liberia 'Packett' I embrace it by writing you these few lines to inform you that I'm still spared & alive, hope they may fine you and your family enjoying good health.

"Jeff is well and haughty, and is on his farm trying by the assistance of the Almighty to make a living, and his children are also well, and expresses their thankfulness to you, for your kind & affectionate influence & contrivance of his being in Africa with them, where they have labored long under fearful apprehensions of ever meeting him in this life. Of the last of our people [i. e.] the Ross Set that came out here twenty-five have died from the effects of the *Cholera* taken in New Orleans on their way out here.

"You will please write me by the first opportunity how all the remaining Ross people are. Old man Hannibald is well & family and wishes to know from, if you have done anything for his daughter Cecelia.

"Now, my dear sir, knowing you were always kindly & friendly disposed towards me, even when Capt. Ross were alive, and I now am old & helpless, can't work, let me intrude upon you, not withstanding past events. Simply by begging you to send me a little Soap, Rappa Snuff & any old clothes that you may judge to be of service to the old man in Africa, and a razor. A number of the last emigrants that is our people died on their passage out here, among whom were as follows: James Cole, Grace Julia [in N. Orleans].

"This settlement [Greenville, Sinoe] is rapidly improving & increasing in population, &c., and have been upon the continual increase ever since I have been here, and I believe the Spirit & necessity of Education have been awakened considerable.

"Now, dear Sir, I hope & trust by the very first opportunity to hear from you and let me hear from all of our people there. Having [no] more of interest to communicate I conclude, praying that the Lord may continue to add his blessings toward you.

"Yours very Respectfully,
"*Hector Belton.*"
"P. S.—Old man Scipio & Sampson is dead." [138]

[138] "Colonization Movement," in *P. M. H. S.*, IX, 401–402. In this place are two other letters from Mississippi negroes who had emigrated to Africa.

There has also been preserved an account of the Mississippi settlement as it appeared about 1852, a few years after its founding.

"The Sinou, a small but placid river, was selected about eighteen years ago by colonists from Mississippi and Louisiana, with a few from South Carolina, who, after acclimating at Monrovia, founded the town of Greenville on the right bank, just above the river's mouth.

"From the sea this settlement presents an attractive appearance . . . Greenville faces the sea, and the river flows behind it. It is regularly laid out, and Mississippi Avenue with a row of dwellings on one side and open to the sea on the other, is a delightful promenade. The houses I considered by far the neatest I had seen—two of them were quite handsome two-story ones; and the gardens were in better condition than those of Monrovia. There are about sixty houses and between three and four hundred inhabitants in the settlement. The churches are the least reputable features of the place; but although unprepossessing in their exterior, their congregations were creditable in costume and deportment. My visit was at the time of the annual Baptist association, and the members of that persuasion thronging the settlement gave it quite a lively appearance.

"There are a number of mechanics in Greenville, particularly carpenters, and in the outskirts of the town I saw a steam saw-mill, to which lumber was rafted from the river by an artificial canal. . . .

"Above Greenville were founded the settlements of Rossville and Readville [Reedville was the proper spelling]; but the country around them, although slightly rolling, is subject to inundation. Other nearby towns were Lexington and Louisiana." [189]

It may not be amiss to include a brief statement of present-day conditions (1930) in Greenville, Liberia, even though this indicates that many of the early hopes have not been fulfilled.

"Greenville is the capital and principal port of Sinoe County, Liberia, and is generally known simply by the name of Sinoe. At present it has a population of about six Europeans, perhaps one hundred civilized Liberians and about two thousand natives. There is practically no business or trade carried on except in connection with small cargoes of miscellaneous supplies landed for local consumption and the shipping of a hundred tons or so of piassava. There are no railroads in Liberia and no roads in Sinoe County except native trails which are impassable to any wheeled vehicles.

"Economically Greenville is suffering from the same great depression which prevails throughout Liberia and in general it may be said that the inhabitants are living only from day to day on home raised garden produce and poultry." [140]

[189] *Report of Commander W. F. Lynch to the Secretary of the Navy*, Sept. 5, 1853 (House Document). In addition to the report just cited, there is a description of Greenville in *Sketches of Liberia* by J. W. Lugenbeel, at one time Colonial Physician and United States Agent in Liberia.
[140] From a letter, dated July 19, 1930, to the writer from C. H. Hall, Jr., American Chargé d'Affaires ad interim, Monrovia, Liberia.

In concluding the history of the Mississippi Colonization Society, a few additional remarks may be proper. The high position of the leaders of the movement has been indicated. If one will but read the correspondence of the few who were especially active in the work, the conviction will be created that they were unselfishly devoted to the cause, and this was in the face of a popular mistrust which developed in the later 1830's and increased until all interest in colonization was lost.

The colonization movement in Mississippi was mainly confined to the southwestern part of the state. It was here that most of the free negroes lived and that most of the criticism against them arose. And it will be remembered that the removal of this class was the primary purpose of the society. It was also in these same counties that .most of the money was raised to finance the work, and from this section came most of the emancipated slaves who emigrated to Africa. The leaders of the movement lived in this part of Mississippi which, significantly, was also a Whig stronghold. The Mississippi Colonization Society might accurately be called the Southwestern Mississippi Colonization Society.

Certain of the tangible accomplishments of the society can be easily listed. About 571 negroes were provided with the necessary equipment and sent to begin their new life on the coast of Africa. The large majority of the emigrants were ex-slaves. It is also certain that a considerable sum of money was contributed; and though the total can never be given, it is probable that a hundred thousand dollars would be a conservative estimate.[141] When the value of the negroes who were emancipated is added to this, the worth of Mississippi's gift to colonization looms large. To complete the record, we should remember the gifts and emancipations offered in good faith which could not be accepted by the society because of legal prohibitions.

One of the main objectives of the Mississippi Colonization Society was to rid the State, particularly its southwestern corner, of free negroes. In this regard the society failed signally. While the free negroes did not keep pace with the great increase in Mississippi's population in the score of years after 1830, this was chiefly due to adverse legislation which caused many of them to move to other

---

[141] In addition to the gifts that have been mentioned earlier, there was also a bequest of $45,000 left to the society by David Hunt, of Adams County.— *American Colonization Society*, p. 63.

States.[142] Colonization may have had an indirect influence on the size of this class by permitting the removal to Africa of slaves who might otherwise have been emancipated within the State by their masters.

One other result of a material nature was the creation and settlement of Greenville on the coast of Liberia, a town that remains to this day as a monument to the Mississippi Colonization Society. The Liberians of this locality doubtless had some share in developing the State of Liberia, in combating the slave-trade, and in civilizing the neighboring parts of Africa.[143] However, such good work as was done seems to have almost ceased. Present-day reports of conditions in Liberia, including Greenville and its vicinity, indicate that the high hopes of the Mississippi Colonization Society have not been fulfilled. Liberians who are descendants of Mississippi emigrants, if we may judge this by their names, are among those whose conduct has recently brought condemnation upon their country.[144] Whatever may be the cause of present conditions, Greenville was settled by a well-chosen group of emigrants who were superior to the average negroes in Mississippi. They were well equipped for their venture, and were sent on their journey by earnest, intelligent, and unselfish citizens of Mississippi.

[142] "Free Negro in Miss.," in *American Historical Review*, XXXII, 769–788.
[143] *American Colonization Society*, chapt. V.
[144] *Report of the International Commission of Inquiry into the Existence of Slavery and Forced Labor in the Republic of Liberia*, pp. 22–23. In 1860 Jefferson Davis avowed his opposition to sending confiscated cargoes of Africans to Liberia on the ground that Liberian colonists excluded uncivilized Africans from participation in churches and schools, and practically enslaved them.— Rowland, *Jefferson Davis, Constitutionalist*, IV, 521.

Davis seems to have known in 1860 what the rest of the world did not learn until 1931.—*Slavery and Forced Labor in Liberia*.

CHAPTER X

CONTEMPORARY OPINIONS—CONCLUSIONS

To the June, 1818, term of the Supreme Court of Mississippi was appealed a case arising from the petition of three slaves for their freedom. In settling this litigation the supreme court used the following language.

"Slavery is condemned by reason and the laws of nature. It exists and can only exist, through municipal regulations, and in matters of doubt, is it not an unquestionable rule, that courts must lean 'in favorem vitae et libertatis.' . . . The defendants say, you take from us a vested right arising from municipal law. The petitioners [slaves] say you would deprive us of a natural right. . . . How should the Court decide, if construction was really to determine it? I presume it would be in favor of liberty. From the view I have taken, I am satisfied, that the petitioners are entitled to have the verdict confirmed, and the motion for a new trial over ruled." [1]

In 1818, George Poindexter, the first and one of the ablest representatives of Mississippi in Congress, "said he fully concurred with the gentleman from New York [Mr. Tallmadge], in his solicitude to expel from our country, whenever practicable, anything like slavery. It is not with us," said he, "a matter of choice whether we will have slaves among us or not: we found them here, and we are obliged to maintain and employ them. It would be a blessing, could we get rid of them; but the wisest and best men among us have not been able to devise a plan for doing it." [2]

Ten years later Governor Brandon, an able and popular man, asserted that "slavery is an evil at best." In support of this he declared to the legislature that slavery had been particularly baneful for the poorer white people, that it had widened the gulf between the rich and the poor, and that Mississippi could never secure a numerous white population and attain her proper rank among other States so long as slavery existed within her boundaries. [3]

[1] Harry *et al v.* Decker and Hopkins, 1 Miss. 36.
[2] *Annals of Congress*, 15 Congrs., 2 Sess., p. 388.
[3] Claiborne, *Mississippi*, p. 386.

Brandon's message indicting slavery evidently did not shock the legislature for no protests were entered. Indeed, prior to 1830 that body spent little time in preparing resolutions or memorials defending slavery. In 1825 a resolution from Ohio proposing a plan for emancipation was received. Although not concurring in this, a "lament that the evil of slavery does exist in any of the United States" was expressed by the law-makers of Mississippi.[4] The following year this body was still willing to admit the imperfections of slavery.[5]

The opinions of Poindexter and Brandon concerning the evils of slavery were shared by many other leaders prior to 1832. In 1800, William Dunbar wrote: "Slavery can only be defended perhaps on the principle of expediency . . ."[6] In 1802, Governor W. C. C. Claiborne wrote to James Madison that the government in its land policy should be careful not to injure independent white farmers while fostering "a few wealthy speculators, who would probably introduce a large number of negroes, a class already formidable for our present population."[7] On another occasion Governor Claiborne wrote in regard to slaves: "This class of population is increasing rapidly, and will, sooner or later, be a great public evil."[8] In 1831, Seargent S. Prentiss penned the following lines to his brother: "That slavery is a great evil, there can be no doubt—and it is an unfortunate circumstance that it was ever introduced into this, or any other country. At present, however, it is a necessary evil, and I do not think admits of a remedy."[9]

Except for advertisements of sales and of fugitives, slavery was seldom mentioned in the press of Mississippi before the 'thirties. The rare exceptions were usually editorials or quotations from other papers and they show a genial tolerance on the part of Mississippi editors toward discussions of either the good or bad elements in slavery. In 1825, the *Woodville Republican* informed its readers that as a result of the revolution in Haiti, "The Domestics of her Black Majesty the Ex-Queen of Hayti, are all white persons."[10] In the same year this paper copied from the *Genius of Universal Emancipation* the following story, with its attendant moral, that would have

[4] *Jour. Gen. Assem. of Miss.*, 1825, House Jour., p. 172.
[5] *Ibid.*, 1826, House Jour., pp. 50–51.
[6] Claiborne, *Mississippi*, p. 145.
[7] *Ibid.*, p. 237.
[8] *Ibid.*, p. 224.
[9] [George Lewis Prentiss], *Memoir of S. S. Prentiss*, I, 107.
[10] *Woodville Republican*, Mar. 15, 1825.

been most disagreeable to slaveholders of later times. A white father sold his own mulatto child. According to this magazine, such things frequently happened and was but one product of slavery, from which America was exhorted to free herself by "a system of operations, which may eventually rid the nation of those evils." [11] While one cannot be sure that the editor approved this view, he was under no compulsion to print it. There was certainly no editorial objection or counterblast. As late as December, 1832, this paper printed a letter from a subscriber which included the sentence: "We, of this country, are unfortunately slave holders." [12] Some years later Olmsted met a Mississippi slave-owner who was an abolitionist at heart. Though at that time and place he was something of a curiosity, Olmsted declared: "It is unnecessary to state his views at length. They were precisely those which used to be common among all respectable men at the South." [13]

These admissions that slavery was not entirely justifiable were all made before 1832. Before the middle of the 1830's many citizens of the State professed a desire to be rid of the institution sometime in the indefinite future; the Mississippi Colonization Society flourished; many slaves were freed and sent to Africa or to the North; and the free negroes in Mississippi became more numerous until the census of 1840. But in the latter part of the 1830's all was changed, and public opinion became nearly unanimous in extolling slavery as an unmixed blessing both for the slaves and the white people. As an example of this change, compare with the quoted message of Governor Brandon, in 1828, one sent to the legislature by Governor Quitman, in 1836. Quitman complained of the "reviews, orations, tracts and even school books, emanating from the non-slave holding states." After mentioning the creation of abolition societies, he concluded:

"The morality, the expediency, and the duration of the institution of slavery, are questions which belong exclusively to ourselves. It would degrade the character and prostrate the dignity of the sovereign State, to step down into the arena of controversy and discuss the morality, the propriety or wisdom of her civil institutions with foreign powers or with selfconstituted associations of individuals, who have no right to question them. It is enough that we, the people of Mississippi, professing to be actuated by as high a regard for the precepts of religion and morality as the citizens of other states, and claiming to be more competent judges of our

[11] *Ibid.*, Feb. 9, 1825.
[12] *Ibid.*, Dec. 22, 1832.
[13] Olmsted, *Back Country*, p. 185.

own substantial interests, have chosen to adopt into our political system, and still choose to retain, the institution of domestic slavery." [14]

Turning to the opinions of the judiciary, the supreme court, which had earlier held that slavery existed only through municipal regulations and that slaves possessed natural rights, later declared that slaves had no rights at all other than those provided by legislation.[15] Furthermore, this body shortly before the Civil War declared that comity between Mississippi and Ohio was virtually dissolved because the latter set free Mississippi slaves brought there for that purpose. Yet this court had earlier approved the emancipation of Mississippi slaves in Mississippi.[16]

Likewise the legislature began to defend slavery, making resolutions and petitions and answering those that came from afar. Among other expressions of opinion, this body, in 1856, branded antislavery resolutions received from Maine and Vermont as "ravings of phrensical fanaticism or the ebulitions of malignant slander." The governor was requested to return the resolutions, together with the legislature's opinion of them, and to follow this precedent when similar documents were received.[17] In 1836, Seargent S. Prentiss, who five years earlier wrote "slavery is a great evil," introduced into the legislature a resolution containing the following words:

"Resolved, That the people of the state of Mississippi look upon the institution of domestic slavery, as it exists among them, not as a curse, but a blessing, as the legitimate condition of the African race, as authorized both by the laws of God and the dictates of reason and philanthropy; and that they hope to transmit this institution to their posterity, as the best part of their inheritance. . . . We hold discussion upon this subject as equally impertinent with discussion upon our relations, wives and children, and we will allow no present change, or hope of future alteration in this matter." [18]

In 1836, Robert J. Walker, representing Mississippi in the Senate of the United States, protested his love for the Union but his bitter opposition to abolitionists. He said: "They may publish document after document, and print after print, but it will all be vain and

[14] Rowland, *History of Mississippi*, II, 643.
[15] George *v.* The State, 37 Miss. 316.
[16] Mitchell *v.* Wells, 37 Miss. 235.
[17] *Laws of Miss.*, 1856, pp. 431–432. For similar opinions of the legislature see, *ibid.*, 1841, pp. 155–156; *ibid.*, 1850, pp. 521–528; *ibid.*, 1854, p. 584; *ibid.*, 1856, p. 434; *ibid.*, 1857, pp. 136–137.
[18] *Woodville Republican*, Apr. 21, 1838.

nugatory. They will not have made the slightest approach towards the grand object of all their efforts. No; our peculiar institutions we will yield only at the point of the bayonet, and in a struggle for their defence we would be found invincible." [19]

Of all phases of slavery, the most difficult to justify was the foreign slave-trade; next to that was the domestic trade. Yet Jefferson Davis declared: "If we had considered the purposes of humanity alone, we should have continued the African slave-trade indefinitely." [20] In 1850, he stated in the Senate that he saw nothing censurable in the slave pens in the District of Columbia.[21] Approving the slave-trade both in this country and abroad, it is but natural that he should have judged slavery as righteous, whether measured by the Constitution, the Bible, or its value to society. He even attempted to prove, as few Southern men did, that slavery was a benefit to the non-slaveholding white men of the South.[22]

As for the newspapers, not a single heated article on slavery appeared in the *Woodville Republican* before November, 1831, when the first tirade, mainly an attack on slavery's opponents, was published. Its writer did not claim that slavery was above reproach, though he asserted that slaves in the South lived under better conditions than did white laborers in the North.[23] By 1835, the abolition movement had become so hated in Mississippi that a letter printed in the *Republican* declared: "The question will not be settled by negotiation, but by the *sword,*—by balls and the *Bayonet.—We can do without the North.*" [24] From August, 1835, through the following year this four-page five-column weekly gave an average of at least a column each issue to discussions of abolition, slavery, and related matters. The agitation continued with lulls but no surrender. The editor and his correspondents were always ready to burst into a vigorous defense whenever slavery was attacked. From July to November, 1848, there were ninety-seven columns filled with discussions of the Wilmot proviso and similar issues.[25]

---

[19] *Congressional Debates,* vol. XII, part I, pp. 690–697.
[20] Rowland, *Jefferson Davis, Constitutionalist,* IV, 522.
[21] *Ibid.,* I, 535–536.
[22] *Ibid.,* III, 320–321, 357.
[23] *Woodville Republican,* Nov. 26, 1831.
[24] *Ibid.,* Aug. 22, 1835.
[25] In the midst of the slavery controversy, waged generally with such deadly seriousness, it is refreshing to discover an attempt at humor. The following letter was an answer to a New Englander's proposal to settle a colony of

At the University of Mississippi there were both a lecture and a trial to show the change that had come over the minds of Mississippians in regard to slavery. Dr. Cartwright, of the University of Louisiana, gave a learned discourse before a convocation of the University of Mississippi in which he declared that anatomy and physiology proved that the negro was not fitted for freedom, but was designed to be a slave.[26] The trial was of Chancellor Frederick A. P. Barnard, who had dismissed a student charged with attacking Jane, a slave. Barnard was then accused of being unsafe on the slavery question because he allowed the testimony of a slave to be used against a white person; and Barnard dared not admit this, for he said he was convinced by other evidence of the student's guilt.[27]

President Augustus Baldwin Longstreet, also of the University of Mississippi, was a member of the committee appointed at the

abolitionists in eastern Virginia for the purpose of improving that slaveholding region.

"Head Waters Tadpole Navigation, Yazoo Swamp
"Mississippi, June 15, 1857

"Hon. Eli Thayer:

"Dear Sir: Having seen a notice to the effect that you were forming a society with the avowed object of colonizing and renovating the worn-out lands lying on the tide waters of Eastern Virginia. Now, sir, the object of this communication is to invite you and your yankee colonists to the more fertile lands lying on the Yazoo River a description of which may not be unnecessary. The Yazoo River is a very small, narrow, muddy stream of great length, and with as many bends, crooks, winds, and twists, as are in a Yankee conscience." After a description of the mosquitoes, alligators and other pests of the region, and a comparison of these to Yankee sins, the writer continues:

"Now this portion of the Yazoo Swamp is not adapted to either white folks, negroes or mules, and we presume it would therefore be a fine country to grow string beans, onions, 'pumpkins,' and Yankees." However, . . .

"You must not cheat or corrupt our negroes.

"On your entrance into the state, you and all your Yankee colonists must take an oath to support the Constitution of the United States, as we do not tolerate treason here. . . .

"Your ob't servant,
"YAZOO SWAMPER."

De Bow's Review, XXIII, 208–209.

[26] This is one sentence from his lecture. "It is this defective hematosis, or atmosperization of the blood conjoined with a deficiency of cerebral matter in the cranium and an excess of nervous matter distributed to the organs of sensation and assimilation, that is the true cause of that debasement of mind which has rendered the people of Africa unable to take care of themselves."—Back Country, p. 94.

[27] Record of the Testimony and Proceedings, in the Matter of the Investigation by the Trustees of the University of Mississippi, on the 1st and 2nd of March, 1860, of the Charges Made by H. R. Branham, against the Chancellor of the University, Jackson, Miss., 1860.

Charleston Commercial Convention to provide orthodox textbooks for use in Southern schools, for books by Northern writers were considered hostile to Southern institutions. The Rev. C. K. Marshall, of Vicksburg, was the prime mover at Charleston in this plan to secure textbooks favorable to the South. Writing probably in 1856, he stated: "The Legislature of Mississippi will act on this matter, I believe, at its approaching session. It would have done so last winter, I think, but for the sudden and protracted illness of the Hon. Wm. L. Sharkey, who took a warm interest in the matter, and was preparing a bill to introduce when taken sick." [28]

It is evident that before 1832 all branches of the government of Mississippi, her representatives in Congress, her newspapers and her private citizens occasionally admitted the evils of slavery and almost never attempted to justify it. After the latter 'thirties there was a complete change. Numerous defensive arguments were evolved, books were written,[29] and an increasing venom was displayed toward opponents of slavery. Eventually it became dangerous for a person from the North to be seen in conversation with negroes in Mississippi.[30] Such a revolution in opinion deserves explanation. The following were among the causes of this change of public opinion in Mississippi toward the institution of slavery.

In the first place, in the middle 'thirties, Mississippi enjoyed the period of greatest apparent prosperity in her history. Cotton sold for a good price; nearly four times as much was produced in 1839 as in 1830. Most of the northern half of the State was thrown open to settlement and there was a remarkable demand for slaves to work this new land. A tremendous number were imported and much of the

---

[28] *De Bow's Review*, XXI, 519; XXII, 104–105. *Back Country*, p. 25.

[29] Among the books in defense of slavery written by Mississippians or published in the State were: T. C. Thornton, *An Inquiry into the History of Slavery* (Washington City, 1841); Matthew Estes, *A Defence of Negro Slavery* (Montgomery, Ala., 1846); John Fletcher, *Studies on Slavery* (Natchez, Miss., 1852); E. N. Elliott, ed., *Cotton is King, and Pro-Slavery Arguments* (Augusta, Ga., 1860); William B. Trotter, *A History and Defense of African Slavery*, n. p., 1861.

As early as 1836 a pamphlet defending slavery on religious grounds was prepared by the Rev. James Smylie, stated clerk of the Presbytery of Mississippi. —*Woodville Republican*, July 23, 1836 to Dec. 24, 1836.

No copy of this has been discovered, though it evoked a reply from Gerrit Smith.—"Letter of Gerrit Smith to Rev. James Smylie of the State of Mississippi," in *Anti-Slavery Examiner*, III, New York, 1837.

[30] Venable, "Down South before the War," in *Ohio Archæological and Historical Publications*, II, 503, 509.

wealth of the State was mortgaged for their payment. There had been no period in the history of Mississippi when the abolition of slavery would have worked greater hardship than in 1835 and 1836.

In the second place, the abolitionist movement aroused considerable excitement in Mississippi during the 'thirties. Seargent S. Prentiss, who was Northern born and who never totally gave his heart to Mississippi, wrote his mother, in 1835, that the excitement over a rumored slave insurrection had about subsided. "During the prevalence of the .alarm, there were, throughout the State, six white men and about fifteen negroes hanged. I think the severe measures which were pursued, will prevent a recurrence of similar events—at least for a long period of time. It ought certainly to serve as a warning to the abolitionists, not only of their own danger but of the great injury they are doing the slaves themselves, by meddling with them." [31] The legislature condemned abolition; [32] the newspapers poured out their wrath upon it; public opinion confused it with colonization; and the latter was forever after unpopular in Mississippi. While the dominant class voiced their hatred of abolition, they also deemed it wise to present to the world a positive brief for slavery. This was done by voice and in writings; and the more zealously slavery was praised, the more impolitic and unpatriotic it became to oppose the hue and cry. Doubtless many citizens who were not sure of the excellence of slavery were convinced by their own and their neighbors' arguments that it was most desirable. [33]

While the abolition question was the first to arouse great anger in Mississippi, other slavery issues—the "gag" rule, the compromises of 1850, the Kansas-Nebraska bill, the rendition of fugitive slaves and the Dred Scott decision—each brought forth its share of excited discussion. Newspapers were little concerned over the justifiableness of slavery except when such issues were before the people. These

[31] *Memoir of S. S. Prentiss*, I, 162.
[32] *Laws of Mississippi*, 1836, p. 101.
[33] Slaves in Mississippi were but little touched by the abolition agitation. A very rare occurrence was described in an editorial that gave the following news and advice. A Wilkinson County planter found in his slave quarters a book of rankest abolition stamp, entitled, *Picture of Slavery*. It was printed in large type, and was filled with engravings illustrating various ways in which slaves were whipped. The editor declared that evidently there were in the community "goats in sheep's clothing," who should be searched for, and, if they were found, "be not too scrupulous in your treatment of them, for it should be looked upon in no other light than as treason against the State."—*Woodville Republican*, Mar. 28, 1846.

repeated blasts of controversy fused opinion into a homogeneous belief in the justice of slavery. Though feeling might become cool, it was generally ready to burst into flame on slight provocation. Olmsted, attempting an academic discussion of fugitive slaves with a Mississippian, was surprised at the warm feeling quickly displayed by his slaveholding companion.[34]

In the third place, two phases of Mississippi's rapid growth of population were significant; through the whole ante-bellum period the slave population was increasing more rapidly than the white, and the growth of both classes was greatest between 1830 and 1840. When slaves were few, the slave code could be simple, exceptions could be made, and a benevolent and liberal attitude could be displayed toward them. After the State was well-nigh swamped with slaves in the 'thirties, a more detailed code of laws for their control was developed, exceptions were frowned upon, paternalism gave place to more systematic government, and slavery became a more fixed institution.

Finally, between 1830 and 1840, Mississippi experienced a change so radical as to almost warrant the use of the word *revolution*. The first constitution of the State, which had been written in 1817, was largely the work of George Poindexter and was permeated with the conservative democracy of the Jeffersonian school. In 1832, a new constitution was adopted which provided for the popular election of judges, for the abolition of property qualifications for voting, and for similar democratic devices, which were detested by Poindexter, Prentiss, and other conservative leaders whose power was waning. But this was only the beginning of Mississippi's swing toward democracy.

In 1832, there were only twenty-six counties, all in the southern half of the State, with public opinion and political power controlled by the planter aristocracy of the Natchez-Vicksburg region. By the end of 1836, twenty-nine additional counties had been created, all in north Mississippi, out of lands recently roamed by the Choctaw and Chickasaw Indians; and the State's population grew between 1830 and 1840 from 70,443 to 179,074.[35] The people of these new counties quickly displayed the aggressive democracy of a frontier region, and the Whigs of the southwest were not slow in sensing the danger to

---

[34] *Back Country*, pp. 172–173.
[35] Dunbar Rowland, *Official and Statistical Register of the State of Mississippi*, 1917, pp. 442–445. *Compendium of the Census of 1850*, p. 45.

their own political supremacy. A great battle was fought over the admission of representatives from the new counties into the legislative halls of the State, and the democracy of the new counties triumphed.[36] In the latter 'thirties Mississippi presents the peculiar spectacle of a State moving backward toward the frontier. The conservatism of the Natchez region was overwhelmed by the new democracy of the northern part of the State.

Jefferson Davis, Jacob Thompson, and the others who controlled Mississippi in the years immediately before the Civil War did not spring from the planter aristocracy of the Natchez region, nor was their party favored there. Their power was based on the young democracy of the frontier parts of the State, the development of which was supposedly dependent on the labor of negro slaves. Though these regions had a much smaller proportion of slaves than the Natchez region, there were high hopes for the future. The leaders of this democracy therefore defended slavery, and they did it with the vigor, the daring, and the uncompromising spirit of the frontier. In brief, before the middle of the 1830's, political power in Mississippi was in the hands of the planters of the southwest, and during this period the evils of slavery were admitted with some frankness; it was not until after southwest Mississippi lost its political dominance that the defense of slavery became popular. Thus the attitude of Mississippi toward slavery moved from the point where a government controlled by the aristocratic owners of many slaves cheerfully admitted the evils of slavery to the point where the political leaders of a new democracy denied the existence of any imperfections in the favorite institution of the South.

But did the increasing reverence in which slavery was held by the leaders of opinion in Mississippi work a hardship on the slaves? For a very small number it did; for as pro-slavery sentiment grew, any movement that tended toward emancipation was, in proportion, frowned upon. Hence, the emancipation of slaves, whether they were to remain in the State or be removed to a Northern State or Liberia, was increasingly unpopular. Eventually it was not allowed under any guise.[37] Since permitting a slave to hire his own time amounted to semi-freedom, this practice likewise met with increasing disfavor.

[36] J. D. Ramsey, "New-County Representation in Mississippi, 1830–1840," MS. thesis.
[37] *Revised Code of 1857*, p. 236.

As a result life became more burdensome for a few intelligent and skilled slaves and at the same time their chances of being able to buy their freedom were lessened. In brief, a slave could hope, in early days, that he might eventually secure his freedom in a legal manner; in later days there was no reasonable ground for hoping to accomplish this.

Other than this, slaves do not appear to have been affected by what their masters thought of the institution; for there seemed to be little relation between the degree to which a man would go in defending slavery and his treatment of his own slaves. Jefferson Davis, uncompromising champion of the institution, was apparently a kind and benevolent master.[38] Another equally kind master opposed the institution, seriously considered colonizing his negroes in Africa, and even thought of going along to aid in the venture.[39] A gentle grandmother who possessed slaves, and whose relatives owned many more, was known by her children and grandchildren to be an abolitionist at heart.[40] On the other hand, an apparently religious mistress of a large plantation woefully overworked her negroes.[41]

The master's treatment of his slaves depended chiefly on his character. The white man's attitude toward slavery was determined largely by the economic interests of his class. Those in Mississippi who chiefly detested slavery owned none themselves. White mechanics regretted the existence of slavery, yet they did not want abolition for, as they said, "nobody couldn't live here then." [42] But the converse was not true. Those who were loudest in the defense of slavery in the years just before the Civil War did not represent the regions in the State where there were most slaves. The great slaveholders had been shorn of their former political power before this time and most of them took little part in the controversy.

Neither slave-owners nor the rest of the white population spent much time debating whether men should or should not own slaves. Those who did not have them envied owners of negroes; the latter were too occupied with the practical problems of making the investment pay to do much theorizing. This does not necessarily mean that the owner looked on his slave only as a machine for making money.

[38] Fleming, "Jefferson Davis, the Negroes and the Negro Problem," in *Sewanee Review*, XVI.
[39] Rowland, *Mississippi*, II, 186–187.
[40] Smedes, *Southern Planter*, p. 97. See *Back Country*, p. 185, for another Mississippi slaveholdng abolitionist.
[41] *Back Country*, pp. 182–183.
[42] *Ibid.*, p. 203. See also pp. 180–181.

He also considered him a person for whom he might have kindly feelings or even true friendship. Dr. M. W. Philips revealed this mixture of business and sentiment, and the varying predominance of these, in the following notations scattered through his diary.

"James with high fever today, unlucky boy, has been down three times."
"Dick died last night, curse such luck."
"I had the misfortune to lose Easter's boy on the night of the 21st."
"Though he [Peyton] was a bad man in many respects, yet he was a most excellent field hand. . . . I wish we could hope for his eternal state."
"Died this morning, Monday, 23rd Sept., Scott, Emily's next to oldest boy—a remarkable child of his age, a pet of us all. I feel as if I had lost some dear relative. We know he is better by the change. . . ." [43]

Philips's attitude seems to have been typical. Most planters had a few slaves who were worthless because of age or disease, and yet they cared for them as well as for able-bodied young field hands. Only one instance has been noted of a slaveholder shirking this responsibility. Mary Ann, an idiot, was deserted by her owner. She was not allowed to suffer, however, for John Thompson, of Monroe County, took care of her and was eventually allowed $10 a month by the county for this act of charity.[44] But negroes were property as well as persons and the first consideration often outweighed the second. In 1846, the steamer "Pride Belle" swamped a skiff containing six "likely" negro men, and they were all drowned. In reporting the accident the newspaper seems to have been chiefly concerned because "they were owned by a couple of young men who had bought and paid for them by the sweat of their brows." [45]

White men, of course, felt that they lived on a higher plane than the slaves. This attitude might take the form of a condescending indulgence toward slaves, as in rewarding a negro for returning a lost bunch of keys; a mere statement of appreciation of the deed was considered sufficient reward for a white man.[46] Also, white men expected slaves to be obedient and respectful to them at all times. There was some difference of opinion as to how to secure this attitude from the slave. A Mississippi editor once expostulated with his readers:

[43] Riley, "Diary of a Miss. Planter," in *P. M. H. S.*, X, 334, 411, 444, 450. Among Philips's negroes was a cripple. Though almost useless, being valued at $25, this slave was decently cared for.—*Ibid.*, pp. 465, 472.
[44] *Laws of Miss.*, 1833, p. 93.
[45] *Woodville Republican*, May 30, 1846.
[46] *Ibid.*, July, 28, 1829.

"There are many persons—and we regret to say it—who think they have the same right to shoot a negro if he insults them, or even runs from them, that they have to shoot down a dog, but there are laws for the protection of the slaves as well as the master, and the sooner the error alluded to is removed, the better it will be for both parties." [47] The supreme court once stated that the insolence and impudence of a slave to a white person was not just cause for killing the slave, particularly when these were habitual and not merely displayed at the moment of the crime. [48]

In their attitude toward slaves and slavery, white persons in Mississippi seldom displayed any fear. Though a servile revolution was anticipated in 1835, the slaves were considered dangerous only in so far as they might be used by white leaders, particularly by the famous brigand, Murrell. Such white leaders were, of course, sometimes called abolitionists, but little or no evidence was ever presented to prove that they were connected with the abolition movement. [49]

What the slave thought of slavery we can only surmise—doubtless as an institution very little. He did not like to be forced to work, he dreaded the lash, and sometimes he ran away to avoid these and other specific evils. He probably felt no disgrace in being a slave, for that seemed the universal lot of negroes; and his thinking dealt with concrete facts rather than with theories and speculations. [50] But in an elementary way, slaves doubtless wondered more than their masters imagined why there was a difference between them. In the somber shadows of a negro burying-ground in Wilkinson County, an aged negro grave-digger addressed a strange but friendly white man:

"Massa, may I ask you something?"

"Ask what you please."

"Can you 'splain how it happened, in the fust place, that the white folks got the start of the black folks, so as to make dem de slaves and do all de work?"

This question alarmed a younger companion of the old grave-

[47] *Woodville Republican*, quoted in Stowe, *Key to Uncle Tom's Cabin*, pp. 254–255.

[48] Jolly *v*. The State, 21 Miss. 223.

[49] Thomas Shackelford, *Proceedings of the Citizens of Madison County, Mississippi, at Livingston, in July, 1835, in Relation to the Trial and Punishment of Several Individuals Implicated in a Contemplated Insurrection in this State*, passim. *Woodville Republican*, 1835 and 1836, passim. J. B. Cobb, *Mississippi Scenes*, pp. 160 ff. *Memoir of S. S. Prentiss*, I, 162. *Southwest by a Yankee*, II, pp. 260–262, 291 ff.

[50] *Southwest by a Yankee*, II, 260–262.

digger, and he broke in: "Uncle Pete, it's no use talkin'. It's fo'ordained. The Bible tells you that. The Lord fo'ordained the Nigger to
work, and the white man to boss."

This mixture of warning and theology crushed Uncle Pete for a
moment. "Dat's so. Dat's so." Then, in a tone of despair joined with
defiance: "But if dat's so, then God's no fair man!" [51]

With the usual qualification as to exceptions, the food and clothing
of Mississippi slaves were reasonably satisfactory. A number of persons who wrote at different times, after observing conditions in
several parts of the State and on large plantations as well as small,
agreed that "the negroes appeared to be well taken care of and
abundantly supplied with the necessaries of vigorous physical existence." [52] Seargent S. Prentiss in a private letter to his brother wrote
that he considered slavery a great evil. "But the situation of the
slaves—at least in this State—is not half as bad as it is generally
represented, and believed to be, in the North. They are in general,
as far as my observation extends, well clothed, well fed, and kindly
treated—and, I suspect, fully as happy as their masters. Indeed, I
have no question, that their situation is much preferable to that of
the free negroes, who infest the Northern cities. To be sure, there
are, occasionally, men who treat their slaves cruelly and inhumanly
—but they are not countenanced by society, and their conduct is as
much reprobated as it would be anywhere else." [53]

These opinions are confirmed by contemporary records of the
amounts and kinds of food and clothing, which were plain, but sufficient. Slave-houses were not as satisfactory, due partly to pioneer
conditions in much of the State, and partly to the fact that the slave's
house was a place to sleep with few other characteristics of a home.

The average slave did not perform an unreasonable amount of
work in a day. Although he stayed in the field from daylight till
dark, movement of body was slow and energy expended was small.
Considered as a machine, the slave turned out about the same product
in a day and used about the same fuel as his free grandchildren of
to-day.

[51] Venable, "Down South Before the War," in *Ohio Archæological and
Historical Publications*, II, 509.
[52] *Back Country*, pp. 74, 14, 15, 53, 140–157. Claiborne, *Life of Quitman*,
I, 85–86. *Southwest by a Yankee*, II, 120–124. Claiborne, *Mississippi*, p. 144.
Wortley, *Travels in the United States*, p. 117.
[53] *Memoir of S. S. Prentiss*, I, 107–108.

The religious and moral training of the slave received considerably less attention than his physical well-being. It may fairly be supposed that few overseers had much interest in such matters, and possibly half of the slaves in the State were under their care. Only a part of the slaves under the immediate supervision of their owners were instructed. On the other hand, few masters objected to religious meetings among their negroes, so long as these gatherings were not a cloak for rowdyism or plotting.

The education of the slaves was almost entirely neglected, though a few masters ignored the laws that prohibited teaching slaves to read or write. There was, of course, training in how to hoe cotton and plant corn; and intelligence directed along practical lines was encouraged. The negro who could get the most work from his mule without galling his shoulders was possibly rewarded. But none were encouraged to meditate on the rights of man or to speculate on the rise of inequality among men.

In both physical and mental life, there was a great difference between the field hands and the domestic servants and town slaves. Undoubtedly, the latter assimilated more than a smattering of the white man's civilization, both good and bad. Field hands, especially on the larger estates, learned how to lift their hats to a white man, to wield the ox-whip, and to guide a plow; otherwise they were little changed by coming to America. They saw the overseer and the planter but seldom conversed with them. Their associates were fellow field hands. Together they remained in a low stage of civilization for generation after generation.[54]

Except for the omnipresent danger of being sold—and no slave was beyond the shadow of this—being a slave was not for the average negro a dreadful lot. Most strangers who witnessed slavery for the first time were surprised at the cheerfulness of the negroes. Generally, the chief difference between a slave and a free agricultural laborer lay outside the realm of food, clothing, shelter and work. The difference was that the slave was ordered to his work; his food and clothing were allowanced; his movements were restricted; his every act was watched; he was sometimes punished and he might be sold. How distasteful life was under these conditions depended on two very variable factors: the character of the masters and the desire for freedom in the hearts of the slaves.

[54] *Southwest by a Yankee*, II, 254–255.

BIBLIOGRAPHY

MANUSCRIPTS

A. *Library of Congress.*
The three volumes of miscellaneous papers preserved by J. F. H. Claiborne, Mississippi historian, which are in the Library of Congress contain a small amount of information about slavery. Another part of the Claiborne collection is in the Department of Archives and History at Jackson, Miss., and a third part is in private hands.

B. *United States Census Bureau.*
The original returns of the slave population of Mississippi collected for the census of 1860 (now bound in five volumes) supply information concerning the number of slaves held by individuals and also supply data from which a few generalizations not made in the published census can be drawn. In addition, an examination of these manuscript returns inspires caution in the use of some of the statistics in the published census.

C. *Department of Archives and History,* Jackson, Mississippi.
  1. Petitions and Memorials to the Assembly, from 1817 to 1839. Nine volumes, catalogued as I 93 to 101.
  2. Petitions to the Legislature, from 1850 to 1859. One volume, catalogued as I 107. Among these petitions are a number of requests from masters that the legislature sanction the emancipation of one or more slaves. The masters' reasons for making such requests are generally set forth in detail.
  3. Adams County Papers; Auction Sales of Slaves, 1827–1859. Lists of sales of slaves, 1833. Catalogued as G 170. Supplies data about prices, traders, and several practices of the trade in slaves.

D. *Chancery Clerk's Office,* Adams County, Mississippi.
Both the records of wills and of deeds contain much valuable information about slavery in the old and wealthy Natchez region. In this study citations have been made to Will Books 1 and 2, and to Deed Book B.

E. *Library of the University of Mississippi.* Unpublished theses.
  1. Guess, Richard M., "Henry Hughes, Sociologist." Hughes' *Treatise on Sociology* (1854), possibly the first book by an American to include the word *sociology*, is one of the most unusual as well as one of the least-known defenses of slavery.
  2. Jobe, Mrs. E. R., "Social History of Ante-Bellum Mississippi." Contains some information about slaves though chiefly concerned with their masters.

3. Ramsey, Jack Davison, "New-County Representation in Mississippi, 1830–1840." A study of sectionalism in Mississippi during the decade when the Whigs of Natchez succumbed to the Democrats of north Mississippi.

4. Stokes, Rebecca, "History of Grenada, Mississippi." Presents a small amount of data about slavery in this town.

F. *Library of the University of Wisconsin.* Unpublished thesis. Rowland, T. B., "Legal Status of the Negro in Mississippi, 1832–1860."

G. *In private hands.*

1. Bowles MS. A typical plantation diary kept during the year 1851 by G. M. Rushing, overseer of the Lafayette County plantation of Mrs. Green Berry Bowles. It is now in the possession of the latter's granddaughter, Mrs. Bem Price, Oxford, Miss.

2. Leflore MSS. A number of papers relating to slavery and to Indian affairs left by Greenwood Leflore, last chief of the Choctaws before their removal to the West, are in the possession of his great-granddaughter, Miss Florence R. Ray, Memphis, Tenn. The papers dealing with slavery consist of a very fragmentary plantation account book and a large number of loose sheets recording purchases of slaves.

3. Forbes MS. Spooner Forbes, who owned a few slaves and who had a store at Port Gibson, Miss., kept a diary of his activities during the years 1858–1865, which is now in the possession of Mr. H. H. Chrisler, editor of the Port Gibson *Reveille.*

4. Leigh MSS. Peter Randolph Leigh owned a plantation in Yalobusha County adjoining that of President James K. Polk, the operation of which is recorded in Bassett's *Plantation Overseer.* A diary of plantation events during the 1850's together with numerous accounts were entered by Leigh in two large books and these are now in the hands of a son, Armistead Claiborne Leigh, Los Angeles, Cal.

5. McArn MS. The amounts of cotton picked daily by his slaves in 1857 and the following years and a few other records were entered in a plantation book by Duncan McArn, of Jefferson County, Miss. The same book records transactions between McArn and his ex-slaves during the reconstruction period. This manuscript is owned by a descendant with the same name who lives at Fayette, Miss.

6. Meek MS. A book kept by S. M. Meek, of Columbus, Miss., and containing the records of his transactions as guardian of several estates is now in the possession of Mrs. B. K. Sessums, Columbus, Miss.

7. Rainwater, P. L., "Mississippi—Storm Center of Secession, 1856–1861." A recently completed, scholarly, and thorough study of the secession movement in Mississippi; based to a large extent on MS. sources.

8. Wailes Diary. Twenty-eight volumes of a diary kept during the 1850's by B. L. C. Wailes, of Washington, Miss., are now in the possession of a descendant, Mrs. Charles G. (Nellie Wailes) Brandon, of Natchez and eight volumes are in the Department of Archives and History at Jackson, Miss. This diary is of great value, for Wailes was a planter who was interested in the history and geology of his region.

In addition he traveled extensively and knew most of the leading men of southwest Mississippi as well as a number in other parts of the nation.

9. Wheeless MS. A slightly mutilated account book, chiefly valuable for its records of amounts of cotton picked by slaves, was loaned by Mr. Robert Wheeless Collins, of Yazoo City, Miss. The plantation was owned by F. W. Wheeless, and the accounts were chiefly kept by an overseer.

10. Will of Elizabeth Green, dated Oct. 29, 1833, in the possession of Miss Laura Baker, Adams County, Miss.

11. Will of Caleb Stowers, dated June 12, 1860, loaned by his great-grandson, Mr. Samuel Stowers Abbott, of Natchez, Miss.

12. Will of Cornelius Vanhouten, of Holmes County, Miss., dated Oct. 9, 1850, in the possession of Mr. Augustin F. Magruder, Starkville, Miss.

NEWSPAPERS

Grenada *Bulletin*, 1836.
Natchez *Daily Courier*, 1859.
Natchez *Daily Free Trader*, 1858–1859.
Natchez *Mississippi Free Trader*, 1852.
Natchez *Mississippi Herald*, 1802.
Natchez *Mississippi Messenger*, 1805–1807.
Natchez *Mississippi Republican*, 1818–1821.
Natchez *Weekly Chronicle*, 1808–1810.
Port Gibson *Southern Reveille*, 1852.
Vicksburg Sentinel, 1841.
Vicksburg *Sentinel and Expositor*, 1844.
Vicksburg *Weekly Sun*, 1860.
Washington Republican and Natchez Intelligencer, 1816.
Woodville Republican, 1823–1833, 1835–1848. During 1831 this paper was called the *Mississippi Democrat* and during 1832 it bore the name *Southern Planter*.

PRINTED SOURCES OTHER THAN NEWSPAPERS

African Repository, and Colonial Journal, official organ of the American Colonization Society (Washington). Publication began March, 1825, and one volume appeared each year thereafter. The first thirty-seven volumes were used in this study.
Anti-Slavery Examiner, III (New York, 1837).
BANCROFT, FREDERIC, *Slave-Trading in the Old South* (Baltimore, 1931).
BASSETT, JOHN SPENCER, *The Plantation Overseer* (Northampton, Mass., 1925).
Biographical and Historical Memoirs of Mississippi, 2 volumes (Chicago, 1891).

BIRNEY, WILLIAM, *James G. Birney and His Times* (New York, 1890).
BRANDON, NELLIE WAILES, and W. M. DRAKE, eds., *Memoir of Leonard Covington by B. L. C. Wailes* (Natchez, 1928).
Brief History of the Ross Slaves, issued by the New York State Colonization Society (New York, 1848).
BROWN, WILLIAM W., *Narrative of William W. Brown, a Fugitive Slave,* written by himself (Boston, 1847).
CARROLL, THOMAS BATTLE, *Historical Sketches of Oktibbeha County, Mississippi* (Gulfport, Miss., 1931).
CHAMBERS, WILLIAM, *American Slavery and Colour* (London and New York, 1857).
CLAIBORNE, J. F. H., *Life and Correspondence of John A. Quitman,* 2 volumes (New York, 1860).
——————, *Mississippi, as a Province, Territory and State* (Jackson, Miss., 1880).
COBB, JOSEPH B., *Mississippi Scenes* (Philadelphia, 1851).
COLLINS, W. H., *The Domestic Slave Trade of the Southern States* (New York, 1904).
Cuming's Tour to the Western Country, 1807–1809, Volume IV of *Early Western Travels, 1748–1846* edited by Reuben Gold Thwaites (Cleveland, Ohio, 1907).
DAVENPORT, F. G., "Judge Sharkey Papers," in *Mississippi Valley Historical Review,* Vol. XX (1933).
DAVIS, REUBEN, *Recollections of Mississippi and Mississippians* (Boston, 1891).
DE BOW, J. D. B., ed., *The Commercial Review of the South and West,* 31 volumes (New Orleans, 1848–1853).
——————, *Industrial Resources . . . of the Southern and Western States,* 3 volumes (1852–1853).
DU BOIS, W. E. B., *The Suppression of the Slave-Trade to the United States of America* (New York, 1904).
ELLIOTT, E. N., ed., *Cotton Is King, and Pro-Slavery Arguments* (Augusta, Ga., 1860).
Emigrants from New Orleans, n. p., n. d. (A 4 page pamphlet that is mainly a reprint of items that were originally published in the *New Orleans Observer* in 1835.)
ESTES, MATTHEW, *A Defense of Negro Slavery* (Montgomery, Ala., 1846).
FLEMING, W. L., "Jefferson Davis, the Negroes and the Negro Problem," in *Sewanee Review,* Vol. XVI (1908).
FLETCHER, JOHN, *Studies on Slavery* (Natchez, 1852).
FOOTE, HENRY S., *Bench and Bar of the South and Southwest* (St. Louis, 1876).
——————, *Casket of Reminiscences* (Washington, 1874).
FOX, E. L., *The American Colonization Society, 1817–1840,* Johns Hopkins University Studies in Historical and Political Science, series XXXVII, number 3 (Baltimore, 1919).

GURLEY, R. R., *Mission to England in Behalf of the American Coloniza-tion Society* (Washington, 1841).

HALL, BASIL, *Travels in North America, in the Years 1827 and 1828,* 3 volumes (Edinburgh, 1829).

HALL, JAMES, "A Brief History of the Mississippi Territory," in *Publica-tions of the Mississippi Historical Society,* Vol. IX (1906). (A re-print of Hall's *History* which originally appeared in 1801.)

HAMAN, T. L., "Beginnings of Presbyterianism in Mississippi," in *Publi-cations of the Mississippi Historical Society,* Vol. X (1909).

HAWES, RUTH B., "Slavery in Mississippi," in *Sewanee Review,* Vol. XXI (1913).

[INGRAHAM, J. H.], *The Southwest by a Yankee,* 2 volumes (New York, 1835).

INGRAHAM, J. H., ed., *The Sunny South; or, The Southerner at Home* (Philadelphia, 1860).

JENKINS, WILLIAM DUNBAR, "The Cholera in 1849," in *Publications of the Mississippi Historical Society,* Vol. VII (1903).

Liberty, anon., n. p., 1837.

LUGENBEEL, J. W., *Sketches of Liberia* (Washington, 1853).

LYELL, SIR CHARLES, *A Second Visit to the United States of North Amer-ica,* 2 volumes (New York, 1849).

MARSHALL, C. K., *The Exodus: Its Effect upon the People of the South, An Address Delivered Before the Board of Directors of the American Colonization Society* (Washington, 1880).

MAYES, EDWARD, *History of Education in Mississippi* (Washington, 1899).

Mississippi, State of, *Code of Mississippi, 1798–1848,* cited as *Hutchin-son's Code* (Jackson, 1848).

————, *Journal of the General Assembly of Mississippi,* Senate and House Journals, 1817–1860.

————, *Laws of Mississippi.* One volume for each session of the legislature, 1817–1863.

————, *Reports of Cases adjudged in the Supreme Court of Mis-sissippi,* cited in this work as *Miss.,* preceded by the volume number. The following table will furnish the names of reporters and the cor-responding volume numbers:

1 Miss.	1 Walker
2 Miss.—8 Miss.	1 Howard—7 Howard
9 Miss.—22 Miss.	1 Smedes and Marshall—14 Smedes and Marshall
23 Miss.—29 Miss.	1 Cushman—7 Cushman
30 Miss.—39 Miss.	1 George—10 George

————, *Report of the Mississippi Penitentiary for the Year 1859.*

————, *Revised Code of the Laws of Mississippi,* cited as *Poin-dexter's Code* (Natchez, 1824).

————, *Revised Code of the Statute Laws of Mississippi,* cited as *Revised Code of 1857* (Jackson, 1857).

————————, *Statutes of the Mississippi Territory* (Natchez, 1816).

North Carolina, *A Collection of All the Public Acts of Assembly of the Province of North-Carolina: Now in Force and Use. Together with the Titles of All Such as Are Obsolete, Expired, or Repealed* (Newbern, N. C., 1752).

OLMSTED, FREDERICK LAW, *A Journey in the Back Country* (New York, 1863).

————————, *A Journey in the Seaboard Slave States* (New York, 1856).

PHILLIPS, ULRICH B., *American Negro Slavery* (New York, 1918).

————————, *Life and Labor in the Old South* (Boston, 1929).

————————, ed., *Plantation and Frontier Documents: 1649–1863*, Volumes I and II of *A Documentary History of American Industrial Society*, 10 volumes (Cleveland, 1909).

P. M. H. S. This abbreviation has been used in citing the *Publications of the Mississippi Historical Society*.

[PRENTISS, GEORGE LEWIS], *A Memoir of S. S. Prentiss*, 2 volumes (New York, 1856).

Proceedings of the Meeting in Charleston, S. C., May 13–15, 1845, on the Religious Instruction of the Negroes, etc. (Charleston, 1845).

Proceedings of the Mississippi Baptist State Convention, for the years 1856 through 1860 (Jackson, 1856–1860).

RAMSDELL, CHAS. W., "The Natural Limits of Slavery Expansion," in *Mississippi Valley Historical Review*, Vol. XVI (1929).

RAY, FLORENCE R., *Greenwood Leflore* (Memphis, 1927).

Record of the Testimony and Proceedings, in the Matter of the Investigation by the Trustees of the University of Mississippi, on the 1st and 2nd of March, 1860, of the Charges Made by H. R. Branham, Against the Chancellor of the University (Jackson, 1860).

Report of the International Commission of Inquiry into the Existence of Slavery and Forced Labor in the Republic of Liberia (Washington, 1931).

RILEY, FRANKLIN L., "A Contribution to the History of the Colonization Movement in Mississippi," in *Publications of the Mississippi Historical Society*, Vol. IX (1906).

————————, ed., "Diary of a Mississippi Planter," in *Publications of the Mississippi Historical Society*, Vol. X (1909).

ROBINSON, SOLON, "Notes of Travel in the West," in *The Cultivator*, n. s., Vol. II (Albany, N. Y., 1845).

ROWLAND, DUNBAR, *History of Mississippi*, 4 volumes (Chicago-Jackson, 1925).

————————, ed., *Jefferson Davis, Constitutionalist, His Letters, Papers and Speeches*, 10 volumes (Jackson, 1923).

————————, *Mississippi*, 3 volumes (Atlanta, 1907).

————————, *Official and Statistical Register of the State of Mississippi* (Madison, Wis., 1917).

————————, ed., *Official Letter Books of W. C. C. Claiborne, 1801–1816*, 6 volumes (Jackson, 1917).

ROWLAND, ERON, *Life, Letters and Papers of William Dunbar* (Jackson, 1930).

SHACKELFORD, THOMAS, *Proceedings of the Citizens of Madison County, Mississippi, at Livingston, in July, 1835, in Relation to the Trial and Punishment of Several Individuals Implicated in a Contemplated Insurrection in This State* (Jackson, 1836).

SHIELDS, JOSEPH D., *Life and Times of Seargent Smith Prentiss* (Philadelphia, 1883).

SMEDES, SUSAN DABNEY, *Memorials of a Southern Planter* (Baltimore, 1888).

SOUTHALL, E. P., "The Attitude of the Methodist Episcopal Church, South, toward the Negro from 1844 to 1870," in *Journal of Negro History*, Vol. XVI (1931).

South-Western Journal, a Magazine of Science, Literature and Miscellany, volume 1, number 2 (Dec. 30, 1837). Published semi-annually by the Jefferson College and Washington Lyceum. (Printed at Natchez.)

STILL, WILLIAM, *The Underground Rail Road* (Philadelphia, 1872).

STOWE, HARRIET BEECHER, *The Key to Uncle Tom's Cabin* (London, n. d.)

SYDNOR, CHARLES S., "Life Span of Mississippi Slaves," in *American Historical Review*, Vol. XXXV (1930).

—————, "The Free Negro in Mississippi before the Civil War," in *American Historical Review*, Vol. XXXII (1927).

THORNTON, T. C., *An Inquiry into the History of Slavery* (Washington, 1841).

TROTTER, WILLIAM B., *A History and Defense of African Slavery* (n. p., 1861).

Twenty-eighth Annual Report of the American Colonization Society (Washington, 1845).

United States, *Annals of Congress* (1789–1823).

—————, *Atlas of American Agriculture*, prepared by Department of Agriculture (1918).

—————, *Census Reports*, through the census of 1860.

—————, *Congressional Debates* (1823–1837).

—————, *Report of Commander W. F. Lynch to the Secretary of the Navy, Sept. 5, 1853* (House Document).

—————, *Report of the Naval Committee to the House of Representatives, August, 1850, in Favor of the Establishment of a Line of Mail Steamships to the Western Coast of Africa.*

—————, *Supreme Court Reports*, 15 Peters, which contains the case, Groves *et al. v.* Slaughter. See also, Walker, Robert J.

WAILES, B. L. C., *Report on the Agriculture and Geology of Mississippi* (n. p., 1854).

WALKER, ROBERT J., *Argument of Robert J. Walker, Esq., Before the Supreme Court of the United States . . . in the Case of Groves et al. v. Slaughter* (Philadelphia, 1840). Walker's argument is mentioned, but not printed, in the official report of this case in 15 Peters.

WARREN, CHARLES, *The Supreme Court in United States History,* 3 volumes (Boston, 1922).

[WELD, THEODORE DWIGHT], *American Slavery as it is: Testimony of a Thousand Witnesses* (New York, 1839).

WENDER, HERBERT, *Southern Commercial Conventions, 1837–1859,* Johns Hopkins University Studies in Historical and Political Science, series XLVIII, no. 4 (Baltimore, 1930).

WORTLEY, LADY EMMELINE STUART, *Travels in the United States* (New York, 1855).

WRIGHT, ANNE MIMS [Mrs. Wm. R.], *A Record of the Descendants of Isaac Ross and Jean Brown,* and allied families (Jackson, 1911).

VAN BUREN, A. DE PUY, *Jottings of a Year's Sojourn in the South* (Battle Creek, Mich., 1859).

VENABLE, W. H., "Down South before the War," in *Ohio Archæological and Historical Publications,* Vol. II (1888–1889).

INDEX

Abbey, R., 14 *n.*, 16 *n.*
Aberdeen, 150
Adams County, 43, 170, 203, 221, 231
    ratio of slave to whites and free negroes in, 5-6
    slave trade in, 152-154
Adams, Peter, 230
Adams, Wesley, 230
African Repository, 215
African tribes, slaves from, preferred, 141
American Colonization Society, 205-206, 213-232
Antislavery sentiment in Mississippi, 239-241, 249
Arkansas, fugitive slaves jailed in, 128
Atwood, T. G., 182 *n.*

Bailey plantation, slave houses on the, 42 *n.*
Bancroft, Frederic, estimates of, concerning slave-trade, 147
Baptist Church, religious instruction of slaves by the, 59
Barksdale, William, 143
Barnard, F. A. P., 244
Barrum, 155
Bascom, Rev. H. B., 213-214
Bass, J. H., and Company, 50
Bearly and Robert, slave-traders, 128, 156
Beaumont, J., 209
Belton, Hector, 235
Big Black River, 39
Birney, James G., 212, 214, 217
Bisland, William, 209
Black, Senator John, 166
Blackburn, L. P., 53
Blackwell, Murphy and Ferguson, 156
Blennerhassett, Harman, 110
Bloodhounds, 117
Boatner, Henry, 230
Boley, Newton, 168
Bolles, Edward and Susan, 230
Bonus contracts with overseers, 69
Bowles plantation, 67 *n.*
    care of slave children on the, 64
    cotton production on the, 195
    food supplies on the, 33-34
    privileges and rewards on the, 97

    punishments on the, 93
    sickness on the, 46
Bradford and Crafford, 155
Bradley, James, 53
Bradley, Robert, 152, 154
Branding of slaves, 92-93. *See* Punishment
Brandon, Gov. Gerard C., 207, 239-241
    opinion of, on slavery, 161, 162
Brandon, Matthew N., 110
Brazeale, Drury W., 231
Brenham, A. H., 53
Brien *v.* Williamson, 167
"Brierfield," 43, 74. *See* Davis, Jefferson, plantation of
Brown, A. G., 143
Brown, William W., 148
Bullock, Mrs., 221, 223
"Burleigh," 93. *See* Dabney plantation
Burling, Walter, 184 *n.*
Burr, slave of S. S. Prentiss, 4-5
Burruss, Rev. John C., 209
Butler, Rev. Zebulon, 208, 223, 227
Buying of slaves. *See* Slave-trade
Byrne, J. B., 230

Campbell, Walter L., 155
Cannon, Mrs. A. M., 177-178
Cannon, Henry E., 175-178
Cannon, Robert L., 178
Carson, Charles, 107
Carson, James G., 209
Cartwright, Dr., 244
Catechism for slaves, 60
Centerville, 230
Chain gang, 92, 124
Chamberlain, Rev. J., 208
Charleston Commercial Convention, 245
Charleston, S. C., slaves purchased through, 141
Chase, Rev. Benjamin, 209
Chew, William L., 209
Chickasaw Indians, 164
Children, slave,
    food for, 65
    names of, 65-66
    nurseries for, 64
    work of, 20, 65
Choctaw Indians, 128, 131, 164

263

(1)

CPSIA information can be obtained at www.ICGtesting.com
Printed in the USA
LVOW06s0125141013

356715LV00006B/10/P